'Allegri's Miserere' in the Sistine Chapel

'Allegri's Miserere'
in the Sistine Chapel

Graham O'Reilly

THE BOYDELL PRESS

© Graham O'Reilly 2020

All Rights Reserved. Except as permitted under current legislation no part of this work may be photocopied, stored in a retrieval system, published, performed in public, adapted, broadcast, transmitted, recorded or reproduced in any form or by any means, without the prior permission of the copyright owner

The right of Graham O'Reilly to be identified as the author of this work has been asserted in accordance with sections 77 and 78 of the Copyright, Designs and Patents Act 1988

First published 2020
The Boydell Press, Woodbridge

ISBN 978 1 78327 487 1

The Boydell Press is an imprint of Boydell & Brewer Ltd
PO Box 9, Woodbridge, Suffolk IP12 3DF, UK
and of Boydell & Brewer Inc.
668 Mt Hope Avenue, Rochester, NY 14620–2731, USA
website: www.boydellandbrewer.com

A CIP catalogue record for this book is available
from the British Library

The publisher has no responsibility for the continued existence or accuracy of URLs for external or third-party internet websites referred to in this book, and does not guarantee that any content on such websites is, or will remain, accurate or appropriate

This publication is printed on acid-free paper

Typeset in Warnock Pro by
Sparks Publishing Services Ltd—www.sparkspublishing.com

Printed and bound in Great Britain by
TJ International Ltd, Padstow, Cornwall

CONTENTS

List of illustrations   ix
List of tables   xii
List of music examples   xiii
Acknowledgments   xiv
Note on the text   xvi

Introduction: myth and reality   1

PART ONE: THE SIXTEENTH AND SEVENTEENTH CENTURIES

1 Context   7
    The College of Papal Singers   7
    Voice types   13
    Repertoire   17

2 Creation   19
    Tenebræ   20
    The Misereres of 1514   21
    The first hundred years   25
    Gregorio Allegri   29

3 Transformation   37
    Allegri's *Miserere*   37
       The four-part verses   39
       The five-part verses   41
       Burney's edition   42
    Tommaso Bai   45

PART TWO: THE EIGHTEENTH CENTURY

4 Show business   55

5 Eighteenth-century sources 1 – Blainville and Mozart   71
    Blainville (1767)   71
    Mozart (1770)   73

6	**Eighteenth-century sources 2 – The Paris and Manchester manuscripts**	77
	Background and provenance	77
	Louis Mesplet and the singers of the Papal Chapel	80
	The publication of 1838	95
	Origins and sources of the manuscripts	99
	A related manuscript in Milan	108
7	**'Con suoi rifiorimente, come si deve eseguire' –What the earliest ornamented manuscripts show**	111

PART THREE: THE NINETEENTH CENTURY

8	**The Papal Choir in the nineteenth century 1 – Giuseppe Baini**	121
	Baini's life and career	121
	Difficult times	126
9	**Nineteenth-century sources 1 – British Library Add. MS 31525 and related manuscripts**	135
	A new version	135
	Complete sources	135
	Partial sources – first group	138
	Partial sources – second group	140
	Different singers, different ornaments	142
	A preliminary note on pitch	144
10	**Nineteenth-century sources 2 – Alfieri's *Il Salmo Miserere* of 1840**	147
	A 'secret' publication	147
	Layout, musical content and sources	152
	The explanations	156
	Pitch	156
	The relation of Bai's Miserere *with that of Allegri*	159
11	**The Papal Choir in the nineteenth century 2 – Domenico Mustafà**	163
	More difficult times	163
	Mustafà's life and career	165
12	**Nineteenth-century sources 3 – The Vatican manuscript of Domenico Mustafà**	169
	The final source	169
	What Mustafà's manuscript shows	176

PART FOUR: PERFORMING THE *MISERERE* IN THE TWENTIETH CENTURY

13 **The current 'popular' version of 'the Allegri': the 'English Miserere'** 185
    The five-part verses 185
    The four-part verses 187
    Misereres in England 1 – early days 190
    Misereres in England 2 – Rockstro in the ascendant 195
    Misereres in England 3 – other ideas 207

14 **Introduction to the editions** 215

15 **Aspects of performance practice 1 – Performing pitch** 217

16 **Aspects of performance practice 2 – Expression** 227
    Dynamics 227
    Rubato 231
    Ornamentation 232
        Gruppetti 233
        Portamento 234
        Appoggiature 238
    Prosody 238

17 **Aspects of performance practice 3 – Performing forces** 241
    Soloists 241
    The *cantus planus* verses 244
    Castrati 247

18 **Conclusion** 251

PART FIVE: APPENDICES, EDITIONS AND NOTES

List of appendices 257
    1 Allegri's 'original' version of verse 1 a5, Cappella Sistina 205 (1661) 258
    2 Biordi's rewriting of Allegri's five-part verses in Cappella Sistina 263 (c.1715) 259
    3 'Allegri's *Miserere*' from Cappella Sistina 340–1 (1748) 261
    4 Bai's *Miserere* from Cappella Sistina 340–1 (1748) 270
    5 *Miserere del Sgr Allegri* in Blainville's *Histoire Générale* (1767) 281
    6 The Paris and Manchester manuscripts *come si deve eseguire* (1798) 283
    7 The Milan manuscript (c.1815) 286
    8 Source **A** (1820s manuscripts): a summary of the sources 288

9	Source **A**: verses 1, 3 and 5, with variants	293
10	Source **A**: verse 3 from British Library Add. MS 31525/1	298
11	Alfieri's published *abbellimenti* (1840)	300
12	Alfieri's manuscript – Berlin, Staatsbibliothek Mus. ms. Alfieri 1	302
13	The performing editions	306
	EDITION 1: Bai/Allegri (Mustafà)	306
	Commentary	324
	EDITION 2: 'Allegri's Miserere' based on Source **A**	328
	Commentary	349

Bibliography 351
Index 363

✳ List of illustrations

1. The Sistine Chapel, engraved by Filippo Juvarra for Andrea Adami's *Osservazioni per ben regolare il coro de i Cantori della Cappella pontificia* (1711), frontispiece — 9
2. The signature of Josquin des Prez, carved into the west wall of the *Cantoria* of the Sistine Chapel © Evan MacCarthy — 11
3. The northern exterior wall of the Sistine Chapel, showing the enclosed corridor which leads to the singers' entrance into the *Cantoria* and the square window at the back of it — 13
4. The Papal Choir in 1898, showing seven *castrati*, by permission of the Fondazione Giovanni Pierluigi da Palestrina — 15
5. Engraving of Gregorio Allegri, in Andrea Adami, *Osservazioni per ben regolare il Coro de i Cantori della Cappella Pontificia* (1711), 198 — 30
6. Tribute to Allegri in Adami, *Osservazioni per ben regolare il Coro de i Cantori della Cappella Pontificia* (1711), 199–200 — 31
7. Harmonic analysis of Allegri's *Miserere* after Lundberg, 'The *Tonus Peregrinus*', 278 — 35
8. Mock funeral inscription of Tommaso Bai printed in *De Viris Illustribus Crevalcorii* (1857), Comune di Crevalcore — 48
9. The Sistine Chapel in Rome (1869), Ph. and F. Benoist, *Rome dans sa grandeur: vues, monuments anciens et modernes, description, histoire, institutions*, vol. 2, *Rome chrétienne* (Paris, 1870), 276 © Bibliothèque nationale de France, K-1574 — 61
10. Title page in Louis Mesplet's hand, *Collection de musique tirée de la chapelle Sixtine appartenant à Mesplet* (Paris) © Bibliothèque nationale de France, MS D.14499 — 78
11. Title page to Allegri's *Miserere*, John Rylands Library, University of Manchester, MS Italian 45, fol. 70r © University of Manchester — 79
12. Giuseppe Baini, *Memorie Storico-Critiche della Vita et delle Opere di Giovanni Pierluigi da Palestrina* (1828), n. 562 (vol. 2, 165–6), recounting the extraordinary concert in the Vatican in early 1798 organised by Mesplet — 83

13	Anonymous caricature of Louis Mesplet, made around 1803 by a member of Ingres' circle of friends by permission of the descendants of J.-F. Gilibert	88
14	Attestation concerning Mesplet in the hand of Nicola Binder, *Diario Sistina* 228 (1807), by permission of the Biblioteca Apostolica Vaticana	91
15	Mesplet: *Six Ouvertures célèbres* (Paris, n.d.) © Bibliothèque nationale de France, département Musique, Vma-3893	93
16	Lithograph of Giovanni Baini, by permission of the Fondazione Giovanni Pierluigi da Palestrina	125
17	Photograph of Joseph Warren by permission of Philippe Jacquet	136
18	Mariano's 'frivolous' ornament, *The Parthenon*, a magazine of Art and Literature (1826), 29	143
19	Extract from Mendelssohn's letter of 16 June 1831, by permission of the Paul Sacher Foundation, Basel	157
20	Domenico Mustafà's gravestone in Montefalco, showing him leading his singers in the *Cantoria* of the Sistine Chapel, by permission of the Fondazione Giovanni Pierluigi da Palestrina	170
21	Alessandro Moreschi (drawing by Paul Renouard) *Rome pendant la semaine sainte* (Paris, 1891), 161 © Bibliothèque nationale de France, K-167	172
22	CS 375: *Miserere di Bai ed Allegri*, in the hand of Domenico Mustafà, verse 1, by permission of the Biblioteca Apostolica Vaticana	176
23	CS 375: *Miserere di Bai ed Allegri*, in the hand of Domenico Mustafà, verse 3, by permission of the Biblioteca Apostolica Vaticana	177
24	CS 375: *Miserere di Bai ed Allegri*, in the hand of Domenico Mustafà, verse 20a, by permission of the Biblioteca Apostolica Vaticana	179
25	CS 375: *Miserere di Bai ed Allegri*, in the hand of Domenico Mustafà, first page of the first soprano part in *Coro 2°*, showing verses 3 (Allegri) and 7 (Bai), by permission of the Biblioteca Apostolica Vaticana	180
26	Rockstro's reconstruction of verse 3 as printed in the first three editions of Grove's *Dictionary* (1880, 1907 and 1929), showing its sources	189
27	Sir Ivor Atkins, by permission of the Library of Congress, Prints & Photographs Division LC-B2- 6079-13	196
28	Roy Goodman aged nine at King's College, Cambridge, c.1960, by permission of Roy Goodman	199

29	Reunion at King's College for the fiftieth anniversary of Roy Goodman's recording (Saturday 16 February 2013), by permission of Roy Goodman	201
30	Prosody given in George Guest's edition (1976) for verses 15 and 17	205

Acknowledgments: Biblioteca Apostolica Vaticana (Figs. 14, 22–5), Bibliothèque nationale de France (10), John Rylands Library, University of Manchester (11), Fondazione Giovanni Pierluigi da Palestrina (4, 16, 20), Sammlung Rudolf Grumbacher Basel (19), Comune di Crevalcore (8), Evan MacCarthy (2), Descendants of J.-F. Gilibert (13), M. Philippe Jacquet (17), Roy Goodman (28, 29), Author (3); others (1, 5, 6, 7, 9, 12, 15, 18, 21, 26, 27, 30) in the public domain.

List of tables

1	Misereres in Cappella Sistina 205–6	26
2	Index and concordances of the Paris manuscript of 1798	103

List of music examples

1	'And this they call an *appoggiatura*'	112
2	'An earthly music, indeed sung by Italians'	113
3	Palestrina's *Improperia* transcribed by Mendelssohn in 1831	114
4	'A clear impression of Papal fifths'	115
5	'*Nil sub sole perfectum!*'	115
6	Mendelssohn's transcription of the *embellimenti* sung in the Misereres of Allegri and Bai	145
7	Fanny Mendelssohn's transcription of part of the *Improperia* as heard in 1840	146
8	First bar of Baini's *Miserere* in B minor transcribed by Mendelssohn	157
9	Nicolai's transcription of the *abbellimento* heard in 1839	159
10	Papal Choir gracing in polyphonic music according to Mendelssohn	232
11	Different notations of *gruppetti* in manuscript **M**	234

✴ Acknowledgments

During the long gestation of this book, I have been lucky enough to be able to call on the help of many people – friends and acquaintances as well as the staff of various institutions – all of whom have given freely of their time and goodwill.

For being the catalysts: Hugh Keyte for the idea, Richard Bethell of NEMA for the occasion of writing its first iteration, and Michael Middeke of Boydell & Brewer for its final form.

For reminiscences and other input, particularly for Chapter 13 (in alphabetical order): Robin Boyle, Ed Breen, Charles Brett, Tim Brown, Ben Byram-Wigfield, Peter Cairns, Nicholas Clapton, Alison Cooke, Anthony Dawson, Sally Dunkley, Michael George, Roy Goodman, Colin Hawke, Edward Higginbottom, John Holt, Alastair Hume, the late Jean Lionnet, Tom Moore, John Nixon, John North, Peter Phillips, Gerald Pointon, Robert Quinney, Nicolas Robertson, Patrick Russill, Jacob Sagrans, Jonathan Seers, Gavin Turner, Stephen Varcoe, Peter Vizard, Laura Xella.

For particular help in resources and research (in alphabetical order): Colin Brownlee (Archive of Recorded Church Music), Professor Jeremy Dibble (Durham University), Marco Gambini (Fondazione Giovanni Pierluigi da Palestrina), Luciano Luciani (Rome), Professor Federico Pirani, Signor Marco Pratelli (Musei Vaticani, for guiding my visit to the Cantoria of the Sistine Chapel), Chantal Prevot (Fondation Napoléon), Professor Graham Sadler (Birmingham City University), Canon Stephen Shipley (BBC), Dr Shirley Thompson (Royal Birmingham Conservatoire).

For access to archives of chapels and cathedrals: King's College Cambridge (the late Sir Stephen Cleobury, Margaret Hebden, David Allsopp and Patricia McGuire), New College Oxford (Jennifer Thorpe), Worcester Cathedral (David Morrison).

For unfailing politeness and help at the following libraries and other institutions: Bibliothèque nationale de France (François-Pierre Goy), British Library (Sandra Tuppen), John Rylands University Library of Manchester (John Hodgson), Bodleian Library, Oxford (Martin Holmes), Sammlung Rudolf Grumbacher Basel (Heidi Zimmermann), Universitäts-Bibliothek Basel (Monika Studer), Österreichische Nationalbibliothek, Vienna (Andrea Harrandt), Sächsische Landesbibliothek, Dresden (Christine Sawatzki), Hochschule für Musik und Tanz Bibliothek Köln (Markus Ecker), Staatsbibliothek zu Berlin (Birgit Busse and Marina Gordienko), Bayerische Staatsbibliothek, Munich (Veronika Giglberger), Leipziger Stadtbibliothek (Silke Tefs and Brigitte Geyer), Biblioteca Apostolica Vaticana, Musée Ingres de Montauban (Brigitte Alasia), Il Comune di Crevalcore.

For translations and textual help: A special mention to Peter Hicks of the Fondation Napoléon in Paris, not only for his translations from Italian and Latin, but for his unfailing readiness to help in all sorts of ways, to Paul Willenbrock and Karin Teepe for texts in German, Adrian Shaw and Liz Cencetti for overviews of my translations from French, and Virginia Lloyd-Owen for properly punctilious proof-reading.

To Tom Shorter for his expert music setting. To *Early Music* and Jenny Roberts for permission to re-use musical examples and appendices which first appeared in my article of February 2016.

And to the wonderful singers of the Ensemble William Byrd, among them our stratospheric soprano Catherine Greuillet and my exceptionally patient wife Brigitte Vinson, who helped me bring this music to life.

⁕ Note on the text

In musical citations, **pitch** is given using Helmholtz notation (octaves reading upwards from eight-foot pitch (changing on c) are C, c, c′ (middle c), c″, c‴).

Note values (in italics): *b* = breve, *s* = semibreve (whole note), *m* = minim (half-note), *c* = crotchet (quarter-note), *q* = quaver (eighth-note), *sq* = semiquaver (sixteenth-note), *d* = demisemiquaver (thirty-second-note). A dot is given as . (e.g. *q.sq* = dotted quaver-semiquaver).

The performing editions in Appendix 13 are reproduced by permission of Shorter House (www.shorterhouse.com), from whom they are available individually or in performance packs.

Translations from Latin and Italian are by Peter Hicks, from German by Paul Willenbrock and Karin Teepe. The author is responsible for all translations from French.

Introduction: myth and reality

Few musical works have as interesting a history, and are nowadays so little understood, as the famous *Miserere* associated with the name of Gregorio Allegri. It is largely known today from performances in English chapels and cathedrals by choirs of men and, mostly, boys, and in concerts by professional choirs including women. But in its heyday, the eighteenth and nineteenth centuries, visitors came from throughout the world to hear it sung by the College of Papal Singers in the Sistine Chapel. There the higher parts were always performed by *castrati*, whose presence in the choir is documented from 1562. Their particular vocal skills were important for many aspects of the choir's unique performing style, and it was their contribution more than anything else that made the *Miserere* famous. Its popularity meant that a small part of the music of the Roman polyphonic school remained always in the public eye before the rediscovery of Palestrina in the nineteenth century.

After hearing the *Miserere* in 1770, Leopold Mozart wrote that 'the manner of performance contributes more to its effect than the composition itself.'[1] Later the same year, Charles Burney echoed the same thought almost word for word, albeit by hearsay, writing that 'its beauty and effect … owes more to the manner in which it is performed, than to the composition'.[2] Even this may be understating the case. The history of the *Miserere* shows it to have been one of those rare works which only really existed within a performance context. The notes of what we suppose to be Allegri's original composition can of course be transcribed from Vatican sources (see Appendix 1) but reveal little or nothing of what made it renowned throughout Europe. Within fifty years it was said to have become unrecognisable because of the ornamentations added by the singers, and within a hundred the five-part verses (1, 5, 9, 13, 17 and the first part of 20) had been recomposed; the first published edition – Burney's, in 1771

---

[1] Letter dated 14 April 1770, in *The Letters of Mozart & his Family*, trans. and ed. Emily Anderson (London, 1938), vol 1, 187. For the context, see Chapter 5.
[2] *The Present State of Music in France and Italy*, 1st edn (London, 1771), 275.

– gives a version of those verses which has been modified out of all recognition from Allegri's original.³

The work commonly sung nowadays, referred to hereinafter as the 'English Miserere', combines that source (different in many details to Vatican manuscripts) with a fanciful reconstruction of the four-part ones (verses 3, 7, 11, 15 and 19) dating from late nineteenth century, which contains the famous 'high Cs'. It is wholly misleading insofar as it pretends to represent the work as performed in the Sistine Chapel by the Papal Choir: not only are most of the notes wrong, but it sheds almost no useful light on interpretative matters such as dynamics and tempo. On questions such as the pitch of performance, the number and placement of the singers, the prosody of the recited sections and even the method of performing the *cantus planus* (even-numbered) verses, it is almost entirely erroneous. Very few members of the numerous public that flocked to the Sistine Chapel in the eighteenth and nineteenth centuries to hear it sung by its original interpreters in their own performance space could have recognised it.⁴

The very particular performing style in which 'Allegri's Miserere' was sung was its most distinctive feature. Listeners convinced that they had heard it could not know that most of the notes were the work of other composers – in some cases entirely so. In 1711 a new *Miserere* by Tommaso Bai was performed for the first time. Its harmonies were conceived to allow the incorporation of ornamentations particularly identified with Allegri's work. That indeed was its *raison d'être*; and as the works performed in the Chapel were never announced, the public had no way of knowing that it was not Allegri's. Henceforward it was given every year, sometimes complete, but more often in combination with the Allegri, in ways which will be discussed in Chapters 3 and 10. For the public, however, there was only one *Miserere*, and Allegri was its composer. In the words of the nineteenth-century writer Ludovic Celler:

> Today it was his, but when it is not his, it is the same, we heard it. Ask three people who were in the Sistine on three different days, they will all say they heard the one and only, the unique, the amazing *Miserere*.⁵

---

³ Verse numbers here follow the Latin version of Psalm 50, which contains twenty verses. *The Book of Common Prayer (BCP)* has only nineteen, as the first two are combined into one. It should be noted also that in *BCP* the *Miserere* is Psalm 51 (because Psalm 9 is divided into two).

⁴ Still sung and recorded with enthusiasm by the best choirs in the land, the 'English Miserere' has taken on a life of its own, like 'Albinoni's Adagio' and 'Caccini's Ave Maria'. Recent editions of it, while acknowledging some of the problems, have done little to correct them.

⁵ 'Aujourd'hui c'était lui, mais lorsque ce n'est pas lui, c'est la même chose, on l'a toujours entendu. Demandez à trois personnes qui ont été à la Sixtine trois jours différents, toutes les trois ont toujours entendu le seul, l'unique, le

This study starts from the premise that the only useful editions of 'Allegri's Miserere' are those which show the particularities of the Papal Choir's performing style and thus give some idea of what that enthusiastic public heard. The earliest source which sheds any light dates from the second half of the eighteenth century. Much of the discussion of performance practice is thus necessarily restricted to the period between the middle of the eighteenth century and the beginning of the twentieth, when the choir was disbanded. To what extent we can extrapolate backwards into the seventeenth is one of the questions which will be considered.

Two such editions, both intended for performance, are proposed with this book. The first is a transcription of a manuscript dating from 1892 discussed in Chapter 12, written by Domenico Mustafà, star *castrato*, composer and finally, from 1878 until 1898, *direttore in perpetuo* of the choir. It gives a version based almost entirely on Bai's *Miserere*, which seems for Mustafà to have been the ideal 'Allegri Miserere'. It must be very close to that which was performed by Alessandro Moreschi, the 'Angelo di Roma', possessor of the only castrato voice preserved on record.[6] Mustafà aimed to show future singers and directors everything they needed to know for its re-creation, and this edition conforms to that wish. If any score of the *Miserere* can be said to be Urtext it is this one.

The other edition takes as its starting point the work which in the early nineteenth century still had Allegri's name attached to it on paper, even though much of it had been heavily revised a century earlier. It draws upon a series of manuscripts from the 1820s (discussed in Chapter 9) which give decorations similar to those heard by Mendelssohn, Spohr, Nicolai and others. They were performed and partly created by one of the greatest exponents of the 'high Cs', the *castrato* Don Mariano Padroni. Editorial additions and suggestions are given freely, based on practices found in all the sources hereinafter examined, but particularly those in Mustafà's manuscript. It is my contention that the style shown there had hardly changed for at least a century, and these editions are both for singers who wish to re-create it and for listeners who wish to understand it.

The earliest source so far discovered with evidence of the choir's execution (included in a very particular *Histoire ... de la Musique* of 1767) is considered in Chapter 5. Its provenance, however, is uncertain, and it is in many ways untypical of those that follow. More important are three manuscripts treated in detail in Chapter 6 – two of which date from 1798 and the other doubtless from within the following twenty years or so – which can be shown to originate inside the Papal Choir. The performance practice found there is discussed in Chapter 7. Comparing them with later manuscripts, it is striking

---

prodigieux *Miserere*.' Ludovic Celler [*nom de plume* of Ludovic Leclerc], *La Semaine Sainte au Vatican; Etude musicale et pittoresque* (Paris, 1867), 43.

[6] Entitled *The Last Castrato*, the recording was released on CD in 1987 (Pearl 'Opal' PRL9823), with numerous reissues.

how little some aspects of the performing style evolved during the following century. Discussion of their provenance also sheds light on a crucial period in the choir's history, when its very existence was threatened by the Napoleonic invasions of Rome.

In the nineteenth century, the evolution of the choir and its performance habits was heavily bound up with the careers of two of its directors, Giuseppe Baini and Domenico Mustafà, whose stories, together with an assessment of their influence on the institution, are the subjects of Chapters 8 and 11. Chapter 10 examines the only Italian nineteenth-century printed version of 'the Miserere'. This comes, albeit indirectly, from the Vatican, and although it contributes little new in the way of different notes, its preamble on performance matters is highly valuable. It also had a tangential, if unwitting, role in the creation of the 'English Miserere', whose history and evolution is discussed in detail in Chapter 13, together with the place of Psalm 50/51 in the Anglican liturgy.

The threads are drawn together in Part Four, a summary of all the issues of performance practice which have arisen in study of the sources. It seeks not only to explain to modern listeners how it was done, but to modern performers how to recreate it – a handbook for the use of the editions, and a guide to conductors in the preparation of their own interpretations.

PART ONE

THE SIXTEENTH AND
SEVENTEENTH CENTURIES

1

Context

※ The College of Papal Singers

THE official name of the choir of the *cappella papale* was the *Collegio dei Cappellani Cantori della Cappella Pontificia* – the College of the Chaplain Singers of the Pontifical Chapel. The Pontifical Chapel was where the Pope presided, and from 1483, when it was inaugurated, this was the Sistine Chapel – the *Cappella Sistina*.[1] Taking its name from Pope Sixtus IV, for whom it was built, it replaced the crumbling *Cappella Magna* of similar proportions. The singers were eventually identified with the space in which they generally sang, and during the nineteenth century became known in English as the Choir of the Sistine Chapel.[2]

Although various groups of singers provided music for papal offices from perhaps as early as the seventh century, notably the *Schola Cantorum*, and much fine music-making doubtless took place during the Avignon papacy in the fourteenth century, the modern history of the Papal Choir effectively begins after the end of the Great Schism in the 1420s. It was definitively re-established in Rome in 1443 by Pope Eugene IV. In the five years from 1479 to 1484, Sixtus IV increased expenditure on the choir by 50 per cent, and its numbers were increased from thirteen to twenty-five.[3] By 1494, under Alex-

---

[1] From around 1620, offices were sometimes sung in the newly completed Pauline Chapel in the Palazzo Quirinale (then the summer palace of the Popes), the dimensions and layout of which are virtually identical to those of the Sistine, both supposedly reproducing the exact proportions of the Temple of Solomon in Jerusalem. Only the placement and size of the *Cantoria* was slightly modified (see pp. 242–3).

[2] The term was possibly invented by Franz Xaver Haberl, editor of the first complete edition of Palestrina's music. What is now called the 'Sistine Chapel Choir' (the *Cappella Musicale Pontificia 'Sistina'*) is an entirely different institution, created at the beginning of the twentieth century after the dissolution of the College of Papal singers. The term 'Papal Choir' is used in this book, translated from the Latin shorthand *Cappella Pontificia* and therefore, like it, capitalised.

[3] See Richard Sherr, 'The Papal Chapel ca.1492–1515 and its Polyphonic Sources' (PhD diss., Princeton University, 1975). Much of Sherr's later research on the choir can be found in the collection of his articles reprinted in *Music and*

ander VI, numbers had dropped to eighteen, and over the next few decades it was the enthusiasm for music of each pope more than anything else which determined the size of the choir.

In 1545 Pope Paul III drew up its most important constitution, the *Constitutiones Cappellæ Pontificiæ*, which fixed thirty-two as the ideal number of singers.[4] Those on a full salary were known as *partecipanti*. There was also provision for a certain number of *soprannumerarî* – young singers who were paid less and were waiting for a fully salaried place. After twenty-five years' service (extended in 1848 to thirty), the *partecipanti* could retire on full pay, having attained the status of *giubilati*. They could continue to sing if requested, but were under no obligation to do so. Sometimes they were asked to assume a *secondo servizio*, generally for ten years and with an increase in pay. For long periods of the choir's history, and particularly during the nineteenth century, these numbers remained theoretical, and the choir was rarely at full strength. Weekday services were organised on a rota basis, but the full complement was required to be present for all the major feasts.[5]

Musicians in Renaissance Rome and Other Courts (Farnham, 1999), each noted separately in the bibliography. His article in *Grove Music Online* ('Rome', 2: 'The Renaissance'), https://www.oxfordmusiconline.com/grovemusic/, is also a valuable resource, as is its bibliography.

[4] Sherr has shown that this constitution was heavily dependent on previous documents in the Vatican archive, one dating from before 1527 and another from between 1530 and 1540. See 'The Singers of the Papal Chapel and Liturgical Ceremonies in the Early Sixteenth Century: Some Documentary Evidence,' in *Rome in the Renaissance: The City and the Myth*, papers of the 13th Annual Conference of the Center for Medieval and Early Renaissance Studies, ed. P.A. Ramsey, *Medieval and Renaissance Texts and Studies*, 18, Binghamton, NY, 1982, 249–64 (reprinted in Sherr, *Music and Musicians in Renaissance Rome* as article XI), 249–50. Events shortly after 1545, detailed in Sherr, 'Competence and Incompetence in the Papal Choir in the Age of Palestrina,' *Early Music*, 22/4 (November 1994), 607–28 (reprinted in *Music and Musicians in Renaissance Rome*, article XIV), imply that twenty-four was soon seen as perhaps a more ideal number.

[5] Sherr ('The Singers of the Papal Chapel', 253) gives a list of the fifty offices of the church year at which the full chapel (Pope, Curia, etc.) was present, taken from the writings of Paride de Grassi, *cerimoniere pontificio* to Pope Leo X (1513–21). All but eight of them took place in the Sistine, and would certainly have required the full choir. (The original *Grassis Diarium* is in the Biblioteca Apostolica Vaticana (the Vatican library), Miscellanea, Armadio XII, Nos 17–21, reproduced in *Il diario di Leone X di Paride Grassi*, ed. Mariano Armellini, Rome, 1884).

For much documentation on how the choir functioned, see volumes 4 and 6 of *Storia della Cappella Musicale Pontificia* (vol. 4/1: Claudio Annibaldi, *Il Seicento, 1590–1644* (Rome, 2011); vol. 6: Leopold Kantner and Angela Pachovsky,

Fig. 1 The Sistine Chapel, engraved by Filippo Juvarra for Andrea Adami's *Osservazioni per ben regolare il coro de i Cantori della Cappella pontificia* (1711). The *Cantoria*, from which the choir always sang, can be seen on the right, with its large double-sided music stand in the middle. The image was re-used by Charles Burney for his volume of Holy Week music published in 1771

The College of Papal singers was unique, or at least exceptional, in a number of ways. Firstly, it sang only in the presence of the Pope, or in his chapel. When he visited other churches, it went with him, displacing any local choir there happened to be. Thus it was that when Pius VI was kidnapped in 1798 by the French, it no longer had any function and was temporarily disbanded.[6] Secondly, in the Sistine Chapel it always sang *a cappella* – unaccompanied.[7] By the second half of the eighteenth century, this made it almost certainly unique (apart perhaps from some closed orders) in the world of Western Christianity. Thirdly, it was composed exclusively of adult singers, the upper parts being sung firstly by falsettists and later by *castrati*.[8] Fourthly, it always numbered composers among its singers: the most famous in the early days were Guillaume Du Fay and Josquin des Pres. Josquin's autograph can still be seen (Fig. 2) carved on the western wall of the *Cantoria*, the gallery where the singers were placed (see the front and back covers and Figs. 1 and 9). Later Palestrina was briefly a member, and Allegri joined in 1629. The fact that some of these composers – including Allegri – were mediocre singers seems to have been accepted as the price to be paid for creating an exclusive repertoire; no doubt with thirty-two singers altogether (albeit often only theoretically), it was felt that the few less able could be carried for the sake of their other talents.

L'Ottocento (Rome, 1998). For a good overview in English, see chapter 5 of Nicholas Clapton, *Moreschi and the Voice of the Castrato* (London, 2008).

[6] See Chapter 6. It was restored in July 1801, when the next Pope, Pius VII, was allowed to enter Rome, but when he in his turn was taken prisoner in July 1809, there was another hiatus, this time until May 1814. A final pause came after the revolutions of 1848 (between November 1848 and April 1850) because of the absence of Pius IX.

[7] This is probably the origin of the term *a cappella*: *alla cappella sistina* – as in the Sistine Chapel, where there has never been an organ. By the eighteenth century, the meaning of the term had evolved to include fairly simple works given with instrumental doubling of the vocal parts, so long as the instrumental parts were not clearly independent. See Jen-yen Chen, 'The Tradition and Ideal of the *Stile Antico* in Viennese Sacred Music, 1740–1800' (PhD diss., Harvard University, 2000), especially his analysis of Fux's *Gradus ad Parnassum* of 1725 (20–6), for discussion of this use in Vienna; and Jean-Paul Montagnier, *The Polyphonic Mass in France 1600–1780: The Evidence of the Printed Choirbooks* (Cambridge, 2017) for its application in seventeenth- and -eighteenth-century France. This supplementary meaning never applied to the Papal Choir, and by the late eighteenth century had more or less died out with the end of the style which it described.

[8] According to Sherr ('Rome' in *Grove Music Online*) abortive attempts may have been made in 1425–7 and again in 1436–7 to introduce boys, although it is not certain that all the *pueri* referred to in the documents were children (the term could also designate adolescents or servants).

Fig. 2 The signature of Josquin des Prez, carved into the west wall of the *Cantoria* of the Sistine Chapel (photograph by Evan MacCarthy, 2004)

Finally, as a college, it was largely self-governing, a status jealously guarded until the very end in 1905.[9] It elected its own officers and enforced its own discipline. Auditions were conducted before the whole choir, and decided by vote. Although the titular *maestro* was the ecclesiastical administrator of the whole of the *Sacro Palazzo Apostolico*, from 1586 the singers elected every year a *maestro pro tempore* from their number. His function was concerned not with musical direction but with organisation, both of the repertoire and of the singers.[10] Conducting performances in the modern sense was not considered

---

[9] This date marks the reform of the constitution of the *Cappella*, reinforced by the *Motu Proprio* of 30 June of that year (Kantner and Pachovsky, *L'Ottocento*, 57).

[10] In 1514 or soon afterwards, Pope Leo X named a composer, Eleazar Genet, known as Carpentras, to the post of *maestro*, but this arrangement does not seem to have endured. (See Richard Sherr, 'Ceremonies for Holy Week: Papal Commissions and Madness (?) in Early Sixteenth-Century Rome', in *Music in Renaissance Cities and Courts: Studies in Honor of Lewis Lockwood*, ed. Jesse Ann Owens and Anthony M. Cummings, Detroit Monographs in Musicology/Studies in Music 18 (Warren, 1997), 391–403; reprinted in *Music and Musicians in Renaissance Rome*, article X, 391–2). The change in 1586 was at the insistence of Pope Sixtus V (one of many reforms he instituted), and the first *maestro pro tempore* was Giovanni Antonio Merlo, the subject of Sherr's 'From the Diary of a 16th Century Papal Singer', *Current Musicology*, 25 (1978), 83–98; reprinted in *Music and Musicians in Renaissance Rome*, article IV, esp. 90–1.

necessary, although a *tactus* (essential for singing from choirbooks) could be indicated by the senior singer (*decano*) of the part that began the polyphony. If the music was homophonic it was the *decano* of the basses who gave the *tactus*. He was usually stationed by the little window (or more accurately, a hinged panel in the wooden fretwork; see back cover) to the side of the *Cantoria*, with a view of the altar. Known therefore as the *basso al finestrino*, from this vantage point he could follow the ceremonial and indicate the right moment for the responses, often following cues given by the master of ceremonies stationed close to the celebrant. Once the performance had started, his role was to ensure that its end coincided with that of the ceremonial, for which purpose he would vary the speed of the *tactus*.[11] It will be seen that the functional role of the choir, ensuring the smooth running of the office, was at least as important as its artistic one.[12] No doubt this was one of the reasons that the Pope took it with him when he celebrated mass elsewhere.

The choir also elected a secretary *(segretario-puntatore)* and an administrator-chamberlain *(camerlengo)*. The main job of the *puntatore* was to mark unauthorised absences and errors in performance with a black mark *(punto)* against the singer's name, which resulted in fines. He also kept the *Diario della Cappella Sistina* (henceforward *Diario Sistina*, or *DS*), in which, by the eighteenth century, was noted not only *punti* but events in the life of the choir. It is a particularly valuable source for understanding the impact of the Napoleonic invasions of Rome, the subject of Chapter 6. From about 1700 he was nominated in order of seniority; then after holding the post for a year he automatically became *maestro pro tempore*, having effectively functioned as administrative assistant to the previous *maestro*.

Some *maestri* went on to become *camerlengo*, whose job involved liaising with the Vatican authorities – principally the *maestro* and the *maggiordomo-prefetto* of the *Sacro Palazzo Apostolico*. The political skills necessary for this role were not negligible, so it is perhaps not surprising that the *camerlengo*

---

[11] Grassi included instructions for the choir about this, which on occasions could also involve repeating chants or singing them very slowly (Sherr, 'The Singers of the Papal Chapel', 258). As the celebrant was reading the texts aloud at the same time as the choir was singing them (and the Pope, when present but not officiating, also read certain texts aloud), perfect timing was both largely the responsibility of the choir and very difficult to achieve. See Richard Sherr, 'Speculations on Repertory, Performance Practice, and Ceremony in the Papal Chapel in the Early Sixteenth Century', in *Studien zur Geschichte der papstlichen Kapelle: Tagungsbericht Heidelberg 1989*, Cappellae Apostolicae Sixtinaeque Collectanea Acta Monumenta Collectanea 2, ed. Bernhard Janz (Vatican City, 1994), 103–22; reprinted in *Music and Musicians in Renaissance Rome*, article XII, esp. 113–16.

[12] I am grateful to Luciano Luciani, musicologist and former member of the *Cappella Pontificia Musicale 'Sistina'*, for his many detailed explanations and elucidations of past and present practice.

Fig. 3 The northern exterior wall of the Sistine Chapel, showing the enclosed corridor which leads to the singers' entrance into the *Cantoria*. The square window is that in the middle of its back wall, visible on the back cover of this book (photograph by the author)

tended to remain longer in his post.[13] As a result, he became over time in many ways the real master of the choir, as Giovanni Baini did when he was nominated to the post in 1817. In 1830 Baini was referred to as *camerlengo e direttore*, the first time this term had been used, and finally *camerlengo e direttore perpetuo* in 1841.[14] Never before had the choir been led by what could properly be called a *maestro di cappella*.

✳ *Voice types*

The thirty-two singers of the Papal College comprised four voice types, eight of each. In the fifteenth and early sixteenth centuries the top part appears to have been sung by falsettists, known as *alti naturali*, and the second part, generally

---

[13] The practice of confirming by simple acclamation the continuation in office of a capable *camerlengo* was made official in 1802 (Kantner and Pachovsky, *L'Ottocento*, 22).
[14] Kantner and Pachovsky, *L'Ottocento*, 30.

marked *altus*, by high tenors. The third part was sung by lower tenors: the range was more or less that of the modern baritone, but no doubt their sound was lighter and clearer.[15] Basses needed a solid lower range.[16]

This formation, common in Renaissance music throughout Europe, was brought into question by the availability of *castrati* during the sixteenth century. A *castrato* was a male singer who, as a result of an operation performed shortly before puberty, retained the vocal cords, and hence the *tessitura*, of a boy, allied to the lung capacity of an adult. The use of this practice for musical reasons may date from as early as the fourth century AD in the Eastern Church, whence after surviving in Sicily following the sack of Constantinople in 1204 it was rediscovered early in the sixteenth century, perhaps by the Spanish in their kingdom of Naples.[17] From that moment *castrati* took musical Europe by storm, dominating its opera houses for more than two hundred years. Although their use on the stage hardly survived the end of the eighteenth century, they were found in church choirs throughout Italy and elsewhere until the mid-nineteenth century, and in the Papal Choir they lasted even longer. Seven are visible in a photograph taken in 1898 (Fig. 4), and an end to further recruitment was not officially decreed until 1902.[18]

---

[15] Confirmation that the *altus* and *tenor* parts were sung by the same kind of voice is provided by the research of Josef Llorens, in 'Cristobal de Morales, cantor en la Capilla Pontificia de Paolo III (1535–1545)', *Anuario musical*, 8 (1953), 39–69, esp. 46. Seeking to know the voice types of all the singers of the Papal Choir in 1544, Llorens noted from the *Diario Sistina* which singers replaced others (some of whose voice types are known) on their days off. By a process of elimination he was able to identify almost all of them. But whereas sopranos only replaced other sopranos, and basses other basses, the singers of the *altus* and *tenor* parts interchanged freely. The reference and explanation is provided in Richard Sherr, 'Performance Practice in the Papal Chapel during the 16th Century', *Early Music*, 15/4 (November 1987), 452–62; reprinted in *Music and Musicians in Renaissance Rome*, article XIII, esp. n. 40.

[16] This was still the case in 1640, when Giambattista Doni noted the prevalence in Rome of deep basses, *'da altri finalmente alla copia maggiore de' Bassi profondi, che più qui che altrove, si trovano'*, which contributed to, or perhaps were needed for, the low pitch used there (*Annotazioni sopra il Compendio de' Generi, e de' Modi della Musica*, Rome, 1640, 182).

[17] For interesting information on the earliest instances of their employment in Italy, by Duke Gugliemo Gonzaga in Mantua in the 1550s, and further comment on the origins of these singers and their use in florid secular music, see Richard Sherr, 'Gugliemo Gonzaga and the castrati', *Renaissance Quarterly*, 33 (1980), 33–56; reprinted in *Music and Musicians in Renaissance Rome*, article XVI. Matjaž Matošec, '*"Female Voices in Male Bodies": Castrati, Onnagata, and the Performance of Gender through Ambiguous Bodies and Vocal Acts*' (MA thesis, Utrecht University, 2008), 40, contains further discussion and references.

[18] See Clapton, *Moreschi*, 164–5, and Kantner and Pachovsky, *L'Ottocento*, 57. In general *castrati* tended to be either shorter or taller than average, as this

Fig. 4 The Papal Choir in 1898, showing seven *castrati*. *Seated on left*: Domenico Mustafà (numbered 26, 1829–1912); *middle row standing*: Giovanni Cesari (13, 1843–1904), Domenico Salvatori (15, 1855–1909), Alessandro Moreschi (16, 1858–1922) and Vincenzo Sebastianelli (18, 1851–1919); *front row standing*: Gustavo Pesci (24, 1833–1913) and Giuseppe Ritarossi (25, 1841–1902)

The Papal Choir was one of the first institutions to employ *castrati* in Italy. The date of 1562 given above for their first appearance there is taken from John Rosselli, and coincides with the appointment of Francisco Soto de Langa, the first *soprano eunuco* to be acknowledged as such.[19] Rosselli points out that 'Spanish falsettists' recruited for the Papal Choir earlier may have been

---

photograph shows. Both characteristics were associated with their physical appearance in the eighteenth century.

[19] 'The Castrati as a Professional Group and a Social Phenomenon, 1550–1850', *Acta Musicologica*, 60/2 (May–August 1988), 143–79. This article was reprinted virtually complete as chapter 2 of Rosselli's *Singers of Italian Opera* (Cambridge, 1992). For a detailed examination of the historical aspects, as well as consideration of the social and philosophical questions surrounding *castrati*, see Martha Feldman, *The Castrato: Reflections on Natures and Kinds* (Oakland, CA, 2015), which also includes (in chapter 1 nn. 5 and 6) many further references. Valeria Finucci, *The Manly Masquerade: Masculinity, Paternity, and Castration in the Italian Renaissance* (Durham, NC, 2003) also contains

undeclared *castrati*.²⁰ Their presence in the *Cappella Giulia* (the choir of the Basilica of S. Pietro) was authorised by Pope Sixtus V in a Bull dated 1589. This necessitated some mental gymnastics, as members of the choir were required to take minor orders, which were in principle forbidden to *castrati*.²¹ The terminology concerning the *castrato* voice is curious and often contradictory, depending largely on the point of view of the writer. Sometimes it is called *forzate* – a 'forced' voice, as opposed to a *voce autentice* or *naturale*; at other times *voce sincero* – genuine, no doubt in contrast to a *falsetto*, a false voice.²² The term generally employed in the *Diario Sistina* is more down to earth: *soprano evirato*.

Initially the *castrati* in the Papal Choir were restricted to the highest parts, where they quickly replaced most of the *alti naturali*.²³ However, it seems that the higher range offered by the *castrati* soon encouraged the choir to perform some polyphony at a higher pitch.²⁴ With the *altus* parts (the second highest) thus becoming progressively more difficult for the high tenors, the *alti naturali* were enabled to find themselves a new role. Becoming scarce by the second half of the seventeenth century, they were unofficially boosted in numbers by

---

interesting reflections on the latter questions. See also the ends of Chapters 4 and 17 below.

[20] Among them were the Bustamente brothers from Naples, admitted on the same day in 1558 (Enrico Celani, 'I cantori della Cappella Pontificia nei secoli XVI–XVIII', part 2, *Rivista Musicale Italiana*, 14 (1907), 753, and see n. 23 below). Evidence which may show that as early as 1506 singing boys (*caponado*) were being selected for castration at Burgos Cathedral is cited in Simon Ravens, *The Supernatural Voice: A History of High Male Singing* (Woodbridge, 2014), 53.

[21] Bodily mutilation for any purpose other than medical necessity was forbidden by canon law, but this prohibition could be sidelined by treating castration as a kind of sacred sacrifice (see Feldman, *The Castrato*, xii–xv). No doubt it was this interpretation that allowed some of them to become priests or monks in later life (Rosselli, 'The Castrati', 150).

[22] Viadana used this sense when he contrasted *falsetti* with *soprani naturali* (castrati and/or boys) in the preface to his *Centi Concerti ecclesiastici* (Venice, 1602, 3). Even more confusingly, *falsetto* was later used in a technical sense, by Pier-Francesco Tosi, *Opinioni de' cantor antichi e moderni* (Bologna, 1723), 14, and his successors, to describe the head register of a voice, as opposed to the *voce di petto*.

[23] According to a manuscript compiled by the papal singer Matteo Fornari, the 'ultimo soprano falsetto' admitted to the choir was Giovanni Santos, in 1588. Much of Fornari's '*Narrazione istorica dell'origine, progresso et privilegi della Pontificia Cappella ... con catalogo dei Cantori ... 1749*' is the source for Celani's articles 'I cantori della Cappella Pontificia' in *Rivista Musicale Italiana*: parts 1 and 2 are in vol. 14 (1907), 83–104 and 752–90, and part 3 in vol. 16 (1909), 55–112.

[24] It seems to have been left to the *decani* of the different parts to fix the pitch, but the actual mechanics of how they did so is unclear. See p. 223, n. 21.

the recruitment of *castrati* altos. The voice-range of a *castrato*, like that of a boy or a woman, could of course be high or low, and many of the most famous operatic *castrati* sang mostly in the alto range. The first *castrato* so engaged in the choir was Giovanni Francesco Grossi in 1675, because of '*la scarsezza dei contralti naturali*'.[25] In the eighteenth and nineteenth centuries there were many. As an understanding of pitch changes in performance is vital in the story of the *Miserere*, it will be dealt with fully in Chapter 15.

✳ Repertoire

The hiring of composers during the expansion of the choir under Sixtus IV in the 1480s increased the amount of polyphonic music in the choir's repertoire. Gaspar von Weerbeke, Bertrandus Vaqueras and Marbrianus de Orto were among the most prolific, and they were joined in 1489 by Josquin des Prez. In 1490 a scribe was engaged to copy the music that they had either brought with them or composed in Rome, to be added to older music by Guillaume Du Fay, Antoine Busnois and Johannes Ockeghem, and to more recent additions by Loyset Compère, Heinrich Isaac and Johannes Martini. At the end of the fifteenth century, it can be shown that the choir had a repertoire of 64 masses, 14 mass movements, 54 motets, 14 Magnificats and 76 hymns.[26]

The choir's principal repertoire was however *cantus planus* – Gregorian chant, or plainsong – but they did not always sing it in a plain way. When reciting psalms and canticles, especially on special occasions, harmony was sometimes added to it from the late fifteenth century onwards using the technique of *falsobordone*. Similar in usage, if not method, to *fauxbourdon*, a *falsobordone* is created by the addition of three harmony parts to a psalm-tone, using mostly root-position chords.[27] The origins of the practice may lie in the improvisation

---

[25] Celani, 'I cantori', part 1, 87 (for the background), and part 3, 65 (for Grossi's career). As *castrati* were officially restricted to the soprano parts, he was listed in the archives as a soprano. Grossi, known as *Siface* after one of his early operatic roles, came to England in 1687, where Henry Purcell wrote a mock lament, *Siface's Farewell*, on his subsequent departure. See pp. 247–8 for John Evelyn's appreciation of his singing.

[26] Jesse Rodin, *Josquin's Rome: Hearing and Composing in the Sistine Chapel* (New York, 2012), 100–1.

[27] According to Otto Nicolai, who spent 1834–6 in Rome as organist of the German Chapel and took great interest in the Papal Choir, *fauxbourdon* – a succession of 6-3 chords, albeit with modified cadences – was still sometimes used for chanting the psalms. Nicolai, ‚Italienische Studien: Über die Sixtinische Capelle in Rom', *Neue Zeitschrift für Musik*, 6 (1837), 47 (modern edn in *Musikalische Aufsätze*, ed. G.R. Kruse, Regensburg, 1960). One of Nicolai's examples is reproduced in Richard Boursy, 'Historicism and Composition:

of harmonised cadences to Gregorian chant, known as *more gregoriano* – the Gregorian manner. Writing these cadences down, and concurrently adding chords to the reciting note, was all that was necessary to produce a repertoire of *falsobordoni*. Each of the two sections of each verse is made up of homophonic recitation on that first chord followed by a harmonic cadence – the first generally a half-close (either what would now be called an imperfect cadence, or with a chord on one of the recognised co-finals of the mode of the chant) and the second a full close. A single Anglican psalm chant displays the same principles, with the difference of not generally being composed around a pre-existent melody.

Falsobordone is one of the earliest compositional genres which necessitated thinking vertically (harmonically) rather than horizontally (melodically). It is thus a striking example of 'the monumental change taking place in the late 15th century from successive to simultaneous composition' with its 'clarity of form, *a cappella* style, triadic writing, four-part harmony, homophonic texture (especially in the recitations) and a bass line that moves by 4ths and 5ths.'[28] Usually only alternate verses of a psalm or canticle were sung in *falsobordone*, the others – which could be either the even- or the odd-numbered verses – remaining in *cantus planus*. Allegri's *Miserere* started life as a *falsobordone* setting of Psalm 50.

Giuseppe Baini, the Sistine Chapel Choir, and Stile Antico Music in the First Half of the 19th Century' (vol.1 text, vol.2 transcriptions; PhD diss., Yale University, 1994), 49.

[28] Murray C. Bradshaw, 'Falsobordone', *Grove Music Online*, which also contains a bibliography of his extensive writings on the long history and different manifestations of it. Improvising *contrappunto alla mente* on a Gregorian antiphon remained one of the tests undergone by candidates for the choir until 1870 (Kantner and Pachovsky, *L'Ottocento*, 21).

2

Creation

THE year 1513 saw the election of a new pope, Leo X. He was well known for his love of music and the arts, a quality not always looked upon with approval by his contemporaries. In the words of one of the less sympathetic of them, the Sienese canon and diarist Sigismondo Tizio:

> Many were of the opinion that it was bad for the Church that her Head should be absorbed in amusements, music, the chase and buffoonery, instead of being occupied by the thought of the needs of his flock and bewailing its misfortunes.[1]

After the inauguration of the Sistine Chapel in 1483, decoration of it had proceeded at pace, and Michelangelo's vault frescoes were completed in 1512.[2] Leo was thus able to make it the centre of his personal ceremonial in the Vatican, and one of his first decisions was to increase the role of the choir. He decreed that in Holy Week 1514 the *Miserere* at the end of the offices of *Tenebræ* should be sung in a special way, perhaps as an aid to meditation and reflection. *Tenebræ* was already one of the most important religious ceremonies of the church year which took place there; from now on it would be an increasingly important artistic one as well.[3]

---

[1] 'Male igitur cum ecclesia esse actum multi arbitrabantur, cum ecclesiæ caput cantilenis, musicis, venationibus et delusionibus vacet hominum dementium, cum sapere virum oporteret et suarum ovium calamitatibus miserescere et illacrymari.' *Historiæ Senenses* (Chigi Library, Rome, Cod. G, II., 37, fol. 325), trans. (by R.F. Kerr) in Ludwig Pastor, *History of the Popes*, vol. 7 (London, 1908), 6–7. As Leo was a Medici from Florence, one could hardly expect a Sienese to be the most unbiased of observers. It is nevertheless true that Leo, who reigned until 1521, was said to have used up the income of three papacies – the preceding one and the following one as well as his own – such was his extravagance.

[2] His *Last Judgment* on the west wall, executed between 1536 and 1541, was still in the future.

[3] Leo had already ordered polyphonic settings by Carpentras of the Lamentations of Jeremiah to be sung on all three days of *Tenebræ*, despite the ban on

 Tenebræ

Tenebræ was a very ancient office celebrated three times in Holy Week. It was in fact two offices in one, combining Matins and Lauds for the three days known as the *Triduum sacrum:* Maundy Thursday, Good Friday and Easter Saturday. From about the thirteenth century, it was celebrated not in the mornings of those days but the preceding evenings: that of Maundy Thursday on Wednesday evening, that of Good Friday on Thursday evening, and that of Easter Saturday on Friday evening. Starting therefore in the late afternoon and finishing after nightfall, it quickly acquired the name *Tenebræ*: shadows, or darkness. The name doubtless also refers to the fifth of the nine Responsories at Matins on Good Friday – 'Tenebræ factæ sunt, dum crucifixissent Jesum Judaei' ('There was darkness when the Jews crucified Jesus'). Matins on these days consists of nine psalms, each with its own lesson (the first three are taken from the Lamentations of Jeremiah), responsory and antiphon. Lauds has four psalms and two canticles. So in the combined office there are fifteen pieces in all: thirteen psalms and two canticles. *Miserere mei, Deus* (Psalm 50 in the Catholic psalter), the most important of the seven Penitential Psalms, is the first psalm at Lauds on the first day.[4] The rubric also required it to be recited 'alte legendo sine nota usque ad finem' ('read out aloud continuously to the end without notes') at the very end of *Tenebræ* on all three days.[5]

No longer part of Catholic liturgy, the office of *Tenebræ* was highly theatrical. A large triangular candelabrum with fifteen candles – called in Italian the *Saetta delle Tenebre* after its shape resembling an arrow-head – was set up beside the altar.[6] To echo the disappearance of the daylight outside with a reduction of illumination inside, a candle was extinguished at the end of each psalm or canticle. The last of the fifteen was the canticle *Benedictus*. In the Papal Chapel, after each of its twelve verses one of the tall candles – six on the altar and six on the rood screen (the *Balustrata*) – was extinguished. Then the

---

figural music between Palm Sunday and Easter Sunday (Sherr, 'Ceremonies for Holy Week', 396).

[4] Indeed in principle it is the first psalm at Lauds on all penitential days, which no doubt explains why in some uses it was the first psalm on all three days of *Tenebræ*. In this part of the office, it was sung in *cantus planus* like all the other psalms.

[5] Sherr, 'Ceremonies for Holy Week', 397.

[6] The English name for it, the *Tenebræ* hearse, is also descriptive, but of a different aspect. *Hearse* is a variant of Middle English *herse* and Old-Middle French *herce*, a harrow, an ornamental framework over (or under) a coffin – whence its most common modern meaning, also a portcullis; probably derived from Latin *hirsutus*, prickly, and ultimately from Samnite *hirpus*, a wolf (Eric Partridge, *Origins: A Short Etymological Dictionary of Modern English*, London, 4th edn, 1966, 282). The Latin name is *Candelabrum Tenebræ*.

fifteenth candle at the top of the *Saetta* – the so-called 'Christ candle' made from superior whiter wax – was taken away and hidden behind the altar during the repeat of the antiphon *Traditor autem*.[7] The final antiphon 'Christus factus est pro nobis obediens usque ad mortem' ('Christ is made for us obedient unto death') was said or intoned in almost total darkness. Then the Lord's Prayer was recited in *secret* (privately), the Miserere was read, the 'Christ candle' was brought out from behind the altar, and the office ended in a silence broken only by the sound of the congregation departing.

❋ The Misereres of 1514

Pope Leo's idea of singing the Miserere at the end of the office instead of reciting it seems to have aroused the interest and enthusiasm of the singers straight away. Paride de Grassi recounted the first Misereres of 1514 in his diary, which Giuseppe Baini reproduced in his monumental book on Palestrina.

> Paride Grassi, Leo X's master of ceremonies, has left in his manuscript diary a valuable record of the first year in which our singers began the change whereby they sang the psalm *Miserere* at the end of the office of Tenebræ Matins during Holy Week as a falsobordone. This took place in 1514, during the Pontificate of Leo X. Here are his words: *At the Office of Tenebræ, Wednesday 1514. At the end, the singers chanted the psalm Miserere in a new way; the first verse they sang in harmony, and thereafter [the verses] alternately, and it was well and devoutly done.*[8]

---

[7] 'At *Tenebræ*, there are always 15 candles mounted on a triangular candelabrum; 7 on the left, 7 on the right, made of yellow wax; and 1 on top, made of white wax. This last, which represents Jesus Christ, is hidden at the end of the *Benedictus* to signify his death, and brought out again after the *Miserere*, to show his resurrection.' ('A Ténèbres, il y a toujours 15 cierges sur un candélabre triangulaire; 7 à gauche, 7 à droite, en cire jaune; 1 en haut, en cire blanche. Ce dernier, qui représente Jésus-Christ, est caché au dernier verset du *Benedictus*, pour signifier la mort, puis après le *Miserere*, on le rapporte pour exprimer la résurrection.') Celler, *La Semaine Sainte*, 39.

[8] 'Paride Grassi, maestro di ceremonie di Leone X, nel suo diario MS, ha segnato la preziosa notizia del primo anno, in cui i nostri cantori modulavano in falsobordone il salmo *Miserere* nel fine dei mattutini delle tenebre nella settimana santa. E fu nell'anno 1514 sotto il pontificato di Leone X. Ecco le di lui parole. *Officium tenebrarum. Die Mercurii 1514. In fine cantores dixerunt psalmum Miserere cum novo modo; nam primum versum cantarunt symphonizando, et deinde alternatim, quod fuit bene et devoto.*' Giuseppe Baini, *Memorie Storico-Critiche della Vita et delle Opere di Giovanni Pierluigi da Palestrina* (Rome, 1828), n. 577 (vol. 2, 194–5). Baini, effectively the director of the Papal

The following day, however, the singers seem to have over-reached themselves. Baini continues:

> The happy outcome of the first evening encouraged both the creator and the performers. They immediately wanted to add more for the Thursday evening, and they merited the following comment: *On Thursday* (continues Grassi's Diary) *at the Tenebræ service, the singers in the end, when they wished to sing in harmony with more learning than sweetness, were not praised.*[9]

So for the third office of *Tenebræ*, on Good Friday, they reverted to the version given on Wednesday.

> Hence on the third evening, they were obliged with shame to return to the first falsobordone. Who was the author of this idea, and of the composition made in this way, I know not.[10]

Andrea Adami, in his important book *Osservazioni per ben regolare il coro de i Cantori della Cappella pontificia* (1711), seems to have noticed only the negative reaction.

> The Great Pontiffs ... have always procured for their Chapel the best men in Europe; and these men, seeing the deformity of music in those times, exercised all of their ability to render it in the best form possible, trying whenever possible to create new compositions in the real ecclesiastical style. As proof of this, see the diary of Paride de Grassi in the time of Pope Leo X, in the year 1514, where on Holy Wednesday the singers of the Chapel sang a new *Miserere*, the first verse *Sinfonizando* and the second *Alternando*. And despite the fact that this was pleasing only slightly, or indeed not at all, these men of virtue should nevertheless not be deprived of praise because of this, since for their part they acted with all the necessary diligence.[11]

Choir from 1817 until his death in 1844 (see Chapter 8), is known nowadays largely for his biography of Palestrina, a book which also contains a wealth of generally reliable detail concerning the operation of the College. (It should be noted that Baini's copious footnotes run continuously through the two volumes, but the page numbers restart for vol. 2).

[9] 'Il felice incontro della prima sera incoraggì l'inventore, e gli esecutori. Vollero questi subito nel giovedì sera aggiungere alcuna cosa di più, e meritarono, che si scrivesse di loro così: *Die Jovis* (continua il diario del Grassi) *Officium Tenebrarum. Cantores in fine cum vellent symponizare doctius, quam suavius, non fuerunt laudati.*'

[10] 'Onde la terza sera dovettero tornar con vergogna al primo falsobordone. Chi fosse l'autore di questa invenzione, e di siffatta composizione, nol so.'

[11] 'Li Sommi Pontefici ... hanno sempre procurato d'aver per la loro Cappella i migliori soggetti d'Europa, quali conosciuta la deformità della Musica di

Who the creators of the Misereres of 1514 were is impossible to say. It was not usual to write down in the *Diario Sistina* the names of composers whose works were performed, and in any case the relevant volume, and much else, was destroyed by fire during the sack of Rome by Emperor Charles V in 1527. Neither can we tell how much embellishment there may have been. Was the second *Miserere* merely a more decorated version of the first, badly received because the ornamentation was incompetently executed or excessive? Or was it another, more harmonically ambitious, setting? We cannot tell. But it is clear that a desire to 'gild the lily', which would create the myth of 'the Miserere' lasting nearly four hundred years, was present from the very beginning.

By Adami's time, the end of the service had become increasingly formalised. For example, he informs us that the soprano responsible for the *Benedictus* antiphon *Traditor autem* had to make sure that it lasted long enough for the Pope to rise from the floor and kneel in front of the *faldistorio* – the folding chair which could also serve as a *prie-dieu*. Then out of the darkness inside the chapel the final antiphon *Christus factus est* was sung by two high voices in unison. Upon confirmation from the master of ceremonies that the Pope had finished reciting the Lord's Prayer to himself, the *basso al finestrino* signalled to the chosen singers and the *Miserere* began.[12] When it was finished, the Pope

---

quei tempi, impiegorno tutta la loro abilità per ridurla nella miglior forma possibile, cercando di quando in quando con nuove composizioni il vero stile Ecclesiastico, come in prova di ciò si legge nel Diario di Paride de Grassi nel Tempo di Papa Leone X nell'anno 1514, che nel Mercordì Santo i Cantori della Cappella cantorno un nuovo *Miserere*, il primo Verso *Sinfonizando*, ed il Secondo *Alternando*, e benche poco, o nulla fosse gradito, non per questo quei virtuosi Uomini deono esser privi di Iode, avendo dal canto loro fatte tutte le necessarie diligenze.' Adami, *Osservazioni*, 36–7. Adami (1663–1742) was a *castrato* singer in the Papal Choir from 1689. His book was still in use in the Papal Choir in the mid-nineteenth century: a copy used by Giovanni Battista Baccellieri when *maestro pro tempore* in 1849–50 shows his interesting manuscript annotations, including those discussed in Chapter 10 below. It is his copy which is published in facsimile by Libreria Musicale Italiana Editrice (Lucca, 1998) with an introduction by Giancarlo Rostirolla.

[12] The full description is taken from Adami (*Osservazioni*, 35–36), the same source subsequently used by Burney for his famous account in *The Present State of Music in France and Italy*. It reads: 'Tutte le Antifone si intonano da i Soprani, e l'Anziano di essi avvisa di mano in mano quei Soprani che vuole che l'intonino; egli però deve intonare la prima d'ogni Mattutino, la prima delle Laudi, e quella del *Benedictus*. L'ultimo Verso del *Benedictus* và terminato, quando è smorzata l'ultima candela dell'Altare, e l'ultima Torcia della Balaustrata, ed immediatamente da i due Soprano Anziani si dee intonare la repetizione dell' Antifona *Traditor autem*, che deve durare fin tanto, che il Papa sceso dal Soglio siasi inginocchiato avanti al Faldistorio, ed allora il Signor Maestro deve far cenno alli due Soprani Anziani, che subito intoneranno il Verso *Christus Factus est* nel qual tempo dovrà egli far preparare i Cantori

recited the final prayer, 'Respice, quaesumus, Domine, super hanc familiam tuam ...' ('Look down, we beseech thee O Lord, on this thy family ...'), and then he and his cardinals rose and dramatically broke the silence by making a great noise (*strepitus*) with their feet on the floor. This was supposed to illustrate the earthquake at the sixth hour – or perhaps the chaos of the world deprived of its Redeemer, depending on which commentary you preferred.[13] Only then was the Christ candle fetched from behind the altar, and all dispersed in silence.

---

    eletti, seconda la lista, per cantare il *Miserere* a due Cori di Gregorio Allegri libro 88. a carte 49. Avvertendo di non farlo cominciare, se non avuto il cenno dal Maestro di Ceremonie dopo che Sua Santità averà detto secretamente il *Pater noster.*'

    The *Christus factus est* was still being sung by the two senior sopranos in unison in 1856 (James Jackson Jarves, *Italian Sights and Papal Principles Seen through American Spectacles*, New York, 1856, 224). Jarves' testimony is found in Richard Boursy, 'The Mystique of the Sistine Chapel Choir in the Romantic Era', *Journal of Musicology*, 9/3 (Summer 1993), 321. This article, which brings together a wealth of descriptions of Holy Week in Rome in the eighteenth and nineteenth centuries, is another version of chapter 2 of Boursy's thesis, 'Historicism and Composition' (see pp. 17–18, n. 27). Mendelssohn, however, who attended all three *Tenebræ* services during his visit to Rome in 1831, described hearing a soloist sing it. (*Felix Mendelssohn: Letters*, ed. and trans. G. Selden-Goth, London, 1946, 139). Mendelssohn's letters to his family and to his teacher Professor Zelter include extensive descriptions of his visit; see particularly those of 1 December 1830 and 4 April and 16 June 1831.

[13] Mendelssohn quoted another explanation for this tradition from a little book he had acquired 'which explains the sense of all the solemnities': 'This noise is symbolical of the tumult made by the Hebrews in seizing Christ.' He went on: 'It may be so, but it sounded exactly like the commotion in the pit of the theatre, when the beginning of a play is delayed, or when it is finally condemned.' *Letters*, 140.

    Ludovic Celler (*La Semaine Sainte*, 88) had yet another one, even more ingenious: 'In the old days, when the bells were silent [between the end of Mass on Maundy Thursday and Easter Day], people were called to the Offices by wooden clappers; it is said that the noise made by the cardinals after the Miserere is an echo of the noise of the clappers, to remind you of the despair that meant that there was no other way to communicate.' ('Anciennement, on frappait des tablettes de bois pour appeler aux offices les jours où les cloches s'abstenaient à sonner, et l'on prétend que le bruit que les cardinaux font après le Miserere est un souvenir de l'agitation des claquettes, et rappeler le désespoir qui interdisait tout autre moyen de communication.') The tradition of wooden clappers replacing bells on Good Friday and Easter Saturday endured in the French provinces until at least the 1960s.

✳ The first hundred years

The performance of the *Miserere* at the end of *Tenebræ* seems to have immediately become an important moment in the choir's musical year, and an apparent desire – already evident in 1514 – to give a different version on each of the three days would have prompted a steady demand for new settings if it had continued. However, even in 1518, Grassi expressed misgivings. 'At the end of the office, I was not pleased because the singers sang the psalm Miserere in falsobordone, and the pope wanted it thus.'[14] It may be that the nascent Miserere tradition was temporarily discontinued after Leo's death in 1521. The Constitution of the choir in 1545 specifically prohibited figural music of any kind in the *Tenebræ* services,[15] and it will be seen below that there is a large gap between the first known setting, by Costanzo Festa in 1517, and those that follow. The sack of Rome in 1527 was also a difficult moment for the choir. It may be that the tradition was not restarted before 1550 at the earliest, the year of the death of Pope Paul III.

Thirteen of the earliest Misereres are preserved in the paired Vatican choirbooks Cappella Sistina (hereafter CS) 205 and 206, which assemble six different layers from different periods and in different hands (see Table 1, to which the numbers below in bold refer). Its title page can be dated to 1631, when Loreto Vittori, the famous operatic *castrato*, whose name is given on the title page as *Magister*, was *maestro pro tempore*. All the works are given in choirbook format – that is to say, although they are copied in separate parts, each shows all the music for entire verses (one or more) at each opening.

The details supplied by Baini about some of the composers, notably the years in which they joined the Chapel, allow some conclusions concerning dates of composition. The unattributed earliest setting in CS 205–6 (**1**) is, according to Baini, that of Costanzo Festa (c.1485–1545), who joined the choir of the Chapel in 1517 and composed prolifically for it.[16] It is a more elaborate *falsobordone* psalm than was the norm, having two versions of the odd-numbered verses which alternated with the even-numbered ones sung in *cantus planus*. *Coro Primo* (the first choir, given in CS 205) sang verses 1, 5, 9, 13 and 17, *Coro Secondo* (CS 206) verses 3, 7, 11, 15 and 19. All the even numbered

---

[14] 'In fine officii mihi non placavit quod cantores cantassent psalmum Miserere per falsum bordonum licet devote et papa sic voluit.' Original and translation from Sherr, 'The Singers of the Papal Chapel', 256 and n. 31. Sherr points out that the earliest use of *falsobordone* by the choir appears during the papacy of Leo X.

[15] Ibid., n. 41.

[16] Baini, *Memorie*, n. 578 (vol. 2, 195–7). James Haar ('Festa, Costanzo', *Grove Music Online*) classifies Festa's authorship as doubtful due to lack of evidence, but there is no particular stylistic reason to doubt Baini's attribution. It is included in *Costanzo Festa omnia opera*, vol. 5 (1979), ed. Albert Seay, Corpus Mensurabilis Musicae 25 (American Institute of Musicology), No. 52.

Table 1 Miserees in Cappella Sistina 205–6

No.	Title	Layer	Coro 1° (CS 205)	Coro 2° (CS 206)	Notes
–	Palestrina *Improperia*	A	2^v–5^r a4	2^v–9^r a4	Complete.
1	*Miserere* [Costanzo Festa]	A	5^v–7^r a4 ($c_1 c_1 c_3 c_4$)	9^v–12^r a5 ($c_1 c_1 c_3 c_4 c_4 f_4$)	*Miserere Primus*, attrib. Baini.
2	*Miserere* [Luigi] Dentice	A	7^v–10^r a5 ($c_1 c_3 c_4 c_4 f_4$)	12^v–14^r a4 ($c_1 c_3 c_4 f_4$)	*Miserere Secundus*.
3	*Miserere* [Francisco Guerrero]	A	10^v–12^r a4 ($c_1 c_3 c_4 f_4$)	14^v–16^r a4 ($c_1 c_3 c_4 f_4$)	*Miserere Tertius*. 'F.G.' in source. Attrib. Baini, 206: notes added at end of B part for v. 20b (*Tunc imponent*) marked 'Tutti'.
4	*Miserere* Palestrina	A	12^v–14^r a4 ($c_1 c_1 c_3 c_4$)	16^v–19^r a5 ($g_2 c_2 c_3 c_4 f_4$)	*Miserere Quartus*. 206: 'Palestrina feria 6' 206: v. 20b as **3** but with rhythmic indications, marked 'Omnes'.
5	*Miserere* Theophilus [Gargari]	A	14^v–16^r a4 ($c_1 c_1 c_3 c_4$)	19^v–22^r a5 ($c_1 c_3 c_4 c_4 f_4$)	206: v. 20b as **4**.
6	*Miserere* [Giovanni] Francesco Anerio	B	20^v–28^r a4 ($c_1 c_1 c_3 c_4$)	24^v–30^r a5 ($c_1 c_3 c_4 c_4 f_4$)	206: 1623 (lower right corner of title page). Also 'A[nno] 1634 3e sera', '1669 3e sera' and '1676'. First setting to give rhythms in chanted sections and to set v. 20a.
7	*Miserere* Felice Anerio	C	29^v–34^r a4 ($c_1 c_1 c_3 c_4$)	31^v–37^r a5 ($c_1 c_3 c_4 c_4 f_4$)	'Felicis Anerii venerdi' v. 20b a9. 'Tibi soli peccavi' (at beginning of v. 5 for the 2 choirs in alternation) crossed out in pencil in all parts (see n. **41**). Sets v. 20a.
8	*Miserere* Anon.	D	37^r a4 ($c_2 c_3 f_3$)	39^r a4 ($c_1 c_2 c_3 c_4$)	Vv. 1 and 3 only (some text of v. 5 over notes of v. 1). Possibly added after **11**.
9	*Miserere* [prob. G.M. Nanino]	D	37^v–39^r a4 ($c_1 c_2 c_3 c_4$)	39^v–42^r a5 ($g_2 c_2 c_3 c_4 f_4$)	First half of each *Coro* from **4**. v. 20b a9. Attrib. Gio. Maria Nanino (Baini), but Palestrina in Biblioteca Vallicelliana MS. Sets v. 20a.
10	*Miserere* [Santo Naldini]	D	39^v–41^r a4 ($c_1 c_1 c_2 c_3$)	42^v–44^r a4 ($c_2 c_3 c_3 f_4$)	'S.C.Feria 5'. Attrib. Baini. v. 20b a8.
–	Palestrina *Improperia*	D	41^v–42^r a4	44^v–45^r a4	Incomplete, no versicles.
11	*Miserere* [Luigi Dentice]	D	42^v–45^r a5 ($c_1 c_3 c_4 c_4 f_4$)	45^v–47^r a4 ($c_1 c_3 c_4 f_4$)	205: 'Denticis', 206: 'Domin. Nanini fer. 6.' v. 20a a9. Omitted by Baini. = **2**, with rhythmic amendments, probably by G.M. Nanino. v. 20b a9 (but only 5 real parts).
12	*Miserere* Ruggero Giovannelli	E	46^v–49^r a5 ($c_1 c_3 c_4 c_4 f_4$)	49^v–52^r a4 ($c_1 c_1 c_3 f_4$)	206: 'Di cappella di papa e questo libro quae il 2° coro'. v. 20a a8.
13	*Miserere* Gregorio Allegri	F	50^v–56^r a5 ($c_1 c_3 c_4 c_4 f_4$)	54^v–60^r a4 ($c_1 c_3 f_3$)	v. 20a a9. Title page dated 1661.

verses, including 20, were sung in *cantus planus*. The *Coro 1°* book would have been laid on one side of the swivelling double-sided music stand in the *Cantoria*, with the appropriate singers grouped around it, that with the *Coro 2°* on the other. Festa varied the texture of his two choirs, setting *Coro 1°* for four high voices (two sopranos and no bass), and *Coro 2°* for five preponderantly lower voices, with two tenors and a bass. This was the template for the settings that followed, most of which alternated choirs of four and five voices and/or varied the texture between them.

Luigi Dentice (c.1510–1566) was a Neapolitan nobleman who may have been in Rome for several years from 1533, again briefly in 1547–8, and finally from about 1557 until his death. Perhaps his *Miserere* (**2**) dates from the latter period.[17] Baini clarifies the manuscript's laconic 'F.G.' for *Miserere* **3** by describing the composer as '*Francesco Guerrero di Siviglia, famosissimo musico*'. One supposes that it dates from Guerrero's brief visit to Rome and was therefore composed for Holy Week of 1582.[18] The *Miserere* ascribed to Palestrina (**4**) is one of the simplest in the collection. If this part of CS 205–6 was compiled chronologically, it must date from after Guerrero's, so probably well after his very brief period of membership of the choir in 1555.[19]

Around the turn of the century the rate of production seems to have abruptly increased, although the assemblage of the following layers does not appear to be chronological (layers **B** and **C** may both be out of place). Teofilo Gargari (**5**, c.1570–1648) joined the choir at the second attempt in 1601, and his *Miserere* precedes the only one with a date: that of Giovanni Francesco Anerio (**6**, c.1567–1630), which is marked 1623 in CS 206. If this is the date of its composition it must belong after **9**, although it may merely signify a performance.[20] *Miserere* **7** is by his elder brother Felice Anerio (c.1560–1614, appointed composer to the choir in 1594), and includes, perhaps for the first time, a final half-verse for both choirs.[21] It remained in use well into the eighteenth century. After *Miserere* **8** (an anonymous fragment), **9** is an adaptation and expansion

---

[17] Much information about Dentice will be found in Richard Wistreich, *Warrior, Courtier, Singer: Giulio Cesare Brancaccio and the Performance of Identity in the Late Renaissance* (Farnham, 2007).

[18] Guerrero was in Rome for a year from October 1581.

[19] From 1565 onwards his pension from the Chapel was increased in return for occasional compositions (see Lewis Lockwood, 'Palestrina, Giovanni Pierluigi da', *Grove Music Online*, para. 3, quoting Jeppesen in *Musik in Geschichte und Gegenwart*). He was active in this regard in 1587, when he composed a set of Lamentations for the choir (see Chapter 6, particularly n. 57). This *Miserere* is given in volume 31 of F.X. Haberl's *Pierluigi da Palestrina Werke* (Leipzig, 1892), 24–7.

[20] CS 205 also gives 1634, 1669 and 1676 for this *Miserere*, obviously dates of subsequent performances. 1623 is the last possible date of composition, as the following year Anerio left Rome for the last time to go to Poland.

[21] If it preceded that by Giovanni Francesco, it also preceded it in setting for the first-time verse 20a (the first part of verse 20). Misereres **3**, **4** and **5** all have a bass part (several low A's followed by a d) added in pencil in CS 206 for verse

of Palestrina's, attributed by Baini to Giovanni Maria Nanino (1543–1607), who joined the choir in 1577, which also includes a final verse a9.[22] Miserere **10** is the work of Sante Naldini (c.1595–1666), who joined the choir in 1617. **11** bears a double attribution, to 'Denticis' in CS 205, and to 'Domin. Nanini' in CS 206. It is in fact the same work as **2**, but with more rhythmic detail in the chanted sections of each verse.[23] Ruggero Giovannelli (c.1560–1625) gave up the post of *maestro di cappella* of the *Cappella Giulia* (the choir of S. Pietro) to join the Papal Choir in 1599. His *Miserere* (**12**) is one of the most interesting.[24]

20b, but the notes given do not come from those settings, nor from any of the others. **4** and **5** give rhythmic indications for the final word: vi- s. tu- m los b.

[22] 'In nono luogo vi sono il sopramenzionati due versi di Pierluigi alquanto variati, e con la giunta dell'ultimo verso à 9. voci: opera di Gio. Maria Nanini.' ('The ninth [*Miserere*] consists of the two verses by Pierluigi mentioned above but significantly varied, with the last verse for nine voices added: the work of Gio. Maria Nanino.') Baini, *Memorie*, n. 578 (vol. 2, 196). The same work is attributed to Palestrina in a manuscript in the Biblioteca Vallicelliana. If Nanino's setting predates that of Felice Anerio, perhaps it is he who should receive the credit for first setting verse 20b for the two choirs together. Like **4**, it can be seen in volume 31 of *Pierluigi da Palestrina Werke* (28–34). In 1905 it was published under Palestrina's name by Novello, adapted into English by W. Barclay Squire for use in Anglican offices (see Chapter 13, pp. 194–5). It was subsequently performed frequently, particularly in Oxbridge colleges.

[23] It is omitted in Baini's list. The final verse a9 is achieved by simply doubling the parts of *Coro 1°* in *Coro 2°*. It is also found in the Vatican Library, Ott. lat. 3388 (fols. 57^v–58^r), under the title 'Miserere mei Deus Fabritii Dentice cum responsione Joannis Maria Nanini' (see Luciano Luciani, *Sussidio per la consultazione dei cataloghi Boezi e Llorens dei fondi Cappella Giulia e Cappella Sistina della Biblioteca Vaticana*, Rome, 2014, esp. 507). This would tend to confirm that the mention of 'Domin. Nanino' (otherwise unknown) in CS 206 is a simple mistake or misreading and that G.M. Nanino was responsible for the amendments. Fabrizio Dentice (c.1539–1581), a renowned lutenist, was Luigi's son, and the *Miserere* was included in a posthumous edition of his sacred music entitled *Lamentationi ... aggiuntovi li responsori, antiphone, Benedictus, & Miserere*, published in Milan in 1593. It was also given with *passaggi* in Francesco Severi's *Salmi passaggiati* (Rome, 1615; see p. 37) and in Giovanni Domenico Viola, *Delli responsorii* (Naples, 1622). As father and son worked together in Naples and elsewhere, it seems most likely that Fabrizio 'borrowed' his father's work, and the compiler of Ott. lat. 3388 was unaware that it was originally the work of Luigi.

[24] Part of the same tradition is the *Miserere* by Matteo Simonelli (1618–1696), the 'Palestrina del secolo XVII', which was performed on Thursday 30 March 1684 ('30 Giovedì Santo ... A conclusione, venne cantato il Miserere di Matteo Simonelli a due cori', *DS* 103, fol. 9^{r-v}. Reproductions of some pages of this diary can be found at http://www.handelforever.com/docs/saggi/dongregoriodegiudici/8ildiario.htm). Only the five-part verses (1, 5, 9, 13 and 17 and 20) from his *falsobordone* survive in CS 192. In that year, Allegri's *Miserere* was sung on Wednesday and Felice Anerio's on Good Friday. A somewhat different

✳ Gregorio Allegri

Miserere **13**, the last in these manuscripts, is Gregorio Allegri's setting, added to the collection in 1661.[25] Born in Rome in 1582, Allegri (Fig. 5) was between the ages of nine and fourteen a member of the highly reputed choir school of S. Luigi dei Francesi under Giovanni Bernardino Nanino.[26] Bernardino had succeeded his elder brother, Giovanni Maria, a respected colleague and contemporary of Palestrina, who often returned to help with the boys, so Allegri must have benefited from instruction from them both. When his voice broke, Gregorio was replaced in the choir by his younger brother Domenico, but after five years absence he returned in 1601 as a tenor and occasional trombonist.[27]

In 1605 he took holy orders and soon afterwards accepted the post of singer and composer at the cathedral of Fermo, near the Adriatic coast in the Marches, one of the most distant of the Papal States. While there he published at least three volumes of motets for small forces and continuo, in the new style of Viadana, and contributed to various collections.[28] No doubt these publications served to keep him in the eye of the Roman musical world. However, by the time he returned to Rome in 1628 to become *maestro* at the Roman church of Santo Spiritu in Sassia, he found himself outshone by his younger brother Domenico, who had been *maestro* at S. Maria Maggiore since 1610.

---

work is Palestrina's *Miserere a tre cori*, from the Altemps collection. It remains a *falsobordone*, albeit on a very large scale. However, if it had ever been sung at *Tenebræ* by the Papal Choir, Baini would surely have mentioned the fact in his discussion of it (*Memorie*, vol. 2, 338–9). Another work even further from the Sistine Chapel *Tenebræ* tradition is Josquin's psalm-motet *Miserere* a5, composed in Ferrara in 1503–4 (after he had left the choir), which is a through-composed motet with very original formal features; it is found in CS 38 (begun in 1563).

[25] It is preceded by its own dated title page: 'Sedente ALEXANDRO VII PONT. OPT. MAX / Bonaventura Argenteo Magistro Cappellæ Pontificiæ pro tempore existente / Iustus Romanus Scripter 1661.'

[26] The notes on his life which follow are taken largely from the commentary by Jean Lionnet included with a CD of his music by the French ensemble A Sei Voci (Astrée-Audivis E8524), and from the article 'Allegri, Gregorio' in *Grove Music Online* by Jerome Roche (rev. Noel O'Regan).

[27] Jean Lionnet, 'Quelques aspects de la vie musicale à Saint-Louis-des-Français: de Giovanni Bernardino Nanino à Alessandro Melani (1591–1698)', in *Les fondations nationales dans la Rome pontificale: actes du colloque de Rome (16–19 mai 1978)* (Rome, 1981), 354.

[28] His volumes were all published in Rome: two books of *Concertini* (1618 and 1619) for two to five voices, and one of *Motecta* (1621) for two to six voices. According to Baini (*Memorie*, n. 475, vol. 2, 36) there was also an earlier volume of *Motecta* dated 1620. Baini lists as well unpublished works in the Altemps collection, and in the Biblioteca Vallicelliana.

Fig. 5 Engraving of Gregorio Allegri, in Andrea Adami, *Osservazioni per ben regolare il Coro de i Cantori della Cappella Pontificia* (1711), 198

Everything changed the following year. Domenico died suddenly, and Gregorio auditioned for the Papal Choir, into which he was accepted on 6 December 1629. Although by all accounts a mediocre singer, he was undoubtedly worth his place as a composer. Over the next twenty-two years until his death in 1652, he added five masses (for five, six and eight voices) to its repertoire, as well as motets, hymns and Lamentations.[29] In 1640 he was asked by his colleagues in the choir to revise Palestrina's hymns for the new texts decreed by Pope Urban VIII, showing his status as Palestrina's 'worthy successor and guardian of the stile antico'.[30] In the words of Jerome Roche, his *prima prattica* music shows that 'the stile antico, far from being insipid, could be the vehicle

---

[29] For more on Allegri's Lamentations, two of which stayed in the choir's repertoire until 1815, see Chapter 6, pp. 101–2.

[30] This phrase, together with the reference to his revision of Palestrina's hymns, was added by Noel O'Regan in his revision of Jerome Roche's *Grove Music Online* article on Allegri.

for superbly controlled sonority and counterpoint, using syncopation to lead to a climax and with a bass line entirely harmonic in function'.[31]

His standing in the eyes of his contemporaries is clear in Andrea Adami's tribute to him, which reproduces almost word for word the entry in the *Diario Sistina* recounting his death (Fig. 6).

> Fù la perdita di queſto grand'Uomo ſentita con infinito rammarico da tutto il noſtro Collegio. Appreſe, come ſi è detto di ſopra, la Muſica Teorica dal Nanini, già Cantore della noſtra Cappella, e tanto s'avanzò nell'eccellenza del Contrapunto, e del comporre, che quaſi pareggiò il ſuo Maeſtro ne i più reconditi arcani della medema; di che ne fanno degna fede le ſteſſe ſue Opere con tanta perfezione compoſte per il noſtro Archivio. Era ancora aggiunta alla ſua virtù una ſingolar bontà di coſtumi. Tanto a i poveri, che aveva ſempre alla ſua porta di Caſa, quanto a i carcerati, che quotidianamente viſitava, faceva larghe limoſine, come mi hà atteſtato un ſuo ſcolare ancor vivente Uomo degno d'ogni credito.

Fig. 6 Tribute to Allegri in Adami, *Osservazioni per ben regolare il Coro de i Cantori della Cappella Pontificia* (1711), 199–200

The loss of a man of such merit was felt by the whole of our college with the greatest of sorrow. He had learned musical theory with Signor Giovanni Maria Nanino, who was in his time musician of our chapel, and had become so advanced in the excellence of counterpoint and composition that he had almost equalled his teacher in the *arcana* of music, and future generations will find evidence of this in the works he composed of such perfection which are in our archive. In addition to his virtue, he had singularly good nature. He gave generous alms to the poor, who were always on his doorstep, as well as to prisoners, whom he visited daily, as I was assured by one of his pupils, a man worthy of belief, who is still alive.[32]

Allegri's version of Psalm 50, more harmonically interesting than most of the others (except perhaps that of Giovannelli, which precedes it in CS 205–6), appears to have been well received, its popularity, according to Giuseppe Baini, immediately eclipsing that of all those which had gone before:

---

[31] Roche, ibid. On the other hand he assesses the small-scale motets as 'written in an unambitious post-Viadana idiom, neither melodious in the manner of the best north Italians nor ornamented'.

[32] Adami, *Osservazioni*, 199–200. The entry in *DS* 70 is dated 18 February 1652.

This competition in writing Misereres for our college came to an end with the appearance of Allegri's composition. He himself improved it, even changing the parts, following the logic of the musical expression: subsequently it was altered a great deal more and perfected by other colleagues who were excellent performers and by composers who studied it, hence its execution reached that level of perfection admired by the whole world since the middle of seventeenth century. This *Miserere* of Allegri used to be sung at Matins on Wednesday and Good Friday, and at Matins on the Thursday the Misereres by Felice Anerio and Sante Naldini used to be given in alternation.[33]

Charles Burney's famous account of the *Miserere* tells a similar story, with a 'translation' from Adami's *Osservazioni*.

> After several vain attempts by preceding composers, for more than a hundred years, to set the same words to the satisfaction of the heads of the church; Gregorio Allegri succeeded so well, as to merit eternal praise; and with few notes, well modulated, and well understood, he composed such a *Miserere* as will continue to be sung on the same days, every year, for ages yet to come; and one that is conceived in such just proportions as will astonish future times, and ravish, as at present, the soul of every hearer.[34]

---

[33] 'Questa gara di scriver dei *Miserere* cessò nel nostro collegio all'apparire la composizione dell'Allegri. Egli stesso la ripuli, e cangionne per fino le parti, seguendo la ragion dell'effetto : a molto più fu variata e perfezionata da altri colleghi eccellenti esecutori, e compositori, che sopra vi studiarono, onde si ridusse nella esecuzione a qual grado perfetto, che in essa ammirò tutto il mondo fin dalla metà del secolo XVII. Questo *Miserere* dell'Allegri cantavasi nei mattutino del mercoledi, e del venerdi santo, nel mattutino del giovedi si soleva dire ora il Miserere di Felice Anerio, ora quel di Sante Naldini.' Baini, *Memorie*, n. 578 (vol. 2, 196). Baini's contention that Allegri himself revised his *Miserere*, and may even have modified the voicing, is interesting, and may explain why there is uncertainty about its date of composition. (See p. 34). Given that Baini is here discussing CS 205–6, he is clearly not, as might be supposed, thinking of the later version discussed in Chapter 3. There must in any case have been at least one earlier copy than that in CS 205–6, made during Allegri's lifetime. Perhaps the necessity of a new 'fair copy' in 1661 is a measure of the work's popularity. What is less clear is how Baini could have known about such modifications, unless he had access to an older manuscript which has since disappeared.

[34] *The Present State*, 276. The original is found in Adami, *Osservazioni*, 37–8. This is Burney's own translation, made after his return to England from the copy presented to him by Giuseppe Santarelli, his main source of information about the choir and the *Miserere*. A papal singer since 1749, Santarelli was *maestro pro tempore* in 1770, an administrative post (see p. 11), although Burney mistakenly describes him as '*Maestro di Capella* to his Holiness' and 'chief

Burney's version of the beginning of the passage hardly does justice to previous composers of Misereres. A better translation might be:

> Driven on by this example [that is, of the performers of the very first Misereres of 1514 which, as we have seen above, were not uniformly successful] their successors, endowed with greater ability and better taste, proudly showed one after another their profound knowledge, leaving behind so many beautiful compositions which are the great glory of our Archive. Of all these worthy composers, one who merits eternal praise over and above that for the others, is our one-time colleague Gregorio Allegri who, with few notes but ones which were so well modulated and excellently conceived, composed the *Miserere*, which is sung on the same days every year, and which has become the marvel of our times, being conceived in such proportions as to ravish the soul of the hearer.[35]

It has to be noted that Sir John Hawkins, in his *General History of the Science and Practice of Music*, was considerably less impressed with it than was Burney.

> Allegri was a man of a very devout temper: his works were chiefly for the service of the church ... Among his competitions in the church style is a Miserere in five parts in the key of G with the minor third, which by reason of its supposed excellence and pre-eminence over all others of the like kind, has for a series of years been not only reserved for the most solemn functions, but kept in the library of the pontifical chapel with a degree of care and reserve that none can account for.
>
> Andrea Adami, who might be a good singer, but was certainly a very poor writer, and, as may be collected from many passages in his book, less than a competent judge of the merits of musical composition, has given a character of this Work in the following words: 'Among those excellent composers who merit eternal praise, is Gregorio Allegri, who with few notes, but those well modulated, and better understood, has composed a Miserere, that on the same days in every year is sung, and is the wonder of our times, being conceived in such proportions as ravish the soul of the hearer.'

---

conductor'. Only from the second phrase onwards is Burney's commentary close to being a faithful translation.

[35] 'Da questo esempio animate i successori dotati di miglior abilità, e di miglior gusto, anno fatto pompa l'un dopo l'altro d'un profondo sapere, lasciando tante belle composizioni, che sono il lustro maggiore del nostro Archivio, e tra questi degni compositori merita al par d'ogn'altro una lode eterna il già nostro Compagno Gregorio Allegri, il quale con poche note, ma si ben modulate, e meglio intese hà composto il *Miserere*, che in tal giorno ogn'anno si canta, reso in vero la meraviglia de' nostri tempi, per esser concepito con proporzioni tali, che rapisce l'animo di chi l'ascolta.'

The above eulogium, hyperbolical as it is, will be found to mean but little when it is considered that most men express delight and admiration, rapture and astonishment in the strongest terms that imagination can suggest. The Miserere of Allegri is in its structure simply counterpoint, a species of composition which it must be allowed does not call for the utmost exertions of genius, industry, or skill; and it might be said that the burial service of Purcell and Blow may well stand in competition with it; if not, the Miserere of Tallis, printed in the Cantiones Sacrae of him and Bird in the year 1575, in the opinion of a sober and impartial judge, will be deemed in every respect so excellent, as to suffer by the bare comparison of it with that of Allegri.[36]

Allegri's *Miserere* is usually said to date from 1638, following information given by Alfieri in his publication of 1840 (see Chapter 10). Alfieri's source remains unknown.[37] Another manuscript, now in Venice, gives 1630.[38] Both dates may have some truth in them given that, as noted above, Baini asserted that Allegri 'himself improved it, even changing the parts, following the logic of the musical expression' during his lifetime.[39] In any case it is impossible for the moment to know exactly when it found the form in which it appears in CS 205–6.

Allegri set verses 1, 5, 9, 13, 17 and the first part of 20 for 5 voices, and 3, 7, 11, 15 and 19 for four, the opposite of most of the earlier settings, including Festa's.[40] Following the innovation of Felice Anerio (or G.M. Nanino), the nine voices join together for the second half of the final verse, '*Tunc imponent super altare tuum vitulos*'. Allegri broke new ground in not setting the first part of verse 5 ('*Tibi soli peccavi*') for the two choirs in alternation, before having the

---

[36] Sir John Hawkins, *A General History of the Science and Practice of Music* (London, 1776), vol. 4, 90–1. He had probably only heard the five-part verses, performed at meetings of the Academy of Ancient Music, which he acknowledged were faulty and incomplete (see p, 43, n. 15).

[37] Manuscripts which give this date (e.g. Naples Conservatorio MS 21.6.4) appear to be merely following Alfieri.

[38] Biblioteca Nazionale Marciana, Cod. It. IV, 1339 [=11092] 'scritto per la cappella di S.Pietro in Roma nel 1630'. The mention of the *Cappella di S. Pietro* is surprising. Perhaps the writer was merely confused about the different papal choirs. But it is also possible that Allegri wrote his *Miserere* initially for the *Cappella Giulia* before he had been invited to join the Papal Chapel. Misereres were sung in S. Pietro during Holy Week, and the director of the Cappella from 1626 to 1629 was Paolo Agostini (1583–1629), whom Allegri must have known well from having grown up with him at S. Luigi dei Francesi. If the date of 1630 is correct, these circumstances could explain why his *Miserere* was not incorporated immediately into CS 205–6 when that collection was assembled in 1631.

[39] See n. 33.

[40] Verse 1 from CS 205 is given in Appendix 1, and verse 3 (transcribed from CS 340, but identical) in Appendix 3.

whole verse repeated by *Coro 1°*, a feature of all the other *Misereres* (except the truncated No. 8).[41]

The Gregorian basis of the two *falsobordoni* is not initially clear. According to Bradshaw 'in the second half of the 16th century (about 1570) composers began to treat the psalm tone melody loosely and eventually abandoned it, but the style and form of the *falsobordone* remained intact.'[42] Allegri's *Miserere* is a good example of this practice. In the five-part verses (for SATTB, with the clefs c1 c3 c4 c4 f4,) the tone is found in the first tenor part in the first half, and the soprano in the second. The basis of the *falsobordone* turns out to be the *tonus peregrinus* (sometimes known as 'the wandering tone'), recognisable because the reciting note in the second part of the verse is a tone lower than that in the first part. The *tonus peregrinus* is the only tone with this feature, a characteristic that trumps all others.[43] However, while the reciting notes (*d* and *c*) are maintained throughout, the normal endings are modified for what appear to be primarily harmonic reasons. Fig. 7 shows Lundberg's analysis of the Allegri.

Choir	first semi-verse	second semi-verse
I	G minor (*ténor: d*) – Bb major	F major (*ténor: c*) – D, *tierce de Picardie*
II	G minor – D major	C minor – G, *tierce de Picardie*

Fig. 7 Harmonic analysis of Allegri's *Miserere* after Lundberg, 'The *Tonus Peregrinus*', 27

The endings in fact resemble more closely Tone I (the tone with which the *tonus peregrinus* has the most in common), especially that of the second half. In the four-part verses too, the psalm-tone is carried in different parts in each

---

[41] In Felice Anerio's setting this first phrase has been crossed out in pencil in all parts in CS 205–6. As his *Miserere* remained in the repertoire far longer than any of the others in this source, except of course Allegri's, this modification could date from any time up to the early eighteenth century, although it seems most likely that it closely followed Allegri's innovation in this regard.

[42] Bradshaw, '*Falsobordone*' (see Chapter 1, n. 28), para. 3.

[43] It is one of several psalm-tones which did not confirm to the normal medieval model, but the only one to survive the Middle Ages. See also Matthias Lundberg, 'The *Tonus Peregrinus* in the Polyphony of the Western Church' (PhD thesis, University of Liverpool, 2007), 16. Lundberg has since published a revised version of his thesis as a book, *Tonus Peregrinus: The History of a Psalm-Tone and its Use in Polyphonic Music* (Farnham, 2011). The chapter on Allegri's treatment of the *tonus peregrinus* in the thesis (Ch. 18) appears as Chapter 11 in the book.

half – the first soprano in the first, the second soprano in most of the second; the *tonus peregrinus* is however clearer.[44]

In the later revision of the five-part verses (by Giovanni Biordi, see Chapter 3) any connection to the psalm-tone virtually disappears after the reciting notes. This is perhaps one of the reasons that in most editions of the 'English Miserere' a psalm-tone (Tone II) is suggested for the *cantus planus* verses which has no obvious relationship either with Allegri's original or with later modifications.[45] As will be seen in later chapters (particularly Chapter 17), by the eighteenth century the *cantus planus* verses were sung by the Papal Choir on a monotone; that would also have been a logical solution in the seventeenth century to doubts about the original Tone.

---

[44] Lundberg ('The *Tonus Peregrinus*', 29–31, 57–8, 62–3 and esp. 276–80) notes a particular connection between Psalm 50 and the *tonus peregrinus* in polyphonic music written in Rome in the seventeenth century, due either to a theological connection with Psalm 113 (*In exitu Israel*, related to the *tonus peregrinus* because of its association with wandering) at the very end of Lent, or to a liturgical one with the Benedictus, the last canticle in the office of *Tenebræ* before the Miserere was sung. Tommaso Bai was also inspired by the *tonus peregrinus* in his *Miserere* (see Chapter 3), while treating it in an equally free style.

[45] Curiously, the *Miserere* has been described since the late eighteenth century as being based on Tone II. Among the manuscripts that do so are MS 4385 in the Biblioteca del Liceo Musicale di Bologna, another in the Stadtarchiv of Nördlingen, copied in the nineteenth century by Julius Ruttmann, and one in the library of the Benedictine Abbey in Ottobüren (MS MO117) which describes the Misereres of both Allegri and Bai as follows: 'Duo Miserere. à duplici Choro Toni 2di Primum pro Coena Domini. authore Baji Secundum pro Feria Sexta. Toni 2di & Die Parasceves. auth: Gregorio Allegri.' In the 'English Miserere' of course, the 'trucker's gear-change' moment in the second half of the four-part verses (see p. 190) completely destroys any pretention to a relationship with any known psalm-tone.

3

Transformation

 Allegri's *Miserere*

THE circumstances of performance of *falsobordone* psalms by the Papal Choir – always unaccompanied (like all its performances) and with few rhythmic imperatives apart from those deriving from the text – made them uniquely apt for the application of decoration in performance, particularly at the cadences. Towards the end of the sixteenth century several treatises appeared showing ways of ornamenting *falsobordoni*. Among the earliest was the *Breve et facile maniera d'essercitarsi ... a far passaggi* (1593) by the Papal Chapel singer Luca Conforti, who followed up with three volumes of *Salmi passaggiati* in 1601–03. In 1615 another papal singer, Francesco Severi, published a similar volume with the same title. It may be that this ornamentation was primarily intended for solo singers, with a bass line supplied 'for singing with organ or with other instruments', although it also provided models for different singers within a group to improvise against the accompaniment of the others.[1]

Perhaps more relevant to the singers of the Chapel were the publications of G.-B. Bovicelli (*Regole, Passaggi di Musica* of 1594) and Lodovico Viadana (*Cento concerti ecclesiastici* of 1602), which give many examples of short cadential flourishes. But the most interesting evidence may be Luigi Zenobi's description, in a letter dating from around 1600, of the art of a good singer.

---

[1] Severi makes clear in the introduction that he wished to show a style popular in Rome: 'I well know that similar *passaggi* are customarily improvised by good singers in Rome and elsewhere when they sing services, but [I am publishing my works] because I wish only to please those who desire to see the style adhered to in Rome when singing psalms.' M.C. Bradshaw, 'Performance Practice and the Falsobordone', *Performance Practice Review*, 10/2 (Fall 1997), 232. Severi's publication includes a set of *passaggi* based on the *Miserere* by Luigi Dentice (Misereres 2 and 11 in CS 205–6), published under the name of his son Fabrizio in 1593 (see p. 28, n. 23). A 1994 recording of the Allegri *Miserere* by the French ensemble A Sei Voci gives an imagined reconstruction conceived by the musicologist Jean Lionnet, largely based on Severi, of an early ornamented performance (see pp. 209–10), and a similar one, by Le Poème Harmonique, appeared in 2019.

> He must know when to make *esclamationi* and not apply them indiscriminately nor crudely, as many do. He must know how to ascend with the voice and how to descend with grace, at times holding over part of the preceding note and sounding it anew if the consonance requires and admits it; he must know how to give rise to dissonances (*durezze* and *false*) where the composer has not touched or made them, but left them to the singer's judgement. He must blend and accord with the other voices; he must at times render the notes with a certain neglect [*con disprezzo*], sometimes so as to drag them, sometimes with sprightly motion; he must have a rich repertoire of *passaggi* and good judgement as to how to use them; he must know which are the good ones, starting with those that are made with the greatest artifice of one note, of two, three, four, five, six, seven, and eight. He must know how to use them ascending or descending he must know how to intertwine, connect, and double them; he must know how to emphasize and to avoid a cadence, he must know how playfully to sing detached and legato crotchets; he must know how to begin a *passaggio* with quavers and finish it with semiquavers and begin it with semiquavers and end it with quavers. He must use different *passaggi* in the same songs, he must know how to improvise them in every kind of vocal music, ... he must know which works require them and which do not; when repeating the same thing he must always sing new ones.

Most telling of all is his definition of 'plain' performance. 'He must know how to sing the piece in its simple form, that is, without any *passaggio*, but only with grace [*gratia*], *trillo, tremolo, ondeggiamento,* and *esclamatione.*' Finally, he must know how to express the meaning of the text, and which ornaments are suitable in different styles.

> He must understand the meaning of the words, whether they be secular or spiritual; ... he must know how at times to begin loudly and then to let the voice die gradually; and at times to begin, or end, softly and then enliven it gradually; he must know how to improvise *passaggi* in skips, in syncopation, and in *sesquialtera;* he must know thoroughly which places demand them; he must start with discrimination and finish in time with those who sing or play with him; he must sing in one style in church, in another one in the chamber, and in a third one in the open air, whether it be in daytime or at night; he must perform a motet in one manner, a *villanella* in another, a lamentation differently from a cheerful song, and a mass in another style than a *falsobordone*, an air differently again ...[2]

---

[2] Luigi Zenobi, '*Lettere*', Biblioteca Vallicelliana, Rome, MS R. 45 (*Raccolta di lettere varie Latine, et Italiane*), fols. 199ʳ–204ᵛ, ed. and trans. in Bonnie J. Blackburn and Edward Lowinsky, 'Luigi Zenobi and his Letter on the Perfect Musician', *Studi musicali*, 22 (1993), 61–114. See also p. 234, n. 17 concerning *portamento*.

It is clear that there was a myriad of ways to decorate other than *passaggi*; in fact by 1628 Vincenzo Giustiniani was calling excessive use of them old-fashioned, and other authors (Rognoni, Caccini and Doni) extolled a certain negligent grace – *sprezzatura* – rather than the *affettazione* of *passaggi*.[3]

The four-part verses

It is clear that many of these techniques were applied to Allegri's *Miserere*, and that by the eighteenth century it was this manner of performance by the papal singers – with their own ornaments and various expressive devices kept secret from outsiders – that made it famous, as Charles Burney explained.

> Signor Santarelli favoured me with the following particulars relative to the famous *Miserere* of *Allegri*. This piece, which, for upwards of a hundred and fifty years, has been annually performed in Passion Week at the Pope's chapel, on Wednesday and Good-Friday, and which, in appearance, is so simple as to make those, who have only seen it on paper, wonder whence its beauty and effect could arise, owes its reputation more to the manner in which it is performed, than to the composition: the same music is many times repeated to different words, and the singers have, by tradition, certain customs, expressions, and graces of convention, (*certe espressioni e Gruppi*) which produce great effects; such as swelling and diminishing the sounds altogether; accelerating or retarding the measure at some particular words, and singing some entire verses quicker than others.[4]

Santarelli went on to show the importance of the *espressioni e Gruppi* by telling Burney the experience of the Holy Roman Emperor Leopold I.

> The Emperor Leopold the first, not only a lover and patron of music, but a good composer himself, ordered his ambassador, at Rome, to entreat the Pope to permit him to have a copy of the celebrated *Miserere* of *Allegri*, for the use of the Imperial chapel at Vienna; which being granted, a copy was made by the *Signor Maestro* of the Pope's chapel, and sent to the Emperor, who had then in his service some of the first singers of the age; but, notwithstanding the abilities of the performers, this composition was so far from answering the expectations of the Emperor and his court, in the execution, that he concluded the Pope's *Maestro di Capella*, in order to keep it a mystery, had put a trick upon him, and sent him another composition.

---

[3] Vincenzo Giustiniani, *Discorso sopra la musica de' suoi tempi*, Lucca, Archivio di Stato, MS O. 49, c.1628; Francesco Rognoni, *Selve Passaggi*, vol. 1 (Milan, 1620); Giulio Caccini, *Le Nuove Musiche* (Florence, 1602); Doni, *Annotazioni*.
[4] *The Present State*, 275–6.

Burney gives Santarelli's exact expression in a footnote: '*Quantunque Cantato da Musici soavissimi, fece alla Corte di Vienna la Misera Comparsa di un semplicissimo falso Bordone*' ('Even though sung by the finest of musicians, at the court of Vienna it gave the wretched appearance of the simplest of *falso Bordoni*'). The Emperor's letter of complaint was sufficient to have the poor *maestro* who had prepared it sacked. When he was finally allowed to explain himself – several years later! – he said:

> that the stile of singing in his chapel, particularly in performing the *Miserere*, was such as could not be expressed by notes, nor taught or transmitted to any other place, but by example; for which reason the piece in question, though faithfully transcribed, must fail in its effect, when performed elsewhere. His Holiness did not understand music, and could hardly comprehend how the same notes should sound so differently in different places.

The Emperor therefore asked that some papal singers should be sent to Vienna to instruct his own singers

> in the same expressive manner as in the Sistine chapel in Rome which was granted. But before they arrived, a war broke out with the Turks, which called the Emperor from Vienna; and the Miserere has never yet, perhaps, been truly performed, but in the Pope's chapel.[5]

These passages by Burney were endlessly repeated by later writers. They support Baini's contention concerning the speed with which the *Miserere* had been transformed into something 'rich and strange', for the most likely date for a sudden outbreak of hostilities against the Turks is their invasion of Austria early in 1683 (Leopold fought them on and off throughout his long reign, from 1658 to 1705). If this story, told to Burney by Santarelli, is true – and it was at least three-quarters of a century old when Burney heard it – it states clearly that before the end of the seventeenth century, the embellishments made in performance were already sufficient to render Allegri's basic score unrecognisable.[6]

In his description of the way the choir sang, Burney made no distinction between the verses for four and those for five voices. For listeners who have only ever heard the 'English Miserere', characterized by 'straight' choral verses

---

[5] Ibid., 279–81.

[6] In fact, given the relevance of the techniques outlined by Zenobi, Rognoni, Caccini, Viadana, Bovicelli and others, there seems little doubt that the earliest singers' decorations are contemporary with the creation of the *Miserere*. Furthermore, the enthusiasm of Allegri's patron, Pope Urban VIII, for singers and opera can only have encouraged them; see Laurenz Lütteken, 'Perpetuierung des Einzigartigen: Gregorio Allegris 'Miserere' und das Ritual der päpstlichen Kappelle', in *Barocke Inszenierung: Akten des Internationalen Forschungscolloquiums an der Technischen Universität Berlin, 20.–22. Juni 1996*, ed. Joseph Imorde, Fritz Neumeyer and Tristan Weddigen (Emsdetten, 1999), 139–42.

alternating with those covered with outbursts of soloistic ornament, this may come as a surprise. It is true that by the nineteenth century most attention was focused on the ornamentation added to the four-part verses to give the famous top Cs, but in Burney's time all the singers in both choirs participated in the *espressioni e Gruppi*. Apart from the *cantus planus* verses, this was music for soloists. Burney noted also that it was 'performed by select voices, who have frequent rehearsals, particularly on the Monday in Passion Week, which is wholly spent in repeating and polishing the performance'.[7] 'Select voices' implies the use of soloists in all the parts. This will be confirmed in the chapters below.

The five-part verses

By Burney's time, not only had the whole *Miserere* been transformed by the singers, but the five-part verses had been completely remodelled by composers. The new version is found first in CS 263, the work of the Chapel singer Giovanni Biordi. A prolific composer in the *prima prattica* style, Biordi (1691–1748) joined the Papal Choir in 1717, and remained associated with it until his death. From 1722 he was also *maestro* of S. Giacomo degli Spagnuoli, a post he won for his compositional skills against some strong candidates.[8] Baini praised Biordi's skill in completing hitherto abbreviated Lamentations settings by Allegri and Palestrina during the reign of Pope Benedict XIII (1724–30) when they would have otherwise been expunged from the repertoire, 'completing the task with great success in very closely imitating the styles of both Pierluigi and especially Allegri'.[9]

Biordi may have begun CS 263, a work-book largely devoted to his own compositions and arrangements, soon after his arrival in the choir, and his version of the five-part verses of the Allegri is the first item. A note at the bottom

---

[7] *The Present State*, 277. This observation is not in the journal. Perhaps it was part of the 'extracts from his own book in MS. relative to several points of musical history, all invaluable as it is utterly impossible to get them elsewhere' given to Burney by Santarelli on 16 November (Charles Burney, *Music, Men and Manners in France and Italy 1770, being the Journal Written by Charles Burney, Mus. D. … Transcribed from the Original Manuscript in the British Museum*, ed. H.E. Poole, London, 1969, 206). Santarelli's description of the music given to Emperor Leopold as 'un semplicissimo falso Bordone' no doubt also figured.

[8] They included Niccolò Porpora. The story is told at some length in Baini, *Memorie*, n. 511 (vol. 2, 63–4).

[9] 'Si presto il Biordi con impegno, e, valorosissimo compositor che egli era, riuscì eccellentemente nell' opera, imitando assai da vicino le maniere tanto del Pierluigi, quanto dell' Allegri.' Baini, *Memorie*, vVol .2, 201. These extra verses, added to Allegri's Lamentations for Thursday and Saturday and to Palestrina's for Friday, are all in CS 263. In 1733 fair copies were made of the originals with Biordi's additions in CS 342. See also pp. 101–2 below.

of the first page reads 'the *primo coro* of the Allegri's *Miserere* changed, the 2do *coro* remains the same as before'.[10] The most important modification is in the voicing: Biordi transformed one of the tenor parts into a second soprano. This had the effect of making the psalm-tone, formerly carried by that tenor, more audible, and also gives a lighter, airier texture, more 'baroque' in feeling. Biordi's setting is also more elaborate. In the second half of the verse it moves into polyphony (in verse 1) after 'secundum ma-' for '-gnam misericordiam tuam'. In the original version 'secundum magnam miseri-' was recited before the composed cadence, consisting only of '-cordiam tuam'. Further modifications followed, and in 1731 a definitive text was copied into CS 185. The canto 1, alto and tenor parts at the end of the second half were rewritten, but the first half, and the harmonic outline of the whole, is Biordi's. Presumably it was to these rewritings that Baini was referring when he described the *Miserere* as being 'perfected by ... composers who studied it'.[11]

Burney's edition

Burney's first journey through Europe in 1770 was undertaken in preparation for his *General History of Music* (which eventually appeared from 1776

---

[10] 'Il primo coro del Miserere dell'Allegri mutato, il 2° coro è l'istesso di prima' (fol. 2ᵛ). The extra verses for the Lamentations, also full of revisions, are found from fol. 20. According to Baini's account, they must date from 1725, the first Holy Week after the accession of Benedict XIII, which gives a *terminus ante quem* to the revisions of the Allegri.

[11] A transcription of verse 1 of Biordi's version is provided in Appendix 2, and it can be compared with CS 341 (identical to CS 185), given complete in Appendix 3. In both cases the important variant in the second half of verses 5 and 13 is also shown. It seems likely that the subsequent revision was also by Biordi, who was still alive, although it is impossible to be sure. The lapse of time between Biordi's first draft (1725 at the latest and possibly up to eight years earlier) and the copying of its definitive version into CS 185 is puzzling. Perhaps there was initial resistance to the fundamental changes it brought to such a well-known and important work. For the sake of completeness, mention must also be made of CS 354 (1705), which, curiously, inverses the choirs: verses 1, 5, 9, 13, 17 and 20a are sung to the four-part music normally used for verses 3, 7, 11, 15 and 19, and those latter verses are sung to the five-part music (the original version as in CS 205) normally used for verses 1, 5, 9, 13, 17 and 20a. Verse 20b is the usual version a9. In the manuscript it follows an extensive setting of *Christus factus est* for four voices by Baldessare Sartori. Sartori was a papal singer who joined the choir in 1698 (Baini, *Memorie*, n. 510, vol. 2, 62), but while *Christus factus est* always immediately preceded the *Miserere* in the office, in the Sistine Chapel it was intoned in plainsong (see above). It seems most likely then that this manuscript was prepared for a particular celebration of *Tenebræ* that took place elsewhere.

onwards), hence his assiduous collecting of music, books and information. Perhaps it was the interest of the English people he met in musical events and gossip that made him realise how popular an account of his travels would be. So the first thing he published on his return, *The Present State of Music in France and Italy*, was an edited version of his journal.[12] Those English people were also, he found, fascinated with the exoticism of the Vatican and of the Papal Choir, and his generous reception by Santarelli no doubt encouraged the idea of collecting and publishing some of its music. In a letter to the actor David Garrick, he wrote:

> As to the Music of the Pope's Chapel, I shall be enabled to speak of it from the best authority my own Eyes & Ears can afford – Sig^r Santarelli the pope's Maestro di Capella has loaded me with Civility & Friendly offices – is now getting made out for me Copies of the best Compositions that are in constant use in the Pope's Chapel.[13]

The fact that one key work, written for the most emotionally charged week of the year, was allegedly embargoed, can only have increased his enthusiasm. The collection appeared in 1771 with the title *La musica che si canta annualmente nelle Funzioni della Settimana Santa nella Cappella Pontificale*.[14] Although the Allegri was no doubt the main selling-point, in fact it is Palestrina's music which takes pride of place, with no less than three works: *Stabat mater* (performed at the distribution of palms on Palm Sunday), *Fratres, ego enim accepi* (sung at mass on Maundy Thursday) and the *Improperia* (for the Adoration of the Cross on Good Friday). Allegri's *Miserere* closes the volume, which also includes Tommaso Bai's *Miserere*. Commentary is restricted to brief biographies of the composers taken mostly from Adami with some input from Santarelli. To supplement the information on the style of Italian singers in *The Present State of Music*, Burney quoted some lines from Giovanni Battista Bontempi's *Istoria Musica* (1695) concerning the training of Roman singers, which Santarelli had allowed him to copy. No doubt this further increased the exoticism-quotient.[15]

---

[12] The journal (in Burney, *Music, Men and Manners*, see n. 7) gives precise dates, as well as sources and context, for many of Burney's most famous comments.

[13] Written from Naples on 17 October, before returning to Rome in November. See *The Letters of Dr Charles Burney*, ed. Alvaro Ribeiro, vol. 1: *1751–1784* (Oxford, 1991), 65.

[14] Burney amused himself with a title page entirely in Italian, including his own name – Carlo Burney. Curiously, it is not listed among Burney's publications in *Grove Music Online*.

[15] There appears to have been at least one manuscript of the Allegri in circulation in London earlier. Ilias Chrissocoidis, in 'London Mozartiana: Wolfgang's Disputed Age & Early Performances of Allegri's *Miserere*', *Musical Times*, 151

It is Burney's version of the five-part verses that is commonly heard in modern performances; however, it contains important differences from that in CS 185 and 341, for reasons which will be examined more closely in Chapter 13 (pp. 185–7). It should also be noted in passing that, despite the fact that much of the reputation and mystique of the *Miserere* in the Anglo-Saxon world comes from his explanations, Burney's account is entirely hearsay. His visits to Rome took place in the autumn: an initial visit from 28 September to 13 October, and a brief return for ten days in November to collect the manuscripts he had requested. He thus never heard the *Miserere* sung in the Chapel, although during his final visit with Santarelli, 'he and his brethren of the Pope's chapel, were so obliging as to execute several beautiful compositions of Palestrina, Benevoli, and Allegri, in order to give me a true idea of the delicate and expressive manner in which they are sung in the chapel of his holiness'.[16] It would be surprising if they had not sung some of the *Miserere* for him, given his keen interest in it. However, none of whatever impression it made on him found its way to the pages of his publication. His edition shows no trace of secret *espressioni e Gruppi*, and the four-part verses are more or less as found in CS 206, a version 'unrecognisable' for more than one hundred years. In the words

---

(Summer 2010), 83–9, documents performances from 1734 onwards organised by the Academy of Ancient Music. The Academy apparently used a score brought back from Rome in that year by the Hon. Robert Hamilton, brother of the Earl of Abercorn; it was popular, and remained in the repertoire until at least the 1760s. A notice for a performance in 1749, 'Motet *for five Voices. / Part of the LIst Psalm* [by] Signor Allegri', shows that the manuscript gave only the *Coro 1°*, i.e. not the verses with most of the *abbellimenti*.

On the other hand, the contiguity of the date with the copying of CS 185 three years earlier suggests that it may have been the new version which Hamilton obtained, in which case the insistence on Allegri's name rather than Biordi's is perhaps a measure of the mystique which already surrounded the 'Allegri Miserere'. According to Hawkins (in 1776), 'the few copies of the Miserere of Allegri till lately extant are said to be incorrect, having been surreptitiously obtained, or written down by memory, and the chasms [sic] afterwards supplied: such it is said is that in the library of the Academy of Ancient Music' (*A General History*, vol. 4, 90n). This manuscript is not in the collection of material from the Academy recently found at Westminster Abbey (see H. Diack Johnstone, 'Westminster Abbey and the Academy of Ancient Music: A Library Once Lost and Now Partially Recovered', *Music & Letters*, 95/3 (August 2014), 329–73. Neither is it the version given in British Library, Egerton MS 2468, as is suggested (by former owner Edward Goddard?) on fol. 59, as there the five-part verses as found in CS 205 are adapted to four parts, and the verses from CS 206 are included. None of the other manuscripts of the Allegri in the British Library can be dated to earlier than Burney's publication.

[16] *The Present State*, 372.

of Giuseppe Baini seventy years later, Burney's publication contains only 'the bare notes, the skeleton of the two Misereres'.[17]

※ Tommaso Bai

By the early eighteenth century, then, less than a hundred years after its composition, the 'Allegri Miserere' had already very little to do with Allegri: the five-part verses were in process of being radically modified, and all the verses, particularly the four-part ones, were almost obscured by embellishments. It was to hear these that the public thronged the Sistine Chapel three times every Holy Week. As the music to be performed was never announced, visitors who happened to be there on a day when a different Miserere was given went away disappointed. It was perhaps for this reason that from the second half of the seventeenth century it was usually programmed twice, on Wednesday and Good Friday, with that of either Felice Anerio or Naldini given on Thursday.

Even a *Miserere* by Alessandro Scarlatti, arguably of far greater musical quality, seems to have aroused little enthusiasm when it was performed in 1708, although it replaced Naldini's for a while.[18] It is an interesting and in many ways original work, but it laboured under the huge disadvantage of not sounding like Allegri's, because the ornamentations which drew the crowds could not be adapted to it. Perhaps Tommaso Bai listened, observed and reflected. Just three years later, in 1711, he found the solution to the problem of the third day of *Tenebræ*, by the simple expedient of tailoring his setting to that of Allegri, so that the same ornamentations could be used:

> '[On Holy Thursday] was sung the *Miserere* of Signor Tomaso Baij, a singer in the Vatican Basilica, [and] afterwards it was presented to His Holiness, who was pleased to accept it, and sent it on to the eminent Cardinal Protector so

---

[17] 'le note semplici, le scheletto dei due miserere'. Letter of 30 March 1841 addressed to the *Maestro del Sacro Palazzo Apostolico*, F.D. Buttaoni, concerning Alfieri's forthcoming publication of the Misereres of Allegri and Bai (CS 658, fol. 45ʳ). See p. 148 and n. 3.

[18] Baini dated this work to 'around 1680', when Scarlatti was in Rome as *maestro di cappella* to Queen Kristina of Sweden. However, Luca Della Libera has recently proposed 1708 as the date of composition in his edition of it in a volume of Scarlatti's *Selected Sacred Music* (Recent Researches in the Music of the Baroque Era, Middleton, WI, 2012, viii). There was certainly a performance of it in that year (see p. 245, n. 14), and the problems in performance on that occasion suggest that it may have been the first. Three years later, in 1711, a fair copy was made for the Chapel archives (CS 188–9), the usual procedure after acceptance by the choir, and in the same year Adami (*Osservazioni*, 41) listed it as a possible *Miserere* for the second evening of *Tenebræ*.

that, having been accepted for the purpose, it was sung, which resulted in general applause.'[19]

Baini confirmed its favourable reception, while mistaking the date.

> And at the request of the college, Tommaso Bai, of Crevalcuore near Bologna, *maestro* of St Peter's Basilica, wrote in 1714 a new *Miserere* with one verse for 5, the other for 4, and the last for 8 voices, based on the phrases of the *Miserere* of Allegri, and since he made slight variations also for the other verses, with very fine, simple, and sublime music, he gained the greatest applause and his perpetual glory on the basis of this work alone. From 1714 until 1767 inclusively, the two Misereres of Allegri and Bai on the three services of Tenebræ Matins shared the applause of the public, and the Misereres of Felice Anerio and Scarlatti were never sung again in our chapel.[20]

Bai (born c.1636, died 1714 or later; often spelt Baj, although the j is just a long Italian i) had been a singer in the *Cappella Giulia* since 1670, initially as an *altus* and, from about 1696, a tenor. Nothing is known about his early life and education. He apparently led a blameless life as a respected singer, serving no less than five different *maestri* of that *cappella* – Orazio Benevolo, Ercole Bernabei, Antonio Masini, Francesco Beretta and Paolo Lorenzani. His vocation as a composer seems to have come relatively late, but surviving works include two masses and about twenty motets. At the very end of his life, in November 1713, he was appointed *maestro* of the *Cappella Giulia*, succeeding Lorenzani on the latter's death.

---

[19] 'Fù cantata il Miserere del Sig^r Tomaso Baij cantore della Basilica Vaticana, quale avendolo p'ima presentato a N. S. si compiacque accetarlo, e lo mando all em° Protet're ; accioche riconosciutolo al proposito, fosse fatto cantare, quale riuscho di commune applauso.' *DS* 131 (1711), fol. 20^v (2 April).

[20] 'Quindi ad istanza del collegio Tommaso Bai, di Crevalcuore nel Bolognese, maestro della basilica vaticana, scrisse nel 1714 un nuovo *Miserere* con un verso a 5, l'altro a 4, e ultima ad 8 voci sopra gli andamenti del *Miserere* dell'Allegri, ed avendo variato alcun poco, ma con chiarissime, semplicissime, ed insieme sublimi melodie anche gli altri versi, otienne il massimi applauso, e perpetuo la sua gloria con questo sola produzione. Dal 1714 fino al 1767 inclusivamente li due *Miserere* dell'Allegri et del Bai si divisero nei tre mattutini delle tenebre i plausi dell'auditorio, e mai più non si sono cantati nella nostri cappella i *Miserere* di Felice Anerio e dello Scarlatti.' Baini, *Memorie*, n. 578 (vol. 2, 196–7). The earliest Papal Choir manuscript of Bai's *Miserere* (CS 203–4) is dated 1713, the date that Burney also gives. Perhaps Baini thought it had been created for a performance the following year, although its copying into choirbooks about two years after its first performance was normal practice. Two later Misereres are noted by Baini: Giuseppe Tartini's in 1768 and Paschale Pisari's in 1777. According to Baini neither was deemed good enough to be repeated (*Memorie*, n. 513, vol. 2, 65–6) although if that is the case it is strange that Pisari's was immediately added, in particularly ornate script, to CS 340–1, the manuscripts used in Holy Week every year.

On Sunday after the Office of None in the chapter, the *Maestro di Cappella* was declared to be Sig. Tommaso Bai, the oldest musician at S. Pietro, a man of excellence, and whose compositions had often been sung there, and Sig. Scarlatti was named coadjutor.[21]

More detail is given in the decrees of the chapter.

Our most reverend chapter then voted by acclamation ... and elected him unanimously in the place and role of the late, abovementioned Pietro Paolo Lorenzani. But to help him in that task, weighed down as he was by his years, being certainly 75 years old, the chapter executed a secret vote placing the ballots in an urn in the usual way and elected and appointed Domenico Scarlatti as Bai's coadjutor, to succeed him after his death.[22]

His tenure lasted just thirteen months, and according to official sources he died on 22 December 1714.[23]

---

[21] 'Domenica dopo nona in capitulo fu dichiarato Maestro di Cappella il Sig. Tommaso Bai, il più antico musico di S. Pietro, e virtuoso, le di cui composizione già erano state più volte cantate in S. Pietro, e coadjutore il Sig. Scarlatti.' 'Giornal-Vatican fatto di Sige Abbate Colognoni Maestro di Ceremonie della Basilica', vol. 33, 298 (19 November 1713), Archivio Capitolare di San Pietro, Rome, trans. in Ralph Kirkpatrick, *Domenico Scarlatti* (Princeton, 1953), 332.

[22] 'Quibus commotum idem reverendissimum Capitulum viva voce, cuiusque suffragiis nemine discrepante illum elegit in locum et munus supradictum Petri Pauli Laurenzani defuncti. In auxilium autem eius ingravescentis ætatis, annorum nempe 75, in eodem munere per vota secreta ex urna de more collecta illi in coadiutorem cum futura successione post eius mortem elegit et designavit Dominicum Scarlattum.' Archivio Capitolare di San Pietro, Armadio XV, Decreti, 20, cc. 63ᵛ–64ʳ, 19 November 1713, reproduced in Giancarlo Rostirolla, *Musica e musicisti nella Basilica di San Pietro* (Rome, 2014), 476, and online at http://www.storiacappellagiulia.it/p/appendici-documentarie.html. Bai's date of birth is usually given as c.1650, apparently on the assumption that he was sixty-four at his death (as in the funeral inscription in Fig. 8). This however cannot be correct: the chapter is unlikely to have made such a large error and, unless he was gravely ill, it would hardly have been necessary to name a coadjutor if he was indeed only sixty-four. An Italian source apparently gives 10 July 1636, which would be much more likely, but it has not been possible to trace or confirm it.

[23] 'Sabbato morì il signor Tommaso Baj, maestro di cappella di San Pietro, e successe il signor Scarlatti, coadjutor' (Rostirolla, *Musica e musicisti*, 484). The date 22 December 1714 is also given in an entry in the 'Diario effemerides dal 1701' (Lorenzo Meletti, in Biblioteca Communale di Crevalcore, MS 21). Curiously, several other sources – Burney (in *La musica*, iii), two sources of the *Miserere* deriving from the Roman priest and collector Fortunato Santini (Bibliothèque nationale, Paris, D. 670, British Library, Egerton MS 2470) and

THOMAS . BAIVS . SAC .

PHONASCVS . ET . HYDRAVLA . PROBATISS .

ROMAE . IN . SACRA . DOMO . PONTIFIC .

HARMONICES . LAVDE . GREGORIVM . ALLEGRIVM

ET . IOSEPHVM . BAINIVM . AEMVLATVS

ANNOR . LXIV . DEC . A . MDCCXIV .

Fig. 8 Mock funeral inscription of Tommaso Bai printed in *De Viris Illustribus Crevalcorii* (1857)

TOMMASO BAI, PRIEST,
RENOWNED CHOIR CONDUCTOR AND ORGANIST
AT ROME IN THE SACRED HOUSE OF THE PONTIFF.
IN EXCELLENCE OF MUSIC, HE WAS THE EQUAL
OF GREGORIO ALLEGRI AND GIUSEPPE BAINI.
DIED AGED 64 IN 1714[24]

With Bai's *Miserere* in the repertoire of the Papal Choir, listeners were now sure to be satisfied whichever day they came. Like his predecessor, Bai based his *Miserere* on the *tonus peregrinus*, with its characteristic feature of the reciting note of the second part of each verse a tone lower than that of the first part. Allied to that, Bai imitated closely Allegri's chord sequences, notably the same 7–6 progression over E♭ just before the first cadence in the four-part verses, permitting the key ornament, so well-known nowadays, to rise and fall in the same way and at the same moment as in his predecessor's work.

While Bai's *Miserere* has much more variety, it will be seen from the transcription in Appendix 4 that *Coro 1°* (a5) follows the same harmonic scheme as that used by Allegri (given on p. 35) in every verse except the first half of 20. In the four-part verses (*Coro 2°*) Allegri's blueprint is followed only in verses 11, 15 and 19, but verse 7 follows that of *Coro 1°*, and only verse 3, after following it for the first half, introduces a real surprise (as far as the Tone is concerned) by initially taking *d* as the reciting note of the second half over a B♭ chord. The

---

a nineteenth-century MS in the library of the Conservatorio Luigi Cherubini in Florence (E.I.76) – maintain that he died in Rome in 1718.

[24] A style exercise devoted to Crevalcore's famous sons, on the model of the famous textbook *De Viris Illustribus Urbis Romae* (L'Abbé Lhomond, 1775), complete with imitations of Roman funeral inscriptions.

c is merely delayed, however, not discarded. Finally, the first half of verse 20 follows the harmonic scheme of the first half of the *Coro* 2° verses, thus reinforcing the connection with the key moment in Allegri's setting.

In certain verses (9, 13) other characteristic outlines of the *tonus peregrinus* can be discerned; the rise from the reciting note d to e♭ and back, followed by a descent, and in the second half a rise after the reciting note of *c* to *d*, followed also by a descent. It is not always in the same voice however, and even jumps from one to another in the course of the verse. The Bai is suffused with the *tonus peregrinus* rather than based on it, what Lundberg, in another connection, called 'a presentation of the *t.p.* [*tonus peregrinus*] as a "genre" or, to put it differently, the payment of lip-service to liturgical convention'.[25]

Bai's *Miserere* was also notable for its careful word-setting. Burney described Bai as:

> much commended for his attention to prosody, or the accentuation of the words, in which his notation is generally so exact, that the proportion of long and short syllables is as strictly preserved, in singing this psalm, as it could be in reading it.[26]

The 'proportion of long and short syllables' appears to have been very important to the papal singers. From about 1600, the Misereres preserved in CS 205–6 include rhythmic indications for the chanted sections of the verse. *Miserere* 9 (in Table 1, Chapter 2), probably by G.M. Nanino (died 1607) has rhythms which are quite complex and carefully detailed to fit the text, as do 10 (Naldini), 11 (Dentice, revised by Nanino) and 12 (Giovannelli). It is thus curious that Allegri's is the only *Miserere* in CS 205–6 with no rhythmic indications at all: the chanted sections are all given with just one long breve. This appears to reflect an idiosyncrasy of the copyist rather than a sudden change of practice; added to CS 205–6 only in 1661, it has the air of a fair copy made for the archive.[27] The unfortunate effect of its notation has been to mislead modern interpreters of the 'English Miserere' into believing that the chanted parts at the beginning of each half verse should be given in a free rhythm reminiscent of Anglican psalm chant, whereas the evidence of all important sources points

---

[25] The *Tonus Peregrinus*, 282.
[26] *La musica*, iii.
[27] See also p. 32, n.33. CS 205–6 are almost unique among Papal Choir manuscripts in preserving *falsobordoni*, which seem normally to have been deemed not worthy of the scribes' time. It was no doubt only the importance of the performance of the *Miserere* at *Tenebræ* which caused their preservation. The only other manuscript devoted entirely to *falsobordoni* is CS 343 of 1735 (see pp. 244–5).

to the use of rhythmic prosody.[28] Bai's *Miserere* seems to have been considered in this, as in other ways, the culmination of Papal Choir practices in the singing of the Miserere.

Carefully detailed prosody is also present in Scarlatti's setting, as are the musical variations between different verses, and its influence on Bai is clear. Moreover, it is unlikely to be a coincidence that the five-part verses of Allegri's *Miserere* were recomposed so soon after the composition of Scarlatti's and the introduction of Bai's. Biordi may have been put to work on it soon after his arrival in 1717, given that it is at the beginning of his working manuscript, CS 263. The original Allegri must have seemed very old-fashioned in its breadth and ambition by comparison.[29] Even in its revised version, Allegri's *Miserere* clearly remains a *falsobordone* – a liturgical 'means to an end', albeit a fairly elaborate one – whereas Bai's setting, equally impregnated with the *tonus peregrinus*, is virtually a through-composed choral recitation.

Unsurprisingly given their common ornamentation, the two Misereres seem to have been immediately perceived as a pair and present in the same sources: firstly in Vatican manuscripts CS 340 and 341, copied in 1748.[30] It is likely that they were copied to replace the many Cappella Sistina manuscripts now necessary for Holy Week (205–6 for the *Improperia* and *Coro 2°* of the Allegri, 185 for *Coro 1°* of the Allegri and 203–4 for the Bai), so we can be virtually certain that from that date none of the other Misereres in CS 205–6 was ever performed again in the chapel. Subsequently the Allegri and the Bai were united in the publications of both Burney (1771) and Alfieri (1840). It must have been difficult for the public in the Chapel to tell them apart, given that both the ornaments and the harmonic sequences were much the same. And the choir seems to have been happy to add to the confusion by combining them in various ways. Alfieri outlined one of the methods of so doing in his introduction,

---

[28] See pp. 238–9 for more discussion of this question and of the importance of prosody in general.

[29] The fact that Bai's *Miserere* precedes the revision of Allegri's perhaps explains why Bai preserved Allegri's original voicing – SATTB – in the five-part verses. Biordi, on the other hand, adopted the two-soprano solution found in Scarlatti's *Miserere*, although whether that was under its influence cannot be determined.

[30] CS 340–1 follow the same format as CS 205–6: the *Coro 1°* verses from both works in one (in this case CS 341), and the *Coro 2°* verses in the other (CS 340), to allow the singers of each choir to stand on opposite sides of the swivelling music stand in the centre of the *Cantoria*. Complete transcriptions of both Misereres are given in Appendices 3 and 4. Their scribe, Giovanni Domenico Biondini, had also copied the new five-part verses of the Allegri into CS 185 (1731), with which CS 341 (fols. 3ᵛ–10ʳ) gives an identical reading. They also contain Palestrina's *Improperia* complete with its verses, and a *Miserere* by Paschale Pisari added in 1777.

in use, he wrote, for 'many years'.[31] Finally in CS 375, compiled by Domenico Mustafà in 1892 (Chapter 12), the two works are combined exactly as described by Alfieri fifty-two years earlier. To the singers of the Chapel – certainly to Mustafà – Bai's seems to have been considered the final, perfected version of the Miserere. Indeed it will be seen below that in 1815 it may have been described as the 'Miserere della nostra Cappella'.[32] It was only to the public that whatever was given was always 'the Allegri'.

---

[31] For a full discussion of Alfieri's publication and indications, see Chapter 10. The extent of the confusion thereby created is highlighted in British Library, Add. MS 31525 (described on pp. 135–7 and in Appendix 8, **1** and **2**), in which two important versions of the Allegri are misattributed to Bai.

[32] See pp. 123–4 and 162.

PART TWO

THE EIGHTEENTH CENTURY

4

Show business

Throughout the eighteenth and nineteenth centuries, visitors flocked to Rome in Holy Week to hear the amazing Miserere. Descriptions such as the following are typical of their reactions:

> There can never have been music with so natural harmonies so delightfully heard as this Miserere ... It was accompanied by no instruments but is so full and so melodious that it cannot be imitated by anybody just from the score ... in the twilight of the evening as the lights are being put out, in a solemn silence unusual for Italians, this song of lamentation starts. On hearing these melodious tunes, one forgets the earth and is drawn from time to eternity, and can imagine one is hearing the choirs of the saints. (Anonymous, 1783)[1]

> No music makes such an impression on the heart, none other has such profound effects such as the old masters used to say music should have, nor brings the soul to such a feeling of deepest trembling ... as this Miserere. What one feels with this music, and must feel, nobody in the world has yet felt ... This music is unique of its kind. (Carl Ludwig Junker, 1784)[2]

---

[1] 'Aber nie kann man eine natürlichere, harmonischere, entzückendere Music hören, als das Miserere ... Es wird von keinem Instrumente begleitet, aber ist so voll, so melodisch, daß es selbst aus den Noten von keinem nachgeahmt werden kann ... Bey der Dämmerung des Abends, bey ausgelöschten Lichtern, bey einer feyerlichen ungewöhnlichen Stille Italiener hebt dieser Klagegesang an. Man vergißt bey diesen melodischen Tönen der Erde, wird von der Zeit in die Unendlichkeit entrückt, und glaubt die Chöre der Seligen zu hören.' Anon., 'Nachrichten über Italien aus dem Briefe eines Reisenden' ('News about Italy from a traveller's letter'), in Carl Friedrich Cramer (ed.), *Magazin der Musik*, 1/2 (Hamburg, 1783), 989–90; quoted in Julius Amann, *Allegris Miserere und die Aufführungspraxis in der Sixtina* (Regensburg, 1935), 83–4.

[2] 'Keine Musik hat je mehr Eindruck auf das Herz – keine, die großen Wirkungen, die die Alten von ihrer Musik behaupteten, gewissermaßen begreiflich gemacht, keine, je die Seele zu den Empfindungen des tiefsten Schauders ... als dieß Miserere. Das was man bey dieser Musik empfindet, und empfinden muß, hat man noch nie in der Welt empfunden ... Kurz diese Musik ist die einzige

They who have assisted at the office of Tenebrae will not be surprised at the saying of a philosopher, that for the advantage of his soul he would wish that when he was about to render it up to God, he might hear sung the Miserere of the Pope's chapel. (Charles Michael Baggs, 1839)[3]

But a thousand times over I would go to listen to the Miserere in the Sistine Chapel; that spot made sacred by the most sublime works of Michael Angelo ... The music, not only of the Miserere, but of the Lamentations, is solemn, pathetic, religious – the soul is rapt – carried away into another state of being. Strange that grief, and laments, and the humble petition of repentance, should fill us with delight – a delight that wakens these very emotions in the heart – and calls tears into the eyes, and yet is dearer than any pleasure. (Mary Shelley, 1840)[4]

There are innumerable similar statements. Valuable accounts were left by Mendelssohn, Spohr, Nicolai, Herold, Gounod, Liszt and Berlioz, not to mention Goethe, Stendhal, Chateaubriand, Ingres and Germaine de Staël.[5] As the testimony of Cramer and Shelley suggests, it was not just the music that impressed the listeners, but the context.

Some of the great effects produced by this piece, may, perhaps, be justly attributed to the time, place, and solemnity of the ceremonials, used during the performance ...[6]

[I] went to hear the miserere sung at the popes chapel, the Cardinals there. There's a candlestick with 15 candles lighted thus [image of a triangle in dots]. Between every Psalm that is chanted one is put out till they are all out but the middle one, then they put out all the candles in the church, & carry away the middle one lighted. Then the miserere is sung, voices only, which seem to be several sorts of instruments as well as voices, reckon'd the finest peice of musick in the world & 'tis said they cannot divulge the notes under pain of excommunication. At the end of it they make a sort of clapping & ye

---

ihrer Art.' In Carl Ludwig Junker's *Musikalisches Taschenbuch auf das Jahr 1784* (Freyburg, 1784), 101; quoted in Amann, *Allegris Miserere*, 84.
[3] C.M. Baggs, *The Ceremonies of Holy-Week at the Vatican and S. John Lateran's* (Rome, 1839), 47.
[4] Mary Shelley, *Rambles in Germany and Italy in 1840, 1842 and 1843* (London, 1844), vol. 2, 231.
[5] See Boursy, 'The Mystique' for a useful summary of the most interesting.
[6] Burney, *The Present State*, 276–7.

midle candle is brought in again. I beleive it has some relation to ye agony in the Garden.[7]

This [the lamentation] lasts for about three hours, during which time the lights on the altar and the triple candlesticks are extinguished, only six large candles on the railing which divides the chapel in two being left burning in the increasing darkness. The large figures on the ceiling have quite a startling effect in the dim light, and one is oppressed with fatigue from the long monotonous singing, when suddenly, after a long pause, the four voices break into sweet harmony, and begin *piano* with the exquisite 'Miserere'. This would be beautiful under any circumstances, but in these surroundings, and after what has preceded it, the effect is prodigious, and for two hundred years has never failed to produce the strongest impression.[8]

Nothing is more impressive than these ceremonies presided by the Pope, that good and venerable man, and his cardinals. I can't tell you how beautiful they are – rich but at the same time simple. But what I had never heard in my life was music like the Miserere, which is sung on three successive days, or rather is breathed in celestial and divine song, which penetrates the soul and makes the eyes brim with tears. These are verses of vocal harmony, because as you know the pope uses no other instrument for his music – that is what he is known for, and it's all to his advantage, I can assure you …

At last at dusk, when the plainchant part of the office is over, the Pope descends from his throne and prostrates himself on the ground, and there is a great silence which heralds the heavenly voices beginning the Miserere. At that moment, everything is in harmony with that music. The day turns to night – there is no light at all – and one can just glimpse the terrifying painting of the Last Judgement, whose extraordinary effect transmits a kind of terror to the soul. Finally, finally I don't know what else to say – I am unbearably moved just telling you about it – in fact I'm not sure one can speak of it, for you need to see it and hear it to believe it.[9]

---

[7] Letter from Richard Pocock to his mother, dated 21 April 1734, British Library, Add. MS 19939, fol. 10ʳ. Original spelling but some punctuation has been added for clarity. For the original transcription, see Chrissocoidis, 'London Mozartiana', 37 (see pp. 43–4, n. 15).

[8] Diary of Fanny Hensel, Easter Saturday (18 April) 1840, in Sebastian Hensel, *The Mendelssohn Family (1729–1847) from Letters and Journals*, trans. Carl Klingemann, vol. 2 (New York, 1882).

[9] 'Rien n'est si imposant que toutes ces cérémonies que la Pape, ce bon et vénérable homme, préside et tous les cardinaux. Je ne peux pas assez vous dire comme cela est beau, riche et simple tout à la fois. Mais ce que de ma vie je n'avais entendu, c'est de la musique comme le Miserere que l'on y chante trois jours de suite, ou pour mieux dire que l'on y exhale par des chants célestes et divins qui pénètrent l'âme et mouillent les yeux. Ce sont des versets en

The beginning of the onset of night, all the cardinals – everyone – prostrate on the ground, the profound silence, the majesty of the chapel, the darkness, everything comes together to make this moment almost extraordinary.[10]

I have just come from Sistine Chapel, where I was present at Tenebræ and heard the *Miserere* sung … The daylight was failing; the shadows crept slowly across the frescoes of the chapel, and one distinguished but a few bold strokes of Michael Angelo's brush. The candles, extinguished one by one in turns, sent forth from their stifled flames a slender white smoke, a very natural image of life, which Scripture compares to *a little smoke*. The cardinals were kneeling, the Pope prostrate before the same altar where a few days before I had seen his predecessor; the admirable prayer of penance and mercy, which succeeded the Lamentations of the prophet, rose at intervals in the silence of the night. One felt overwhelmed by the great mystery of a God dying that the sins of mankind might be wiped out. The Catholic Heiress was there on her seven hills with all her memories; but, instead of the powerful pontiffs, those cardinals who contended for precedence with monarchs, a poor old paralyzed Pope [Pius VIII, elected three weeks previously], without family or support, Princes of the Church, without splendour, announced the end of a power which has civilized the modern world. The master-pieces of the arts were disappearing with it, were fading away on the walls and ceilings of the Vatican, that half-abandoned palace. Inquisitive strangers, separated from the unity of the church, assisted at the ceremony on their way and took the place of the community of the Faithful. The heart was seized with a two-fold sadness. Christian

---

harmonie de voix, car vous saurez que le pape n'a jamais d'autre instrument à sa musique, c'est son étiquette et il n'y perd pas, je vous assure … Enfin à la chute du jour l'office de plain-chant fini, le pape descend de son siège, il se prosterne, un grand silence se prépare et annonce le commencement céleste de ces voix qui commencent le Miserere. Tout dans ce moment est d'accord avec cette musique. Le jour baisse, aucune lumière, le jour baisse et laisse à peine entrevoir ce terrible tableau du Jugement Dernier, dont l'effet prodigieux imprime une sorte de terreur dans l'âme. Enfin, enfin je ne sais plus que vous dire et je suis tout ému en vous le racontant, si cela se peut se raconter, car il faut le voir et l'entendre pour le croire.' Letter from the painter Ingres, dated 7 April 1807, to his friend Pierre Forestier, in Jean-Auguste-Dominique Ingres, *Lettres de France et d'Italie, 1804–1841*, ed. Daniel Ternois (Paris, 2011), 155. Part of Ingres' commentary on Holy Week of that year is also found in *Ingres raconté par lui-même et par ses amis*, ed. Pierre Cailler (Geneva, 1947), 118–19; quoted in Boursy, 'The Mystique', 319.

[10] 'La nuit qui commence à tomber, tous les cardinaux et tout le monde prosternés, le silence profond, la grandeur de la chapelle, l'obscurité du lieu, tout contribue à rendre ce moment presqu'extraordinaire.' Louis-Joseph-Ferdinand Herold, *Lettres d'Italie, suivies du journal et autres écrits 1804–1833*, ed. Hervé Audéon (Weinsberg, 2008), 217.

Rome, while commemorating the Agony of Jesus Christ, seemed to be celebrating her own, to be repeating for the New Jerusalem the words which Jeremiah addressed to the old.[11]

Suggestive gloom, nostalgia, repentance, tradition, ceremonial, beauty – not to mention smells and bells – all these things worked a powerful spell on visitors, even Protestant ones disinclined to take them at face value:

> Vanity will not allow me to suppose it weakness yet I must confess that though sufficiently aware of the empty senseless pomp, the tricked and tinsel state and pageantry of catholic ceremonies, I never have assisted in any of their great days of Devotion without experiencing a deep, involuntary, impression if not of devotion at least of reverence even for the empty shadow of religion. Afterwards I grant that recollection brings the service back to my mind clad with a thousand absurdities, a thousand whimsical conceits, hid at the time under the awful and imposing solemnity of the

---

[11] 'Je sors de la chapelle Sixtine, après avoir assisté à ténèbres et entendu chanter le *Miserere* ... Le jour s'affaiblissait; les ombres envahissaient lentement les fresques de la chapelle et l'on n'apercevait plus que quelques grands traits du pinceau de Michel-Ange. Les cierges, tour à tour éteints, laissaient échapper de leur lumière étouffée une légère fumée blanche, image assez naturelle de la vie que l'Ecriture compare à *une petite vapeur*. Les cardinaux étaient à genoux, le nouveau pape prosterné au même autel où quelques jours avant j'avais vu son prédécesseur; l'admirable prière de pénitence et de miséricorde, qui avait succédé aux Lamentations du prophète, s'élevait par intervalles dans le silence et la nuit. On se sentait accablé sous le grand mystère d'un Dieu mourant pour effacer les crimes des hommes. La catholique héritière sur ses sept collines était là avec tous ses souvenirs; mais, au lieu de ces pontifes puissants, de ces cardinaux qui disputaient la préséance aux monarques, un pauvre vieux pape paralytique, sans famille et sans appui, des princes de l'Eglise sans éclat, annonçaient la fin d'une puissance qui civilisa le monde moderne. Les chefs-d'œuvre des arts disparaissaient avec elle, s'effaçaient sur les murs et sur les voûtes du Vatican, palais à demi abandonné. Des étrangers curieux, séparés de l'unité de l'Eglise, assistaient en passant à la cérémonie et remplaçaient la communauté des fidèles. Une double tristesse s'emparait du cœur. Rome chrétienne en commémorant l'agonie de Jésus-Christ avait l'air de célébrer la sienne, de redire pour la nouvelle Jérusalem les paroles que Jérémie adressait à l'ancienne.' *The Memoirs of François René Vicomte de Chateaubriand*, trans. Alexander Teixeira de Mattos, vol .5 (London, 1902), 36–7; quoted in Boursy, 'The Mystique', 298. This passage is an extract from *Mémoirs d'Outre-tombe* of 15 April 1829 (Holy Wednesday), part 3, book 30, chapter 6, 390. The author, French ambassador to the Vatican in 1829, conflates his artistic sensibility with nostalgia about the power of the Papal States, then under serious threat from the coming revolutions of 1830.

scene, an effect which the sublimity of catholic music contributed so much to produce.[12]

A better-known Protestant, Felix Mendelssohn, was equally sensitive to the atmosphere.

> People have often both zealously praised and censured the ceremonies of Holy Week, and yet omitted, as is often the case, the chief point, namely the complete whole ... Many ... have taken just the music and then found fault with it, because of the external adjuncts it requires to produce the full effect, were lacking. ... so long as these indispensable externals are there, and especially in such perfection, just so long will it produce its effect. And the more convinced I am that place, time, order, and the vast crowd of human beings awaiting, in the most profound silence, the moment for the music to begin, contribute largely to the effect.[13]

For others, it was the unaccompanied voices that were key.

> Allegri's famed *Miserere*, as sung in the Sistine chapel at Rome, during Easter, justifies the belief that, for purposes of devotion, the unaided human voice is the most impressive of all instruments. If such a choir as that of his Holiness could always be commanded, the organ itself might be dispensed with. This, however, is no fair sample of the powers of vocal sacred music; and those who are most alive to the 'concord of sweet sounds' forget that, in the mixture of feeling produced by a scene so imposing as the Sistine chapel presents on such an occasion, it is difficult to attribute to the music only its own share in the overwhelming effect. The Christian world is in mourning; the throne of the Pontiff, stripped of all its honours, and uncovered of its royal canopy, is degraded to the simple elbow chair of an aged priest. The Pontiff himself, and the congregated dignitaries of the church, divested of all earthly pomp, kneel before the cross in the unostentatious garb of their religious orders. As evening sinks, and the tapers are extinguished one after another, at different stages of the service, the fading light falls ever dimmer and dimmer on the reverend figures. The prophets and saints of Michael Angelo look down from the ceiling on the pious worshippers beneath, while the living figures of his Last Judgement, in every variety of infernal suffering and celestial enjoyment, gradually vanish in the gathering shade, as if the scene of horror had closed forever on the one, and the other had quitted the darkness of earth for a higher and a brighter world. Is it [not] wonderful that,

---

[12] *Italian Journey: Being Excerpts from the Pre-Victorian Diary of James Skene of Rubislaw* (London, International Publishing Co., 1937), 102; quoted in Boursy, 'The Mystique', 291.

[13] *Letters*, 120.

Fig. 9 The Sistine Chapel in Rome, Ph. and F. Benoist, *Rome dans sa grandeur…, deuxième volume – Rome chrétienne* (Paris, 1870), Chapter 2

in such circumstances, such music as that famed *Miserere*, sung by such a choir, should shake the soul even of a Calvinist?[14]

After the end of the Napoleonic wars in 1815, a visit to the Sistine Chapel in Holy Week was once again part of the Grand Tour, and the majority of visitors were English.[15] They were largely there as tourists, hoping to not only imbibe some of the Renaissance and classical culture Italy afforded, but also perhaps have a mystical experience in the romantic archaism of Catholic ritual, the epicentre of which was the Sistine Chapel and the choir that sang there. Some of them marvelled at the tolerance of the Church at this invasion.

To-day was a sort of climax to the religious carnival of the whole week, and the number of sights to be seen in the shape of strange religious ceremonies

---

[14] John Russell, *A Tour in Germany and some of the Southern Provinces of the Austrian Empire in 1820, 1821, and 1822* (Edinburgh, 1824), 149–50. This extract was reprinted in *The Harmonicon*, 3 (1825), 197–8. One sees in such a passage the generalised admiration for what James Garratt has called '*naiv* Catholic art' (*Palestrina and the German Romantic Imagination*, Cambridge, 2002, 50–2), in which the music of Allegri and Palestrina is equated to the art of Raphael, Titian and Michelangelo as representative of a kind of Catholic Golden Age.

[15] In the 1830s and 1840s the number of English visitors has been estimated at around five thousand each year, and the number had doubled by the end of the century. For discussion about their motives, and frequent bad behaviour, see Boursy, *Historicism and Composition*, 59–68.

was really quite embarrassing. The eagerness with which Monsignore ____ urged upon us the curiosity and beauty of these various holy spectacles struck me as very strange. I find it difficult to imagine that frame of mind which rejoices in the unsympathizing presence of crowds of strangers at the sacred services of one's religion; and it is always a marvel to me that the Catholic clergy, and even the people themselves, do not object to the careless show which foreigners make of their places of worship and religious ceremonies.[16]

The author decided that it must be simply a question of commerce, stating, 'To be sure, foreigners are a very considerable item of profit to the Roman people and Catholic places of worship, and so the thing resolves itself into natural elements.'

Roads in the Papal States had been greatly improved by the French during the Napoleonic occupation, and advances in technology – trains and steamboats – made for easier travel. Ludovic Celler described the effect on the city of Rome in the 1860s.

When Easter Day is near, crowds of travellers make their way to Rome, and the physiognomy of the city completely changes. Instead of the sweet solitude ordinarily found there, one is buffeted at every step by bustling tourists. They do not come to Rome for the season, nor even just for a month – they come to experience Holy Week. Some are travelling in Italy, and pass by Rome in the Easter period; others come only for the holy days and go home straight afterwards. The first group are not so smart, because in Rome at that moment there is nothing to see: the galleries are closed, the churches decorated, the parks are shut, and Rome is not as it usually is. The second group, motivated only by piety, are not concerned by artistic aspects, or only tangentially; for them, everything is perfect ...

... The notices for the steamships, posted on the Roman palaces, announce extra sailings; every day at Cività at least four different lines arrive, disgorging onto the little railway line there 2,000 to 3,000 people every twenty-four hours. The hotels are full, people sleep at taverns, and furnished apartments attain legendary prices. If we add to these travellers who come by sea those who arrive by land, from Naples, Ancona and Florence, we can well imagine the number of people hurrying to Rome for the famous days which are about to start. It is said that more than 30,000 travellers have arrived.[17]

---

[16] Fanny Kemble (later Mrs Butler), *A Year of Consolation*, vol. 1 (New York, 1847), 127–8.

[17] 'Lorsque le jour de Pâques est proche, les voyageurs se dirigent en foule vers Rome, et la physionomie de cette ville se modifie complètement. Au lieu de la solitude si douce qu'on y trouve d'ordinaire, on se heurte à chaque pas à des curieux affairés. Ceux-là ne viennent pas à Rome pour y passer une saison ou

It was by no means easy to gain admittance to hear the *Miserere*. Speaking of the first day of *Tenebræ*, Celler wrote:

> Today, for the first time, we go to the Sistine for Tenebræ and the Miserere. To get into the right place at the right time is not easy – it's like a campaign, you need strength, patience and, as well, some luck.[18]

Although entry was by ticket, the crowd was always dense, with a mad scramble at the door and no guarantee of a place; cynics such as Celler said that five times as many tickets were given out as there were places. Charles Dickens, one of many English visitors, failing to gain entry into the Sistine Chapel in 1845, recalled:

> We saw very little, for by the time we reached it (though we were early) the besieging crowd had filled it to the door, and overflowed into the adjoining hall, where they were struggling, and squeezing, and mutually expostulating, and making great rushes every time a lady was brought out faint, as if at least fifty people could be accommodated in her vacant standing-room.[19]

All behaviour was fair to gain admittance.

> One powerful French girl, who wished the situation of an Italian lady of my acquaintance in front of her, abruptly demanded it. Being respectfully declined, she, by a process well known to schoolboys, knocked the lady's

---

> même seulement un mois, ils viennent voir la Semaine Sainte. De ces curieux, les uns voyagent en Italie, et font coïncider leur séjour à Rome avec l'époque de Pâques: les autres ne viennent absolument que pour les jours saints et s'en retournent après. Les premiers sont des maladroits, car à Rome, dès à présent, l'on ne peut plus rien voir: les galeries sont fermées, les églises décorées, les parcs clos, et Rome ne ressemble plus du tout à Rome. Les seconds, poussés par la seule piété, ne s'occupent pas des choses artistiques ou ne s'en occupent qu'accessoirement; pour eux, tout est au mieux ... Les affiches des bateaux à vapeur, placardées sur les palais romains, annoncent des services supplémentaires; l n'y a pas de jour où, à Cività, n'abordent au minimum quatre lignes différentes. Elles versent au petit chemin de fer de 2 à 3,000 personnes par vingt-quatre heures. Les hôtels sont bondés: on y couche sur les tables d'hôte, et les appartements meublés atteignent des prix légendaires. Si, à ces voyageurs venant par mer, on ajoute ceux de la terre ferme des routes de Naples, Ancône et Florence, on comprend quelle quantité de gens accourt à Rome pour les journées célèbres qui vont commencer. On dit qu'il y a plus de 30,000 voyageurs arrivés.' *La Semaine Sainte*, 3–4.

[18] 'C'est aujourd'hui que, pour la première fois, on se rend à la Sixtine pour les Ténèbres et le Miserere. Parvenir en lieu et temps utile n'est pas chose aisée; c'est une véritable campagne; il faut de la force, de la patience, et en plus, un peu de hasard favorable.' Celler, *La Semaine Sainte*, 38.

[19] *Pictures from Italy*, ed. David Paroissien (New York, 1974), 202.

legs from under her by striking her in the hollow of her knees, so that she fell as suddenly as if she had been shot. Before she could recover herself or her presence of mind, her place was gone.[20]

The ceremony was long, lasting several hours, a fact constantly alluded to by those eighteenth- and nineteenth-century tourists who found themselves crammed uncomfortably into the Chapel waiting for the *Miserere*.

> The most enthusiastic among the curious had already arrived at noon, and queued until 2 o'clock; they were then allowed into the Sistine, where they waited again until 4 o'clock. The Lamentations started, and continued until half past six; the wait was really long, but one puts up with anything for Allegri's Miserere, that's what they've all come to hear – nothing else.[21]

This must be a description of Thursday because, as Celler also informs us,

> each day *Tenebræ* starts at a different time: on Wednesday around five, on Thursday around four, and on Friday around half past two in order, on this final day, to allow the Pope to be at St Peter's at dusk to adore the most important relics. In any case, the performance of the Miserere nearly always starts late.[22]

The solution seems to have been to wait until Friday.

> The Tenebræ, which many frequent entirely for the sake of the *Miserere*, lasts upwards of two hours, occupied in simple, unharmonized chaunting; and the experience of every year proved that on the first evening confusion and inconvenience ensue from the eagerness of hundreds to enter the chapel; but by the third day, when the office is much shorter, the lamentations more

---

[20] Jarves, *Italian Sights*, 268; quoted in Boursy, 'The Mystique', 289.
[21] 'Les plus ardents parmi les curieux étaient arrivés à midi, ils avaient fait queue jusqu'à 2 heures; là ils étaient entrés dans la Sixtine, et avaient de nouveau attendu jusqu'au 4 heures. Les Lamentations commencèrent, et durèrent jusqu'à 6 heures et demie; l'attente était bien longue, mais on supporte tout pour le Miserere d'Allegri, car c'est lui que chacun veut entendre, et pas d'autre.' *La Semaine Sainte*, 47.
[22] 'Chaque jour les Ténèbres doivent commencer à une heure différente; le mercredi vers cinq heures, le jeudi vers quatre heures, le vendredi vers deux heures et demie, afin de permettre, cette dernière journée, au Pape, de venir à St Pierre, à la chute du jour, adorer les grandes reliques. Mais l'exécution du Miserere est presque toujours en retard sur l'heure indiquée.' Ibid., 43.

exquisite, and the Miserere in general the best, it is left to the occupation of a few, whom better feelings than mere curiosity inspire with perseverance.[23]

In any case, the ceremony was at the top of almost everyone's list.

> The effect of this service varies, of course, according to the individual temperament. Many do not consider it worthy of the fatigue and exertion it requires; but no-one would consider Rome as visited unless he had heard the Miserere by the Pope's choir in the Sistine Chapel. It can be heard nowhere else, because there alone are those wonderful associations of art that contribute so greatly to its effect.[24]

The attraction, mixed inevitably with a certain amount of prurience, of being able to see and hear *castrati* should not be underestimated. Burney devoted several paragraphs to the subject during his visit to Naples.

> I enquired throughout Italy at what place boys were chiefly qualified for singing by castration, but could get no certain intelligence. I was told at Milan that it was at Venice; at Venice, that it was at Bologna; but at Bologna the fact was denied, and I was referred to Florence; from Florence to Rome, and from Rome I was sent to Naples … all the Italians are so ashamed of it that in every province they transfer it to some other.[25]

In Naples he was assured that the operation was forbidden in the *conservatori* there, and that the boys had all come from Lecce merely to try out their voices. No doubt in Lecce it was said that they all came from Sicily, and in Sicily, from Turkey. Commentators were clearly uncomfortable with the whole question, especially as few really seem to have known exactly what it entailed, and no doubt imagined a more drastic operation than that which was actually necessary.[26] Burney's view was

---

[23] Cardinal (Nicholas) Wiseman, *Four Lectures on the Offices and Ceremonies of Holy Week as Performed in the Papal Chapels, delivered in Rome in the Lent of MDCCCXXXVII* (London, 1839), 12–13.

[24] Jarves, *Italian Sights*, 269–70; quoted in Boursy, 'The Mystique', 321–2.

[25] *The Present State*, 301–2.

[26] A recent summary of the detail is as follows: 'The operation performed in Italy never involved full ablation; in fact, often it did not even involve removal of the testicles (bilateral orchiectomy). At the time of the surgery the boy was given some opium, his carotid artery was compressed to induce a coma-like state, and he was immersed in a bath of milk to soften his genitals or in frozen water to anesthetize the cut. At this point the *vas deferens* [more properly, the *vasa deferentia*], which take the sperm from the testicles to the urethra were severed, just as it is done today for vasectomy. The testicles were then scored with a three-quarter-inch-deep cut so they would atrophy. At times, testicles were

> that the cruel operation is but too frequently performed without trial, or at least without sufficient proofs of an improvable voice; otherwise such numbers could never be found in every great town throughout Italy, without any voice at all, or at least without one sufficient to compensate such a loss. Indeed all the *musici* in the churches at present are made up of the refuse of the opera houses, and it is very rare to meet with a tolerable voice upon the establishment in any church throughout Italy. The *virtuosi* who sing there occasionally, upon great festivals only, are usually strangers, and paid by the time.[27]

As might be expected, Protestant writers were the most critical. In 1834 Joseph Mainzer (1801–51) wrote a series of four articles on the choir for the *Gazette Musicale de Paris*, in which his interest in the music did not always overcome his Protestant distaste of Vatican ritual and practices, particularly in the last instalment of 2 February. *Castrati*, he wrote, 'have been for a long time the object of bitter criticism of the Roman court. Accusations of cruelty and inhumanity have however been vain and useless.'[28] He accused the Church of forbidding women, who would be an excellent substitute, solely because their beautiful voices would

> cause trouble to the pious souls of the cardinals, and distract them with worldly thoughts: everyone knows that the reason for the famous dictum *Mulier tacent in ecclesia* [women should keep silent in church] is not because the Curia hates the female sex, but because they are too susceptible to it.[29]

> simply squeezed or twisted, but results from those procedures were uneven, thus surgery was preferred. Alternately, the scrotum was removed.' Finucci, *The Manly Masquerade*, 245–6.

[27] *The Present State*, 302–4. It is interesting that in the second-last phrase, the journal originally omitted the words 'throughout Italy', which are added in parentheses, followed by 'which confirms what Santarelli had told me in Rome'. By 1770, part of the attraction of good *castrati* was their extreme rarity.

[28] '[Les castrats] ont pendant longtemps été l'objet de reproches amers contre la cour de Rome. Vainement on a taxé cette cour de cruauté et d'inhumanité; tout a été inutile.' 'La Chapelle Sixtine à Rome', *Gazette Musicale de Paris*, 1834, No. 5 (2 February), 38–9.

[29] 'jeter le trouble dans les âmes pieuses des cardinaux, et ne leur rappelassent des idées toutes mondaines: chacun sait en effet que le fameux *Mulier tacent in ecclesia* n'est pas dû tant à la haine de la curie pontificale envers le sexe féminin, que bien plutôt à sa trop grande sensibilité'. *Gazette Musicale de Paris*, 1834, No. 5 (2 February), 38–9.

He found boys' voices equally beautiful ('No castrato can ever replace the charm and beauty of a boy's voice'),[30] although the fact that they change in adolescence made their use in choirs complicated. And he had heard that the English used falsettists, although he was not convinced by their singing.

> I want to talk of male altos and sopranos singing their part in falsetto an octave higher than their natural voice, as I heard done at the English Seminary in Rome in Pitoni's *Dies Irae* and other old pieces. Everyone will agree that such an ingenious artistic invention could only have come from the English. I have to say that they were reasonably at ease with the style, and were not much worse than worn-out castrati; there was, as in the case of the latter, something unnatural about their voices, but at least one did not have to lament their unnatural and deplorable condition.[31]

By 1867 Ludovic Celler could pretend that *castrati* did not really exist.

> The Papal Chapel used to be famous, especially during the heyday of the *castrats* ... Some travellers make out that *castrats* still exist; I don't really know, but I have my doubts, the present Pope having given strict orders to cease this barbarous practice. If we suppose that they still exist, the possibilities for singing the high parts are: *castrats*, 'pretend sopranos' (tenors which sing falsetto), [and] real sopranos (very young); but these different types of voices do not blend well. The falsettists produce a very particular sound, and it is difficult to tell if they are men, women, children or *castrats*; they try to replace the latter, and so try to sing with the same mannerisms. This idea

---

[30] 'Il n'est pas de castrat qui puisse remplacer le charme et la beauté d'une voix de garçon'. *Gazette Musicale de Paris*, 1834, No. 5 (2 February), 38–9.
[31] 'Je veux parler de voix d'hommes alto ou soprano exécutant leur partie avec le fausset à l'octave au dessus de la voix naturelle, comme je l'ai entendu faire à Rome dans un séminaire anglais pour le *Dies Irae* de Pitoni, et d'autres anciens ouvrages. Tout le monde sera d'accord sur ce point, qu'une invention aussi ingénieuse dans le domaine de l'art ne pouvait être imaginée que par les Anglais. Cependant je dois dire que les séminaristes étaient assez exercés dans ce style et que les voix d'alto et de soprano ne faisaient pas un effet beaucoup plus désagréable que les voix de castrats quand elles sont usées; elles avaient bien comme les voix de ces derniers, quelque chose d'anti-naturel, mais au moins n'avait-on pas à gémir sur la condition déplorable et contre nature des chanteurs.' *Gazette Musicale de Paris*, 1834, No. 5 (2 February), 38–9. Mainzer had formerly been a Catholic priest, and expresses himself with all the certainty of the convert. In the last extract it is not clear what distinction he is making between English falsettists and Vatican *alti naturali*.

originally came from the English Seminary in Rome; [the sound they make] is neither natural nor gracious.³²

The reference to English falsettists not only makes clear Celler's debt to Mainzer's articles, but also typifies the general stance on *castrati*, which may be characterised as ignoring them as much as possible. Yet no-one who heard the choir during the years he wrote this, when Domenico Mustafà both directed them and sang, can have been in any doubt about how he did it.

In another description from the 1860s attributed to the Goncourt brothers, the strangeness of the sound seems to be taken as code for the unnaturalness of the means.

> [The choir sang with] voices of bronze, voices thudding on the psalms like earth on a coffin-lid, voices reaching tender heights, voices of breaking crystal, voices swollen by a river of tears, voices taking wing entwined, plaintive voices rising and falling with a quavering moan, pathetic voices, voices of adoring supplication swept away by the tempest of the plainchant, voices trembling in sobbing lament, voices whose swift flight fell suddenly back into a silent abyss whence immediately sprang other sonorous voices, strange and disturbing voices, piping and brimming with tears, voices of neither child nor woman, voices of feminised men, voices with the husk of an adolescent angel, neutral and asexual voices, virgin and martyr voices, fragile and poignant, assailing the nerves with the arresting unnaturalness of their sound.³³

---

³² 'La chapelle papale a été célèbre, surtout à l'époque la plus florissante des castrats ... Quelques voyageurs prétendent qu'il y a encore des castrats; je ne sais, mais je doute que cela soit, le papa actuel ayant donné des ordres formels pour cesser cet usage barbare. En admettant qu'il y en ait encore quelques-uns, il y aurait pour l'exécution des parties hautes: les castrats, les soprani factices (ténors qui se sont fait une voix de fausset), les soprani vrais (très jeunes); mais ces variétés de voix se fondent mal. Les chanteurs en fausset produisent surtout un singulier effet; on ne sait si ce sont des hommes, des femmes, des enfants ou des castrats; ils visent à remplacer ces derniers, et on les exerce aux effets qui leur étaient habituels. L'idée première de ce système appartiendrait au séminaire anglais de Rome; ce n'est si naturel ni gracieux.' *La Semaine Sainte*, 34–5.

³³ 'des voix d'airain, des voix qui jetaient sur les versets le bruit sourd de la terre sur un cercueil, des voix d'un tendre aigu, des voix de cristal qui se brisaient, des voix qui s'enflaient d'un ruisseau de larmes, des voix qui s'envolaient l'une autour de l'autre, des voix dolentes où montait et descendait une plainte chevrotante, des voix pathétiques, des voix de supplication adorante qu'emportait l'ouragan du plain-chant, des voix tressaillantes dans des vocalises de sanglots, des voix dont le vif élancement retombait tout à coup à un abîme de silence d'où rejaillissaient aussitôt d'autres voix sonores, des voix étranges et troublantes, des voix flûtées et mouillées, des voix entre l'enfant et la femme, des

Harriet Beecher Stowe was equally graphic in 1862.

> The long-drawn aisles are now full to overflowing with that weird chanting which one hears nowhere but in Rome at this solemn season. Those voices, neither of men nor women, have a wild, morbid energy which seems to search every fibre of the nervous system, and, instead of soothing or calming, to awaken strange yearning agonies of pain, ghostly unquiet longings, and endless feverish, unrestful cravings. The sounds now swell and flood the church as with a rushing torrent of wailing and clamorous supplication, now recede and moan themselves away to silence in far distant aisles, like the last faint sigh of discouragement and despair. Anon they burst out from the room, they drop from arches and pictures, they rise like steam from the glassy pavement, and, meeting, mingle in wavering clamors of lamentation and shrieks of anguish. One might fancy lost souls from out the infinite and dreary abysses of utter separation from God might thus wearily and aimlessly moan and wail, breaking into agonized tumults of desire, and trembling back into exhaustions of despair. Such music brings only throbbings and yearnings, but no peace; and yonder, on the glassy floor, at the foot of a crucifix, a poor mortal lies sobbing and quivering under its pitiless power, as if it had wrenched every tenderest nerve of memory, and torn open every half-healed wound of the soul.[34]

Others were pithier. Ralph Waldo Emerson was content to acknowledge the quality while making known his feelings about the process: 'Those mutilated wretches sing so well it is painful to hear them.'[35] Stendhal was unwilling to admit even the quality, referring to them as 'hoarse capons'.[36] And even if writers were unwilling to dwell on their situation, it was nonetheless common knowledge. In making the following reference to the servant of M. Mabeuf, Victor Hugo was confident it would be understood.

---

voix d'hommes féminisés, des voix d'un enrouement que ferait dans un gosier une mue angélique, des voix neutres et sans sexe, des voix vierges et martyres, des voix fragiles et poignantes attaquant les nerfs avec l'imprévu et l'anti-naturel du son.' From the *Journal des Goncourt*, by the brothers Edmond and Jules de Goncourt, quoted in Paul Renouard, *Rome pendant la semaine sainte* (Paris, 1891), 95. As Jules, the younger brother, died in 1870, this description must date from the 1860s.

[34] *Agnes of Sorrento* (Boston, 1862), 363.
[35] He was referring to singers that he heard at either S. Pietro or the Chiesa Nuova, possibly both. *Journals of Ralph Waldo Emerson*, vol. 3 (London 1910), 83.
[36] 'Chapons enroués'. Stendhal (Henry Beyle), *Rome, Naples et Florence* (Paris, 1854), 304.

His servant was also a sort of innocent. The poor good old woman was a spinster. Sultan, her cat, which might have mewed Allegri's miserere in the Sistine Chapel, had filled her heart and sufficed for the quantity of passion which existed in her. None of her dreams had ever proceeded as far as man.[37]

---

[37] 'Sa servante était, elle aussi, une variété de l'innocence. La pauvre bonne femme était vierge. Sultan, son matou, qui eût pu miauler le miserere d'Allegri à la chapelle sixtine, avait rempli son cœur et suffisait à la quantité de passion qui était en elle. Aucun de ses rêves n'était allé jusqu'à l'homme.' *Les Misérables*, vol. 3, book 5, chapter 4, 293 (original French edn of *Les Misérables*, Brussels, 1862), trans. Isabel F. Hapgood (New York, 1887).

5

Eighteenth-century sources 1 – Blainville and Mozart

Is it possible to know more precisely what listeners heard in the Sistine Chapel during performances of the *Miserere* in the eighteenth and nineteenth centuries? As we have seen in Chapter 3, vocal ornamentation was almost certainly added from the very first performance, and the most important phrase – that which occurs at the end of the first half of the four-part verses – must have been largely fixed at the latest by 1711, when Bai wrote his *Miserere* around it. But no written trace of those decorations has yet been found from earlier than 1767, when Charles-Henri de Blainville published his *Histoire Générale, Critique et Philologique de la Musique* in Paris.

Blainville (1767)

Blainville (1711–69) was a composer and theorist who attracted some fleeting attention with his 'discovery' of a *mode mixte* – neither major nor minor.[1] His *Histoire* includes sections on the music of the ancient Greeks, Romans, Moors and Turks, similar in many ways to that recently published by Padre Martini in his *Storia della Musica* (1757), but his main interest was clearly the harmony of his time. He seems to have been part of ongoing exchanges about music theory (especially concerning Rameau's *Traité de l'Harmonie*) involving such figures as La Borde, D'Alembert and Rousseau in France, and Padre Martini, Vallotti and Tartini in Italy. The *Histoire* includes a lengthy supplement discussing theories by the latter. Most of the musical examples (sixty-one pages of plates) are either pictures of exotic instruments or harmonic examples. There are just five extracts of composed music, such as Martini would provide in the two volumes of his famous *Esemplare, o sia Saggio fondamentale pratico di contrappunto* (1774 and 1776), and only one is identified – two verses of Allegri's *Miserere*, found on plates XXII–XXIII (hereinafter **B**). It follows a series of short phrases in two, three and four parts, in a quasi-*falsobordone* style, under the heading

---

[1] It was based on a scale starting with a semitone (e.g. E minor without an F♯). See Gérard Geay, *Le troisième mode de Blainville*, Cahiers Philidor 32 (Versailles, 2005).

'Differentes issues [sic] de L'harmonie du Contrepoint'. This is presumably what Blainville describes in the text (p. 74) thus: 'Simple counterpoint is note-against-note, and is properly called *fauxbourdon* in psalms, as I mentioned above.' The Allegri is presented as another example of the same.[2]

Although this 'Miserere del S^{gr} Allegri' is based on the original version found in CS 205–6, it has been considerably modified. Both choirs have been adapted to the clefs of $c_1 c_3 c_4 f_4$ – SATB. In the first verse, originally a5, the two original tenor parts (c_4) have been reduced to one; in verse 3, usually a higher choir notated in $c_1 c_1 c_3 f_3$ (or f_4) (SSABar), the middle parts have been adapted to slightly lower voices. The whole psalm could thus be performed by a single quartet of singers, and perhaps the changes were made for that reason. But it is equally possible that it was taken from hearing a performance. It bears all the characteristics of a recollection – the outer parts easily noted, but the inner ones much less clear. In any case we can be sure that it was never performed thus by the Papal Choir.

The interesting and original aspect is the ornamentation provided for the upper part (and in one place the tenor part) at the cadences in both verses. Most tellingly, it gives the famous ornament on the 7–6 progression over E♭ at the end of the first half of verse 3, so well known nowadays, which rises to a top g (g") and slides gently back down to c♯'. Clearly, whether or not the scribe had access to a manuscript, he must have heard a performance, whence its unique value.[3] It has been transcribed in Appendix 5.

The date of this version is difficult to determine. By 1730 at the latest, Biordi's revision of verse 1 had been incorporated into performance, but this is not useful as a dating device because the adaptation may have been made from an earlier manuscript. It has already been noted that the characteristic ornament in verse 3 must have existed when Bai wrote his *Miserere* around it in 1711. The other ornaments do not provide any more certainty regarding date, although those at the cadences of both halves of verse 3 sound much more French than Italian, an effect heightened by *appoggiature* on the final notes. They would not be out of place in a work by Charpentier!

---

[2] 'Le contrepoint simple consiste à faire note contre-note, & c'est proprement ce que j'ai appellé ci-devant fauxbourdon des psaumes.' Other pieces of music are extracts from the Christmas hymn *Christe redemptor* a4: two settings of verse 1 to illustrate 'contrepoint figuré', one with the *cantus firmus* in the *dessus*, the other in the bass; and a setting of verse 5 (*Hunc coelum terra*) with a walking continuo part shadowing the cantus firmus bass part to show 'contrepoint figuré avec le B.C. sous le plainchant'. Finally there is an *Amen* in free counterpoint, which could be from the same piece or pieces, to illustrate 'contrepoint musical'. All these could have been written by any number of Italian composers in the first fifty or so years of the eighteenth century.

[3] The scribe has also added rhythms for the text on the reciting notes, although they are not always convincing.

Neither can we know where and when Blainville found the transcription. Almost nothing is known of his life or his movements. His evident enthusiasm for Italian music might suggest that he visited the country – Bologna to see Padre Martini, Padua to meet Tartini, even Rome to hear the Papal Choir. On the other hand, his copious exchanges with both French and Italian writers make it just as likely that he acquired it from a correspondent. One thing which is clear is that it is largely superfluous to his theoretical arguments, so he must have included it chiefly because he found it interesting and perhaps unique.

※ Mozart (1770)

Just three years later, another record was made of the *Miserere* in performance, although this one has unfortunately not survived. In 1770 Wolfgang Amadeus Mozart, then aged fourteen, visited Rome during Holy Week. His father Leopold described what happened in a letter to his wife.

> You have often heard of the famous Miserere in Rome, which is so greatly prized that the performers in the chapel are forbidden on pain of excommunication to take away a single part of it, to copy it or to give it to anyone. *But we have it already.* Wolfgang has written it down and we would have sent it to Salzburg in this letter, if it were not necessary for us to be there to perform it. But the manner of performance contributes more to its effect than the composition itself. So we shall bring it home with us. Moreover, as it is one of the secrets of Rome, we do not wish to let it fall into other hands, *ut non incurramus mediate vel immediate in censuram Ecclesiae.*[4]

More detail is found in Friedrich von Schlichtegroll's 1793 *Nekrolog* of Mozart, relying on testimony by Mozart's sister Nannerl (Maria Anna).

> On Wednesday afternoon they accordingly went at once to the Sistine Chapel, to hear the famous *Miserere*. And as according to tradition it was forbidden under ban of excommunication to make a copy of it from the papal music, the son undertook to hear it and then copy it out. And so it came about that when he came home, he wrote it out, and the next day he went back again, holding his copy in his hat, to see if he had got it right or not. But a different *Miserere* was sung. However on Good Friday the first was repeated again. After he had returned home he made a correction here and there, then it was ready. It soon became known in Rome, [and] he had

---

[4] Letter dated 14 April 1770 (Easter Saturday), in *The Letters of Mozart & his Family*, vol. 1, 187.

to sing it at the clavier at a concert. The castrato Christofori, who sang it in the chapel, was present.[5]

It has for some time been fashionable to bring the whole story into question. It is said that the feat of copying the *Miserere* was either so simple that anyone could have done it, or alternatively so difficult that Mozart must have seen a copy in advance.[6] Regarding the second point, apart from the fragment in London and the copies mentioned by Burney,[7] no manuscripts dating from before 1770 are known except for those in the library of the Papal Choir. It was precisely because the music of the *Miserere* was generally unavailable that Burney went to such lengths to find and publish something in 1771. Subsequently it would be necessary to wait until 1838 (see Chapter 6) for the publication of anything not wholly derived from Burney's edition. It must also be remembered that even if Mozart had seen the London fragment, or what Burney acquired later the same year, such a manuscript would have been of little use in preparing a transcription, given the freedom in execution exercised by the singers.

As for the supposed simplicity of the score, it is true that in Allegri's *Miserere* (although not in Bai's) more or less the same music is repeated several times. The prosody of each verse however varies, and with it, as will be seen below, the expression. It is likely that differences in ornamentation occurred as well, as is the nature of ornamentation. Assuming that it was Allegri's *Miserere* that Mozart heard, if he noted just one five-part verse and one four-part one, verses 1 and 3 for example, the changes necessary to adapt his transcription to the different texts of the other verses and add appropriate graces remained only in his memory. Perhaps it was to these variations, as well as particularly subtle graces, that his father was referring when he wrote of 'the manner of performance' which required his presence for a perfect understanding of the composition.[8]

There seems no reason to suppose that the story was invented by Leopold solely to impress the Archbishop of Salzburg, as Luca Bianchini would have us

---

[5] Reproduced in Otto Deutsch, *Mozart: A Documentary Biography*, trans. Eric Blom, Peter Branscombe and Jeremy Noble (Stanford, 1965), 459, and also in Boursy, 'The Mystique', 282–3.

[6] For examples of these different arguments, see Arthur Hutchings, *Mozart: The Man, the Musician* (New York, 1976), vol. 2, 14; Maynard Solomon, 'Mozart: The Myth of the Eternal Child', *19th Century Music*, 15 (1991–2), 96–7; Luca Bianchini, *Wolfgang Amadé Mozart* (2011) on the website www.italianopera.org (the site includes a translation by Robert Newman); and Chrissocoidis, 'London Mozartiana', who argues that Mozart could have seen a copy, and even heard a performance, in London in the 1760s (see pp. 43–4, n.15).

[7] See n. 14.

[8] If he heard the Bai, or some combination of the two, it would have been more difficult. We shall never know.

believe. Rather it seems to have been a plan hatched by Leopold to open doors to his son in Rome. Although the music of the *Miserere* was reputed to be a closely guarded secret and allegedly protected by the menace of excommunication, he seems to have made every effort to proclaim Wolfgang's exploit – hence perhaps the concert – and remained extremely sanguine about possible consequences. When his anxious wife sent him an article which had appeared in the Salzburg press, citing a letter sent from Rome, he replied:

> On reading the article about the Miserere, we simply burst out laughing. There is not the slightest cause for anxiety. Everywhere else far more fuss is being made about Wolfgang's feat. All Rome knows and even the Pope himself that he wrote it down. There is nothing whatever to fear; on the contrary, the achievement has done him great credit, as you will shortly hear. You will see to it that the letter is read out everywhere, so that we may be sure that His Grace hears what Wolfgang has done.[9]

He judged, correctly, that a *succès de scandale* was required, and may even have been slightly disappointed that Pope Clement XIV was sufficiently relaxed about it to award Wolfgang the Golden Spur (the *Militia Aurata*) for artistic distinction. It has even been said that there is no record of a *castrato* called Christofori, but in fact Burney heard him sing twice in Rome in 1770.[10] His full name was Carlo Domenico de Cristofori da Novara, and he had joined the Cappella Musicale Pontificia on 11 March, the second Sunday of Lent in 1770, in plenty of time to sing the Holy Week offices.[11] It is true that the image of a fourteen-year-old Mozart singing it while accompanying himself at the keyboard should give us pause! But other details in Nannerl's recollections ring true: for example, the fact that the same Miserere was sung on Wednesday and Friday, with a different one on Thursday.

The real interest of Mozart's exploit is that he must have written down what he heard, necessarily including the principal ornamentation performed that year and at least some of the *espressioni e Gruppi* which had made it famous. This was, after all, the really secret part. Moreover, as will be shown below, considerable upward transposition was normally practised, and this too, could well have been reflected in Mozart's transcription. If it had survived, it would be the only one ever taken live from a performance apart from the few fragments noted by Mendelssohn, Spohr and others. Its disappearance is an incalculable loss.

---

[9] *The Letters of Mozart*, 201. No doubt if the event also made an impression back in Salzburg, so much the better.
[10] *The Present State*, 364 and 377.
[11] Celani, 'I cantori della Cappella Pontificia' part 3, 101–2.

It has been suggested that Burney's publication might have been based on Mozart's transcription. He had met the Mozarts on 30 August in Bologna, three weeks before his visit to Rome.

> I met with M. Mozart and his son, the little German, whose premature and almost supernatural talents astonished us in London a few years ago, when he had scarce quitted his infant state. Since his arrival in Italy he has been much admired at Rome and Naples; has been honoured with the order of the *Speron d'Oro*, or Golden Spur, by his Holiness, and was engaged to compose an opera at Milan for the next Carnival.[12]

There is no indication that Burney was even aware of Mozart's having copied the *Miserere*. He seems to have considered Mozart to still be 'a little man' not worth talking to, although he 'had a great deal of talk with his father', in the course of which he must have been told about the Golden Spur and the opera in Milan.[13] If Leopold also boasted about Wolfgang's transcription, Burney evidently did not think it worth mentioning. He already had a copy of the *Miserere* from Padre Martini himself; why should he need the scribblings of a 'little German'?[14] It seems likely that it was only when he arrived in Rome that he learned about the importance of the manner of performance and the *certe espressioni e Gruppi* that Mozart's copy must have contained.

---

[12] *The Present State*, 228.

[13] Charles Burney, *Continental Travels 1770–1772*, ed. C.E. Glover (London 1927, 43), reproduced in I. and P. Zaluski, *Mozart in Italy* (London 1999), 119. In his journal, Burney's summary of his impressions is very telling: 'The little man is grown a good deal but is still a little man ... The Pope has knighted the little great wonder.' *Music, Men and Manners*, 98.

[14] 'Padre Martini told me that there were never more than two copies made of it by authority, one of which was made for the late king of Portugal, and the other for himself: this last he permitted me to transcribe at Bologna.' *The Present State*, 278. In the second edition (1773) Burney changed the number of copies to three, having realised that he had forgotten the Emperor Leopold (287–8).

6

Eighteenth-century sources 2 – the Paris and Manchester manuscripts

✳ Background and provenance

GIVEN the loss of Mozart's transcription of the *Miserere* in performance, it is fortunate that another source of information directly from the Papal Choir survives, in the form of two manuscripts created by some of its members for a French public servant called Louis Mesplet.[1] One (henceforward referred to as **P**) is in the Bibliothèque nationale in Paris, with the catalogue number D.14499. It is part of the *Fonds Conservatoire* – that is, it was formerly in the library of the Paris Conservatoire.[2] The other (**Man**) is now in the John Rylands Library of the University of Manchester, where it is catalogued as MS Italian 45.

The title page of **P** (Fig. 10) describes it as a 'Collection de musique Tirée de la Chapelle Sixtine appartenant à Mesplet' ('a collection of music from the Sistine Chapel belonging to Mesplet'). The flourish with which 'Mesplet' is written suggests that the title is in his own hand, a supposition which can be verified by comparison with the summary of his career in the public service which he made in 1824.[3]

Man was once part of the Biblioteca Lindesiana, the large library assembled by Alexander, Lord Lindsay (1812–80), the manuscript portion of which was purchased by the Rylands Library in 1901. It is not typical of the manuscripts collected by Lord Lindsay, and it is not at present known how it came into his

---

[1] This chapter is a recasting of my article '"Per divertimento del Cittadino Mesplet, amatore et conoscitore della vera Musica": Two Early Sources of the *Abbellimenti* Used in Allegri's *Miserere*', *Early Music*, 44/1 (February 2016), 21–44. A third source clearly related to these manuscripts is now in Milan, and is discussed at the end of the chapter.

[2] It was catalogued there as Recueil 32. It can be viewed online at http://gallica.bnf.fr/m/ark:/12148/btv1b53090808m/f1.image;jsessionid=1205AEB9BC2BA131F3E96D78A0CCB7E5.

[3] Mesplet prepared this *Etat de service* (now in the Archives Nationales, A537/71/2) for the *Ecole Royale de Musique et de Déclamation* (as the Paris Conservatoire was named between 1816 and 1830), where he was employed as *chef du bureau de surveillance* from 1821.

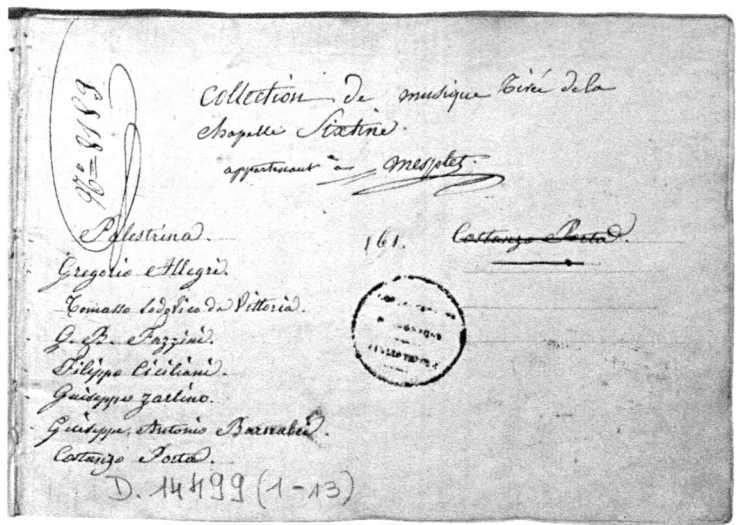

Fig. 10 Title page in Louis Mesplet's hand, Paris, Bibliothèque nationale de France, MS D.14499

collection, as there is no surviving accession register for the manuscripts of the Biblioteca Lindesiana.[4] The paper used is similar to that of **P**, and although slightly smaller now it has been visibly cut down during the binding process.[5]

Both **P** and **Man** give verses 1 (a5) and 3 (a4) of the Allegri *Miserere* in two versions. The first of each, marked *come l'originale*, is clearly derived from Vatican sources – CS 341 for the five-part verses and CS 340 for the four-part ones – with slight differences of detail in repeated notes and underlay (variants are given with the transcription of CS 340–1 in Appendix 3). But the second

---

[4] My thanks to John Hodgson of the John Rylands Library for this and other important information about this MS. Italian 45 is listed as N° 79 in Barry Cooper, 'Catalogue of Pre-1900 Music Manuscripts in the John Rylands University Library of Manchester,' *Bulletin of the John Rylands University Library of Manchester*, 79/2 (1997), 27–101, where more details can be found (available online at https://www.escholar.manchester.ac.uk/uk-ac-man-scw:1m4018). According to Cooper, the binding is English, with an 1804 watermark in the paper of the flyleaf. There were only three other music manuscripts with Italian connections (tentatively datable to 1837, 1841 and after 1832) in the Biblioteca Lindesiana.

[5] **P** measures 175×240mm and **Man** 169×229mm. **Man** has exclusively ten systems per page, with considerable detail differences, whereas more than half of **P** has rather superior paper with just seven staves. The paper of the binding of **P** was manufactured by Fabriano (then as now one of the most prestigious Italian makers) between 1790 and 1810 (personal communication from the staff of the Bibliothèque nationale).

version (transcribed in Appendix 6), which shows 'come si deve eseguire suoi rifiorimenti che s'imparano per tradizione' ('how the ornamentation which is learned by tradition should be performed'), is wholly original and unique, and contains the earliest extant indications from within the Papal Choir of both ornamentation and of the choir's manner of performance.[6] In **P** only, an alternative version of the two decorated soprano parts for the words 'munda me' is given at the end of verse 3. Otherwise the readings in **P** and **Man** are identical. Verse 20 is also present, unadorned but with some dynamic indications.[7] The connection of **Man** with Louis Mesplet (and thus with **P**) is made explicit by the title page of the *Miserere* (Fig. 11), which contains a notably generous dedication to him.

Fig. 11 Title page to Allegri's *Miserere*, John Rylands Library, University of Manchester, MS Italian 45, fol. 70ʳ. Copyright of the University of Manchester

> Miserere mei Deus, from the Sistine Chapel
> By Gregorio Allegri, a Roman,
> With its flourishes as they should be performed
> And have been learned by tradition
> For the entertainment of citizen Mesplet
> Lover and connoisseur of true music

---

[6] While some input from a papal singer into the 1767 version given by Blainville is not impossible, it is far from sure (see Chapter 5).

[7] At the final word 'vitulos', *p* is indicated at 'vi-' followed by *f* at '-tu', no doubt to prepare for a *diminuendo* on '-los', which was famously described by Burney (see p. 230).

The close relationship between the two manuscripts is also clear from their contents. As well as the *Miserere*, both contain works attributed to Gioseffe Zarlino, Giuseppe Antonio Bernabei, Costanzo Porta, 'Tommaso Lodovico da Vittoria' and Giovanni Battista Fazzini, as well as much by Palestrina: among his works are interesting variations (also marked *come si deve eseguire*) on the *Improperia*, sung at the Adoration of the Cross on Good Friday.[8] Every piece in **Man** is reproduced in **P** in virtually identical readings, but while both the Allegri and the *Improperia* are carefully written fair copies in **Man**, the other pieces there show considerable signs of haste and a certain number of corrections; they give the impression of having been collated from the separate parts during the copying process. If that is the case, it seems clear that at least those parts of **Man** were made as a preliminary version of **P**, the manuscript presented to Mesplet. This derivative relationship is confirmed by the fact that **P** has additional music – two Palestrina masses and a large *Veni creator spiritus* a7 by Filippo Ciciliani, together with a little canon between the title page and the score of the latter.

Louis Mesplet and the singers of the Papal Chapel

How did this obscure Frenchman build a relationship with the singers of the Papal Chapel, such that they were willing to write down for him – twice – their most famous work, an action moreover which was said to run the risk of excommunication? How can we be sure that these manuscripts really do originate in the choir? The answer lies in events in Rome during the French invasion of 1798.

Until he arrived in Italy, Louis-Hyppolite Mesplet had lived, as far as can be ascertained, an unexceptional life. He was born in Comines, a town divided in two by the River Lys – which marks to this day the border between northern France and Flanders – on 23 August 1766. His father was a *contrôleur de postes*, at the time a reasonably good position in the public service. Given the cultural interests his later career shows, Louis must have benefited from a good education, but no documentation has yet been traced.[9] Engaged aged eighteen as an

---

[8] Mendelssohn was particularly taken by the choir's performance of the *Improperia* when he visited Rome during Holy Week in 1831 (see his *Letters*, 147–8, and Ex. 3, p. 114). A version *Come è l'Originale* is given in both **Man** and **P** as well as the decorated one. While there is less ornamentation than in the *Miserere*, the precision of the prosody is particularly striking.

[9] Perhaps the most likely source of it would have been as a *garçon de chœur* at the Collégiale St Pierre in Lille, where there had been a *maîtrise* (children's

assistant accountant to the *Payeur de la Guerre* in Lille, Louis was soon transferred to a similar post in Paris.[10] Then followed stints at the *Trésor National* and finally in the *caisse de l'extraordinaire* (the war accounts) under a prominent *fonctionnaire* and former *conseilleur d'état* Antoine Amelot, Marquis de Chaillot. He seems to have left public service in 1793 (coinciding with certain political problems faced by his superior) and is next heard of in 1797, aged thirty-one, as an *employé de l'Armée d'Italie* (employee of the [French] army [stationed in] Italy); there he was probably reunited with Amelot. His artistic talents and interests must have come to the attention of Général Berthier, Bonaparte's chief of staff, because at the end of January 1798 he was asked to make a visual record of the town of Ancona.[11]

---

choir) since 1425. In 1774, eight years after his birth, his parents were married there (it was not uncommon at this time for couples in the working population of cities to remain unmarried), which makes one wonder if they took this step to give their son the *de facto* legitimacy required to join the *maîtrise*, just at the age when they might have wished him to do so. In that case he would have come under the influence of Jean-Albert Devillers, organist of St Pierre from 1760 until the Revolution, described by Burney as 'an agreeable and intelligent man in his profession' (*The Present State*, 10), who also filled in there on the 'cornet d'Espagne' and the serpent. A true polymath, he was also employed at the theatre of Lille, not only as a musician (harpsichordist and cellist) but as an actor, at a time when the repertoire was as good as anywhere in France outside Paris. From the choir school Louis would have progressed to the *collège* of St Pierre, which at this time taught a relatively wide and enlightened curriculum, with plays and concerts given every year. See E. Hautcoeur, *Histoire de l'église collégiale et du chapitre de Saint-Pierre de Lille*, vol. 3 (Lille, 1899), 286–8, and L. Lefebvre (ed.), *Histoire du Théâtre de Lille* (vol. 3 (Lille, 1907). See also n. 13.

[10] This information and most of that which follows is based on the summary of his career in the public service mentioned above (n. 3). The date and place of his birth are confirmed by his marriage certificate (see n. 20). The spelling of Hyppolite (his mother's Christian name) is subject to variation in official documents.

[11] 'An authorisation given to the deceased on *12 pluviôse an 6* [31 October 1798] by General Alexandre Berthier, to create all the views of Ancona that he thinks fit' ('Une autorisation donné le douze pluviôse an six par le Général Alexandre Berthier au défunt de prendre à Ancône toutes les vues qui bon lui semblera') is in the inventory of his possessions made on 17 October 1731, after his death on 21 August of that year (Paris, Archives Nationales, Minutier Central des Notaires MC/ET/XVI/1052), fol. 10 – Papiers, 4ème lot, No. 1. Ancona had been in French hands since 9 February 1797. Mesplet remained throughout his life an enthusiastic painter, mostly of water-colour landscapes and miniatures. This request must be seen in the context of Bonaparte's passion for using art to promote both himself and *la Gloire de la France*. No-one who

The French army invaded Rome on 10 February. Normal practice after invasion was to appoint *commissaires* (or *inspecteurs*) *chargés des objets d'arts* – administrators whose task was to assess the value of artistic artefacts and organise the taking of the best ones to France to 'save them for civilisation'. Mesplet must also have been known for his interest in sacred music, for almost immediately, on 19 February, he found himself nominated as *inspecteur* of the entire musical archive of the Vatican.[12] The following day Pope Pius VI, made a prisoner following his refusal to renounce his temporal power, was taken out of Rome, never to return. The Papal Choir existing only to sing for him, offices in the Chapel were immediately suspended (the final one was sung the following day, 21 February, which suitably enough was Ash Wednesday), and the members of the choir found themselves with neither job nor salary.

If Mesplet was interested in the music of the Chapel before he arrived in Rome, as seems likely, he must have been very disappointed by this turn of events. Was it he who proposed a grand concert in which the choir could sing for the greater glory of the new French Republic of Rome, as Baini suggests in the extract below? Whatever the truth of the matter, he was immediately given the authority and means to organise such a concert. It was an exceptional event, and Giovanni Baini's somewhat breathless account shows not only Mesplet's interest in the choir and its repertoire but also his musical talents.

---

    could hold a paintbrush, it seems, was refused. The much more renowned painter Anne-Louis Girodet wrote to a friend: 'We have all been enlisted even if we don't wear a uniform – paintbrush to the right, pencil to the left, forward march – and we march.' ('Nous sommes tous enrégimentés quoique nous ne portions point l'uniforme. Pinceau à droite, crayon à gauche. En avant marche et nous marchons.') Trans. in Denis O'Brien, *After the Revolution: Antoine-Jean Gros, Painting and Propaganda under Napoleon Bonaparte* (University Park, PA, 2004), 2. The original text is in the French version of the same book, *Jean-Antoine Gros, peintre de Napoléon* (Paris, Gallimard, 2006, 2.)

[12] 'Nomination of the deceased at Rome, dated *1 ventôse an 6* [19 February 1798], to the post of inspector of the musical archives of St Peter's and of the Vatican' ('Une nomination de défunt en date à Rome du premier ventôse an six aux fonctions d'inspecteur des dépôts de musique de Saint Pierre et du Vatican') is also in the inventory, fol. 10 – Papiers, 4ème lot, No. 2. Mesplet's record of service notes that he was 'chargé … de la conservation du dépôt de musique de la chapelle Sixtine pendant la dernière année' ('put in charge of the conservation of the musical archive of the Sistine Chapel for the final year of his service there'), which implies that he had already been in Italy for some time. An interest in the music of the Papal Choir would have been pretty exceptional in eighteenth-century France, particularly among *fonctionnaires*.

Occupata Roma nel 1798. quel signor Mesplet commissario delle belle arti, di cui abbiam ragionato con distinzione di ringraziamenti nella nota 379. volle dare una solenne accademia di musica vocale e strumentale nel palazzo vaticano alla nazione francese. Completò un' orchestra ben numerosa dei primi strumentisti di Roma, e volle per cantori tutt' i cappellani cantori della nostra cappella, e pochi altri dei più distinti della città. Io benchè aggregato dalli 2. Marzo 1795. nella cappella, era tuttavia giovanetto studente di teologia, alunno nel Seminario Romano, fui perciò esentato dall' intervenire a siffatta accademia, bensì uno dei cantori anziani D. Saverio Bianchini di Ceprano, molto mio amorevole seco mi condusse alla prova generale, che si fece pure al Vaticano in un giovedì dopo pranzo. Il primo pezzo, con cui si diè principio fu l'*Ouverture* dell' *Ifigenia* del cav. Cristoforo Gluck, che per la direzione del lodato Sig. Mesplet intendentissimo di musica, fu eseguita d' una maniera veramente squisita. Terminata l'*Ouverture* con piena sodisfazione dell' uditorio, il secondo pezzo da eseguirsi era il *Benedictus qui venit in nomine domini* concertato a quattro sole voci, due soprani, un contralto, ed un tenore della messa *Assumpta est* di Giovanni Pierluigi. Echeggiava ancora il Vaticano allo strepito della grande orchestra, e delle robuste armonie del boemo restauratore della musica drammatica, e quattro de' nostri cantori Biagio Parca di Corchiano, Lorenzo Neroni di monte S. Polo, amendue soprani, D. Giuseppe Pisani di Ferentino di Campagna, contralto (questi tre sono già passati all'eterno canto) e D. Niccola Lamberto Binder romano, tenore, si accingono alla esecuzione del *Benedictus*. Un pallore generale occupa il volto di tutti i cantori presenti della nostra cappella, me compreso; e ci diciamo a vicenda all' orecchio. Pessima disposizione! Dopo una così profonda e tragica composizione da numerosissima orchestra con tanta anima, con sì fino sentimento, qual' effetto potran mai produrre quattro sole voci in un *Benedictus*? Dopo una musica modernamente cuniata da un genio tutto fuoco, qual lusinga di ottenere un buon risultato per un concertino vecchio già di più di duecento anni? Se si voleva un pezzo di musica da stare a fronte della sinfonia dovevasi scegliere un gran mottetto ad otto, o dieci voci di Pasquale Pisari, ovver di Filippo Siciliani moderni nostri cantori, eseguito da tutto il coro. Ma già i quattro cantori destinati al concerto sono in azione. Tutto è silenzio. Dalla seconda nota rimane l'uditorio sorpreso: sembra a ciascuno di essere trasportato in un nuovo mondo di nuovi cieli, di nuova terra: nuove melodie, nuove armonie, nuovi suoni, nuovi accordi, nuove successioni: noi stessi della cappella non riconosciamo il trito *Benedictus*: sono angeli che cantano? Sono uomini? È musica umana? O un divino ritrovato d' impercettibili suoni? Un' estasi generale rende l' uditorio assorto. Chiudesi con l'ultima inaspettata cadenza la composizione, e schiudesi all' istante un plauso indicibile di tutti e di ciascuno. La gran sala, e le camere contigue pienissime di uditori d' ogni ceto, d' ogni sesso, d' ogni età, d' ogni maniera di pensare applaudiscono alla novità dell' insieme di cotal musica, con entusiasmo mai non veduto, peschè mai non si era instituito siffatto parallelo, e tutti ebbero a confessare, che questa era musica che questa musica era la musica della mente e del cuore, e che si elevava sopra l'*Ouverture*, più che l'*Ouverture* si eleverebbe al di sopra de' suoni inconditi di barbare genti. Si continuò quindi nella esecuzione degli altri pezzi di musica stabiliti, ma gli uditori prevenuti dall' effetto sopragrande che produsse il ridetto *Benedictus*, non gradirono altro: e questo stesso prodotto si ebbe, per quanto mi contarono i miei colleghi, la sera dell' accademia, benchè non fosse avvertito pienamente nella gran sala ripiena di persone intente solo per riguardi politici ed economici a corteggiare il Generale, e lo stato maggiore dell' armata francese quivi presenti.

Fig. 12 Giuseppe Baini, *Memorie Storico-Critiche della Vita et delle Opere di Giovanni Pierluigi da Palestrina* (1828), n. 562 (vol. 2, 165–6), recounting the extraordinary concert in the Vatican in early 1798 organised by Mesplet

When Rome was occupied in 1798, M. Mesplet, a Commissioner of Fine Arts, to whom we have expressed our special thanks in note 379 [see below], wished to give a fine concert of vocal and instrumental music in the Vatican Palace in honour of the French nation. He assembled a very large orchestra composed of the best musicians of Rome, all the singers of our chapel, and a few extras from among the most distinguished of the city. Although I had been accepted into the Chapel on 2 March 1795, I was still a student in the Roman Seminary, so therefore could not take part in such an event, but one of our older singers, Saverio Bianchini of Ceprano, with whom I got on well, took me to the final rehearsal, which took place in the Vatican one Thursday afternoon. The first piece, for the beginning of the concert, was the *Overture* to *Iphigenia* by Cav. Cristoforo Gluck, which thanks to the excellent direction of M. Mesplet was performed in a truly exquisite manner.[13]

After the overture was finished to the entire satisfaction of the audience, the second piece to be performed was the *Benedictus qui venit in nomine domini* for four solo voices – two sopranos, alto and tenor from the *Missa Assumpta est* of Giovanni Pierluigi. The Vatican still echoed to the sound of the large orchestra and the fiery harmonies of the Bohemian restorer of dramatic music, and four of our singers, Biagio Parca of Corchiano, Lorenzo Neroni of Monte S. Polo, both sopranos, Don Giuseppe Pisani of Ferentino di Campagna, alto (these three have since joined the heavenly choir), and Don Niccola Lamberto Binder of Rome, tenor, were getting ready to attack the *Benedictus*. A general pallor was evident in the faces of all the singers present from our chapel, including me, and we whispered to each other, 'what an unfortunate arrangement'; after such a profound and tragic composition given by such a large orchestra with such feeling, what effect could be produced by just four singers in a *Benedictus*? After newly created music by a fiery genius, what hope was there for a good result from singing a little piece already more than two hundred years old? If you wanted a piece of music to hold its own after a large symphonic work, it would have been better to choose a grand motet in eight or ten parts by one of our modern singers, Pasquale Pisari or Filippo Siciliani, performed by the whole choir.

But the four men assigned to the piece had already begun. All was silence. After the second note the audience were amazed: each and every one seemed to be transported into a new universe with new heavens and a new earth; new melodies, new harmonies, new accords, new progressions; we of the Chapel hardly recognised the well-worn *Benedictus*. Is it angels

---

[13] Of Gluck's two operas about Iphigenia, *Iphigenia in Aulide* (1774) and *Iphigenia in Tauride* (1779), it is the overture to the latter which is generally better known nowadays. However, it was that of *Iphigenia in Aulide* that Mesplet would later publish, in an arrangement for harp, piano and violin, in his collection *Six Ouvertures célèbres* (see Fig. 15 and n. 30). It is also the one which had been performed in 1782 as part of a '*grand concert instrumental*' at the *collège* of St Pierre in Lille, conceivably towards the end of Mesplet's time there (Hautcoeur, *Histoire*, 289). All of Gluck's operas were given in Lille over the seasons 1781–2 and 1782–3.

singing? Are they men? Is it human music? Is it a divine concourse of imperceptible sounds? A general ecstasy seized the audience. When the composition closed with the last unexpected cadence, there arose an indescribable tumult of applause.

The great hall and the adjoining rooms, filled to overflowing with hearers of every rank, sex, and age, of every mode of thought, rang with unheard-of enthusiasm for the novelty of the combination of such music, because such a juxtaposition had never before been arranged, and all had to confess that this latter was music and that this music was the music of the mind and of the heart, and that it was as far superior to the *Overture* as the *Overture* was superior to the uncouth sounds of barbarous nations.

The rehearsal continued with the other pieces in the programme, but the listeners had been so overcome by the extraordinary effect they had experienced from the small *Benedictus*, that they could not appreciate anything else. And the same thing occurred in the evening at the concert, so my colleagues said, although it was less pronounced in the great hall, [which was] full of people only there for political and economic reasons, and to meet the General and the General Staff of the French Army [who were] also present.[14]

One can well imagine the effect on the singers of Mesplet's having chosen a piece from their most treasured repertoire for his concert and, what's more, convinced a heterogeneous public that it was a good idea to do so. Whatever they thought of this foreigner parachuted into the control of their precious musical archive, he had established his credentials not only as a fine musician but also as a lover and connoisseur of their music.

He did not stop there. Realising that his new friends in the choir were in financial difficulties, he found money for them. In another footnote in his *Memorie Storico-Critiche*, Baini gave him credit for acts of charity to many musicians and singers of Rome, as well as paying tribute to his benevolent role in the preservation of the archives.

> In the first invasion of Rome in 1798, our archive was miraculously saved. Among the administrators who came after the French army, there was a certain man called Sig. Mesplet who came as a Commissioner of Fine Arts. This man, while very busy with the looting of a great number of precious objects, gave little attention to music, although he did do some good things,

---

[14] The story was retold by Nathan Haskell Dole in *Famous Composers* (New York, 1891, repr. 1902), 9–10, the beginning of the chapter on Palestrina, who glosses it as follows: 'The *Benedictus* performed on that gala occasion was composed by Giovanni Pierluigi da Palestrina, called the Prince of Music, and the spectator who so graphically described the effect produced on that brilliant audience was Giuseppe Baini, "Roman priest, Capellan Cantor, and director of the Pontifical Chapel," whose enthusiastic life of Palestrina, written in beautiful Italian, was until a few years ago the repository of all that was known about the great composer' (Fig. 12). His translation has been lightly revised, and extended to include the last paragraph.

notably some acts of charity to a good number of instrumentalists and singers in the city who had been reduced to poverty. As regards our chapel, Mesplet demanded first of all copies of different compositions, which were given to him. Then he requested the keys of the *custodia* (two small rooms, each situated respectively in one of the chapels in the Vatican and in the Quirinale [one in the Sistine Chapel in the Vatican, and one in the Pauline Chapel in the Quirinale] where the music books for the daily service are kept) ... and these keys were given to him. As he was leaving Rome, however, he returned the keys to one of our singers, Giuseppe Censi, without having ever visited the two *custodie*, which he left sealed, and at that moment, at extremely great risk, all the books were spirited away by us and put into safe-keeping.[15]

The horror of the invasion is clear from the rest of Baini's story. The choir's archive was located in the Quirinale Palace on an upper floor above the Pauline Chapel. When Rome was declared a Republic, the French consuls were installed in the Quirinale, and one of them turned the whole of that top floor into a chicken-run, so the archive was 'at the mercy of an old keeper of the chickens' ('il nostro archivio rimase in balia di un vecchio guardapolli'). When Rome was reconquered by an army from Naples in September 1799 the chickens left, but they returned when the French invaded again in 1809. He continues:

> Once Italy and Rome were finally liberated, I was one of the first to get into the Quirinale, and I ran straight away to the archive and I found the door open, and I must say my heart fell to my boots. I pushed open the door and found the locks [of the cupboard doors] hanging on a nail, but the cupboards were closed. I opened the cupboards as I had the keys with me, and I saw, almost not believing my eyes, that everything was intact. Hence I burst out *fecit Dominus potentiam in brachio suo. Oculos habuerunt et non viderunt; manus habuerunt, et non palpaverunt. Dicites dimisit inanes*![16]

---

[15] 'Nella prima invasione di Roma del 1798, il nostro archivio fu prodigiosamente salvo. Seguiva l'armata francese un cotal sig. Mesplet come commissario delle belle arti; questi occupato nello spoglio di tanti preziosi oggetti non curò gran fatto la musica, fece però alcun bene, ed anche qualche caritatevole atto a parecchi suonatori, e cantori della città ridotti in miserie. Per quel che riguarda la nostra cappella, richiese dapprima il Mesplet le copie di vaiig composizioni, che gli furono date: quindi volle le chiavi della custodia (due piccole camerette, ciascuna situata respettivamente in una delle cappelle al Vaticano, ed al Quirinale, ove si tengono i libri musicali per il servigio quotidiano) ... e gli furono consegnate: ei però dopo alcuni mesi in partendo da Roma restituì ad un nostro cantore Giuseppe Censi, le ridette chiavi senza mai visitar le due custodie, che lasciò biffate, ed al momento furon dai nostri con grandissimo rischio involati tutti i libri, e posti in salvo.' Baini, *Memorie*, n. 379 (vol. 1, 278–9).

[16] 'Liberata finalmente l'Italia e Roma, io fui de'primi , che m'introdussi nel Quirinale, corsi tosto all' archivio, e trovai la porta socchiusa, mi cadde, a dir vero, il cuore in terra, spingo la porta, e trovo le serrature appese ad un chiodo,

Corroboration of Mesplet's generosity is found in letters from the painter Jean-Auguste-Dominique Ingres. Ingres was awarded a scholarship to the Académie Française in Rome in 1801, but until 1806, when the state finally found the necessary budget to install him in the recently acquired Villa Medici, he was given, along with other artists, an *atelier* in the former Couvent des Capucines in Paris. It is during this period that he seems to have become a friend of Mesplet, perhaps through connections with other artists installed there who had worked with the army in Italy (such as Antoine-Jean Gros), or with returning officers visiting them there.[17] Mesplet certainly made many friends among Ingres' circle, one of whom sketched a caricature of him (Fig. 13).[18]

When Ingres finally arrived in Rome in 1806, he could indulge his fascination for the ancient world, particularly the Vatican, of which he made several paintings during his lifetime. An excellent amateur musician himself, he made a point of hearing all the Holy Week offices of 1807 in the Sistine Chapel (see his account in Chapter 4) and became friendly with some of the singers. In a letter to Pierre Forestier, a friend of both his and Mesplet's, he wrote:

> I am extremely happy to be able to recount to you something which does credit to the generosity of Mesplet who, during his stay in Rome, was very useful and generous to the poor singers of the Papal Chapel who were starving. These good people brought this up spontaneously while showing us their library, just as I was about to speak of him. They were thrilled to

---

gli armarii però chiusi, gli apro, avendo meco le chiavi, e li riconosco, non credendolo quasi ai miei occhi, intatti; ond'ebbi ad esclamare: *fecit Dominus potentiam in brachio suo. Oculos habuerunt et non viderunt; manus habuerunt, et non palpaverunt. Divites dimisit inanes!*" Given that it is said that the French sack of the Quirinale in 1798 was so complete that not even the doors were left on their hinges, one can understand his relief.

[17] See M.E.-J. Delécluze, *Louis David, son école et son temps* (Paris, 1855), 294–300.

[18] One of Ingres' portraits from this period was catalogued by him later simply as 'un ami de Mesplet' without further explanation. It has recently been convincingly identified by the Ingres scholar Georges Vigne as representing the French composer Albert-Auguste Androt (1781–1804), painted shortly before he left for Rome in 1803 as the very first winner of the *Prix de Rome*. See '"Un ami de Mesplet": le portrait d'Albert-Auguste Androt par Ingres', *Bulletin du Musée Ingres*, 85 (Montauban, April 2013), 17–34. Mesplet also presented Ingres' friend Pierre Forestier with a 'pretty view of the Capucines', a gesture much appreciated by the painter, and remained in contact with Ingres' childhood friend Jean-Pierre-François Gilibert, who studied law in Paris from around 1796 until 1804. Gilibert kept the caricature of Mesplet drawn by one of their circle, and in 1809 Mesplet presented him with a 'petit paysage à la gouache' (a small water-colour landscape) inscribed 'donné à Gilibert par son ami Mesplet 1809' ('given to Gilibert by his friend Mesplet in 1809'). It is described in Marie-Jeanne Ternois, 'Ingres et Montauban' (diss., Ecole du Louvre, 1955), 28–9, n. 4. Both of these water-colours have now disappeared, as has a large oil-painting of the Villa Borghese in Rome, which was among his possessions at his death.

Fig. 13 Pencil sketch: anonymous caricature of Louis Mesplet, made around 1803 by a member of Ingres' circle of friends. The inscription reads 'painter of miniature watercolours Mesplet'. Preserved in the papers of J.-F. Gilibert and now in the possession of his descendants (reproduced with permission)

meet a friend of their benefactor, as they called him, with tears of gratitude in their eyes. This little scene happened in the presence of these independent gentlemen [it is not clear to whom Ingres is referring here]; and I was enchanted by it, although in no way surprised by Mesplet's behaviour because I know well his generous heart. I shall very much enjoy writing to him about this, but I shall always think, 'What a shame!'[19]

The shame to which Ingres refers was a recent scandal involving Mesplet, which may be connected to his subsequent marriage, on 4 May 1807, to

---

[19] 'Mais une chose dont je me plais à vous faire part et qui fait honneur au bon cœur de Mesplet qui, lors de son voyage à Rome, a rendu les plus grands services à ces pauvres chanteurs de la chapelle du pape qui étaient sans pain. Ces bonnes gens, en nous montrant leur bibliothèque musicale et au moment où j'allais leur parler de Mesplet, m'ont prévenu. Ils ont été enchantés de voir en moi l'ami de leur bienfaiteur, c'est ainsi qu'ils le nomment, les larmes aux yeux de reconnaissance. Cette scène s'est passée en présence de beaucoup de ces messieurs les indépendants; et moi en mon particulier j'en suis enchanté, sans que cela m'étonne de Mesplet parce que je lui connais un excellent cœur. Je me fais une fête de lui écrire à ce sujet, mais je dirai toujours de lui: «C'est dommage»...'. Extract of his letter of 7 April 1807, in Ingres, *Lettres de France et d'Italie*, 156. Ingres' account of Holy Week is contained earlier in the same letter.

Adelaïde Marie Louise Thomas Decressy, and the birth of their son, Hyppolite Louis, just three days later.[20] On 17 January 1807, shortly after arriving to take up his scholarship at the Académie de France, Ingres wrote, 'I share your thoughts about M. Mesplet, I'm very upset and sorry for him, but have no reason to hate him, and can't believe him capable of any <u>indiscretion</u>.'[21] On 21 February he wrote again.

> Poor Mesplet, he's caught between Charybdis and Scylla. The picture that you paint of him is horrible. One would have thought that he would be the first to follow the good advice that he usually gives; he's lost, and it's a shame, because he had all the qualities necessary to have a good place in society, with his talents and his amiability. But the more miserable he is, the more he is to be pitied. As things are, please remember me to him if you see him.[22]

Whatever the scandal was, it is clear that the doors to bourgeois respectability were henceforth closed to him. Forestier, for example, refused henceforth to formally receive him, as is made clear when Ingres continues in his letter of 7 April.

> ... at the same time I cannot disapprove of the measures that your prudence has obliged you to take in regard to your relations with him. I also owe him many thanks for the pretty view of the Capucines that he gave you, which made me grateful to him not only for the pleasure it brought you, but also for the kind words you say to me about it. I very much miss my fine studio in the Capucines and the good times we spent together there.[23]

---

[20] The two marriage certificates are in Archives de Paris, État-civil reconstitué 1798–1860, and the birth certificate of his son in Archives de Paris, État-civil, Acte de naissance n° 511700100223111234. See www.généalogie.com (accessed 15 October 2013). The letters from Forestier to Ingres are lost.

[21] 'Je pense comme vous sur M. Mesplet, j'en suis fâché et le plains sans le haïr, je n'en ai pas sujet et le crois incapable d'aucune <u>légèreté</u>.' *Lettres de France et d'Italie*, 134.

[22] 'Ce pauvre Mesplet, il tombe de Charybde en Scylla. Le tableau que vous me faites de lui est épouvantable. Lui, qui donne de si bons conseils ordinairement, devrait être le premier à les suivre, c'est un homme perdu, c'est dommage, car il avait tous les moyens possibles pour avoir dans la société un rang très honorable, par ses talents et son amabilité. Mais plus il est malheureux et plus il est à plaindre. En ce cas, je vous prie de me rappeler à son souvenir, si vous le voyez.' Ibid., 145.

[23] '... et j'approuve bien ce que votre prudence vous a fait faire à l'égard des convenances de lui à vous. Je lui dois aussi beaucoup de remerciements de la jolie vue des Capucines qu'il vous a donnée, il m'a rendu double plaisir, pour le cas que vous en faites et les choses bonnes et bien obligeantes que vous me dites sur cela. Je regrette beaucoup mon joli atelier des Capucines et les moments où j'avais le bonheur de vous y voir.' Extract from letter of 7 April 1807, Ibid., 156.

We can be sure that Ingres did indeed write to Mesplet about his meeting with the singers because, perhaps sensing an opportunity to re-establish some of his reputation, Mesplet asked him to obtain an attestation of his good conduct from the Vatican authorities. Ingres wasted no time in doing so.[24] On 24 June the *camerlengo* of the choir, Giuseppe Censi, informed its members that

> a *penzionato Francese* had made known by a note that 'Monsiur Mesple', now living in Paris, who was in Rome at the time of the ex-Republic as a Commissioner of Fine Arts particularly concerned with music, asked our College to make him an attestation, certifying that he had saved the treasure of our musical compositions from the hands of the Republicans at the time that he held the keys of our Archive.[25]

It was rapidly drawn up by the *segretario-puntatore*, who that year was Nicola Binder (the tenor who had participated as soloist in Mesplet's grand concert), and was ready on 8 July.

> In witness to the whole truth, we the undersigned, chaplain singers of the Reverend College of the Papal Chapel, state in full and in undoubted faith that we very well remember, that when the French army occupied this Ecclesiastical State in the year 1798, it happened that one of the Commissioners who looked after the Fine Arts was the very worthy Signor Mesplet, who among his wide knowledge possessed particular expertise in the science of music. This well-respected person gave himself the task of scrupulously conserving all the Books of Music which were in the *Custodia* of the Papal Chapel; while in Rome he always looked after the keys of the said *Custodia* and upon his departure he handed them over to two of the singers, hence nothing was missing. Therefore, for love of Justice, and in gratitude, we believe we have a duty to supply to the praiseworthy Signor Mesplet the present Testimonial, in its most authentic form, furnished with the seal of Our College, and signed with our own hands. Dated the 8th of July at our College in Rome, in the year of our salvation 1807, and the 8th year of the reign of our most clement and sovereign Pontiff, Pius VII. Benedetto Barsanti, Maestro della Cappella Pontificia, D. Nicola Binder, Segretario, e Puntatore.[26]

---

[24] In his next letter to Forestier, dated 29 May the same year, Ingres notes, 'I am writing to M. Mesplet and I am going to look after his business.' ('J'écris à M. Mesplet et vais m'occup[er de] son [affaire].') Ibid., 164 (the paper was torn by the seal).

[25] 'un penzionato Francese per mezzo di un Viglietto [sic] li aveva fatto intendere, che Monsiur Mesple ora dimoranti in Parigi commissario in Roma nel tempo dell'estinta Republica sopra le belle arti, e segnatamente sopra la Musica pregava il Nostro Collegio di farle un attestato, che lui aveva salvato da[l]le mani de' Repu[b]blicani il tesoro delle nostre composizioni Musicali nel tempo che il medesimo riteneva le Chiavi del nostro Archivio.' *DS* 229 (1807), fol. 52ᵛ.

[26] The attestation (Fig. 14) was actually ready on the 4th, but the Sacro Palazzo Apostolico insisted that it 'should only be in the name of those members [of the

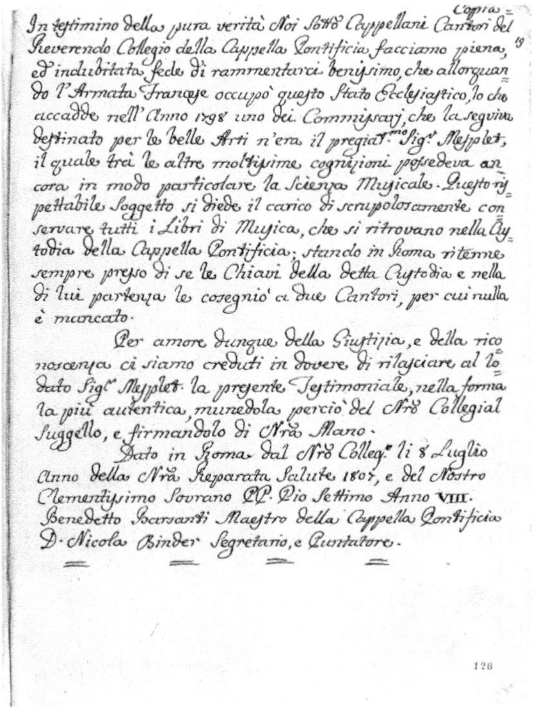

Copia

In testimonio della pura verità Noi Sott.i Cappellani Cantori del Reverendo Collegio della Cappella Pontificia, facciamo piena, ed indubitata fede di rammentarci benissimo, che allorquando l'Armata Francese occupò questo Stato Ecclesiastico, lo che accadde nell'Anno 1798 uno dei Commissarj, che la seguiva destinato per le belle Arti n'era il pregiat.mo Sig.r Mesplet, il quale tra le altre moltissime cognizioni possedeva ancora in modo particolare la Scienza Musicale. Questo rispettabile Soggetto si diede il carico di scrupolosamente conservare tutti i Libri di Musica, che si ritrovano nella Custodia della Cappella Pontificia; stando in Roma, ritenne sempre presso di se le Chiavi della detta Custodia e nella di lui partenza le consegnò a due Cantori, per cui nulla è mancato.

Per amore dunque della Giustizia, e della riconoscenza ci siamo creduti in dovere di rilasciare al lodato Sig.r Mesplet la presente Testimoniale, nella forma la più autentica, munendola perciò del N.ro Collegial Suggello, e firmandolo di N.ra Mano.

Dato in Roma dal N.ro Colleg.o li 8 Luglio Anno della N.ra Reparata Salute 1807, e del Nostro Clementissimo Sovrano P.P. Pio Settimo Anno VIII.

Benedetto Barsanti Maestro della Cappella Pontificia

D. Nicola Binder Segretario, e Puntatore.

128

Fig. 14 Copy made for the papal archive of the attestation concerning Mesplet in the hand of Nicola Binder, *Diario Sistina* 228 (1807), addendum, fol. 126^{v}

Baini described Mesplet in admiring tones.

> The above-mentioned Sig. Mesplet, via a certain Sig. Ingres, one of the students at the French Academy at the Villa Medici, asked our College for an attestation that he had jealously guarded our musical treasures during the occupation of Rome, and it was graciously granted him on 8 July 1807. In addition to this service, to give pleasure to Sig. Mesplet, or if he is no longer among the living, to his descendants, I give him honourable mention for the charity which he showed to certain Roman *professori* of music, and

choir] who had been present in the time of the ex-Republic' ('che l'avessero sottoscritto soltanto quelli Sig^{ri} Compagni che si erano trovati presenti in tempo dell'estinta Republica', *DS* 229 (1807), fol. 57^{r} (14 July)), so a modification was made. It was then given to Ingres to be sent to Mesplet, who certainly received it, as it was among his possessions at his death: 'A certificate in Italian from the musicians of the Sistine Chapel in Rome certifying that the deceased conserved the music of it intact and with the greatest care' ('Un certificat délivré en italien par les musiciens de la Chapelle Sixtine à Rome constatant que le défunt en a conservé la musique intact et avec le plus grand soin'). Inventory, fol. 10 – Papiers, 4ème lot, No. 5.

for the moderation with which he behaved towards the singers of the Apostolic Chapel, and towards the *custodie* and the archive of the books during the nineteen months of wild inhumanity, barbarous despoliation and violent theft of his superiors.[27]

One wonders if Mesplet's 'moderation' did not win him much favour from his superiors; his principal job as a *commissaire* was, after all, to decide which treasures were to be taken for the state, and it appears that from the musical archive of the Vatican, none were. Moreover it may be that his 'charity' was exercised with money raised in imaginative ways. For example, he was apparently responsible for the sale at auction of the entire library of the Villa Albani.[28] As there is no reason to suppose from his background that he was rich enough to be generous with his own money, perhaps some of the takings were 'diverted' towards the singers and musicians of Rome. In any case, for reasons unknown he was reassigned in October 1798 to other, more prosaic posts in the French army in Italy: *inspecteur des fourrages* (in charge of the provision of fodder), and then his old job, *agent des finances*.[29] These were certainly posts out of which considerable money could be made, but Mesplet must have felt them to be very far from his brief moment of glory at the centre of the musical life of Rome. He then disappears entirely from view until around the time of his disgrace, when he started arranging and publishing music (Fig. 15).[30]

[27] 'Il soprannominalo sig. Mesplet noli' anno 1807. per mezzo di un cotal sig. Ingres uno dei pensionati dell'accademia di Francia a villa Medici richiese al nostro collegio l'attestato di aver gelosamente nella occupazione di Roma conservato il nostro tesoro musicale, e gli fu per compiacimento rilasciato in data degli 8. di Luglio 1807. Oltre cotal' officio gradisca anche il sig. Mesplet, o s' egli mai non fosse più tra' vivi , gradiscano i suoi questa , che io gli rendo, onorevole rammemorazione del di lui nome, della di lui carità verso alcuni professori romani di musica, e della moderazione usata verso il collegio de' cappellani cantori apostolici, e verso le custodie e l'archivio de' loro libri nei diciannove mesi della furibonda inumanità, del barbaro spoglio, e della violenta rapina del suo direttorio.' Baini, *Memorie*, n. 397 (vol. 1, 279). The nineteen months referred to are from February 1798 until September 1799. The story of Mesplet's generosity must have been impressed on Baini many times for him to feel obliged to pen such a tribute to someone he never knowingly met.

[28] See Jeanne Bignami-Odier, 'Christiniana', *Mélanges d'archéologie et d'histoire*, 80 (1968), 709.

[29] The relevant orders are found in the inventory, fol. 10 – Papiers, 4ème lot, No. 3 and extra note. The first (dated 13 October 1798) is a passport to travel; the second, dated 13 November 1798, was delivered in Milan.

[30] A volume of *Six Ouvertures célèbres ... arrangées pour harpe, piano et violon ... par Mesplet* is undated, but has been assigned tentatively to the beginning of the century (see Fig. 15). The earliest dated publication is a piano arrangement of Méhul's *Chanson de Roland* in 1806, and in 1813 followed two volumes of

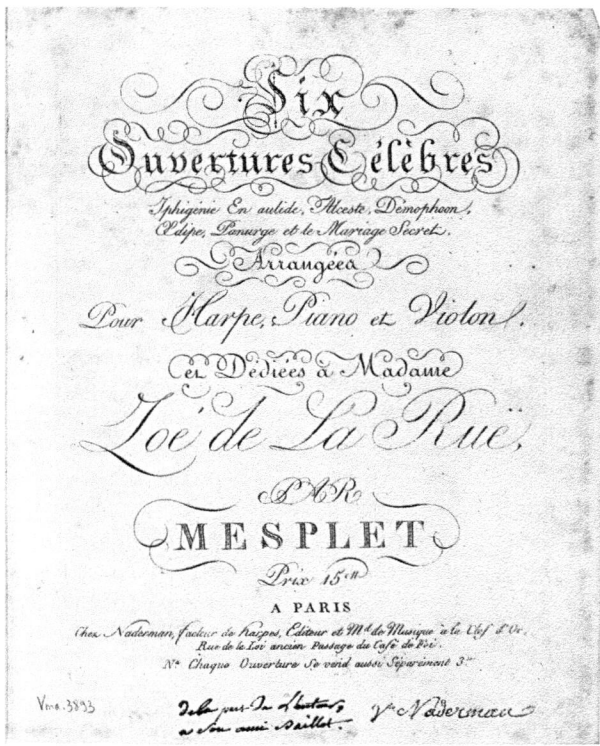

Fig. 15 Mesplet. *Six Ouvertures célèbres* (n.d.)

The end of his story is quickly told. From 1815 he was *sous-chef à l'Etat-major* [the administration] *de la Garde Nationale à Paris* and finally, from the beginning of 1821 until his death ten years later, he was employed in the administrative post of *chef du bureau de surveillance* at the Ecole Royale de la

---

'Douze adagio, andante, menuets et trio tirés des symphonies de Haydn et arrangés pour le piano, avec accompagnement du violon, par Mesplet ... chez les marchands de musique', which was announced in the *Journal Général de la Littérature de France* of that year. They are listed in the *Bibliographie Musicale de la France et de l'Etranger* of 1822, now classified as a 'Pot-pourri', and available 'chez l'Auteur', living at 38 rue Bleue. They remained available throughout Mesplet's life, and at his death he still had twelve unsold copies.

Pierre Baillot, the famous violinist and later conductor of both the Paris Opéra and the Concert Spirituel, to whom Mesplet presented the overtures (from the author to his friend Baillot – 'de la part de l'auteur, à son ami Baillot'), worked in the Ministry of Finances from 1791 to 1795, where he may well have encountered Mesplet. He was later a colleague at the *Ecole Royale de la Musique*.

Musique et de Déclamation under its director Cherubini.[31] The post involved noting absences, punctuality and behaviour of both students and their teachers, a sometimes delicate job for which his evident human qualities would have stood him in good stead. Perhaps it was at this time that he placed his manuscript in the library of the *Ecole Royale* for safe keeping.[32]

Despite his fall from grace, Mesplet attempted to stay in contact with members of the choir. In 1830 François-Joseph Fétis, by this time a colleague at the *Ecole Royale*, wrote to Baini to compliment him on his recently published biography of Palestrina.[33] In his letter, he transmitted greetings from Mesplet, who asked also to be remembered to the singers. He added a list of requests from Mesplet for the library of the *Ecole Royale*, including scores of pieces for 16, 24, 32 and 48 parts by Antonelli, Agostini, Soriano and others, as well as copies of books by Andrea Adami (no doubt his *Osservazioni per ben regolare il coro de i Cantori della Cappella pontificia*, which had been Burney's chief source for his description of *Tenebræ*), Giuseppe Santarelli, who had also helped Burney and published *Della musica del santuario e della disciplina de' suoi cantori* in 1764, and Baini himself. Baini replied civilly to Fétis, while managing to send as little as possible (except for a copy of his own *Memorie Storico-Critiche*), but did not mention Mesplet by name – perhaps surprising given the generous tribute to him in his book, and the fact that he seems not to have known until receiving this letter that Mesplet was still alive. The request for the historical works by Adami and Santarelli, of which he must have been made aware either by a perusal of Burney,[34] or by having been introduced to them during his time in Rome, shows the extent to which Mesplet remained interested in the music of the choir, and makes one wonder if he was working towards publishing

---

[31] See M. Lassabathie, *Histoire du Conservatoire imperial de musique et de declamation* (Paris, 1860), 440, and Mesplet's own *Etat de service*. The Conservatoire had readopted its old title of *Ecole Royale* after the Restoration in 1815. Various letters, including what may be a recommendation for the post by the Marquis de Lauriston, are found in the inventory fol. 10 – Papiers, 6ème lot.

[32] He had already sent music to the *Conservatoire* (as it was then called) from Rome. On *28 pluviôse an 7* (16 February 1799] the authorities there noted his gift of Frescobaldi's *Toccate d'Intavolatura di Cimbalo et organo* (the acknowledgment is in the inventory, fol. 10 – Papiers, 4ème lot). Given that the *Conservatoire* had only been founded in 1795, and its library was not begun until 1801 (the foundation stone was laid on 4 October), this perhaps indicates to what extent Mesplet was part of that Parisian musical world before his voyage to Rome.

[33] There is a *précis* of this letter, dated 30 April, in Adrien de La Fage's posthumously published *Essais de diphthérographie musical* (Paris 1864), 518, as well as one of Baini's reply of 18 July.

[34] Burney's work had appeared in French in 1809 as *De l'Etat présent de la Musique en France et en Italie*, translated by Charles Brack and published in Genoa.

his manuscript version of the *Miserere* with a historical note, a project which would have been cut short by his death the following year.

※ The publication of 1838

The manuscript of the *Miserere* did however eventually find its way into print, published by Bobœuf et Cie, rue Cadet 23, Paris, as part of *Sainte Cécile, premier semestre 1838, collection de musique religieuse* under the title *Miserere de Gregorio Allegri. Exécuté le Mercredi et le Vendredi saints dans la Chapelle Sixtine*. *Sainte Cécile* begins with Burney's 1771 edition of the Allegri, which is reproduced exactly, except that rhythms have been inexpertly imposed on the opening chanted parts of those verses (all except 1 and 3) which Burney had left in breves. Then follows a careful copy of manuscript **P**'s *Version Originale* and finally the version with *rifiorimenti*, precise even to the extent of copying inexactitudes – for example the imprecise pitch of the *appoggiature*.[35]

There is an extensive *Avant-Propos*, which begins by placing the Allegri in context.

> This piece has an immense reputation in the Christian world. We know that, apart from its great beauty, this Miserere, as well as the other sacred pieces like it, draws much of its powerful effect from its place in the ceremonies of the Papal Chapel. We can add here another interesting fact: this *Miserere* was for a very long time communicated to nobody, and it was strongly forbidden to give it, or to take a copy of it; however, towards the end of the eighteenth century a Prince, who had been very moved when he heard it, persuaded the *Holy Father* to send him a copy of the famous *Miserere* … [36]

---

[35] The pitch of the *appoggiature* is much more carefully indicated in **Man**. The Paris print also follows the bass parts in the first bars of verses 1 and 3 of the 'flowery' versions, where they make fifths with the soprano. In **P**, these have been amended with lighter ink (difficult to see in reproduction), no doubt by a later hand.

[36] 'Ce morceau jouit d'une immense célébrité dans le monde Chrétien: On sait que, indépendamment de ses grandes beautés, ce Miserere, ainsi que les autres Cantiques de cette nature, emprunte une partie de son effet puissant à l'ensemble des cérémonies de la Chapelle Pontificale. On cite même, à cette occasion un fait assez curieuse: ce *Miserere*, pendant fort longtemps, ne fut communiqué à personne, et il était sévèrement défendu d'en donner ou d'en prendre copie; cependant, vers la fin du 18ème siècle, un Prince, qui avait entendu ce morceau avec une vive émotion, obtint du *Saint Père* qu'il lui serait expédié une copie du fameux *Miserere* …'

Probably based on the gloss of Burney in François-Joseph Fetis's recently published *Biographie universelle des Musiciens* (Paris, 1837),[37] the preface continues with the story of Leopold I transplanted a century later ('vers la fin du 18ème siècle'), no doubt to make it sound more up-to-date.[38] After listing (from Fétis) the composers whose Misereres are found in CS 205–6, together with Bai (1714), Giuseppe Tartini (1768), Pasquale Pisari (1777) and Baini (1821), the music is introduced as follows: 'We present here *Allegri's Miserere*, as it was published in London in 1771 by Burney. But we also add a kind of duplicate, a very interesting piece, about which here is a short preamble …'[39]

> At the time of the first invasion of Italy by *Bonaparte*, MM. *Mesplet, Monge, Kreutzer, Denon and others* were sent to Rome as commissioners responsible for *objets d'arts*. M Mesplet, being taken to the two little rooms containing the Pontifical Archives, ordered them to be immediately sealed. They all remained intact, and when the French left, M Mesplet returned the keys of this precious repository. The Roman Court was extremely grateful to our compatriot for his scrupulous conduct, for which he was presented with a certified testimonial. Pius VII's *Maître de Chapelle*, M Baini, gave M Mesplet a little manuscript as a present, which he subsequently presented to the Library of the Conservatoire, and which is an authentic volume of pieces sung in the *Sistine* Chapel during Holy Week.
>
> Among the pieces of hallowed music [in this manuscript] is Allegri's Miserere, *in the author's original version*. We print here this original text without barlines, in the manner of plain-chant; and in addition another piece at least as precious: the same *Miserere* written rhythmically, and with the embellishments gradually introduced and preserved by tradition. We believe that everyone will be grateful to us for having unified these different versions and made them known.[40]

---

[37] Article on Allegri, vol. 1, 72–4.

[38] See pp. 39–40.

[39] 'Nous donnons ici le *Miserere d'Allegri*, tel qu'il a été publié à Londres, en 1771, par Burney; mais nous y joindrons une sorte de Duplicata, pièce infiniment curieuse, dont voici une courte Notice …'

[40] 'Lors de la 1ère invasion d'Italie par *Bonaparte*, MM. *Mesplet, Monge, Kreutzer, Denon &c.* furent envoyés à Rome en qualité de Commissaires chargés des objets d'Arts: Mr Mesplet, s'étant fait conduire à deux petites chambres qui contenaient les Archives Pontificales, ordonna qu'on y apposât immédiatement les scellés Tout demeura intact, et au départ des Français, Mr Mesplet remit les clefs de ce précieux dépôt. La Cour de Rome sut un gré infini à notre compatriote de sa conduite scrupuleuse, dont il lui fut délivré une attestation légale. Le Maître de Chapelle de Pie VII, Mr Baini, fit don à Mr Mesplet d'un petit manuscrit, légué par lui à la Bibliothèque du Conservatoire, et qui contient un recueil authentique des morceaux chantés dans la Chapelle *Sixtine*, durant la Semaine Sainte. Parmi ces morceaux de Musique consacrée, figure

It is clear that the anonymous writer of this preface did not have all the facts at his disposal. The manuscript cannot have been presented by Baini because in 1798 he was not even a full member of the choir, let alone one with authority to give away its manuscripts; it was only from around 1817 that he began to become in any sense *maître de chapelle*. In any case, he exiled himself from Rome for the whole period of the French occupation.[41] Furthermore, Pius VII was not elected until 1800 and did not come to Rome until the following year. Finally, of the 164 pages of actual music in **P**, only thirty-nine (the *Miserere*, the *Improperia* and the Lamentations) are devoted to music for Holy Week, albeit arguably the most interesting parts. Errors like this make it likely that the author of the preface was neither a musicologist nor a historian. In fact, given his intimate knowledge of some things (the testimonial from the Vatican) and his sketchy acquaintance with others (Baini's early career in the choir, the faulty prosody of the Miserere text imposed on Burney's version), the most likely candidate is perhaps Mesplet's son, Hyppolite Louis. He had already published music in his own name,[42] and he could easily have claimed access to the manuscript in the Conservatoire library belonging to his father.[43] In 1838 he was aged thirty-two.

Whoever the publisher was, he must have been disappointed by what happened next. At the end of 1838, when all the issues of *Sainte Cécile* for the year

---

le Miserere d'Allegri, *conforme au texte original* de l'Auteur. Nous joignons ici ce texte original, écrit sans barres de mesure et comme le plain-chant; et de plus, une autre pièce non moins précieuse: c'est le même *Miserere*, mesuré, et avec les fioritures successivement introduites et conservées par la tradition. Nous pensons qu'on nous saura gré d'avoir réuni ces documents, et de les faire connaître.'

[41] He retired to Castel Sant Elena near Perugia until Rome's liberation by the Neapolitans in September 1799. See Boursy, 'Historicism and Composition', vol 1, 116–17. According to Pietro Alfieri, 'in 1798, having taken priestly orders, he left the seminary and went to Castel di S. Elena near Perugia, perhaps to escape the tumult of the capital invaded as it was by the French.' ('Nell' anno 1798, ricevuto l'ordine sacerdotale, usci dal seminario, e recossi al Castel di S. Elena nel Perugino, forse per isfuggire i rumoridella capitale invasa dai francese.') Pietro Alfieri, 'Biografia di Monsignor Giuseppe Baini', *Gazzetta Musicale di Milano*, 14 (1856), published in eight parts in every second issue from 18 May to 24 August, part 2, 177.

[42] 'Marche nocturne du troisième acte de l'opéra de *Virginie*, musique du chevalier Berton' was announced for sale in Fétis's *Revue Musicale*, 3 (1828), 288, 'arrangé pour le piano ... par Mesplet fils' and available at his father's address, 38 rue Bleue. Berton was a colleague of his father at the *Ecole Royale*.

[43] It is not clear when, or indeed whether, Mesplet gave up his ownership of the manuscript to the Conservatoire.

were collected into one volume, the *Miserere* number was entirely reset.[44] In the process, both the *Version Originale* and that *come si deve eseguire* disappeared entirely, despite reference to them still being made in the unchanged *Avant-propos*. What remained was simply Burney's 1771 version, with the rhythms incompetently imposed on the chanted parts of the verses suppressed and Burney's breves reinstated.

Given the widespread curiosity at the time, in France as much as anywhere, about the work and about the institution where it could be heard, this is extremely puzzling. Collectors from Germany and England vied with each other for manuscripts which purported to reveal the ornamentation used by the singers, the famous *abbellimenti*.[45] Burney's edition had been published in Leipzig in 1809, and it was frequently reprinted and widely pirated throughout Europe.[46] An extensive interview with Baini by G.L.P. Sievers appeared in the journal *Cäcilia* in 1825,[47] and he also wrote at length about the choir in seven weekly instalments of *Allgemeine Musikalische Zeitung* the same year.[48] Joseph Mainzer's four articles about 'La Chapelle Sixtine à Rome' had been published in the *Gazette Musicale de Paris* in 1834 (see pp. 66–7), and Fétis wrote at length about various aspects of the institution in his *Biographie universelle des Musiciens*. Yet no sooner was this fascinating version in the public domain than it was suppressed.

The source of virtually all the information in these aforementioned publications was Giuseppe Baini, who, from his position of absolute power within the College of Papal Singers, gave out information with the utmost parsimony. His almost visceral resistance to letting any hint of the inner workings of the choir leak into public gaze other than under his control can be seen in his vituperative reaction to Alfieri's projected publication of 1841, detailed in Chapter 10. Neither would he lend anything from the archives, illustrated by his refusal to permit Mainzer, in 1834, to take a copy of his own *Miserere*, or to allow access

---

[44] They are catalogued in the Bibliothèque nationale as follows: first semester Vm⁷ 112118, and annual volume Vm¹ 561(1).

[45] The term appears to have been used for the first time by Pietro Alfieri, in his *Il Salmo Miserere posto in musica da Gregorio Allegri e da Tommaso Bai, Publicato cogli Abbellimenti per la prima volta* (Lugano, 1840). See Chapter 10.

[46] The German version was published by Peters Edition under the title *Musica Sacra quæ Cantatur Quotannis per Hebdomamam Sanctam Romæ in Sacello Pontificio* (Leipzig, n.d. [1809]). Burney's *The Present State of Music in France and Italy* had been translated into German as soon as 1772 (by Christoph-Daniel Eberlin) under the title *Tagebuch einer Musikalischenreise durch Frankreich und Italien* (Hamburg), and into French in 1809 (see n. 34).

[47] 'Das Miserere von Allegri in der Sixtinischen Capelle in Rom', *Cäcilia, eine Zeitschrift für die Musikalische Welt*, N°5 (1825), 66–82. The article itself is dated July 1824.

[48] 'Die päpstliche Kapelle zu Rom', *Allgemeine Musikalische Zeitung* (1825), Nos. 19–25 (May–June).

to the collector Fortunato Santini.⁴⁹ The commentary of Adrien de La Fage, who not only was Baini's pupil but also counted himself a friend, concerning Baini's reply to Fetis's letter of 1830, is telling: 'Baini, while declaring that fine things are by their nature created in order to be made known, forgets the extent to which he participated in preventing their dissemination.'⁵⁰

The widespread distribution of Burney's publication seems to have pained him considerably, as would the circulation of numerous manuscripts in the 1820s had he known about them. The Paris publication would have come as a particularly unpleasant surprise given that it is unlikely that he had more than the vaguest idea of what music Mesplet had taken away with him in 1798.⁵¹ In Paris, however, Baini had powerful friends, and all of them – the restricted circle of musicologists and historians interested in the choir and the *Miserere* – were beholden to him for the information he fed them. All were honoured to call him a friend. It would thus have been a simple matter, and entirely in character, for him to pull the necessary strings to ensure that Allegri's Miserere *come si deve eseguire* disappeared from public view. If the editor was indeed Mesplet *fils*, he would have been powerless to prevent it.

※ Origins and sources of the manuscripts

It is clear from the story told here that both of these manuscripts – the one brought back to Paris and the one now in Manchester – were created by papal singers who were grateful for Citizen Mesplet's generosity in difficult times, and inspired by his enthusiasm for the traditions of the choir. This is clearly expressed both in the title page of the *Miserere* in **Man** and in the attestation they drew up for him, not to mention Baini's record of the esteem in which he was clearly held. These are extraordinarily expansive tributes, especially to the representative of a hostile foreign power, which show that Ingres' testimony of the singers 'with tears of gratitude in their eyes' was no exaggeration. It is of a piece with the 'love of Justice', 'gratitude' and 'duty' which underlies the singers' generous testimonial to the 'praiseworthy' and 'well-respected' Signor

---

⁴⁹ The tenseness of their relationship is shown in Kantner and Pachovsky, *L'Ottocento*, 34–5.

⁵⁰ 'Baini, en disant que le beau est par sa nature fait pour être répandu, oublie qu'il contribuait pour sa part à empêcher cette diffusion.' See p. 94 and n. 33.

⁵¹ No doubt the singers, aware of his sensitivities, took care not tell him about the manuscripts they had prepared for Mesplet. Baini seems to be merely repeating what he had been told when he writes: 'As regards our chapel, Mesplet demanded first of all copies of different compositions, which were given to him' (see p. 86). There is no evidence that he was given anything other than the two manuscripts described here.

Mesplet.⁵² No doubt in normal times even this would not have been sufficient incentive for the singers to give such a manuscript to an outsider, but in 1798 the choir had been disbanded, Rome was occupied by a powerful enemy, and this outsider was not only protecting their archival heritage, but saving some of them from starvation.

Although these circumstances alone would be enough to underline the authenticity of the provenance of these manuscripts in the Papal Chapel, their contents add further confirmation. Apart from the performing versions of the *Miserere* and the *Improperia* – clearly the finest gift the singers could think of – there is much by Palestrina, the composer at the very centre of the choir's repertoire. **Man** has two motets (*Veni sponsa Christi* and *Salvatorem expectamus*, the latter misattributed to Allegri), three *Benedictus*, a canonic *Sicut erat* and three Lamentations (although only one is in fact by him), to which **P** adds two masses. These are in the composer's sunniest vein, the second being one of the few (7 of 104) which is based on a secular madrigal; its two equal upper parts give it quite a modern feel.

Papal Choir habits may explain the presence in both manuscripts of no less than six *Benedictus qui venit*, three by Palestrina, one by Victoria and two by Fazzini. The *Benedictus* of the mass was usually written for a reduced number of voices, and therefore normally reserved for soloists.⁵³ It was thus a moment for them to regularly show their vocal skills and musicality. By the end of the eighteenth century, it seems to have been common practice during sung mass to insert a *Benedictus* from a different setting as an Elevation motet. CS 279 (1777) contains no fewer than sixteen of them assembled for precisely this purpose: 'Quos in Missae elevatione inoleverant cantus' ('which were sung during mass incorporated at the Elevation'), including the two by Fazzini in **Man** and **P**. Some *Benedictus* may even have become 'star vehicles' for the soloists of the Chapel, which may explain why it was a *Benedictus* (from Palestrina's *Missa Assumpta est Maria*) that the papal quartet sang in Mesplet's concert in the

---

⁵² It is curious that the fulsome dedication to Mesplet is not in the manuscript (**P**) which was actually presented to him. Perhaps the score of the *Miserere* in **Man** was originally intended to be for him, but was put to one side when a later decision was made to present him with all the other works as well, and the dedication was forgotten in the haste to finish it if, for example, his transfer out of Rome came at short notice.

⁵³ Noel O'Regan has shown that from at least the beginning of the seventeenth century it was the normal practice in the choir during the office of the mass to sing the *Benedictus*, as well as other movements for smaller forces, with solo voices ('The Performance of Palestrina: Some Further Observations', *Early Music*, 24/1 (February 1996), 145–54). This article affirms much of the pioneering work of Jean Lionnet, especially 'Performance Practice in the Papal Chapel during the 17th Century', *Early Music*, 15/1 (February 1987), 4–15.

Vatican, on the face of it an unusual choice. Sure enough, it is present in the manuscripts.[54]

Many of the other works in **Man** and **P** have clearly been chosen as examples of compositional artifice. They can all be found in Padre G.-B. Martini's famous *Esemplare, o sia Saggio fondamentale pratico di contrappunto*.[55] Perhaps Mesplet expressed an interest in such works, or maybe one of the singers brought them to his attention. Four come from volume 1 of that work, which treats 'contrappunto sopra il Canto Fermo'. Two are exactly that, Zarlino's *Veni creator spiritus* (originally published in his *Institutioni harmoniche*) and Porta's antiphon *Angelus autem Domini*. Palestrina's *Veni sponsa Christi* is given there as an example of the use of Tone VII, and the extract (*Sicut erat in principio*) from the same composer's *Magnificat* on Tone IV is a triple canon, with imitations at the octave and the fifth. The most complex work is Giuseppe Antonio Bernabei's *Ave Regina Cælorum* a7, which consists of three canons with a seventh part *ad libitum*. It appeared in volume 2 of the *Esemplare*, concerned with 'Contrappunto Fugato'.

It seems highly likely that Martini's work was the source used by the compilers of **Man** and **P**. It may even have been a source for Papal Choir repertoire: two of the *Benedictus* in these manuscripts are not in fact *Benedictus* at all, but adapted from works printed by Martini. That on page 61 of **P**, with its canon at the fifth between the two tenor parts, was originally the *Gloria patri* of Victoria's first setting of the *Magnificat* in Tone VIII; that on page 81 was originally the *Deposuit* of a Palestrina *Magnificat* in Tone II. Both these works are printed in their original form in volume 1 of the *Esemplare*. These adaptations may also illustrate the strong demand for suitable *Benedictus* settings, although, given that there are no copies of the adaptations in the Chapel archive, we cannot be certain that they were sung there.

It is the three Lamentations ascribed to Palestrina which show most clearly the intimate relationship of these manuscripts with the Papal Choir. They consist of settings of the first lesson only for each of the three days of *Tenebræ*, but only that for Friday is in fact by him; those of Thursday and Saturday are by Allegri. Palestrina's setting was, according to Baini, composed in 1587 specifically for the Chapel and reserved for its exclusive use; it did not appear in any of his published collections of Lamentations. It could thus only have been sourced from the choir's own archive.[56] Until 1815 these three were the only

---

[54] In fact, puzzlingly, it is copied out twice in **P**, as is the *Benedictus* from the *Missa Brevis* which follows it, although this is not the case in **Man**. The differences between the readings, although slight, are sufficient to suggest that they were taken from different sources, particularly that from the *Missa Brevis*.

[55] Published in Bologna in two volumes, the first in 1774 and the second in 1776.

[56] Its earliest printing was as an appendix to volume 4 of Pietro Alfieri's *Raccolta di Musica Sacra* (Rome, 1843), with the description 'quam in usum Cappellae Apostolicae an 1587 composuit Praenestinus'. Another, probably earlier, version,

Lamentations heard in the Chapel because, as Baini explains, only *Lectio I* was sung in polyphony.⁵⁷

Two other works are worthy of note: the motet *Salvatorem expectamus* a6 which is ascribed to Allegri, and Filippo Ciciliani's grandiose *Veni creator spiritus* a7, which is in **P** only. Between the latter's title page and the work itself has been inserted an anonymous *Canon a Tre retrogrado* to the text 'Se difensore tu sei per noi ancor la Musica ravviverà' (If you are a defender for us, Music will live again'). Its placement suggests strongly that Ciciliani composed it. The choice of text, its meaning neatly illustrated by the retrograde canon, can hardly be without significance. It may not be fanciful either to assume that the text of *Salvatorem expectamus* is equally meaningful: 'We await the Saviour, our Lord Jesus Christ, who will transform our lowly body to be like his glorious body.'⁵⁸

Table 2 gives an index of **P**, as well as concordances both with **Man** and with the main Vatican sources.

Although the music in **P** appears to have been written over a short period with the same ink, it is clearly in two different hands, which are identified in the table below as Scribe A and Scribe B.⁵⁹ Most works also have a separate title page (not systematically noted in the table below) which appears to be in the

---

with a different opening phrase ('Incipit Lamentatio …') and longer versions of the Hebrew letters and of 'Jerusalem, convertere' at the end, is found in autograph in S. Giovanni Laterano, MS 59 (Rome) (see Haberl, *Pierluigi da Palestrina Werke*, vol. 31, 125–31). Laterano 59 is available in reproduction in Giancarlo Rostirolla and Luciano Luciani (eds.), *Il codice 59, autografo di Giovanni Pierluigi da Palestrina*, Palestrina, 1996.

⁵⁷ Baini's account of the creation of Palestrina's Lamentations is in *Memorie*, vol. 2, 190ff., and the adoption of the two by Allegri in 1651 in vol. 2, 200–1. Curiously, the titles of Friday's and Saturday's are exchanged in both **Man** and **P**; the titles are thus in the right order, but not the music. This is a strange mistake for papal singers to make, but perhaps understandable in a hurried collation of different sources given that both commence with the text 'De lamentatione', and in both 'Jerusalem, convertere' is set for five voices.

⁵⁸ Allegri wrote a mass based on this motet, but the motet itself is certainly by Palestrina. It was not printed, and the earliest attribution is found on fols. 83ᵛ–90 of a lavish manuscript formerly in the Vatican dated 1727, now in the library of the Catholic University of Washington, where it is catalogued as MS 202; see C.A. Dower, 'Cappella Sistina Codexes in the Catholic University of America Library', *Notes*, 36/3 (1980), 615–23. The motet also appears, unattributed, in the large composite choirbook CS 72, in the script of Lucas Orpheo Fanensis. The earliest manuscript by him in the choir archive can be dated to 1582 and there are none after 1599, which is far too early for Allegri. No doubt the compiler(s) of Mesplet's manuscript was (or were) confused because of the mass based upon it.

⁵⁹ I would like to thank François-Pierre Goy of the Music Department of the Bibliothèque National for his discussions with me on this subject.

Table 2 Index and concordances of the Paris manuscript of 1798

Page	Work	Manchester (**Man**)	Concordances and Notes
1	*Messa a cinque voci Di Pier Luigi da Palestrina* Chirie–Christe–Chirie, Gloria, Sanctus and Hosanna, Agnus Dei I (missing Credo, Benedictus et Hosanna, Agnus Dei II) Scribe A	Absent	= *Missa dilexi quoniam* (*Missarum Libro VI*, 1594); the copies in CS 132 (1753) and 286 (1791) are missing the same movements.
25	*Messa a cinque voci Di Pier Luigi da Palestrina* Kyrie–Kyrie, Gloria, Sanctus and Hosanna, Agnus Dei I (missing Christe, Credo, Benedictus and Hosanna, Agnus Dei II) Scribe A	Absent	= *Missa Quale il più grande Amor* (*Missarum Libro XII*, 1601).
45	*Miserere mei Deus Di Gregorio Allegri Romano con suoi Rifiorimenti, come si deve eseguire Li quali d'imparano per tradizione* Scribe B **i** *Primo coro, come L'Originale* **ii** *Secondo coro detto concertino, come L'Originale* **iii** *Primo coro, come si deve eseguire suoi rifiorimenti, che s'imparano per tradizione* **iv** *Concertino Secondo Coro* (with alternative ending) **v** Last half-verse *Tunc imponent* a 9	fols. 70ʳ–75ᵛ	Title page of **Man** adds 'Per divertimento del Cittadino Mesplet, amatore et conoscitore della vera Musica' Fair copy in **Man** **i** = CS 185 and 341, with detail differences **ii** = CS 206 and 340, with detail differences **iv** Alternative ending not in **Man** **v** Unique reading, closest to Burney's
59	*Benedictus qui venit posta in Musica di diversi autori*		Title page, missing in **Man**.
61	[Benedictus] *Di Tommaso Lodovico da Vittoria* a6 Scribe A	fols. 46ʳ–49ᵛ	Adapted from *Gloria patri* of *Magnificat* Tone VIII (odd verses). CS copy of 1576 print (CS 212) shows extreme signs of use. Also in Martini, *Esemplare*, vol. 1, 190–95.
66	[Benedictus] *Di Gio: Battista Fazzini* a6 Scribe A	fols. 62ʳ–65ᵛ	= CS 279 (1777). Title page in **Man**: *del Fù D. Gio. Battᵃ Fazzini, Cantore della Cappella*.
71	[Benedictus] *Di Gio: Battᵃ Fazzini* a5 Scribe A	fols. 66ʳ–69ᵛ	= CS 279 (1777).

Page	Work	Manchester (*Man*)	Concordances and Notes
73	[Benedictus] *Di Pier Luigi da Palestrina* a4 Scribe A	fols. 17ʳ–19ʳ	from From *Missa Assumpta est Maria* (1585–6), unpublished, CS 76, 137, 127, etc.
76	[Benedictus] *Di Pier Luigi da Palestrina* a4 Scribe A		Another copy of that on p. 73; one minor variant.
79	[Benedictus] *Di Pier Luigi da Palestrina* a3 [c₁ c₃ c₄] Scribe A		From *Missa Brevis* (*Missarum Libro III*, 1570), CS 280 (1724), CS 247 (1749).
81	[Benedictus] *Di Pier Luigi da Palestrina* a3 Scribe A	fols. 13ʳ–14ʳ	Adapted from verse 7 (*Deposuit*) of *Magnificat II* in Martini, *Esemplare*, vol. 1, xxx–xxxi.
83	[Benedictus] *Di Pier Luigi da Palestrina* a3 [g₂ c₃ c₄] Scribe A	fols. 15ʳ–16ᵛ	Another copy of that on p. 79; one different clef, one minor variant, extra slurs (as in **Man**).
89	*Veni creator spiritus A sette voci Di Filippo Ciciliani* Between the title page (p. 89) and the work itself (p. 93) is a *Canon a Tre Retrogrado* to the text *Se difensore tu sei per noi ancor la Musica ravviverà* Scribe A	Absent	= CS 331 (copied in 1790).
115	*Veni creator spiritus a tre Di Giuseppe Zarlino* Scribe B	fols. 60ʳ–61ᵛ	*Versetto a 3 Voci sopra l'Inno di Pentecoste* in **Man**. In Martini, *Esemplare*, vol. 1, xxix–xxx.
119	*Veni sponsa Christi Motetto a quattro Di Pier Luigi da Palestrina* Scribe B	fols. 1ʳ–5ʳ	= *Motecta festorum …* (1563, 1570 and 1591); CS 100 (1659), 302 (1742), in Martini, *Esemplare*, vol. 1, 144–8.
129	*Sicut erat in principio a sette con artificio di Canone Di Pier Luigi da Palestrina* Scribe B	fols. 6ʳ–12ʳ	= last verse of *Magnificat IV Tono*, in Haberl, Vol XXVII *Magnificat Octotonum* (Bk. 3, pp. 188–91), in Martini, *Esemplare*, vol. 1, 80–7.

Page	Work	Manchester (*Man*)	Concordances and Notes
139	*Salvatorem expectamus Motetto di Gregorio Allegri a6* Scribe A	fols. 76ʳ–81ᵛ	Part 1 only. By Palestrina. Anon. in CS 72, (prob. end 16ᵗʰ cent.) Attrib. to him in Washington Catholic University MS 202 (83ᵛ–90), formerly in CS (1727).
147	*Ave Regina celorum ~~Di Giovanni Animuccia~~ Di Giuseppe Antonio Bernabei Canone* [a7] Scribe A	fols. 50ʳ–57ʳ	Attrib. Animuccia in **Man**. In Martini, *Esemplare*, vol. 2, 251–64 (correctly attributed)
159	*Angelus autem Domini Antifona Di P: Costanzo Porta a4* Scribe B	f.58ʳ- fols. 58ᵉ–59ᵛ	In Martini, *Esemplare*, vol. 1, 164–5.
165	*Lamentazioni a quattro Per la Settimana Santa Di Pier Luigi da Palestrina* Scribe B		Title page, not in **Man**, although all 3 lessons are attributed to him there.
167	*Lamentazioni Prima per il Giovedi Lectio I* Scribe B	fols. 20ʳ–25ʳ	By Allegri (1651), fair copy in CS 342 (1733) with additions by Giovanni Biordi.
178	*Lamentations for Holy Saturday, entitled by mistake Venerdi santo Lectio I* Scribe B	fols. 26ʳ–31ʳ	By Allegri (1651), fair copy in CS 342 (1733) with additions by Giovanni Biordi.
181	*Lamentations for Good Friday, entitled by mistake Sabato santo Lectio I* Scribe B	fols. 32ʳ–39ʳ	By Palestrina, composed for the Chapel in 1587. Fair copy in CS 342 (1733) with additions by Giovanni Biordi.
193	*Improperii Di Pier Luigi da Palestrina* (Title page) Scribe B	fol. 40ʳ	*Improperii Del Celebre Pier Luigi da Palestrina* in **Man**, which gives a fair copy.
195	*Come à l'Originale* Scribe B	fols. 40ʳ–41ᵛ	
198	*Come si deve eseguire* Scribe B	fols. 42ʳ–45ᵛ	

hand of Scribe A. Among the papal singers at this period, two stand out as possible copyists: Don Nicola Binder and Filippo Ciciliani. As *segretario-puntatore* of the Papal Choir in 1807 Binder kept that year's *Diario Sistina*, which allows us to see his writing hand in the attestation for Mesplet (Fig. 14). Furthermore, his musical hand is visible in a manuscript in Rome, and it shows certain similarities to that of Scribe A.[60] Binder was received into the choir in 1785, at the age of twenty-seven. Despite being accepted by thirty-three votes to eight, he seems not to have immediately impressed the *maestro*,

> who told him in front of the whole College that he must study, since he was in need of it, and if he did not do it on his own, the College would oblige him to do so by assigning him a teacher, and making him pay for it out of his own salary.[61]

Whatever the problem was, it appears to have been quickly rectified. Perhaps his learning did not yet match his vocal skills, the quality of which are attested by his participation as soloist in Mesplet's grand concert, despite being one of the more junior members, and not yet even a *partecipante*. It follows that during his exceptionally long career, he must often have sung the *Miserere*.[62] He died in 1840, aged eighty-three. The fact that on the day following his death another tenor (Domenico Cesare Caramici) was made *partecipante* indicates that he retained an active role until the very end. He may also have been the donor of a later manuscript of the *Miserere* now in Milan, showing the *Rifiorimenti Che si usano nella Cappella Pontificia* (see below), although it does not appear to be in his hand.

Filippo Ciciliani (1757–1815), composer of the *Veni creator spiritus* a7 added to **P**, is an even stronger candidate for identification as Scribe A. A '*soprano evirato*', Ciciliani was born in Fabrica di Roma, around forty miles north of the city, and was accepted into the choir in 1778 by an almost unanimous vote

---

[60] The manuscript is a copy of *Laudate pueri A 4° con[cer]to Del Sigr Giovanni Masi*, in the library of the *Conservatorio della Santa Cecilia* (Rome) under the call mark G.Ms.44.

[61] 'il sig. Maestro] disse al sud.° tenore presente a tutto il Coll.°, che dovesse studiare, mentre ne aveva di bisogno e che se non l'avesse fatto da sé il Coll.° gli è lo avrebbe fatto fare per forza, con assegnarli un Maestro, e poi pagarlo con le sue provenienze' (*DS* 208 (1785), fol. 48^r–48^v). A candidate needed two-thirds of the votes plus one to be automatically accepted.

[62] He finally attained the rank and salary of *partecipante* in 1803. In 1810 he became a *giubilato*, and from 1832 was *decano* not just of the tenors, but of the whole choir (*DS* 248 (1832), fol. 7^v). In past centuries the *decano* had been responsible for training young singers in plainchant, and although this part of his function had largely died out by the nineteenth century, the honorary aspect of it, similar to 'Father of the House' in the British House of Commons, remained.

(thirty-eight for and only one against). He made his mark as a composer with an eight-part mass in 1788 and, according to Baini, his *Veni creator spiritus* (1790) made a great impression on Pope Pius VI.[63] A copy of his oratorio *Ruth*, now in Rome, is said to be autograph, and the hand of Scribe A has much in common with it.[64] It is also likely that it was he who added his own *Veni creator* to **P**, together with the canon *Se difensore* which precedes it. In that case he is almost definitely Scribe A in **P** as well as of the whole of **Man**.[65] It may be that he was the prime mover in the whole enterprise, responsible among other things for the selection of works from Padre Martini's *Esemplare*, which, as a composer, he may have acquired in order to perfect the fugal techniques subsequently displayed in his *Veni creator*.[66] The strong bonds of affection and respect between him and Mesplet are clear. It is also evident that he was supported by most of his colleagues, as is shown by the attestation that Binder drew up on their behalf. Scribe B of **P** must be another colleague, drawn into the project under time pressure. For the moment it has not been possible to identify him, except to note that he had a neat and practised, if not necessarily professional, hand, with a curious way of writing ties. There are some aspects of this hand in the manuscript in Milan (see below) but not enough to identify him as the same person.

A final question presents itself. Does the use of the phrase 'for the entertainment of Citizen Mesplet' imply that the fair copies of the *Miserere* and

---

[63] *Memorie*, vol. 2, 19. For much of the information presented here about Ciciliani and Binder I am indebted to Professor Federico Pirani, who has generously shared with me his research on papal singers prepared for volume 5 (*Le Settecento*) of *Storia della Cappella Musicale Pontificia*, which awaits publication. Ciciliani's writing hand can be seen in *DS* 224 of 1803, when he was *puntatore*.

[64] It is in the *Archivio della Congregazione dell'Oratorio di S. Filippo Neri* (Rome) (MS F.III.4), and was doubtless composed for the *Congregazione*. What appears to be the same hand, of the title pages at least, is found in the British Library, MS R.M.23.f.20, which contains, among other things, unadorned versions of both the Allegri and the Bai. By a curious coincidence, it belonged at one point to the pianist and conductor Sir William George Cusins (1833–93), later Master of the Queen's Musick. In his youth, Cusins studied in Brussels with François-Joseph Fétis, sometime colleague of Louis Mesplet at the *Ecole Royale de la Musique* in Paris. It is not impossible that Ciciliani maintained contact with Mesplet and sent him manuscripts, one of which may have been presented to Fétis, and thence to Cusins.

[65] One wonders if it was Ciciliani who was appointed by the *maestro* to instruct Binder after his audition – as a composer, he would have been ideal for the job – and that this perhaps accounts for the many similarities between their hands. Much of **Man** is very roughly written, which makes identification difficult, but there are similarities with hastily written parts of *Ruth*.

[66] The scribe of **P** took the trouble of drawing attention to the *cantus firmus* in verse 3 by copying it out in square notation, as if with a pedagogical purpose.

the *Improperia* were made for a special private performance for the singers' benefactor? Mesplet must have been disappointed that the suspension of the choir's activities meant that he could not hear the Holy Week music sung in the Sistine Chapel. In what better way could they have shown their gratitude for his support than by singing these cornerstones of their repertoire for him in a special, one-off, performance? If so, preparations cannot have been a simple matter. In fact, these manuscripts may represent the first attempt to put into full score the singers' elaborate interpretations. The implications of the problems they must have faced will be discussed further below, particularly in Chapters 7 and 10.

※ A related manuscript in Milan

Another interesting manuscript, evidently closely related to **P** and **Man**, is now in the Biblioteca del Conservatorio G. Verdi in Milan, catalogued as MUSA MS 2-2 (hereinafter **Mil**). Its title is *Rifiorimenti / Che si usano nella Cappella Pontificia / Al Miserere / Di Gregorio Allegri,* and another hand has marked 'Ricevuto dall' Abb.ᵉ Niccola'. Like **Man** and **P**, it gives verses 1 and 3 and the second half of 20, but without the 'plain' versions. A transcription is provided in Appendix 7. Close inspection shows it to be almost certainly in a different hand from the earlier manuscripts, although it has some features in common with Scribe B of Source **P**.

It is unknown to whom the manuscript may have originally been given, and the library knows nothing of its provenance. The version of the ornaments it gives has so much in common with **Man** and **P** that it clearly comes from the same tradition. All three manuscripts give very precisely the word rhythms of the chanted sections in more or less identical form, complete with the parallel *portamenti* found there, as well as numerous *appoggiature*. The ornamentation is similar to, if often smoother than, the earlier sources. Occasionally chords are held longer; for example, the length of the penultimate bass notes of the first section is doubled in both verses 1 and 3. It may of course be that at these places there was flexibility for the soloists to decide the speed of the ornaments, and the extra length merely makes metrical an implied pause. The similarities are so pronounced that its origin must also be a papal singer. In that case, the phrase 'Abbate Niccola' suggests one in particular: Don Nicola Binder. He is the only 'Niccola' among Chapel singers of this period who was an *Abbate*, i.e. ordained.[67]

Two significant details suggest that **Mil** represents an evolution from **Man** and **P**. The first is the presence of the melodic phrase a′c″e♭″g′ in the highest

---

[67] The complete list of nineteenth-century singers is in Kantner and Pachovsky, *L'Ottocento,* chapter 5.

part at bar 20 of verse 3, also found in the series of manuscripts dating from the mid-1820s (labelled Source **A** and discussed in Chapter 9). The second is the substitution of the indications *a piacere* (at the chanted sections of each verse) and *a misura* (at the subsequent 'composed' parts) with *for* and *dol*. In **A** these become systematically *f* and *p*. Their probable meaning in this context will be discussed more fully in Chapters 7 and 16. It may well be that **Mil** dates from after 1815, when new singers, particularly Mariano Padroni, started to have more influence on the execution of the *Miserere*. Unfortunately we can have no guidance on this question from the extent of Binder's career in the choir, owing to its extreme length.

7

'Con suoi rifiorimente, come si deve eseguire' – What the earliest ornamented manuscripts show

As in all *falsobordone* psalms, a large part of the choir's interpretative work lay in the chanted sections, the rhythms of which are precisely given in all three of these manuscripts. The only other source to give such a level of detail is Domenico Mustafà's retrospective manuscript of the *Miserere di Bai ed Allegri* of 1892 (CS 375) described in Chapter 12. That there is so much in common between them all is a measure of how slowly styles evolved in the Chapel. It has been noted above (Chapter 3) how important the 'proportion of long and short syllables' had been to the singers since at least 1600, but what is found in these manuscripts is much more complex – true choral recitative.

Given the level of ornamentation in nearly all the parts of both choirs, it is clear that this was music for soloists. In the 'composed' sections embellishments are added frequently, as well as liberal indications of *appoggiature*, particularly in the upper parts. Only the lowest voices in each choir have no ornaments at all apart from in the chanted text. With the exception of the famous descending phrase in verse 3 and both versions of the phrase for duetting sopranos at the end of it, the decorations are composed largely of simple turns, *gruppetti, appoggiature* and other graces, many of them consistent with those found in seventeenth-century sources such as Rognoni and Bovicelli.[1] This not only accords with Mendelssohn's description of the choir's performances when he visited in 1831 – 'little ornaments and trills such as were popular at the beginning of the last century'[2] – but is not incompatible with Zenobi's instructions of 1600 (see p. 38) for singing 'plainly', using 'grace, *trillo, tremolo, ondeggiamento,* and *esclamatione*'. The actual ornaments may have evolved (and some are difficult to express on paper), but the spirit of 'rendering the notes with a certain neglect, sometimes so as to drag them, sometimes with sprightly motion' is clearly shown. Most noticeably, the famous phrase with

---

[1] See Chapter 3. Was the second version in **P** discovered at the last minute in someone's memory, or perhaps even invented during the preparation of a performance for Mesplet? As it was still in use in 1840 when it was printed virtually unchanged by Alfieri, one may suppose that in 1798 it was a recent development. **Mil** gives this later version as well, albeit with even quavers rather than dotted ones.

[2] *Letters*, 95–6, referring particularly to the music of Palestrina. See also pp. 232–3 and Ex. 10.

which the *Miserere* is now associated, which rises to the highest note in the soprano soloist's part before gradually descending, is present in a form virtually identical to that in which it would be heard throughout the nineteenth century, as in Blainville's version of 1767. It too was prescribed accurately for Zenobi's ideal singer: 'He must know how to ascend with the voice and how to descend with grace, at times holding over part of the preceding note and sounding it anew if the consonance requires and admits it'.

Mendelssohn also wrote of the frequent use of *appoggiature*, which seems to have been part of the singing technique of the *castrato*.

> I was struck with the meaning they attach to the word *Appoggiatura*. If the melody goes from C to D or from C to E they sing thus:

Ex. 1 'And this they call an *appoggiatura*.' (Mendelssohn, *Letters*, 95–6)

> And this they call an *appoggiatura*. Whatever they may choose to call it, the effect is most disagreeable, and it must require long habit not to be discomposed by this strange practice which reminds me very much of our old women at home in church: moreover the effect is the same.[3]

Rather than as an *appoggiatura* – an ornament with an harmonic and/or melodic function – we would nowadays describe this ornament as an *acciaccatura*, a notated vocal gesture used for reasons both technical (managing the transition between the chest and head registers, which happened around c″ in *castrato* voices) and expressive (an emotional exaggeration).[4] The phenomenon can be clearly heard in recordings made in 1902 and 1904 by 'the last *castrato*' Alessandro Moreschi and also, if less frequently, in those of other singers of that period.

---

[3] *Letters*, 143–4.

[4] It is however included under the heading *appoggiature* in Gilbert Duprez's Italian-influenced *L'Art du Chant* (Paris, 1845), described as a 'crushed note' ('note brisée'). 'One must move very quickly to the following note, which thereby becomes much more accented' ('on doit passer avec une extrême rapidité à celle qui la suit; celle-ci dès lors en devient beaucoup plus accentuée'). It is also very similar to that described by Domenico Corri in *The Singer's Preceptor* (London, 1810), lesson VIII, as 'the leaping grace'. For a detailed discussion of this and similar 'graces', see Chapter 16 (in the discussion of *portamento*). For discussion of the vocal registers in *castrato* voices, see the testimony of Domenico Mancini's singing lessons with Moreschi (pp. 249–50).

Many of the more musical commentators noted the frequent use of parallel fifths and octaves introduced on the reciting chords, among them Otto Nicolai and Ludwig Spohr. The latter was particularly outraged in 1817.

> Five solo voices intone the C minor triad in a beautiful five-part chording, tender and pure, like a harmony from another world. Never has a simple chord made such a powerful impression on me. But then all too soon one was reminded that one was hearing an earthly music, indeed sung by Italians: for already in the second bar the ear was tortured by a horrid succession of fifths. The theme was doubtless after this manner

Ex. 2 'An earthly music, indeed sung by Italians' (*Louis Spohr's Biography*, vol. 2, 36)

But was given by the singers in the following barbarous manner

I wouldn't have believed anybody, not even my own ears, that it could be possible to sing like that in the Sistine Chapel had I not myself heard that very section of the piece repeated four more times. Is this perhaps the mysterious manner of performing these old compositions, of which it is said that it has been passed on by tradition from one singer to another and is only known to this choir? Surely not! Only the newer (breed of) Italian singers can sing like that, as they clearly have a feeling for melody, but no idea about harmony.[5]

---

[5] *The Musical Journeys of Louis Spohr*, trans. and ed. H. Pleasants (Norman, OK, 1961), 190; quoted in Boursy, 'The Mystique', 306. This is a translation

Clearly it did not occur to Spohr that *all* the notes not part of the C minor chord were additions! This effect is systematically noted in all three manuscripts, albeit with just one grace note rather than two, and exactly the same indications are found in Mustafà's manuscript (CS 375) of 1892.

It was an effect not reserved just for the *Miserere* but a Papal Choir speciality. Mendelssohn heard it used in Palestrina's *Improperia* during the Adoration of the Cross on Good Friday (Ex. 3), a fact that should not surprise us, given that it is clearly marked in the version *come si déve eseguire* of this work in **P**.

Ex. 3 Palestrina's *Improperia* transcribed by Mendelssohn in 1831

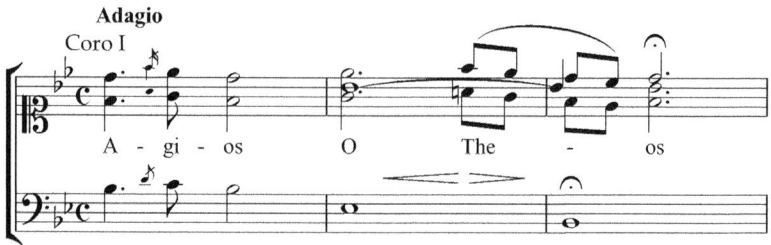

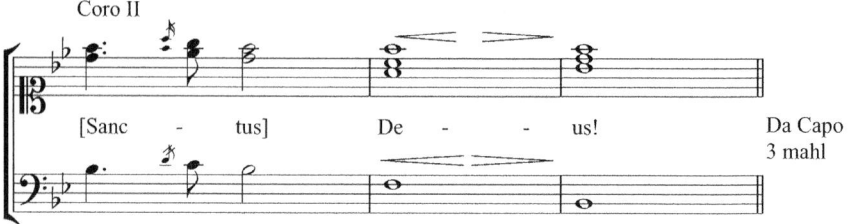

'Such passages as that at the commencement, where all the voices sing the same embellishment, repeatedly occur, and the ear becomes accustomed to them.'[6]

When Fanny Hensel, Mendelssohn's sister, visited Rome in 1840, she had been forewarned by her brother: 'Pay attention to the horrendous fifths the Papal singers make when all 4 voices are ornamented with coloratura at the same time.' She was not disappointed.

---

from Spohr's article in *Allgemeine Musikalische Zeitung* (1817, 676), which is reproduced in Amann, *Allegris Miserere*, 47–8. The story reappears in different words in Spohr's *Selbst-biographie*, translated anonymously as *Louis Spohr's Biography* (London, 1878), vol. 2, 36, which also gives the musical examples and their explanation interpolated here.

[6] *Letters*, 148. For the Papal Choir the *Improperia* seems to have held a place as important as the *Miserere* in its repertoire of Lenten music: it appears twice in CS 205–6 among the early Misereres, in CS 340–1 (which served as the Sistine reference copy of Holy Week music from 1748) and in Burney's *La musica*.

I already received a clear impression of Papal fifths at Christmas. This is the perpetual refrain:

Ex. 4 'A clear impression of Papal fifths'

And if those aren't fifths, then I don't know what fifths are.[7]

Otto Nicolai too disliked the parallel chords and, particularly, the ornament which went with it:

It will be easy for you to understand that if different voices add passing notes to the harmony, each according to his caprice, the result must often be repulsive. The following figure was often particularly annoying to me

Ex. 5 'Nil sub sole perfectum!'

which is abundantly used and is also still a significant ornament used by the latest Italian singers. At first I found the heartrending octaves and fifths, which they sing with all their might, for example

A - men.

quite unbearable. So there is still something left to be desired. However, *Nil sub sole perfectum* [nothing is perfect under the sun]![8]

---

[7] Felix's letter of 4 January 1840, followed by Fanny's comment, in Hensel, *The Mendelssohn Family*, letter 116, n. 9, 286–8.
[8] 'Es wird Ihnen leicht erklärlich sein, daß, wenn bei verschiedenen Stimmen jeder nach seiner Willkür durchgehende Noten anbringt, die Harmonie oft

All these manuscripts have interesting remarks about tempo. The scribe of **Mil** thought that the following indication was sufficiently important to put it on the front cover: 'Avvertimento: Nell'eseguire questo Miserere non si usi il tempo in precisione' ('Warning: in the interpretation of this Miserere do not use a strict tempo'). **Man** and **P** are slightly more nuanced, carefully marking *a piacere* ('with freedom') at each reciting moment, despite the carefully marked rhythms. It is clear that the correct prosody is necessary but not sufficient: it must then be sufficiently flexible to echo the meaning of the words. At the 'composed' sections, the instruction is *a misura*, which we can take to mean 'with a regular *tactus*'. The same markings are found in Mustafà's manuscript of almost a century later. Santarelli was no doubt describing their effect when in 1770 he described to Burney how the singers were 'swelling and diminishing the sounds altogether; accelerating or retarding the measure at some particular words, and singing some entire verses quicker than others'.[9]

Mil is as precise rhythmically as **P** and **Man**, although the rhythms given are generally a bit more relaxed, but it does not have *a piacere* or *a misura*. Instead, as noted in Chapter 6, dynamics are marked. The reciting chords at the beginning of the second half of each verse (1 and 3) are marked *for[te]*, which gives way to *dol[ce]* at the 'composed' sections. One wonders if these indications are not in some way equivalent to *a piacere* and *a misura*: *forte* standing for dramatic, following the meaning of the text (i.e. *a piacere*), and *dolce* meaning 'gently', following the written notes, i.e. *a misura*. This may seem fanciful, but given that exactly the same indications are found in the manuscripts of the 1820s, where they are present in every verse irrespective of the sense of the words, it seems unlikely that they mean merely 'loud' and 'soft'. This reasoning will be expanded in Chapter 16.

Finally, questions need to be asked about the sources of these ornamented versions of the Allegri. If it was indeed the singers – Ciciliani, perhaps Binder, and no doubt others – who organised them, where did they get their information? With the notable exception of Mustafà's much later manuscript, there are no sources with *abbellimenti* in the Vatican. Not much has disappeared

---

widerwärtig werden muß. Besonders lästig ist mir oft die Figur [...] gewesen, die im Überfluß angewandt wird und auch noch eine Hauptverzierung des neuesten italienischen Gesanges ausmacht. Die herzzerreißenden Oktaven und Quinten, wenn sie so recht nach Leibeskräften, z. B. intonieren, [...] waren mir in der ersten Zeit ganz unerträglich! – So ist denn auch einiges zu wünschen: indes *Nil sub sole perfectum!*' Otto Nicolai, 'Italienische Studien', in Kruse, *Musikalische Aufsätze*, 73–4. Many of Nicolai's other writings about his long stay in Rome are summarized in Ulrich Konrad, 'Otto Nicolai und die Palestrina-Renaissance', in *Palestrina und die Idee des klassischen Vokalpolyphonie in 19. Jahrhundert: Zur Geschichte eines kirchenmusikalischen Stilideals*, ed. Winfried Kirsch, Palestrina und die Kirchenmusik im 19. Jahrhundert, 1 (Regensburg, 1989), 117–42.

[9] *The Present State*, 275–6.

from that archive over 500 years, so one would imagine that if there were such a manuscript, there would be some trace of it. Baini claimed that they were always sung entirely from memory, but when he was obliged to teach it in 1815 after the five-year break caused by the second French invasion, it seems hardly conceivable that he taught all the singers all of the parts entirely by example.

In the choirbook format used in the Chapel, each verse was visible in the same opening, albeit written as separate parts rather than as a score. The two choirbooks, one for *Coro 1°* and another for *Coro 2°*, would have been mounted on the double-sided music stand in the *Cantoria*, above and to the side of the listeners. The singers would face each other on either side of the stand.[10] Those singers who felt it necessary – those singing it for the first time, for example – could easily carry loose sheets of paper on which ornamentation and other detail could be notated. Such 'cribs' would have been very useful in 1798 to supplement the memories of the singers who remained in Rome (many had fled the French invasion), in order to prepare the score – and perhaps a performance – for Mesplet. Alternatively, perhaps they were created as a first step to making a score for Mesplet, as the singers jotted down their own personal recollections. In any case, this score, quite probably the first ever made, can only have been based upon any of these 'cribs' that could be found or created from the singers' collective and individual memory. In this they were preparing the path for the manuscripts of the 1820s, and for Mustafà and the other singers who in 1892 created the last one in exactly the same way.

---

[10] The stand swivels easily, and it may be that before 1815 it jutted out less from the *Cantoria* into the Chapel space than it does now, as in the etching by Filippo Juvarra of 1711 (Fig. 1). The whole screen, and no doubt much else, had to be reconstructed after 1815, because the French had removed it altogether.

PART THREE

THE NINETEENTH CENTURY

8

The Papal Choir in the nineteenth century 1 – Giuseppe Baini

WHEN peace returned to Europe after the final defeat of Napoleon in 1815, the phenomenon of the Grand Tour resumed with renewed vigour and enthusiasm. Rome, a cradle of European civilisation, was an obligatory stop and, seeking to combine the exoticism of ancient ruins with that of Catholic ritual, Holy Week in the Vatican was a favourite rendezvous. The 'Allegri Miserere', sung by the Papal Choir in the Sistine Chapel, was once again the focus of all music-lovers and culture hunters. Its evolution through the century, like that of the choir, revolved around two very large personalities, Giuseppe Baini and Domenico Mustafà.

Baini's life and career

Giuseppe Baini (1775–1844) was admitted into the Papal Choir in 1795, having been noticed by some of the Papal singers when he joined in with them during a visit of the Pope to the *Collegio Inglese* for the feast of St Thomas of Canterbury the previous year. During his early years he received special dispensation to continue his training in the seminary of the *Collegio Romano* while singing in the choir.[1] He had to teach himself to read music, having been allowed to study only solmisation and Gregorian chant in the seminary, and he received singing lessons from Saverio Bianchini, one of the basses of the Chapel. His first composition teacher was his uncle Lorenzo, *maestro* at various churches in Rome and Venice, and later at the cathedrals of Terni and Rieti, but his

---

[1] It is made clear in his account of Mesplet's concert in Chapter 7 that he could not be considered a full member of the choir until his ordination. Most of the information here is taken from Boursy, 'Historicism and Composition', vol. 1, chapter 3, which is itself based on La Fage, 'Notice sur la Vie et les Ouvrages de Joseph Baini', 17–49, the first part of his *Essais de diphthérographie musical*, Detail has been verified in Kantner and Pachovsky, *L'Ottocento*, esp. 25–31 and the entry on Baini in the 'Schede biografiche dei cantori' (141–3).

true master was Giuseppe Jannaconi, who from 1802 instructed him in his preferred subject, *stile antico* Palestrinian counterpoint.[2]

Soon after the French invaded Rome in February 1798, Baini left for Sant'Elena, near Perugia, where he stayed until they were driven out in November of the following year.[3] Of a serious disposition, he distinguished himself immediately upon his return by persuading the other members of the choir, which had been disbanded since the invasion, to reunite and sing the traditional *Missa de Spiritu Santo* regularly during the long conclave to elect the successor to Pius VI, who had died in August 1799.[4]

The choir was reconstituted after the new Pope, Pius VII, was finally allowed to enter Rome on 3 July 1801. Once again Baini took the initiative. A certain number of endowed masses and other offices which had previously served as rehearsal time for the singers of the Chapel had been suppressed by the French, so Baini instituted twice-weekly rehearsals at his home of music *alla Palestrina*. The same year he wrote his first compositions for the choir.

Relations between Pius VII and Bonaparte were never good, and in February 1808 French troops once again occupied Rome. Offices continued in the Vatican until June 1809, when Pius was dethroned and the Papal and Cardinalate chapels were suppressed, although the *puntatore* of the choir insisted on June 10th in the *Diario Sistina* that 'our Chapel cannot be said to be dissolved'.[5]

---

[2] Jannaconi (1740–1816) was a renowned contrapuntist and a pupil of the Papal Choir composer Pasquale Pisari (1725–78), whom Padre Martini called 'the Palestrina of the 18th century'. Jannaconi was twice passed over for the post of *maestro* of the *Cappella Giulia* (the choir of S. Pietro) in favour of more 'worldly' composers, before finally achieving it just four years before his death (Rostirolla, *Musica e musicisti*, 627–8, 643, 671, 693–708). He was a prolific composer of *prima prattica* sacred music, most of which is now in the Santini collection in Munich.

[3] See p. 97, n. 41.

[4] The conclave lasted from 30 November until 14 March 1800. *DS* does not confirm Baini's role as unique instigator of these events, but he was certainly closely involved. For political reasons the conclave was held not in Rome but in Venice, under the protection of the Austrian government. The choir sang these services at the Chiesa Nuova, where the singers had a chapel with a tomb and memorial for deceased members. Its plaque, now removed, used to have carved into it a perpetual canon for five tenors by Allegri to the text *Cantabimus canticum novum*, which has survived only because Pier Francesco Valentini, the learned contrapuntist, wrote a diatribe supposedly showing its inadequacies ('Il Canone che stà... sopra la lapide del sepolcro de musici Ponteficj è questo', included in *Due discorsi et una epistola, opere musicali di Pierfrancesco Valentini Romano*, Biblioteca Apostolica Vaticana, MS Barberini 4418).

[5] 'Il nostro Collegio non può dirsi disciolto.' *DS* 230 (1809–14), fol. 68.

Finally on 6 July, the Palazzo Quirinale was attacked and the Pope was taken to France as a prisoner. The singers of the Papal Choir were again unemployed, and this time the hiatus lasted for nearly five years, until May 1814.

Baini must have made a great impression with his leadership qualities during the years 1801–9. How else to explain the fact that when the choir was once again surplus to requirements, he was apparently approached to take up an important position in sacred music in Paris? Much uncertainty surrounds this story. The approach is said to have come through the French *directeur de la musique des fêtes religieuses* Alexandre-Etienne Choron, who had been given the task of re-opening the *maîtrises* (choir schools) lost at the Revolution. Perhaps it was also, among other things, a way to neutralise in Rome a personality who was implacably opposed to the French occupation and who had gained a large following as a confessor. In any case, Baini turned the proposition down, although he did not forget in 1815 to point out to the *Reverendo Collegio* (the term generally used to refer to Vatican authority) the sacrifice he had made, which allowed him to be the only singer who had refused to be employed by the French to be indemnified for his loss of salary.[6]

When on 24 May 1814 Pius VII returned to Rome, the offices of the Papal Choir resumed their ancient rhythms. 'And as Baini was estimated by his colleagues to be the most expert in music, they gave him the position of Director, a post never attributed before.'[7] Over the next few years his work would involve reorganising the archive and renewing the repertoire. In preparation for the Pope's arrival offices were sung at the Chiesa Nuova, the first one on 16 May was said to have gone 'very well despite the interruption of five years of perfect silence'.[8] By Holy Week 1815 the choir was ready to sing *Miserere* three times, although it was not without its drama. Napoleon had escaped from Elba, and a Neapolitan army commanded by the former Maréchal Murat, now

---

[6] Altogether twenty-four *partecipanti* and *supranumerari* refused to be 'corrupted' by taking a salary from the French authorities, while fourteen (eleven of them *giubilati*) accepted. When those singers who had refused asked for payment for the five years lost, they were turned down flat, just as they had been in the same circumstances in 1801. The correspondence between the singers and the authorities is given in Kantner and Pachovsky, *L'Ottocento*, 27–8. See also Clapton, *Moreschi*, 88–9.

[7] 'E poichè il Baini era stimato da' suoi colleghi il più esperto nella musica, percio gli conferirono l'incarico di Direttore, quantunque a nessuno prima di lui fosse stato concesso.' Alfieri, 'Biografia', part 3 (29 June 1856), 201. This post appears to have been entirely unofficial. Alfieri, no friend of Baini (for reasons which will become clear in Chapter 10), used his biography to give a more balanced view of his qualities than some of the more hyperbolic tributes which followed his death in 1844.

[8] 'assai bene non ostante l'interruzione di anni 5 di perfetto silenzio'. DS 230 (1809–14), fol. 88.

King of Naples, was marching towards Rome. On Holy Wednesday, 22 March, Pius VII fled to Viterbo, but the singers continued with the offices, singing the *Miserere della nostra Cappella*. On Thursday and Friday they sang Bai's *Miserere*, before closing down until Corpus Christi on 15 May.[9]

Another 'restoration' followed with Pius VII's return to Rome on 7 June 1815, and Baini wrote a motet *Oremus pro nostro Pontifice Pio* for the occasion.[10] In a similarly triumphant vein, his *Te Deum*, one of his most ambitious compositions, was given in S. Pietro on 8 September.[11] In 1816 his turn came to be *segretario-puntatore*, and, following usual practice, he automatically became *maestro pro tempore* for the year 1817.[12] Finally in 1819, on the death of Giuseppe Censi, he was elected *camerlengo*, a post in which he was confirmed by acclamation every year until his death in 1844. In 1830 he was referred to as *camerlengo e direttore*, and in 1841 he was made a Monsignor and given with it the honorary status of *cameriere d'onore in abito pavonazzo* (an honorary title similar to Gentleman of the Bedchamber) as well as *camerlengo direttore perpetuo*.[13]

It is clear that the main reason that Baini found himself in effective charge of the college of singers was that he was seen as someone who understood, and could restore, the old traditions. His research into the repertoire and history of the choir had begun in 1801 and resulted in numerous tracts over the next eight years concerning the Gregorian modes, the singing of the lessons, improvised counterpoint on Gregorian chant (*Breve notizia istorica e regole del contrappunto solito farsi da' Cantori pontificj nel cantare il canto gregoriano*) and canonic devices.[14] Much of Jannaconi's teaching had involved transcribing into

---

[9] *DS* 231 (1815), fol. 35ᵛ. The French composer Herold was sure that the choir sang the same piece on all three days in 1815 (see p. 162).

[10] Both Alfieri ('Biografia', part 3, 201–2) and La Fage ('Notice sur la Vie', 28n.) suggest that Baini wrote only the introduction to this motet, with the rest taken from an unknown seventeenth-century work, an assertion supported by Boursy ('Historicism and Composition', vol 1, 154–8).

[11] An extensive dedication, giving the date, precedes the work in CS 450.

[12] His nomination for these posts followed seniority, just as it would have done if his perceived leadership qualities had not already given him an expanded role in directing and rehearsing performances. Taking his turn like everyone else meant that he succeeded in each post Bernardino Cianchetti, who had officially joined the choir just a day earlier than he had.

[13] He was also an honorary member of academies throughout Europe (Sweden, Vienna, Paris) and Italy, and was even offered, in 1829, the role of Rector in the *Collegio Urbano di Propaganda Fide* (College for the Propagation of the Faith), which shows the extent to which he was valued by several different popes for the manner in which he carried out his religious duties.

[14] A list of these writings, all of which remain in manuscript in the Biblioteca Casanatense (Rome), is given in *Grove Music Online* ('Baini, Giuseppe' by Sergio Lattes). La Fage also gives a list in his *Essais de diphthérographie*, 54–8.

Fig. 16 Lithograph of Giovanni Baini

score music by Palestrina, and this method both formed his understanding of the *prima prattica* style and informed his own compositions and teaching: 'few rules, many examples' ('peu de préceptes, beaucoup d'exemples').

His research carried on unabated after the hiatus of 1809–14, and eventually led to the work for which he is best known today, his monumental *Memorie Storico-Critiche della Vita et delle Opere di Giovanni Pierluigi da Palestrina* of 1828. Despite containing 'many failings in historical and philological method and ... inaccuracies of fact',[15] it is nevertheless one of the earliest biographies deriving from archival research. Many of its judgements about Palestrina and his music have not worn well, but it remains uniquely valuable for its illumination of context. Baini's projected history of the *cappella*, like most of his monumental edition of Palestrina's works, never appeared. Perhaps he decided instead to include in the *Memorie Storico-Critiche* the material he had

[15] Lattes, 'Baini, Giuseppe'.

gathered as footnotes, the limitations of which are confined to those of the Vatican archive, to which he had at the time unique and unrivalled access.[16]

✴ Difficult times

The early years after the restoration of Pius VII in 1815 were difficult for the choir, largely because of a dearth of singers, especially good *castrati*. Some had left Rome to take posts elsewhere, and some had died. For the first offices the choir was obliged to call upon the services of the many *giubilati* to raise a quorum until new singers could be recruited.[17] Moreover salaries in the Vatican had not kept pace with the outside world, and even when good singers could be found, they were easily enticed away. As an emergency measure, nine new *soprannumerarî* were taken on in 1814, and immediately thrown into the round of daily services, but three of the best singers, two of them *castrati*, had left within three years for better paid posts elsewhere.[18] A note in the *Diario Sistina* of 1820, describing a rehearsal for Holy Week, makes clear one of the problems.

> Last to be sung was the Miserere of Tommaso Allegri [sic!], which for some years has not been done well because of a scarcity of good voices, and which

---

[16] In the words of Lewis Lockwood, 'Despite its severe limitations, [it] ranks even now as not only the first, but still the most comprehensive, study of Palestrina, and a landmark in the field of musical biography. Its major fault lies in the discrepancy between the source material assembled by Baini (much larger than that of any predecessor) and his lack of critical thinking with which to interpret it' (introduction to his edition of Palestrina's *Pope Marcellus Mass*, Norton Critical Scores (New York, 1975), 34). The footnotes, on the other hand, needed little or no interpretation. They are so numerous and detailed that in the German edition of Baini's work, *Über das Leben und die Werke des G.P. da Palestrina*, trans. F.S. Kandler and ed. R.G. von Keisewetter (Leipzig, 1834) they were extracted from the main text and grouped together in an appendix.

[17] When *DS* 230, which had been started in 1809, resumed (fol. 82) after the hiatus, it gave no new list of singers, and curiously, the diary for 1815 (*DS* 231) makes no distinction between *participanti*, *giubilati* and *soprannumerarî*, listing simply 45 *cappellani cantori* (11 *soprani*, 11 *alti*, 12 *tenori*, 10 *bassi* and one unspecified voice).

[18] Domenico Bertozzi (tenor) went to the Teatro Real in Palermo, Domenico Laureti (soprano) took a post in Lisbon, where he would be the last *castrato* to sing in the cathedral, and Francesco Reali (soprano) joined the Portuguese Royal Chapel in Rio de Janeiro (Kantner and Pachovsky, *L'Ottocento*, 30–1 and 'Schede biografiche dei cantori', individual entries).

today has become almost monotonous, because in it there are no variations in [the music of] the first verse.[19]

The writer is complaining that the singers lacked the skill to grace their parts with decorations in the five-part verses (which in the Allegri are all identical on paper). One good *castrato* was enough to carry off the four-part ones, but the five-part ones also needed some imagination and expertise.

Baini reacted in two ways. Firstly he initiated a concerted drive to recruit more *castrati*, which resulted in two new singers being found in the following three years.[20] He also composed a *Miserere* of his own, first performed in 1821. The *Diario Sistina* described the event as follows:

> The *reverendo collegio*, which takes very much to heart the exact execution of all the functions of our Chapel, noticing that in the Holy Week, and especially the performance of the Misereres of Allegri and Bai, because of the scarcity of voices, could not have a happy outcome, strongly begged the reverend Signor Don Giuseppe Baini, experienced in this kind of work, to apply the sublimity of his genius and the talent that he has demonstrated in other circumstances, to create a new composition ... this new Miserere for ten voices was executed, and the difficult challenge produced an extraordinary effect, both as a melodious work, and in its admirable feeling.
>
> In these favourable circumstances it would be a hateful thing, and not fitting, to compare the ancient Misereres of Allegri, and Bai with the new production of our above-mentioned colleague Signor Baini, but an essential observation should not be neglected. The Misereres of Allegri and Bai are limited to the artful arrangement of only three verses, extremely embellished by our singers, whereas in that of Baini every verse is treated with faithfulness to the meaning that the specific words of this psalm deserve, and as far as the execution of the music is concerned, it incited applause greater than that for the famous old masters.[21]

---

[19] 'E stato cantata in fine il Miserere di Tommaso Allegri, che di qualche anno non riesce bene par la scarszezza delle buone voci, quasi redendosi in oggi monotono, perché in esso non v'è alcuna variazione dal primo verso.' DS 236 (29 March 1820), fol. 26ᵛ. Reproduced in Kantner and Pachovsky, *L'Ottocento*, appendix II, 216.

[20] They were Donato Leoni and Feliciano Dominici, both described by Alessandro Gabrielli as 'having voices suitable for singing in the choir, nothing more' ('erano voci di coro, corista, nulla di più'). A. Gabrielli, 'Riassunto delle conversazioni sulla storia delle cappelle musicali romane' *Rassegna Dorica*, 10 (1938–9), 238 (cited in Kantner and Pachovsky, *L'Ottocento*, 25).

[21] 'Il r[evere]ndo collegio, a cui sta molto a cuore l'esatta esecuzione di tutti le funzioni della nostra Cappella, prevedendo, che in quella della Settimana santa, e specialmente nell'eseguire i Miserere dell'Allegri e Bai, per la scarszezza delle voci, non potesser' avere un esito felice, ne prega vivamente il r[evere]ndo

In other words, because his setting was more 'composed' with special attention to the meaning of each word, the simple performance of the notes on the page was sufficient: little or no embellishing skills were required of the soloists who sang it.[22]

For some this was a handicap.

The Miserere which followed was Baini's, which is well known. The main difference between it and that of Allegri is that Allegri's is more concerned with the general impression than with the detail, whereas Baini tries to wring meaning out of each word; this leads to a striking lack of simplicity and a too pronounced striving for effect. Baini's Miserere is not divided up in the same way as Allegri's, and does not make a noteworthy impression. In Allegri's, each verse is divided in two parts: the first starts with the voices chanting which develops into an imperfect cadence on a simple chord; the second part of each verse, in contrast to the first, has richer chords and finishes with a final crescendo.[23]

---

sig[no]r D. Giuseppe Baini la di lui sublimità d'ingegno e di talento del pari erasi in altre circostanze, in questo genere sperimentata, acciò si occupasse per una nuova composizione ... si è eseguito il nuovo Miserere a dieci voci sott'oggi col massimo impegno, avendo prodotto en effetto straordinario, per il melodioso concerto, che in esso mirabilmente si è sentito.

In questa favorevol circostanza sarebbe cosa odiosa, e non conveniente, paragonare gli antichi Miserere dell'Allegri, e Bai colla nuova produzione del sud[ett]o nostro collega sig[no]r Baini, ma non dee trascurarsi un'essenziale osservazione. I Miserere dell'Allegri, e Bai, sono limitati all'artificio di tre soli versi, ed abbelliti fuor di modo dalli stessi nostri cantori, quello però del Baini vien trattato in ciascun verso, con quella fedeltà, che meritano le distinti parole del d[ett]o Salmo, che dal canto dall'esecuzione ancore riguardato, ha fatto riscuotere al med[esim]o un applauso maggiore degli 'antichi celebri maestri.' DS 237 (1821), fol. 21^v (20 April), reproduced in *L'Ottocento*, 216. The mention of 'tre soli versi' is puzzling. Perhaps the writer meant three kinds of verses, a5, a4 and the final a8 or a9, although Baini's textures, all a10, hardly offered more variety.

[22] This does not necessarily mean that there was no embellishment at all. Mendelssohn's statement in 1831 concerning all three Misereres that 'it is quite immaterial which they sing, for the embellishments are pretty much the same in all three' (*Letters*, 140, and see p. 161). No doubt some 'little ornaments and trills' (*Letters*, 95–6), and the 'parallel *portamenti*' in the reciting sections of each verse, which the choir apparently applied systematically to their whole repertoire, were present.

[23] 'Le Miserere, qui vint après, était celui de Baini; composition renommée. La grande différence entre celui-ci et celui d'Allegri, c'est qu'Allegri s'occupe moins des détails que de l'expression générale, tandis que Baini recherche le sentiment attaché à chaque mot; il en résulte pour son œuvre un manque de simplicité très-frappant et une trop grande recherche des effets. Le Miserere

The future Cardinal Wiseman, who heard the work conducted by the composer himself in the 1830s, agreed, and at considerably greater length.

> The difference of style which I have remarked between the old and the modern composers is here strongly observable. Baini's, I believe, generally pleases the uninitiated most; and would be a grand and beautiful composition anywhere, but appears less so under the roof against which Allegri's strains are accustomed to die away. Every verse is varied, and betrays art. At the words *Et exultabunt ossa humiliata*, there is air, or rather time, upon the first part of the verse, in a rising, joyful movement, succeeded by a low, deep and sepulchral expression in the rest of the phrase. The verse *incerta et occulta sapientiae tuæ manifestasti mihi*, begins with a soft stealthy expression, to convey the idea of concealment and uncertainty: then at the *manifestasti*, 'thou hast declared,' part succeeds to part, till a grand burst of full declaration is made. Every verse proceeds upon the same principle, and the mind is thus kept undecided between different feelings, watching the art and skill of the composer, now held in suspense, and heaving upwards on a majestic swell, then falling suddenly, by its breaking, as a wave, on an abrupt and shortened cadence; and you arrive at the conclusion with a variety of images and feelings, the mind, like a shivered mirror, retaining only fragments of sentiments and emotions.
>
> How different is the effect of Allegri's, upon the soul of one, who, kneeling in that silent twilight, and shutting up every sense, save that of hearing, allows himself to be borne unresisting by the uniformly directed tide of its harmonies. It is but a chaunt twice varied: one verse being in four parts, and another in five, till both unite in the final swell of nine voices. The written notes are simple and unadorned; but tradition, under the guidance of long experience and of chastened taste, has interwoven many turns, dissonances and resolutions, which no written or published score has expressed. At first, the voices enter into full but peculiar harmony, softly swelling in emphasis on each word, till the middle of the verse, when a gradual separation of each part takes place, preparing for the first close; you hear them, as though weaving among themselves a rich texture of harmonious combination; one seems struggling against the general resolve, and refusing more than a

---

de Baini n'est pas coupé de même que celui d'Allegri et n'en possède pas un effet célèbre. Chez Allegri, chaque verset est divisé en deux parties, la première est dite d'abord par les voix qui se divisent pour la terminaison faite par une cadence retardée et l'accord parfait, la deuxième partie du verset est plus riche comme accords, fait opposition à la première et se termine par un crescendo final.' Celler, *La Semaine sainte*, 96. This commentary echoes in many ways the different schools of criticism of 'Palestrinian polyphony' in France at the time. See Katharine Ellis, *Interpreting the Musical Past: Early Music in Nineteenth Century France* (New York, 2005), esp. 22–31 and chapter 6, 'Defining Palestrina'.

momentary contact with another, but edging off upon delicious dissonances, till the whole, with a waving, successive modulation, meet in full harmony upon a suspended cadence. Then they proceed with the second portion of the verse, upon a different, but even richer accord, till once more they divide with greater beauty than before. The parts seem to become more entangled than ever. Here you trace one winding and creeping, by soft and subdued steps, through the labyrinth of sweet sounds; then another drops, with delicious trickling falls, from the highest compass to the level of the rest; then one seems at length to extricate itself; then another, in imitative successive cadences; they seem as silver threads that gradually unravel themselves, and then wind round the fine, deep-toned bass which has scarcely swerved from its steady dignity during all their modulations, and filling up the magnificent diapason, burst into a swelling final cadence, which has no name upon earth. After verse has thus succeeded to verse, ever deepening the impression once made, without an artifice or an embellishment to mar the singleness of the influence, after the union of the two choirs has made the last burst, of condensed, but still harmonious, power; and that affecting prayer, 'Look down, O Lord, upon this thy family,' has been recited in melancholy monotony amidst the scarcely expired echoes of that enchanting, overpowering, heavenly strain, the mind remains in a state of subdued tenderness and solemnity of feeling, which can ill brook the jarring sounds of earth, and which make it sigh after the region of true and perfect harmony. I hardly think that once or twice hearing the Misereres of Allegri and Bai can impress the feelings which I have feebly endeavoured to describe.[24]

Examination of the score makes clear that, like many other works by Baini, it was not as new as all that.[25] Many verses – 7 (*Ecce enim veritatem*), 11 (*Cor mundum*), 17 (*Quoniam si voluisses*) and, particularly, the second half of 20 (*Tunc imponent*) – are more or less ten-voice adaptations of Bai's *Miserere*, in which 'every verse is [indeed] treated with faithfulness to the meaning that the specific words of this psalm deserve'.[26] Like the Bai, Baini's *Miserere* is more a kind of choral recitation than a *falsobordone*. Every verse is for all ten singers, and there is no place for extravagant *abbellimenti*. Mendelssohn, who heard it in 1831, was not impressed, describing it as 'a composition devoid of life and strength, like all his works; still it had chords and music, so made an

---

[24] Wiseman, *Four Lectures*, 86–90.
[25] It is transcribed from CS 483 in Boursy's 'Historicism and Composition', vol. 2, 155–77.
[26] Baini had a high regard for Bai, jokingly referring to his own surname as a diminutive of Bai (Sievers, 'Die päpstliche Kapelle', 400, cited in Boursy, 'Historicism and Composition', vol. 1, 123, n. 48).

impression'.²⁷ He had considerable reservations about Baini as a man also, as he wrote in a letter to his father at the beginning of his stay.

> I also intend to thoroughly savour Baini, who is the craftiest priest one could imagine, and at the same time the most popular confessor in all of Rome; he creates an artificial halo around himself, and I think he takes me for a *brutissimo Tedesco*, so that I can get to know him quite splendidly. Of course his compositions are nothing much, as is the case with all the music here.²⁸

There is doubtless a certain amount of Protestant disdain included in this opinion. The truth is probably that Baini could be extremely generous, but also had a very strong opinion of his own worth and was extremely jealous of his status, as will be shown by his treatment of Alfieri in Chapter 10.

It can be no surprise that during Baini's time in charge *stile antico* polyphony, either in original creations like Palestrina's, or in 'modern copies' like his own works, predominated in the repertoire of the Papal Choir. Given that accompaniment of any sort was out of the question, any director would have had little choice but to follow this course, so it was as well to have a director interested in it. But by the end of the eighteenth century, *stile antico* in general musical culture had become virtually moribund, reserved for the expansive fugues found in the closing movements of Gloria and Credo settings, in which composers liked to show off their serious training. Until the 1830s, when German and French musicians and historians started to become interested in this tradition, the Papal Choir was virtually alone in taking it seriously.

It is perhaps no coincidence that many of those at the heart of this reawakened interest, which led in turn to the Cecilian movement (see p. 170), were pupils of Baini – Ferdinand Hiller, Carl Proske (and his pupil Franz Xaver Witt, the founder of the Allgemeiner Cäcilien-Verein) and Otto Nicolai; nor that their taste was close to his. Boursy, in his discussion of Baini's compositions, shows at some length that Baini's style had more in common with the gestures of Palestrinian style than with its essence.²⁹ Baini himself was only really interested in the simpler, more monophonic works: the *Improperia*, *Stabat mater*, sets of Lamentations and the *Missa Papae Marcelli*.

> Oh how very different Pierluigi the author of the Lamentations is from Pierluigi the author of the five aforementioned masses [from the *Missarum Liber Primus* of 1554]: there all art, here all nature; there full of trifles, here of seriousness. There meaningless cold, here all fire, all spirit, all truth. There

---

[27] *Letters*, 140. He is contrasting it with the hours of Gregorian psalmody which preceded it.
[28] Letter to his father, 7 December 1830, in *Mendelssohn: A Life in Letters*, ed. Rudolf Ewers, trans. Craig Tomlinson (New York, 1986), 145.
[29] 'Historicism and Composition', chapter 4.

overloaded with strain and labour, here fluid and smooth, without interruption or any difficulty. There the imitator of various manners not his own, here the imitator of nature, with styles all his own.[30]

By 1831 Baini's role as conductor was an established fact, and Mendelssohn was able to give the lie to the popular legend that the choir was undirected. Climbing a handy ladder in the Pauline Chapel on Maundy Thursday, he 'saw plainly enough the shadow of Baini's long arm moving up and down; indeed he sometimes struck his music-desk quite audibly'.[31] The previous year, the American painter Rembrandt Peale recounted that for the *Miserere*

> two great candles were lighted in the choir, the singers took new positions, the leader waved his paper scroll, and the feminine voice of the first singer commenced a pathetic strain; the choir gradually combining their varying and subordinate tones, to produce the most affecting and delightful harmony that was ever heard from human voices.[32]

Baini seems to have embraced the role of conductor-interpreter with enthusiasm, impressing Nicolai considerably.

> The director often varies the tempo according to the meaning of the words, his own sensibility and the tradition that has come down to him; he lets *rallentando* and *stringendo* and *crescendo* and *diminuendo* happen, where Baini's quite particular art and the exceptional obedience of the singers – who already know every movement of his finger and how to interpret it – really cannot be admired enough.[33]

---

[30] 'Oh! Quanto mai il Pierluigi autor delle lamentazioni è diverso dal Pierluigi autor delle cinque sopramenzionate messe: Là tutt'arte; quì tutto natura: là pieno d'inezie, quì di serietà. Là freddo insignificante: quì tutto fuoco, tutt' anima, tutto verità. Là ricolmo di sforzo e di fatica: quì fluido e corrente, senza arresto o difficoltà veruna. Là imitatore di varie maniere non sue: quì imitatore della natura, con foggie tutte sue proprie.' Baini, *Memorie Storico-Critiche*, vol. 2, 425 (trans. in Boursy, 'Historicism and Composition', vol. 1, 153). Baini's attitude prefigured that of the German 'Cecilians' later in the century.

[31] *Letters*, 142.

[32] *Notes on Italy* (Philadelphia, 1831), 174.

[33] 'Der Direktor wechselt oft dem Sinn der Worte, eigener Empfindung und der ihm überkommenen Tradition gemäß das Tempo, läßt rallentando und stringendo und crescendo und diminuendo machen, wo denn wirklich die ganz eigentümliche Kunst Baini's und die ungemeine Folgsamkeit der Singenden, die jede Bewegung seines Fingers schon kennen und zu deuten verstehen, nicht genug bewundert werden kann.' Nicolai, 'Italienische Studien', *Musikalische Aufsätze*, 71–2. Baini's own *Dies Irae* (transcribed by Boursy, 'Historicism and Composition', vol. 2, 53–89, discussed in vol. 1, 162–4) is heavily marked with

No doubt this precision of gesture allowed his performances to be highly expressive, although it is arguable that this was not a new style. The practice of 'accelerating or retarding the measure at some particular words, and singing some entire verses quicker than others' had been reported to Burney by the Papal Chapel singer Santarelli in 1770.[34] The difference, perhaps, is merely in the means by which the performance was achieved.

It was not efficient in all areas, however. Mendelssohn could also say that 'even the Papal singers are growing old, are almost completely unmusical, and don't even get the traditional pieces right.' Things were no better when his sister Fanny heard them in 1840.

> During this ceremonial [Good Friday morning] the Improperie are sung to Palestrina's music ... It sounded very soft and sweet, partly because the first soprano, though very powerful, was particularly sweet in tone. The alto was very bad, and got terribly flat. They began the 'Miserere' and the 'Improperie' in Friday in B major, and ended in G; indeed on Friday, it was almost F minor.[35]

The choir's frequent problems of tuning were remarked upon by many musical witnesses, together with poor diction and unpleasant shouting, all of which does little to enhance Baini's reputation as a director.

---

expressive indications (*maestoso, expressivo, grave, dolce, vivace, risoluto*, etc.), dramatic pauses and sudden changes in metre, key, tempo and character, as well as *sforzandi* and extreme dynamic changes in short spaces of time.

[34] Much of this tradition is still evident in Mustafà's manuscript of the *Miserere* made in 1892, and in performances by the modern version of the *Cappella Musicale Pontificia* as recently as the 1980s.

[35] Hensel, *The Mendelssohn Family*, Vol. 2, 98. For her musical example from the *Improperia*, see p. 146, Ex. 7.

9

Nineteenth-century sources 1 – British Library Add. MS 31525 and related manuscripts

✳ A new version

AFTER the dramas of the Napoleonic era came to an end in 1815, a new generation of singers brought new interpretations of 'the Miserere'. In the mid-1820s a new version started to circulate, now known from twelve closely related manuscript copies (listed in detail in Appendix 8, to which the numbers in bold in the discussion below refer). Two are in the British Library, but most of the others are in German-speaking countries. They have been collated to produce what is called here Source **A**, transcribed in part in Appendix 9. It is the basis of the performing edition of Allegri's *Miserere* included with this book, Edition 2 of Appendix 13.

Complete sources

British Library Add. MS 31525 contains sources **1** and **2** bound together. It belonged formerly to the English organist, collector, musicologist and editor Joseph Warren (1804–81; see Fig. 17), whose name is found on the title page.[1] It was part of a large collection of manuscripts that were acquired from him by Julian Marshall, and sold on to the British Library in 1881.

The first manuscript, Add. 31525(1), is marked *Come si eseguisce nella Cappella Pontificia Di Roma* [as it is executed in the Papal Chapel in Rome] *In Roma presso Bened Morganti Via de Crociferi N°119* and is misattributed to *Sig*ʳ

---

[1] Warren was one of the most active writers and editors of the nineteenth century. His re-edition of Boyce's *Cathedral Music* (1849) was widely praised, with many extra works, added organ parts and short biographies. Organist at St Mark's Catholic Chapel in Chelsea from 1834, he was a key figure in the revival of early English music, and published guides for madrigal singers, organists and composers, as well as a method for the concertina. In later life he fell upon hard times and was obliged to sell his valuable library before being rescued from destitution by the musicologist W.H. Cummings. (My thanks to Philippe Jacquet for sharing with me the family archive, and granting permission to reproduce the photograph in Fig. 17.)

Fig. 17 Photograph of Joseph Warren

M^{ro} *Baj*. The second, Add. 31525(2), in a different hand, shows more signs of haste and is unattributed except in pencil (to Bai) in a later hand (which may be Marshall's), no doubt misled by the false attribution of the first version.[2] But its title, simply *Miserere*, is in the same hand as the whole of **1**, so we can probably safely assume that Warren acquired them together, probably in Rome in the mid-1820s.[3] Both contain all the verses, and the second has more numerous

---

[2] The misattribution was first noted by Ben Byram-Wigfield, in his essay on the Allegri, 'A Quest for the Holy Grail?' (2012 and subsequent revisions), available at http://www.ancientgroove.co.uk/essays/sources.html. His judgement that its being by Allegri rather than Bai makes it 'infinitely more than that' is one with which most nineteenth-century singers of the Papal Chapel, not least Domenico Mustafà, would have taken issue.

[3] Proof that he visited Rome in the 1820s remains elusive, but his activities between 1822, when he resigned from the conductorship of an amateur orchestra, and October 1826, when he married in London, are otherwise

dynamic markings. Morganti was a seller of books and manuscripts, some of them copied to order, and his name is found in numerous sources dating from around 1800 to the 1830s. Although the British Library catalogue still refers to the manuscript as eighteenth-century, its experts consider that the paper dates almost certainly from the early nineteenth century.[4]

It is Source **2** – Add. 31525(2) – that gives a musical text which is virtually the same as nine other contemporary sources and one important later copy, all apparently prepared by or for German collectors.[5] The enthusiasm of travellers' accounts had led to German performances of the *Miserere* in the early nineteenth century – in Leipzig in 1810 and Kassel in 1812. Burney's edition, published in 1809 by Peters in Leipzig, presumably provided the music, no doubt performed in a suitably reverent manner by a large choir.[6]

Two of these sources, almost complete (missing v. 20) and virtually identical, are now in Vienna (**3**, Österreichische Nationalbibliothek Mus. Hs. 15604) and Munich (**4**, Bayerische Staatsbibliothek Mus. ms. 671). They both bear the description 'notated by a Papal singer, with all ornaments and indications, as it is sung in the Sistine Chapel (that is, since 1824)'.[7] The Vienna manuscript (**3**) gives three versions of the *Miserere*, and the first two, on facing pages, allow the reader to compare the decorated one with Burney's complete plain one.[8] Verses 1 and 3 with decorations were printed by Robert Haas in his *Aufführungspraxis der Musik*, who noted that it formerly belonged to Michael Hauber.[9] Munich

---

unaccounted for. A few annotations in Add. 31525(2) suggest that he may have heard a performance of the *Miserere*.

[4] My thanks to Sandra Tuppen of the British Library for this information and for allowing me to photograph the watermarks.

[5] Although the five-part verses in Add. 31525(1) are very similar, it gives a unique version of the four-part ones (3, 7, 11, 15 and 19), transcribed separately in Appendix 10.

[6] For more on this, as well as notes concerning the importance of the *Miserere* as a stimulant to interest in Roman polyphonic music, see Garratt, *Palestrina and the German Romantic Imagination*, esp. 41–2. For the German edition of Burney see p. 98, n. 46.

[7] 'Von einem päbstlichen Sänger, mit allen Verzierungen und Andeutungen des Vortrags aufgesetzt, wie es in der Sixtinischen Capelle gesungen wird (d. h. seit 1824).' The date indicates a relationship of these manuscripts with **6–9**, below.

[8] The copy of Burney's includes verse 20. As verse 20b a9 never contained ornaments, it was not necessary to reproduce it in version 2, but it is surprising that 20a is not given in ornamented form there. The third version, used in Salzburg Cathedral ('Wie es in Salzburg in der Domkirche gesungen wird'), is Allegri's original (as in CS 205–6) and is provided with a thoroughly figured bass. Curiously it too is lacking verse 20a (the text is provided, as it is for the other *cantus planus* verses).

[9] *Aufführungspraxis der Musik* (Potsdam, 1931), 157–60. Johann Michael Hauber (1778–1843), editor (with Caspar Ett) of *Cantica Sacra in Usum studiosae*

671 (**4**) bears the name of Anton Friedrich Justus Thibaut, a passionate advocate of Roman polyphonic music and founder of the Heidelberg Singverein. Its description contains the supplementary phrase 'auch bey dem Anhören revidiert' ('and revised after listening'), although its readings are virtually identical with those of Vienna 15604. Source **5**, now in the Biblioteka Uniwersytecka in Warsaw (RM 6027), was almost certainly copied by the German musicologist Emil Bohn (1839–1909) from Munich 671.[10] A particularity of all these complete sources is the use of an asterisk * after important syllables in the unrhythmicised recited sections of each verse, the meaning of which is made clear in sources **6–9**.

Partial sources – first group

There are no fewer than seven incomplete sources, all of which give readings essentially the same as the complete ones. They can be divided into two groups. Four derive from a copy (or copies) apparently made or acquired by 'the Palestrina of Berlin' Bernhard Klein (1793–1832), during his honeymoon in Rome in 1824.[11] Both **6** (Berlin, Staatsbibliothek Sammlung Teschner 119) and **7** (Dresden, Sächsische Landesbibliothek Mus. 1474-E-3) are said in pencil notes to be very close copies of it, and are described as 'Allegri's Miserere (with all the ornaments, as it is sung in the Sistine Chapel during Holy Week in Rome)'.[12] They give only four verses – 1, 3, 5 and 7 – together with the first soprano part only of verse 20a, and the first two chords of 20b, to which, oddly, the text

---

juventatis (Munich, 1855), was an important figure in the early Cecilian movement in Munich.

[10] It was formerly in the Musikalisches Institut bei des Universität, Breslau (now Wrocław), under the call mark Mf. 5132, and is part of the large collection of manuscripts and transcriptions assembled by Bohn. It is important because Julius Amann, in his *Allegris Miserere*, used it as the basis of his transcription of verses 1 and 3 of this version (50–2), and also for his detailed list of variants (53–5) between the manuscripts discussed here of which he had knowledge. Amann did not take account of British Library Add. 31525 (**1** and **2**), no doubt because of its misattribution in the British Library catalogue, nor was he aware of Cologne R1038/2 (**9**), Leipzig PM 5618 (**11**), or Bodleian MS M. Deneke Mendelssohn d.70 (**12**). The *Miserere* is the last piece in RM 6027, a collection of twenty-two works by Allegri, Bai, Anerio, Festa, Palestrina and Biordi, all probably copied from Munich sources.

[11] Klein also supplied manuscripts to Thibaut. See Richard D. Green, 'Klein, Bernhard', *Grove Music Online*.

[12] 'Miserere von Allegri (Mit allen Verzierungen; so wie es in der heiligen Woche zu Rom in der Capella sixtina gesungen wird).'

'Gloria patri et filio' has been added.[13] Both manuscripts bear the place and date Rome, February 1825, and the note 'This is as much as was in the exemplar from which this copy was made.'[14]

Source 8 (Munich, Bayerische Staatsbibliothek Mus. Ms. 3268(2)) could be a copy of Teschner 119, having identical contents and readings, although with fewer marks of expression and no descriptions of any kind, and a slightly later source with interesting individual features is Cologne R1038/2 (**9**). Its title is the same as that of **6** and **7**, as is the explanation for its brevity, but it does not contain the *Gloria patri* sketch. The description of its origin is also somewhat different: 'Obtained in the year 1830 from Bernhard Klein, who received it from the Kapellmeister of the Papal Chapel during his presence in Rome.'[15] One wonders therefore if the abbreviated version of verse 20 might have been a sketch added by Klein himself, and that later he supplied the owner of Cologne R1038/2 with a copy of his original version without it.[16]

The Cologne manuscript is interesting also because it contains rubrics derived from a variety of sources. Concerning the even-numbered verses, it is stated in **6** and **7** that 'Il populo risponde l'altro verzo' [sic], and at the end the use of a monotone is specified: 'Thus the remaining verses are alternated between *Coro* I and II and the *risposten* [responses, i.e. the plainsong verses] are sung on one note which fits with the verse.'[17] These instructions

---

[13] Another manuscript in Dresden (Mus. 1474-E-1), described by Amann (*Allegris Miserere*, 110) and lost in the Second World War, apparently contained the whole of the psalm adapted to the music of the five-part verses, with differences thought by Amann to be 'so fundamental that the composition can hardly be regarded as Allegri's Miserere' ('Die Abweichungen dieser Handschrift sind so wesentlich, daß die Komposition kaum noch als Miserere von Allegri angesprochen werden darf'). It also contained an adaptation of the *Gloria patri* to the same music, although whether it was in any way an influence on 1474-E-3 and the other manuscripts cannot now be verified.

[14] 'Soweit führte das Exemplar, nach welchem diese Copie gemacht, Rom im Februar 1825, Bernh. Klein.' G.W. Teschner, whose name is found on the front cover of Teschner 119, was a singing teacher and prolific editor of old music, a pupil of Klein (and of Mendelssohn's teacher Carl Friedrich Zelter) in Berlin from 1824 until about 1829.

[15] 'Erhalten im Jahr 1830 von Bernhard Klein welcher dieselben von dem Capellmeister der päpstlichen Capelle bei seiner Anwesenheit in Rom empfing.'

[16] It is hard to believe that the creator of any Roman source would imagine that the music of verse 20b should be sung to the *Gloria patri*. A later owner of R1038/2 was Nikolaus Joseph Hompesch (1830–1902), who was one of the first graduates from the Conservatorium der Musik in Cologne and who taught piano there from 1854 to his death. It was he who presented it to the Cologne library in 1878.

[17] 'Also werden die übrigen Versette mit Abwechselung des Coro I° und II° und den Risposten, in einem Tone nach dem Versmaaße abgesungen.'

are reproduced in R1038/2, with the additional note 'Il populo risponde quasi parlante l'altro verso come segue' – followed by octave Ds (d and d' on a c₃ clef) suitable for tenors and basses – a rubric which appears to be derived from sources 10, 11 and 12. It also gives (not entirely convincing) detailed rhythms for the *cantus planus* text in verse 2 and part of verse 4, the only source which suggests any rhythmicising of these verses.

These four sources are unique in the use of a strange sign resembling a small vertical dumb-bell at most of the same places in the text as 1–4 (and 5) give *, described (in 6, 7 and 9) as a 'segno di Appoggiatura'. No doubt it indicates the famous Papal Choir 'parallel portamento', described by Spohr, Nicolai and Mendelssohn (see Chapter 7).

Partial sources – second group

The descriptions in these three manuscripts are entirely in Italian, and they may be later than the others. They all describe *Coro 1°* a5 as the *Coro maggiore*, and *Coro 2°* a4 as the *Coro minore*, a terminology found nowhere else.[18] 10 (Basel, Universitäts-Bibliothek kk XII 22:3) is entitled *Miserere di Gregorio Allegri*, 'with all the different ornaments as it is sung in the Sistine Chapel on Wednesday, Thursday and Friday of Holy Week',[19] and is dated 'Roma, il 30 Ottobre [18]29'. It contains verses 1, 3 and 20a, all with ornaments, as well as 20b (without) in the version given by Alfieri in his edition of 1840 (see Chapter 10).

Source 11 (Leipziger Stadtbibliothek – Musikbibliothek PM 5618) gives text and descriptions identical to Basel kk XII 22:3, to the extent that it is impossible to be sure which is more original, except that verse 20b is not included. It was possibly formerly owned by Ernest Friedrich Richter (1808–79), composer, editor and teacher at the Leipzig Conservatoire and Kantor at the Thomasschule. Concerning the even-numbered verses, after noting that 'Il populo risponde l'altro verso', both 10 and 11 specify that they are to be sung by 'Tutti i Tenori e Bassi' on the note d (which is given on a stave with a bass clef). At least some of the information about these verses given in 9 may come from one of these sources.

The third manuscript in this group, MS. M. Deneke Mendelssohn d.70 (12), has only come to light relatively recently, having been donated to the Bodleian Library, Oxford, by a descendant of the composer in 1973. It is in the hand of Franz Xaver Gleichauf, a Frankfurt music teacher and Bach enthusiast who came into the family circle because of the help he gave the composer with

---

[18] The Vatican terms, at least in the nineteenth century, are generally *Concertone* (a5) and *Concertino* (a4).

[19] 'con tutti quelli ornamenti come si canta nella capella sistina nel giorni Mercoldi [sic], Giovedi e Venerdi della Settimana santa'.

his edition of Bach organ works in 1845–6. The descriptions and the musical texts are the same as those found in **10** and **11**, but it lacks the note D in the instruction concerning the monotone verses. Like **10**, it gives verse 20b in Alfieri's version,[20] although it reverses the order of the two choirs on the page compared to that edition. There are also rhythms given for the reciting chords of each verse, but they are incompetently done by a non-latinist (verse 3: *ab inquitate* for *ab iniquitate*, verse 20b: *oblatum* for *oblationem*). Interestingly, the manuscript also includes the same settings of the Lamentations, by Allegri and Palestrina, that are found in Mesplet's manuscript described in Chapter 6, although they do not appear to derive from that source. None of these three manuscripts use either the * or the 'dumb-bell' symbol found in the others, although in **10** and **11** these places are marked with an x in verse 20a only.

While it is certain that all these sources are interconnected, their lineage is far from clear. The two German-derived complete manuscripts **3** and **4** are puzzling insofar as most of the obvious errors occur in the first two verses and are corrected in later ones. For example, in bar 3 of verse 3 every single source except **2** (and **1**, which is very different at this point) gives $c''d''c''e(\flat)''$ for notes 2–5 of soprano 1, and every one changes it to $c''d''b(\flat)'d''$ in the later verses (except of course **10–12**, which give verses 1, 3 and 20 only). One might think therefore that **3** and **4** could be based on the Klein derived **6–9**, which also give these differing readings in verses 3 and 7, except that those sources also contain a blatant error, unique to them, in the following bar (the first note in soprano 2 is *m.*, which means that the subsequent semiquavers coincide with those in the alto part). And yet all these manuscripts have so much in common that they must have a common origin. Was it a Papal singer, as described in **3** and **4**? Did Klein really obtain his copy from the 'Kapellmeister' of the choir, as stated in **9**? Perhaps both these statements are true, as they could easily describe the same person.[21] In any case, it is unlikely that any of these sources were ever used for performance, so they must respond simply to musicological curiosity, showing vividly how much interest there was at this period in the *Miserere*

---

[20] See the end of Appendix 13 for further discussion of the different versions of verse 20b.

[21] Kantner and Pachovsky, *L'Ottocento* gives a list of the *maestri pro tempore* in appendix 9 (271), but there is no suggestion that any of those from these years faced any particular problems with their positions, as they surely would have done if Baini had been aware of them giving away the choir's precious archives (see Chapters 6 and 10). The *maestro pro tempore* in 1824 was Don Francesco Tifoni (1771–1848), a tenor who joined the choir in 1803. He was described after his death as 'an excellent colleague who was untiring in his duties, and in short was blessed with that rare combination, a true gentleman distinguished by a priestly character' ('ottimo collega istancabile à' suoi doveri, e dotato insomma di tutte quelle rare prerogative, che costituiscono il vero galantuomo, insignato del carattere sacerdotale')., Ibid., 186.

and its performance by the Papal Choir. That being the case, it is telling that they are all based on Allegri's *Miserere*, little performed by the choir in the nineteenth century compared to Bai's (see Chapter 10). The power of the title 'Allegri's *Miserere*' for those collectors is clear.

For the edition of **A**, it is **2** – Add. 31525(2) – that gives the most reliable readings for all verses. Despite his evident haste, its scribe was clearly musical, and capable of hearing what he was writing and checking it. I have therefore given it precedence. Appendix 9 gives a transcription of verses 1, 3 and 5, noting such variants as there are between sources **1**–**4**. As **1** provides a unique reading of verse 3, I have included it as Appendix 10, despite its being generally less satisfactory musically than the others.

✳ Different singers, different ornaments

The evolution from the versions given by the manuscripts in Manchester, Paris and Milan (and Alfieri, which although later appears to give largely an earlier version) to these ones is shown mostly in the presence of extra passing notes, and a tendency towards smoother vocalises rather than short ornaments. We can see this process already underway in **Mil**, described in Chapter 6. These features may be related to the presence in the choir at this time of the famous *castrato* Don Mariano Padroni (b. 1776), who had been admitted to the choir in 1801. He was heard by G.L.P. Sievers in 1824, Mendelssohn in 1831, Nicolai in 1839 and, probably, Fanny Hensel in 1840, by which time he must have been around sixty-four. This fine singer, to whom we owe (via a letter of Mendelssohn) the 'top C phrase' with which the *Miserere* is now associated (Ex. 6), sang, according to a witness in 1826, with 'a beautiful simplicity'. His ornamentation was never 'in the slightest degree inconsistent with the dignity of the subject', and his 'art of swelling and diminishing the tones by almost imperceptible gradations' was widely admired. Sievers wrote that he had thought that Mariano's voice was finished when he previously heard him singing oratorio, but in the *Miserere* he provided

> a triumph of the real art of singing … who can imagine my surprise when, from the first measure of the *Miserere*, he showed the smoothness of his voice, the way he had of carrying it, and a solidity of the sound, in comparison with which all voices I have heard before are but outbursts of the roughest nature? My admiration mounted with each measure – I would even say with every note, and if I had less self-control and more fantasy, I would have taken Mariano's singing for the voice of an angel, coming from

the clouds ... How much comes from him and how much from his predecessors I cannot say, but each of his *abbellimenti* reflects the nobility of the subject.[22]

The part of Sievers' article concerning *castrati* was summarised and expanded in *The Parthenon* in 1826. Describing him as 'almost 50 years of age', the article continues:

> Mariano has the greatest compass. He sings only ... on extraordinary occasions, and enjoys a very high reputation in Rome. The impression he produces in singing the *Miserere*, is said to be wonderful ... there is a beautiful simplicity in Mariano's execution. He introduces no ornament, in the slightest degree inconsistent with the dignity of the subject. A foreign musical critic, whose Essay on the State of Music in Italy, has furnished us with many of the facts we here state, points out the following, as the only passage to which, on hearing Mariano sing the *Miserere*, he thought a more serious character might have been given.[23]

Fig. 18 Mariano's 'frivolous' ornament

---

[22] 'Mariano's Vortrag ist der Triumph der wahren Singkunst ... Wer schildert mein Erstaunen, als er gleich im ersten Tacte des Miserere einen Schmelz des Organs, ein Tragen der Stimme, ja eine Gediegenheit des Klanges hören liess, gegen welche mir alle bisher gehörten Stimmen nur Ausbruch der rohesten ungebildetsten Naturen gewesen zu sein schienen? Meine Bewunderung steig mit jedem Tacte, ich möchte sagen mit jedem Tone, und wenn mir weniger kaltes Blut und mehr Phantasterei eigen wäre, ich hätte den Gesang dieses Mariano wirklich für eine Engelstimme, aus den Wolken erschallend, nehmen können ... Wie viel von dem, was Mariano als Melodie vorträgt, sein, oder ihm von seinen Vorgängern überliefert worden ist, vermag ich nicht zu bestimmen, aber wohl behaupte ich, dass keine seiner Verzierungen, der Würde des auszudrückenden Gegenstandes unangemessen sind.' Sievers, 'Das Miserere von Allegri' (see p. 98, n. 47.), 78–9.

[23] Anon, 'Soprano singers', *The Parthenon, a magazine of Art and Literature* N°2 (18 June 1826), 29. Sievers described the phrase as 'zu galant' – by which he presumably meant too frivolous (or perhaps too theatrical) – in other words, not sufficiently serious.

It is interesting that Sievers picked out for disapproval a variation of the very phrase which made the reputation of the *Miserere*! It will be noted, from comparison with the phrases Mariano sang for Mendelssohn (see below) and Nicolai (reproduced in Chapter 10), as well as the two versions in Add. 31525, that he seems to have made a point of varying it every year.

Mariano was also admired by the German writer Franz Kandler, in an article published under the title 'Present State of Music in Rome' in *The Harmonicon* of 1828. His words are clearly derived from Sievers.

> Of all the sopranos in the Pontifical chapel, Mariano Patroni [sic] is the most esteemed. Though now at an advanced age, he still continues to sing, though it is only on musical solemnities of importance. The delicate *chiaroscuro* of his song, and his art of swelling and diminishing the tones by almost imperceptible gradations, constitute this singer's chief merit; added to which, his perfect knowledge of musical tradition, of the manner in which the master-pieces of the old composers are to be given, render him the soul of the chapel, and cause him to be looked upon by his brethren as a kind of oracle of music.[24]

There is no doubt that Mariano was something of a *prima donna*. Almost immediately after the restoration of the choir in 1814 he attempted to retire, no doubt to follow a more lucrative career as a singer of oratorio. His colleagues were distraught, convinced that his capacity to sing very high solos was irreplaceable. Finally a compromise was reached, whereby he sang only at Christmas and Easter. This he did until 1843. Mendelssohn noted in 1831 that 'he came from the mountains to Rome expressly to sing on this occasion, and it is to him I owe hearing the *embellimenti* with their highest notes'.[25] In 1840 it can be supposed that it was Mariano who impressed Fanny Hensel in the *Improperia*. 'It sounded very soft and sweet, partly because the first soprano, though very powerful, was particularly sweet in tone.'[26] After that he gradually withdrew, first from the Christmas offices, then from those of Easter. In 1846 he was excused the *Miserere* as well, and he died the following year.

A preliminary note on pitch

The example in *The Parthenon* is given in B♭, a minor third higher than written pitch. Observant readers will already have noted that the first chord transcribed

---

[24] *The Harmonicon*, (1828), 151. The article was published in three extracts. It was also translated into French in volume 3 of Fetis's *Revue Musicale* (1828).

[25] Letter to Zelter, 6 June 1831, in *Letters*, 142. See also Kantner and Pachovsky, *L'Ottocento*, 171–2.

[26] Hensel, *The Mendelssohn Family*, Vol. 2, 98, and see p. 133.

by Spohr in 1817 (Ex. 2 in Chapter 7), complete with the 'disgraceful' parallel fifths, was a fourth higher, in C. By the nineteenth century, the *Miserere* seems to have been habitually subject to upward transposition of at least a third. Although the first printed reference to the practice is found in Alfieri's edition of 1840, witnesses attest to it from at least 1792.

On Wednesday of Holy Week.
The famous *Miserere* by Allegri was today sung for the first Feast [of Tenebrae] in the pontifical *Capella Sistina*. I hope they sing it better tomorrow and the day after when the Pope will be there, today they sang very badly and lost pitch so that having started in *B flat* they finished in *F#*.[27]

In 1815 the French composer Herold heard it in C.[28] On the title page of Add. 31525(2) is a pencilled note probably in Joseph Warren's hand, which reads, 'It ought to be sung four tones higher – in C.' It is this transposition which gives the soloist a top C, during the first part of the verses a4, and is the reason which there is one in Mendelssohn's famous phrase heard in the 'English Miserere' nowadays.

Ex. 6 Mendelssohn's transcription of the *embellimenti* sung in the Misereres of Allegri and Bai (letter to Professor Zelter, 16 June 1831)

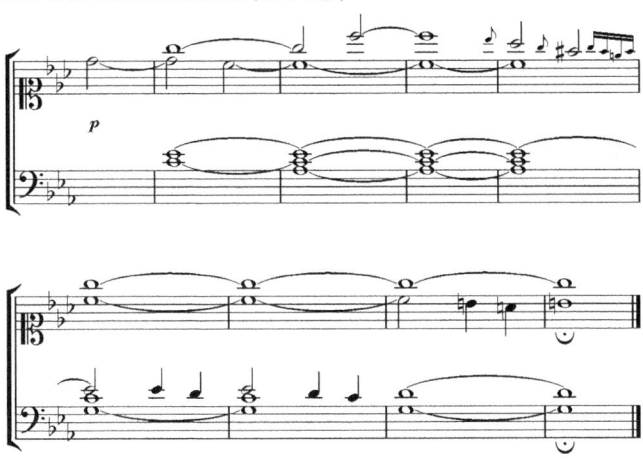

---

[27] '*Am Mittwoch der Heiligen Woche. Das berühmte Miserere von Allegri ward heute zum ersten Mahl in der päbstlichen Capella sistina abgesungen. Ich hoffe sie singen es morgen und übermorgen, wenn der Pabst gegenwärtig seyn wird, besser Heute sangen sie sehr falsche und zogen so herunter, dass sie die B angefangne Musik in Fis schlossen.*' 'Briefe aus Rom 6', *Musikalisches Wochenblatt*, ed. J.F. Reichardt, Vol. 1, N°10, 76 (the entire journal was repr. in *Studien für Tonkünstler und Musikfreunde ... fürs Jahre 1792*, Berlin, 1793, with the original pagination preserved). The writer had already complained about the tuning of the castrati in his previous communication (N°9, 66).

[28] See p. 158. Herold also noted a serious loss of pitch.

Ex. 7 Fanny Mendelssohn's transcription of part of the *Improperia* as heard in 1840 (Hensel, *The Mendelssohn Family*, 98)

It is not clear how old this tradition was, or why it began. It should be noted too that it did not apply only to the *Miserere*; Mendelssohn's phrase from the *Improperia* (Ex. 3 in Chapter 7) is also transposed a fourth higher than the written key. When Mendelssohn's sister Fanny heard it in 1840, it started higher still before sinking (Ex. 7). Like Herold and her brother, Fanny observed that the choir could not maintain this pitch. 'They began the "Miserere" on Thursday and the "Improperie" on Friday in B, and ended in G minor; indeed, on Friday it was almost F minor.'[29] Further discussion will have to wait until Chapter 10, when we examine Alfieri's publication and, particularly, Chapter 15. It can be noted here however, that in 1824, when the transposition was 'only' a minor third, Mariano profited from the lower pitch to take his phrase higher than ever, up to D♭.

---

[29] Hensel, *The Mendelssohn Family*, Vol. 2, 97.

10

Nineteenth-century sources 2 – Alfieri's *Il Salmo Miserere* of 1840

✳ A 'secret' publication

AFTER Burney's publication of 1771, there was no new edition of the *Miserere* until 1838, when the Paris publication (described in Chapter 6) briefly appeared. But the next was not long in coming. In 1840 the Vatican publisher Pietro Alfieri (1801–63) issued *Il Salmo Miserere posto in musica da Gregorio Allegri e da Tommaso Bai, Publicato cogli Abbellimenti per la prima volta*. It is significant because it is the only one by a Roman editor, although Alfieri published it 'incognito' under the name of Alessandro Geminiani, and in Lugano, Switzerland, rather than in Rome.[1]

Perhaps he doubted that permission for it would be given by the Vatican authorities, and so decided to pre-empt their refusal. It seems he was right. The following year, perhaps ill at ease with his subterfuge, he asked to be allowed to publish in Rome. In a modified preface he attempted to argue precedent, as well as repeating the argument already made in his Lugano publication concerning the need for explanations.

> Publications similar to these were made last century by Dr Charles Burney in England, together with all the other pieces sung in the Apostolic Chapel during Holy Week, since they were given to him by a certain Giuseppe Santarelli, soprano of the said Chapel. But now, since copies can no longer be found, and imprecise copies are circulating in divers parts of the world, and [which are] deprived of the necessary clarifications, I thought it would be good to republish them with the greatest diligence.[2]

---

[1] 'Alessandro Geminiani' takes the first name of Alfieri's father and the family name of his mother. The publication can be consulted online at http://hz.imslp.info/files/imglnks/usimg/b/b5/IMSLP279617-PMLP453942-alfieri_il_salmo_miserere_1840.pdf, which is taken from the copy in the British Library (catalogued as G.539). See also p. 152 and n. 13.

[2] 'Cotali produzioni furono publicate nello scorso secolo del Dottore Carlo Burney in Inghilterra con tutte le altre composizioni della Settimana Santa, che cantansi nella Cap[pella] Ap[ostolica] per avergliele date certo Giuseppe Santarelli soprano della menzionata Cappella. Ora però non rinvenendose

As Alfieri must have expected, the authorities immediately showed the projected publication to Baini, who did not mince his words in his reply to Padre Domenico Buttaoni, Master of Ceremonies of the Apostolic Palace.

The two Misereres in the Pontifical Chapel, of whose renown everyone is familiar, had always been jealously guarded in the Chapel archive. A *castrato*, G. Santarelli, found the means of copying them secretly and sold them to an English Jew, C. Burney, who immediately had them printed in London for huge profit. This betrayal greatly displeased Rome, and it even displeased the Pontiff himself – Clement XIII – who, if he hadn't been prevented by dying, would have given Santarelli the punishment he deserved. From that day until now all music publishers sell either in print or lithograph or manuscript the two aforementioned Misereres. Today it carries on and another of our colleagues, Signor ____, made friends with Signor Alfieri and crudely betrayed the Chapel for similar interests. Santarelli sold to the Jew the bare notes, the skeleton of the two Misereres. Signor ____ sold to Alfieri the *adornamenti*, which by aural tradition have dressed them, and which I taught to Signor ____, some of which he was never able to reproduce with his voice. In consequence how could Signor Alfieri have understood them were it not that they had been executed for many years defectively by his associate? How could he even have written them if he had not understood them? Furthermore, the same Signor ____ sold to Alfieri private information of our College known only to us and that Signor Alfieri published by an invasive statement in his preface. What shameful thirst for gain among men of the Church! To betray those who fed him! And sell what was given to him as a secret in good faith for base, personal gain![3]

---

più esemplari, e girando per le varie parti del Mondo delle inesatte copie, e scuore [? = prive] dei necessari schiarimenti ho creduto di ristamparli con ogni diligenza.' This text is preserved in CS 658, fol. 42^v–42^r.

[3] 'Li due Miserere della Cap[pella] Pont[ificia] di quella fama che ognun sa, erano stati sempre conservati gelosamente nell'Archivio della Capp[ella]. Un tal musico evirato G. Santarelli trovato il mezzo di nascostamente copiarli, li vendè ad un ebreo inglese C. Burney, che tosto li fe' stampare in Londra con immenso lucro. Questo tradimento dispiacque a Roma, e dispiacque eziandio al som[mo] pont[efice] Clemente 13, che se non era impedito dalla morte, voleva darne al Santarelli il merito gastigo. Da quell'epoca fino al di d'oggi tutte le copisterie di musica vendono sia in istampa, sia in litografia, sia in m[ano] s[critto] i due cit[ate] Miserere. Oggi il progresso va innanzi, ed un altro n[os]tro collega il s^r ____ fatta amistà con il s[igno]r Alfieri tradisce per simile interesse più crudamente la Cappella. Il Santarelli vendè all' ebreo le note semplici, le scheletto dei due miserere ; il s^r ____ vende all'Alfieri gli adornamenti, onde per tradizione verbale sono rivestiti: adornamenti, che io insegnai al s^r ____, ed alcuni de' quali egli mai non seppe con la voce eseguire ; in conseguenza come mai il s[igno]r Alfieri li ha intesi se non sono stati eseguiti da molti anni per

A further letter to a more senior cleric – Monsignor Francesco Saverio Massimo, Secretary of State and Prefect of the Apostolic Palace – shows even more animosity, and suggests that Alfieri had tried to publish in Rome previously.

> Since last year Alfieri has been boasting that he is printing and publishing the two Misereres of Allegri and Bai together with those *adornamenti* that show exactly what is sung in the Papal Chapel. Some of the more zealous among us notified at once the worthy Padre Maestro Buttaoni, complaining against the attack of Alfieri wanting to publish our private compositions, begging him to prevent such audacity. On learning about this complaint and petition, Alfieri went silent. This year, he has spread around the same news, saying that he would print the two Misereres with explanations and the *adornamenti* that are used in the Chapel, now that he knows them all; and adding that to prevent another attempted interdiction, had already commissioned the printing in Florence; he would finally rend the veil, and reveal its secret, and the monopoly of the Chapel, now decrepit and ancient, would make way for the progress of today. Faced with such threatening words there was a real fear that any day would bring the news of the sale of the two Misereres even here in Rome.[4]

---

difetto del suo socio? Come mai li ha potuti scrivere se non li ha intesi? Di più il medesimo s^r ___ vende all' Alfieri alcune notizie interni del n[os]tro Coll[egi]o, note a noi soli, e chi il s[igno]r Alfieri pubblica per invasione profetica nella sua prefazione. Vergognosa sete di guadagno in persone ecclesiastiche ! Tradir chi lo ha sfamato ! e vender ciò che gli fu affidato segretamente in buona fede per onore proprio e commune!' Letter addressed to Il p[adre] F.D. Buttaoni, Maestro del S[acro] Palazzo Apostolico, 30 March 1841, CS 658, fol. 45^r–45^v. It is reproduced in Kantner and Pachovsky, *L'Ottocento*, 208. There is no evidence that Burney was of Jewish descent, or that Santarelli asked for money, except perhaps to reimburse copyists. Baini's exaggerated indignation gives an idea of what his reaction could have been to the Paris publication of 1838.

[4] 'Fin dall'anno scorso si vanta l'Alfieri di far imprimere e pubblicare i due Miserere dell'Allegri e del Bai con quegli adornamenti co' quali precisamente si cantano nella Capp[ella] Pont[ificia]. Alcuno più zelante dei nostri si presenta tosto al lod[ato] p[adre] m[aes]tro Buttaoni reclamando contro l'attentato dell'Alfieri di voler pubblicare le nostre privative composizioni, e pregandolo di impedire tanta audacia. Risaputosi il reclamo e la petizione, l'Alfieri si tacque. Quest'anno ha egli sparsa l'istessa voce, dicendo che farebbe imprimere i due Miserere con gli adornamenti e con le avvertenze che si usano nella Capp[ella], essendogli oggi noto il tutto; ed aggiungendo, che affine di evitare un nuovo ricorso ad inibizione, ne aveva commessa già la stampa a Firenze; onde finalmente squarcierebbe il velo, si paleserebbe il segreto, e la privativa della Capp[ella] ormai decrepitamente invecchiata darebbe luogo all'attuale progresso. Dietro cotali minacciose parole si stava in qualche timore di sentire di giorno in giorno la vendita dei due Miserere anche qui in Roma.' Letter addressed to Monsignor Francesco Saverio de' Principi Massimo, maggiord [omo] di

He reiterated his argument that Alfieri's publication would traduce the choir because it was not well done.

> The two Misereres of Allegri and Bai which are heard every year in the Papal Chapel are executed with many exquisite *abbellimenti* that never have been written down, so that they cannot be communicated to anyone, and which are handed down by tradition from singer to singer; they are the most beautiful romantic compositions that are known in the *stile osservato*. They have for two centuries formed the glory of august papal functions, and some of the greatest pontiffs have on occasion glorified in them; they have ever been the delight of listeners of every class and every nation; and have gained the admiration of many outstanding amateurs of music from all over Europe who have come to Rome to hear them.
>
> Now Alfieri claims that he can print them and by boasting of being the first to publish them, he has reduced them to a state of misery and indecency, such as to bring shame upon the Chapel, the pontifical functions, and the fame that they have always deservedly enjoyed. Just so that Alfieri can make money from the curious with this novelty, and to be seen as another Columbus, but of music. I see no other reason. Oh! how much better it would have been if he had continued to sit with his father on the little bench in Scarpinello, resoling the shoes of the population, rather than playing at being a scientific arranger continuously disfiguring the works of others, only for financial gain.[5]

---

n[ostro] s[ignore], e prefetto de' s[acri] p[alazzi] a[postolici]', 4 April 1841, CS 658, fols. 48ʳ–49ʳ. Reproduced in Kantner and Pachovsky, *L'Ottocento*, 209–10. Copies at least of the Lugano edition did in fact arrive in Rome during 1841, as is shown by the note on a manuscript of the Allegri now in the British Library (Mus. MS Add. 31395), 'bought by me at Rome in the Corso, 1841, Frederick Blaydes Ch. Ch. Oxon.' Add. 31395 is an exact manuscript copy of Alfieri's edition, although without the page of *abbellimenti*.

[5] 'Li due Miserere dell'Allegri e del Bai che ci ascoltano ogni anni nella Capp[ella] Pont[ificia] sono eseguiti con molti e squisiti abbellimenti che mai non sono stati scritti affinché non possano comunicarsi a veruno, e si tramandono per tradizione in voce de cantore in cantore; essi sono le più belle composizioni sentimentali che si conoscano nello stile osservato. Hanno da due secoli formato la gloria delle auguste funzioni pontificie, e se ne sono gloriati alla circostanza anche più sommi pontefici; sono mai sempre stati la delizia di tutti gli uditori di ogni ceto e di ogni nazion; ed hanno riscosso l'ammirazione di quanti insigni Intendenti di Musica di tutta Europa, sono venuti in Roma e bearsene.

Ora l'Alfieri pretende di farli imprimere, e vantandosi di essere il primo a pubblicarli, li ha ridotti ad uno stato di miseria e di sconcezza da far onta alla Cappella, alle funzioni pontificie, alla fama che han sempre meritamente goduto. Basta all'Alfieri di poter trarre danaro dai curiosi Con la novità, e di esser egli tenuto un altro Colombo in musica, non gli cale di altro. Oh! quanto

And he repeated his accusation against an unidentified member of the choir.

> I looked at it all and noticed that only one of our colleagues could have revealed some of Alfieri's explanations; I knew however also that the traitor was poorly informed, most likely because he knew no more. In fact, instead of the many beautiful *adornamenti* that we execute, I saw there a wretched sketch of a few *diminuzioni* out of the context of their clear naturalness, impoverished by the limits of a constant tempo: moreover I read in the preface some explanations, some false and some offensive to our Chapel, hence I replied immediately to Padre Maestro Buttaoni on 31 March, insisting especially on the deceit that was about to be played on the public, and the offence our Chapel, and via that the sovereign Pontiff, would receive if Alfieri is allowed to print the two Misereres.[6]

He finished with a flourish:

> That Alfieri be authoritatively prohibited from printing the two Misereres, so as not to deceive the public; and not to tarnish the honour of God, the supreme Pontiff, and the Chapel. And if he dares have them printed out of Rome, as he has already boasted, he should even be threatened with imprisonment.[7]

> meglio avrebbe egli continuato a sedere con suo padre al piccolo banco di Scarpinello, e risolare i scarponi dei popolanti, laddove con voler recitare da scienziato raffazzona di continuo le opere altrui sfigurandole alla peggio, solo che possa trarne lucroso partito.' Ibid., 210.

[6] 'Osservai il tutto e mi avvidi, che solo un n[os]tro collega poteva aver palesato all'Alfieri alcune avvertenze; conobbi pero insieme, che il traditore lo aveva mezzanamente informato, forsi, e senza forsi, perché non ne sapeva di più. Di fatto, in luogo di trovare gli adornamenti molti, e bellissimi che da noi vi si eseguiscono, vi riscontrai un cenno miserabile di poche diminuzioni fuori anche della loro franca naturalezza, ed impoverite dai limiti del tempo sempre equale: di più lessi nella prefaz[ion]e avvertimenti parte falsi, parte offensivi della n[os]tra Cappella, onde risposi tosto al p[adre] m[aestro] Buttaoni in dat[a] dei 31 marzo p[rossimo] p[assato], insistendo specialmente sull' inganno che si preparava al pubblico e sull'offesa che ne riceverebbe la Capp[ella] ed in essa sovrano Pontefice se si permettesse all'Alfieri la stampa del due Miserere.' Quite how Baini could identify the one member of the choir who could not only give information to Alfieri, but moreover do it badly, is not clear. Ibid., 209.

[7] 'Si proibisca autorevolmente all'Alfieri di stampare i due Miserere, onde non sia ingannato il pubblico; e non ne patisca l'onore di Dio, del som[mo] pontefice, e della Cappella. E se ardisse egli di farli stampare fuori di Roma, come già si è vantato, gli si minacci eziandio l'ergastolo.' Ibid., 210.

✳ Layout, musical content and sources

Baini's description of Alfieri's publication, 'a wretched sketch of a few *diminuzioni* out of the context of their clear naturalness', is not unjust, for his edition is a strange one. Instead of complete usable scores of the two Misereres with their ornaments written out, as in the manuscripts contributing to Source **A**, it provides merely undecorated versions of them based on CS 340–1, by this time the standard Papal Choir text (it is the only printed edition in the nineteenth century to do so, all others being based upon Burney's amended scores). At the end is a page of appendices, identified by letters, showing the *abbellimenti* to be sung in the four-part verses of each. Each appendix gives all four parts. One set is for the Allegri, the first for the half-close in the middle of the verse (letter **A**), and the other for the final cadence (letter **B**). Another set is provided for the Bai, consisting of three endings, one for the half-close (letter **C**) and two for the final cadence, the first for verse 7 (letter **D**) and the second for verse 19 (letter **E**). Equivalent letters are marked in the full scores to show where they should be sung. Strikingly, these ornaments are virtually identical for the two Misereres: *abbellimento* **A** is the same as **C**, and except for the first bar, which provides a bridge, *abbellimento* **B** is the same as **D** and **E**. This can be seen clearly in Appendix 11, and is a measure of the extent to which Bai's *Miserere* was written around the *abbellimenti* already used in Allegri's and also remained connected to it. The letters given in the full score are incomplete and often wrong, especially in the Bai. In the British Library copy most have been corrected by hand.[8]

Two autograph manuscripts which Alfieri clearly used to prepare his publication are now in the Staatsbibliothek, Berlin, under the call signs Mus. ms. 550/2 and Mus. ms. Alfieri 1.[9] Mus. ms. 550/2 gives the unadorned texts of both Misereres, to which have been added dynamics and other indications, e.g. *Largo* at the beginning, *tutti* before the verses a5 and *soli* before the verses a4, all of which appear in the printed edition. It is noticeable that the *lacunæ* of underlay in this manuscript and in the print are almost identical. The main variations in comparison to CS 340–1 concern the underlay at the ends of verses, in which the final syllables of held notes are aligned with the resolutions of dissonances in other parts.[10] We cannot know exactly from which sources Alfieri worked, as it is clear that Baini saw to it that he did not have direct access

---

[8] In his revised preface (see p. 147) Alfieri mentioned only four letters, **A** to **D**, so one assumes that he made some modifications, and perhaps corrections, to the scores he wished to republish as well as to the introduction. Unfortunately the revised scores have not been found.

[9] They are described in Amann, *Allegris Miserere*, 109 and 108, respectively, but without identifying Alfieri as the scribe.

[10] Presumably these are modifications by Alfieri himself. In both Misereres, it is not done in later verses, as if he forgot as he went along, and some of the

to the Papal Choir archive. Apart from different versions of verse 20b in both Misereres (that given for the Bai shows considerable variants, mostly tending towards simplification), the differences are so slight that they must have been very close to the Papal Choir, perhaps another Vatican establishment such as the *Cappella Giulia*, which also performed the Misereres in Holy Week.[11]

Mus. ms. Alfieri 1 is part of a collection of twenty-five manuscripts from Alfieri's estate acquired by the Staatsbibliothek from the Roman bookseller Josef Spithöver in 1874. They are in two groups, and Alfieri 1 is the first of twelve entitled *Raccolta di Musica Sacra*, no doubt made largely in preparation for his publication of seven volumes under that title from 1841 to 1846.[12] Among its forty-seven works spread over 416 pages are two ornamented versions of verses 1 and 3 – the first (**a**, pp. 63–6) marked *Miserere di Gregorio Allegri con abbellimenti* and the second (**b**, pp. 67–70) *Il medesimo Miserere di Allegri con altri abbellimenti*. Both are based upon the plain version found in Mus. ms. 550/2. As will be seen by the composite transcription in Appendix 12, the ornaments are virtually identical to those reproduced in Alfieri's appendix, although the notation sometimes varies (e.g. in bars 13–14 and 24–6, where appoggiaturas effectively give the same reading as *q.sq*). Despite the fact that Mus. ms. 550/2 is not part of the Alfieri collection in the Staatsbibliothek, and that his autograph hand is unacknowledged in the catalogue, the link between these two manuscripts is clear. It is underlined further by the presence of some ornamentation (*appoggiature* and *gruppetti*) from both **a** and **b** in verse 1 only of the Allegri in Mus. ms. 550/2, added in lighter pen or pencil, as well as a series of *appoggiature* in verse 11 (a4) of the Bai.

It is odd that the prosody of the chanted sections of the Allegri which appear in the print is missing in Mus. ms. 550/2. One wonders if Alfieri's basic sources of both Misereres gave only a breve, as some of the rhythms in the manuscript of the Bai have clearly been added later from CS 340–1, or from someone who knew it. Perhaps this caused Alfieri to add some to a lost final copy of the Allegri sent to the printer – it is noticeable that they are often very similar in the two Misereres, and he underlines in his preface how important he thinks it is to interpret these sections correctly.

---

earlier ones show signs of having been 'corrected'. The printed edition carefully reproduces these variations.

[11] If that is indeed the case, and given that Bai finished his career as *maestro* of that *Cappella*, it may be that Alfieri's publication preserves an earlier, perhaps the original, form of verse 20b.

[12] Catalogued as Mus. ms. Alfieri 1–12, information about them is available only in a handwritten catalogue of autographs and manuscripts in the rare music reading room. The other thirteen manuscripts, all of which contain only Alfieri's own compositions, are known as Mus. ms. autogr. Alfieri, P. 1–13 M, and details are available on *RISM*, http://www.rism.info/home.html. My thanks to Birgit Busse and Marina Gordienko of the Staatsbibliothek for their detailed explanations.

It is also necessary to know ... that the long notes (some of which I have reduced to measure) which from time to time return now in the beginning now in the middle of the verses, are not to be beaten in exact time but are to be regulated according to the number and sense of the words.[13]

It is not clear why Alfieri did not simply incorporate the ornaments found in Mus. ms. Alfieri 1 in the framework supplied by Mus. ms. 550/2 for his edition, rather than the awkward 'mix and match' version he produced. Even if he had given them only in verses 1 and 3 of the Allegri, the extra information supplied – the parallel fifths on the reciting chords (as in **P**, **Man**, **Mil** and **M**), the many *appoggiature* and *gruppetti* in both verses and the *abbellimenti* in 'the context of their clear naturalness' – would have made his edition immeasurably more valuable, as well as placing it more clearly in the progression of the other sources detailed in these pages.[14]

Perhaps he was simply trying to protect his source. If so, he seems to have succeeded, as Baini's letters make clear that he believed that Signor ___ sang the music to Alfieri, rather than writing it down for him.[15] Quite how the renegade singer could have sung the decorations in all four parts is unexplained. Baini's criticism of the printed ornaments as lacking the freedom and 'naturalness' necessary to a good interpretation is an interesting musical comment, but at the same time it shows the extent of his confusion. It seems in any case that he succeeded in forestalling a Roman publication, and perhaps he never

---

[13] 'E' necessario poi sapere ... che le note lunghe (alcune delle quali ho ridotto a misura) che di quando in quando ritrovansi or nel principio, ed or nel mezzo de' versetti, non vanno in battuta esatta, ma vengono regolato secondo la moltitudine, ed il senso delle parole.' The translation given here is that found with the copy in the British Library, written at 'Swift's Court, 15 Castle Street, Liverpool' during the 1860s (and reproduced on *IMSLP*; see n. 1 above). The 1841 version says the same thing, slightly rephrased, see n. 2.

[14] As far as the Allegri is concerned, Mus. ms. Alfieri 1 is striking for giving the same ornamentation as the alternative version in **P** for the duet at the end of verse 3, as **M** for the first soprano at bars 22–3 in the same verse, and as **A** at bars 6–8 in verse 1. As for the Bai, in the absence of any other contemporary sources with ornamentation, the ornaments in verse 11 of Mus. ms. 550/2 are interestingly similar to those given by Mustafà in 1892 described in Chapter 12.

[15] 'Signor ___ sold to Alfieri the *adornamenti*, which by aural tradition have dressed them, and which I taught to Signor ___, some of which he was never able to reproduce with his voice. In consequence how could Signor Alfieri have understood them were it not that they had been executed for many years defectively by his associate? How could he even have written them if he had not understood them?'

knew of the Swiss one. It was only after his death in 1844 that Alfieri felt able to reveal the truth.[16]

The fact that unknown Papal singers were able to produce (or at least provide the information for) manuscripts such as Mus. ms. Alfieri 1 and the different versions of **A** provokes more questions about the material the singers themselves used to perform the *Miserere*, a subject already touched upon at the end of Chapter 7. One of Baini's first priorities when the choir was re-formed in 1814 after six years of inactivity was to prepare a performance of it – the climax of the choir's year – for 1815. In his long interview with G.L.P. Sievers, published in *Cäcilia* in 1825, Baini maintained that he was obliged to teach it to the singers from memory, having no manuscripts of it from which to work. Obviously he meant that he had no manuscripts of the *abbellimenti* from which to work, because there was no shortage of sources of the Misereres unadorned. He insisted moreover that in any case the *abbellimenti* of the Misereres had never been written down, and that the singers had always based their performances entirely on received aural tradition.

As noted in Chapter 7, this is very hard to believe. Maybe it was Baini's way of adding a bit more mystique to the legend of 'the Allegri', or perhaps he was trying to convey the message to would-be thieves that there was nothing to be stolen. It is even harder to believe in reference to 1815, when the singers of all the parts needed instruction. It has been suggested that singers may well have jotted down on loose sheets of paper ornamentation and other detail, or that those who prepared the copy for Mesplet in 1798 began by pooling their collective memory with such 'cribs'. In 1815 it seems most likely that, with the choirbooks as a basis, Baini used these *aide-mémoire*, and perhaps even created new ones from collective memory.

If that were so, it would explain the most curious thing about Alfieri's *abbellimenti*: their similarity to those found in **Man** and **P**. Particularly striking is the likeness between the alternative version (given in **P** only) of the duetting sopranos at the end of verse 3. Whatever the compilers of those manuscripts used in 1798, much of it was evidently still available in 1840, and therefore must also have been to Baini in 1815. Some of it was certainly a bit out of date by then: for example, in *abbellimento* **D**, there is no sign of the melodic phrase

---

[16] On the front cover of a manuscript copy of Alfieri's publication, now in the Biblioteca Greggiati, Ostiglia, near Mantua (Ms. Mus. B 2988), there is a note written by the copyist, Giuseppe Greggiati: 'This copy, made in Mantua 23 September 1851, revised by me, was taken from a printed exemplar lent to me by the Rev. Sac. Giovambattista Candotti, Master of the Chapel in Cividale in Friuli, on which was written in his hand: "Gift of the publisher Monsignor Pietro Alfieri, from Rome, hidden under a false name. September 1846".' ('Mantova 23 settembre 1851. Questa copia, riveduta da me, fu tratta da un esemplare stampato, prestatomi del Rev. Sacerd.ᵉ Giovambattista Candotti maestro di Cappella in Cividale del Friuli, sul quale era scritto di suo pugno, Dono dell'editore M.ʳ Pietro Alfieri Romano nascosto sotto falso nome. Settembre 1846.')

a′c″e♭″g′ in the second part of verse 3 found in the manuscripts of **A**, and even in **Mil**, which probably precedes them. The execution of the Misereres had moved on during the 1820s, under the influence of the main soprano, Mariano. But Alfieri, excluded from direct contact with the choir, was obliged to make do with what he could get. If some of it was no longer entirely up-to-date, no-one outside the Chapel would know.[17]

❋ The explanations

Alfieri attempted to make up for the (perhaps intentionally) limited musical information with two very important explanations, which seem to have made Baini positively incandescent. If the maintenance of secrecy about the Chapel's musical practices was his aim, it is easy to see why, because they give information vital for creating a modern performance. The wish to correct 'inexact manuscript copies without any explanations' was Alfieri's chief justification for his Lugano publication, and in his revised preface he implies that he is referring to pirated copies of Burney's edition, which does not give any practical information at all. It is the 'suitable explanations' of current performance practice that contain the main interest of Alfieri's publication, and certainly compensate for the impractical edition and the mostly relatively old ornaments. They concern performance pitch, and the relationship between the Misereres of Allegri and Bai.

Pitch

Alfieri writes that 'it is necessary to know that in the Chapel the key of G is sung as B'.[18] This is the first 'official' mention of upward transposition, confirming the accounts from witnesses already discussed in Chapter 9. Mendelssohn

---

[17] On the other hand the ornaments given in verse 3 (bb. 22–23 of version **b**) in Ms. Alfieri 1, and in his Ending **D**, are only otherwise found in Mustafa's manuscript (**M**) of 1892, which provokes other questions of the continuity of the tradition. One supposes that Baini was not accusing Mariano of being the conduit of information, partly because the different examples of his ornaments given above show that they were rarely the same as those that Alfieri prints. And it would be strange to accuse him of incompetence, given the mastery of which witnesses speak. However, it was Mariano who had sung the first soprano in the Chapel for the last twenty-five years, and so must have known them most intimately. One wonders if a controlling personality like Baini might not have resented Mariano's licence to sing only on important occasions.

[18] 'E necessario poi sapere, che nella predetta Cappella il tono G si converte in B del Diapason.' In the revised edition he uses this Guidonian nomenclature more precisely: 'E necessario poi sapere, che nella suddetta Cappella il tono di Sol convertesi in Bemi del Diapason.'

Ex. 8 First bar of Baini's *Miserere* in B minor transcribed by Mendelssohn

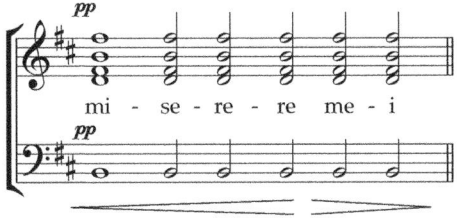

quoted the first bar in B minor in his letter to his family of 4 April 1831 (Ex. 8). In the letter to his teacher Professor Zelter on 16 June, which describes the different offices much more fully, it is clear that he was referring to the first evening, when the choir sang Baini's *Miserere*, but he adds, 'the key in which they sing depends on the purity of the voices. The first day it was in B minor, the second and third in C minor, but each time they finished almost in B flat minor.'[19]

This passage has always been read as 'the second and third in E minor'. The text, as reproduced most recently in Bärenreiter's new edition of the letters, reads 'den ersten Tag was es hmoll, den 2ten und dritten emoll'.[20] However, consultation of the original manuscript, now in Basel, shows that while it is easy to read 'emoll', 'cmoll' is correct (Fig. 19). In the words *canto* and *capella*, both used several times in the same letter, the initial *c* could often be easily read as *e* if the context did not exclude it, whereas there are no *es* at the beginning of words which are not entirely closed.

Fig. 19 Extract from Mendelssohn's letter of 16 June 1831 (Sammlung Rudolf Grumbacher, Basel, Mendelssohn letter Nr. 487)

The context also argues for C minor. Mendelssohn's transcription of the most famous phrase (Ex. 6 on p. 145) appears in the same letter, and clearly describes the second and/or the third evenings. 'The soprano [Mariano] intones the high C in a pure, soft voice, allowing it to vibrate for a time, then slowly glides down …'[21] Moreover, one would expect that such a large difference in pitch – a fourth – between the first and subsequent evenings would have provoked further comment from Mendelssohn, especially with such an extreme loss of pitch in performance – an augmented fourth, even greater than

---

[19] *Letters*, 142.
[20] Felix Mendelssohn Bartholdy, *Sämtliche Briefe*, vol. 2 (Kassel, 2009), 288.
[21] *Letters*, 141.

that (a major third) heard in 1792 (see p. 145). If this misreading is excluded, C minor remains the highest pitch for which there is any testimony.

The French composer Herold, who heard the *Miserere* in 1815, the year marking the restoration of the Pope to Rome and of the Papal Choir, was also struck both by the pitch and by problems of tuning. 'I was surprised that the singers sang so high. The first chord appeared to be C minor, the soprano beginning on G ... [by the end] I noticed that the singers had gone down by at least a tone.'[22] When Otto Nicolai heard Mariano in 1839, he noted the key *abbellimento* in B♭, with the ornamentation considerably modified (see Ex. 9).[23] The following year Mendelssohn's sister Fanny heard it in B minor,[24] and it has already been noted (in Chapter 9) that Spohr heard it sung in C minor in 1817 and Sievers in B♭ in 1824, and that Joseph Warren noted the necessity of transposing it a fourth higher in performance in his manuscript (British Library Add. 31525), which also dates from the mid-1820s.

Despite the fact that most of these accounts are from the nineteenth century, it seems likely that this tradition of upward transposition was already well established much earlier. Given that it existed in 1792, is there any reason to suppose that Mozart did not hear the *Miserere* in a very high key in 1770? What catalyst could have provoked such a practice and, most importantly, when? Could it even date from the seventeenth century? There is also the question of its general use: to how many other works did it apply? As noted in Chapter 7,

---

[22] 'J'ai été étonné que les chanteurs entonnassent si haut. Le 1er accord m'a paru être en *ut* mineur, le soprano commençant par sol ... J'ai remarqué que les chanteurs ont au moins baissé d'un ton.' *Lettres d'Italie*, 217. It is impossible to guess whether Herold based his estimation of pitch on that he had learned in Paris, and if so which of the many pitches there he was thinking of. According to Lassabathie (*Histoire du Conservatoire*, 54) the 'Ancien Ton du Conservatoire' in 1812 was A=460, but according to the researches of the Commission established by the French government in 1858, also recounted by Lassabathie (88–106), the Paris Opéra in 1821 was at around A=431, and pitches in other theatres and churches were all different. The evidence of the original pitches for many French organs suggests that *ton de chapelle* in that country was around A=392 from the beginning of the seventeenth century to at least the beginning of the nineteenth (Bruce Haynes, *A History of Performing Pitch: The Story of 'A'*, Lanham, MD, and Oxford, 2002, 97–8), probably very similar to church pitch in Rome and the Vatican (ibid., 69–75), although how aware Herold would have been of church pitch is a moot point. See Chapter 15 for more discussion.

[23] The transcription is from the second volume of his diaries (*Otto Nicolais Tagebücher*, ed. Wilhelm Altmann, Regensburg, 1937); reprinted in Konrad, 'Otto Nicolai', 124, and in Amann, *Allegris Miserere*, 45. For another version of this phrase by Mariano, again in B♭ minor but with a different ornament to give a higher top note, see Fig. 18 in Chapter 9.

[24] Hensel, *The Mendelssohn Family*, Vol. 2, 98.

Ex. 9 Nicolai's transcription of the *abbellimento* heard in 1839

Mendelssohn also heard Palestrina's *Improperia* transposed up a fourth, and his sister Fanny heard it even higher.[25] Alfieri wrote simply that 'in the Chapel the note G is sung as B'; he did not restrict this rule just to the *Miserere*. We shall consider all this in detail in Chapter 15.

The relation of Bai's Miserere *with that of Allegri*

As well as printing Bai's setting of the *Miserere* in the same volume (as Burney had done), Alfieri's edition shows clearly that the same ornamentation formulæ were applied to both works. It is evident that the use of the same decorations would tend to lead the public to believe that they were always listening to 'the Allegri', that being the name they knew. But the subterfuge went further.

> Though I do not know the reason, for many years they have not sung in order the verses in each piece but in the following manner. On both days [the two days on which Baini's *Miserere* was not given] is always sung for the *Primo coro*, which are the verses for five voices, those of Bai; with the verses for four voices, also known as the *Concertino*, [sung] as found in both compositions, excepting the verse *Amplius* of Bai, in place of which that of Allegri is sung; and finally the *Tunc imponent* of Bai for eight voices is repeated in that of Allegri.[26]

---

[25] Both Mendelssohns apparently had perfect pitch, so we can give credence to their accounts, although whether it was perfect pitch at A=440 is a moot point.

[26] '... ignorandone il motivo, da molti anni non si cantano con ordine i versetti in ciascuna composizione, ma nel modo seguente. Si canta sempre in ciascuno de' due giorni per primo Coro chè è il versetto a cinque voci quello di Bai; rimanendo il versetto a quattro ossia Concertino come si ritrova nell'una, e nell'altra composizione, eccetto il versetto Amplius de Bai, invece di cui si canta quello di Allegri; e per ultimo il tunc imponent a otto voce di Bai ripetesi in quello di Allegri.' In his revised preface of 1841, Alfieri slightly modified these phrases without changing the meaning: 'Si canta in ciascuno dei due giorni, il quale dipende dall'ambitrio dei Cantori per primo Coro, avice il versetto a cinque voci sempre quello di Bai, rimanendo tal quale il versetto a

In other words, in a performance of Allegri's *Miserere*, only the four-part verses would be his, the five-part verses being all Bai's. The final half-verse (*Tunc imponent*) would be sung twice, with Bai's setting added to Allegri's. When Bai's *Miserere* was sung, the first four-part verse, *Amplius lava me* (verse 3), would always be Allegri's, before a return to Bai's music for the rest. In both cases, all but the most informed listeners (such as Mendelssohn) would believe they were hearing 'Allegri's Miserere'. We note with surprise that this meant that the five-part verses attributed to Allegri were no longer performed at all. Neither was Bai's verse 3, and even if you knew both works intimately, you would have to wait until verse 7, the second four-part verse, before you could tell which composition the choir was 'officially' singing that day. It has to be said that Alfieri was hardly a master of the clear explanation, so questions remain about both his accuracy and his real meaning.[27] There is however enough to show a scheme seemingly created for little reason other than to provoke confusion. Given that the fame of 'the Miserere' was intimately bound up with Allegri's name, perhaps this was the secret that Baini was keenest to keep.

The first specific mention of such a practice is in the *Diario Sistina* of 1822, when a *Miserere* was performed in a special concert for Friedrich Wilhelm III, King of Prussia. In that case the first two verses were Allegri's, and the rest Bai's.[28] The first documented performance of a mixed version during Holy Week took place in 1827: 'Tommaso Bai's wonderful *Miserere* was performed,

---

quattro ossia il Concertino nell'una, e nell'altra composizione fuori del versetto Amplius di Bai, invece di cui si canta quello di Allegri, e per ultimo il tunc imponent ad otto voci di Bai si ripete in quello di Allegri.' ('On each of the two days is sung, depending on the choice of the singers, the *primo Coro*, that is the verses for five voices, always that of Bai, with the verses for four voices, also known as the *Concertino*, as found in both compositions, except that in place of the verse *Amplius* by Bai, is always sung that of Allegri, and finally the *Tunc imponent* for eight voices of Bai is repeated in that of Allegri.') CS 658, fol. 42ᵛ. It should be noted that in all Vatican manuscripts *Primo coro* always designates the five-part verses, and *Secondo coro* the four-part ones. The mostly German sources of the 1820s which are the basis of **A** reverse this nomenclature.

[27] This reading assumes that when Alfieri used the term *Primo Coro*, he was referring to the *Concertone* group who sang all the five-part verses, and not just the first verse of the psalm. In this I have differed from the otherwise excellent translation found with the copy in the British Library (see n. 13), which reads, 'On both days is sung for the first chorus the verse for 5 voices of Bai.' For more on the settings of *Tunc imponent* (verse 20b), see p. 350.

[28] The King, together with other dignitaries, had come to Italy for the Congress of Verona, recently concluded. See *DS* 238 (1822), fols. 52–3 (15 December), reproduced in Kantner and Pachovsky, *L'Ottocento*, 217 (appendix II).

interspersed with some verses from Gregorio Allegri's.'[29] Mendelssohn recorded something similar in his letter of 16 June 1831 to Professor Zelter:

> The *Miserere* sung on the first day was that of Baini ... on the second they gave some extracts of Allegri and Bai, on Good Friday – all was Bai's ... However it is quite immaterial which they sing, for the embellishments are pretty much the same in all three. Each chord has its embellishments, and thus very little of the original composition can be detected.[30]

It can be seen that in this year at least the Allegri was not heard complete at all, and it seems likely that this had already become the norm. Other combinations of Allegri and Bai are recorded also, for example that noted in the *Diario Sistina* in 1835: 'they sang Allegri's *Miserere*, with the amazing *concertone* [the verses a5] by Bai'.[31] In 1851, they did the opposite, singing 'Bai's *Miserere* for the *concertino* [the verses a 4], and for the *concertone* [the verses a5] they used Allegri's.'[32] This is the version published in Rome in 1870 as part of a large collection of Holy Week music, mostly by Palestrina and Victoria.[33] It is also the one noted in one of the manuscript amendments made by *maestro* G.B. Baccellieri in 1849–50 in the facsimile reproduction of Adami's *Osservazioni*.[34]

---

[29] '[Fu cantato] il bellissimo *Miserere* di Tommaso Bai con alcuni versetti innestati di Gregorio Allegri.' *DS* 243, fol. 32^r, reproduced in Kantner and Pachovsky, *L'Ottocento*, 114, n. 184. A mixed version was also noted in *DS* in 1828, 1829, 1837 and 1840–2 (Kantner and Pachovsky, *L'Ottocento*, 102).

[30] *Letters*, 140. This appears to contradict his letter to his family of 4 April (1831) to his family, which, according to Selden-Goth's translation, reads: 'On Thursday ... some portions of the Miserere were taken from Baini, but the greater part was from Allegri ... On Friday ... they did Baini's Miserere, which they sang infinitely the best' (*Letters*, 125). However, verification of the original in the M. Deneke Mendelssohn collection of manuscripts (MS d.13, fols. 49–50) in the Bodleian Library, Oxford, shows that each 'Baini' is in fact 'Bai'. The new German edition (*Sämtliche Briefe*, vol. 2, 249) gives the correct reading. Curiously, the same error is found in a French translation of 1870: *Felix Mendelssohn, Voyages de Jeunesse, Lettres européennes (1830–1832)*, reprinted with a preface by Rémi Jacobs (Paris, 1980), 160–1.

[31] 'fu cantato il Miserere di Allegri innestato con brilliantissimo concertone del Baj'. *DS* 251 (1835), fol. 25^r (17 April).

[32] 'il Miserere de Bai per concertino e di Allegri per concertone'. *DS* 266 (1851), fol. 35^{r-v} (13 April).

[33] *Excerpta ex celebrioribus in musica viris, Jo. Petro Aloisio Praenestino, Thoma Ludovice a Victoria Abulensi et Gregorio Allegri Romano ... Romae ... 1870*. It includes Allegri's verse 20b.

[34] See p. 22, n. 11. On page 41, Baccellieri replaces mention of Alessandro Scarlatti's *Miserere* for Thursday of Holy Week with the note 'Si canta un verso di Allegri et uno di Bai', and on Friday (page 47), to the printed rubric 'Il Miserere

Herold, who went on all three days in 1815 expecting to hear three different works, got quite upset about it. About Thursday's performance, he wrote: 'I heard more or less the same Miserere as yesterday. It is said to be a different one, but in that case I want to know why I heard all the same passages? We'll see tomorrow if it's the same again.' On Friday he was convinced. 'This evening I am sure that it was the same one as yesterday's.'[35] As 1815 was the first year in which the choir had performed in Holy Week choir since 1809, it may, exceptionally, have been true that they sang the same *Miserere* three times that year. In the midst of the drama of the Pope fleeing to Viterbo after Napoleon's escape from Elba, the *puntatore* wrote in the *Diario Sistina* that on Wednesday the choir sang the *Miserere della nostra Cappella*. On both Thursday and Friday the 'Miserere di Bai' was given, so Herold was correct about that.[36] If Wednesday's was indeed the same, as Herold thought, then Bai's had already replaced Allegri's as the *Miserere* of choice in *nostra Cappella*. We cannot know if Allegri's verse 3 ('Amplius lava me') was already routinely inserted into Bai's work, but if it was, the mixture of the two pieces described in 1840 by Alfieri and 1892 by Mustafà was already in use in 1815. It seems in any case that for the Papal Choir the two Misereres were endlessly interchangeable, and that between them they provided all the combinations necessary for the three *Tenebræ* offices of Holy Week. However, as Celler observed, whatever was sung, for the public it was always 'the Allegri'.[37]

---

a due Cori è di Gregorio Allegri a carte 49 col Secondo Coro al lib. 88. carte 52' he adds the phrase 'di Tom. Bai', which comes to the same thing.

[35] 'J'ai entendu à peu de chose près le même Miserere qu'hier. On dit que c'en est un autre; en ce cas je demanderai pourquoi j'ai trouvé tous les mêmes passages? Nous verrons demain si ce sera la même chose … ce soir je suis bien persuadé que c'était le même qu'hier.' *Lettres d'Italie*, 218. In 1841 the same thing happened, according to Fanny Hensel: 'they sing the same "Miserere" both on Thursday and Friday' (Hensel, *The Mendelssohn Family*, Vol. 2, 98).

[36] *DS* 231 (1815), fol. 35ᵛ.

[37] See p. 2. Celler also wrote (*La Semaine Sainte*, 103) that from 1821, Baini's version eventually superseded Bai's ('a fini par écarter celui de Bai'). This surprising statement could perhaps be understood if Celler had ceased to distinguish Bai's *Miserere* from Allegri's because they were so intertwined as to be thought one and the same – an understandable error if they were indistinguishable until verse 7. It should be noted however that Celler appears to contradict himself, having noted elsewhere (ibid., 46) that the choice is between Allegri, Bai and Baini, with occasionally one by the current *maestro* ('quelquefois cependant un du maître de chapelle en exercice'); and Celler is writing well after the event, in 1867. According to Kantner and Pachovsky (*L'Ottocento*, 103), from 1855 until 1870 the three Misereres heard were those of Mustafà, Baini and a combined Allegri–Bai.

11

The Papal Choir in the nineteenth century 2 – Domenico Mustafà

✳ More difficult times

However great Baini's achievements as *direttore perpetuo* of the Papal Choir had been, he did not leave it in a healthy state on his death on 21 March 1844. The problem of recruiting and keeping singers of the necessary quality, which had dogged the choir since 1815, had not been resolved, largely because Papal salaries had not kept pace with inflation. By 1848, for example, no fewer than ten positions were vacant – almost a third of the choir – especially but not only among the higher voices.[1] Had it not been for many singers undertaking a *secondo* or even a *terzo servizio*, the situation would have been much worse, but of course this meant that the average age was inexorably rising. The best singers could still carry the group, but they were also in constant demand in other churches and for concerts and salons.

New hope came with a new Pope, Pius IX, in 1846, who wasted little time in expressing his dissatisfaction with the 'notable deterioration that he found in the Papal Choir' ('notabile deterioramente in cui trovasi la Cappella Pontificia'). The following year the singers organised a 'conference for the improvement of the institution' ('congresso per il miglioramento dell'instituzione'), after which they drew up a summary for the Pope, setting out the causes of the present problems and suggesting some solutions. Pointing out that their salaries would have to be doubled to restore the quality of life they had enjoyed in 1590, they nevertheless contented themselves with asking for an augmentation of 30 *scudi* per month for the *partecipanti* and 18 for the *soprannumerarî*. In the face of a tendency to restrict membership to priests, they also asked for confirmation that minor orders were sufficient for membership, as in the past, thereby allowing singers to be married. One respected member of the

---

[1] Only twenty-two out of the thirty-two posts were filled (Kantner and Pachovsky, *L'Ottocento*, 46); the summary of the situation post-Baini which follows is largely based on chapter 3.1 of that book. According to Fanny Hensel, on Good Friday 1840 there were just nineteen of them, 'for I counted them as they passed through the ladies' tribune to their posts in the choir' (Hensel, *The Mendelssohn Family*, Vol. 2, 98).

choir, Mariano Astolfi, composer and director at S. Lorenzo in Damaso and friend of Donizetti, Spontini and Mercadante, went even further, proposing the recruitment of twenty *secolari*, who would be free not only to marry but also to practise a profession outside the Chapel. While this idea was unsurprisingly rejected, it may have helped to concentrate minds, and in February 1848 the salary increase was granted, although with a sting in the tail: for all future recruits active service was extended from twenty-five to thirty years before a singer became a *giubilato*. The singers protested vigorously, but in vain.

There was also a problem related to the conducting of performances. Baini had been such a strong musical personality, and during his years as *direttore perpetuo* had made the choir such an expression of himself that his death left a huge gap. Even if in the eighteenth century interpretation was subject to extremes of tempo and dynamics, as Burney suggests, there is no doubt that more than twenty-five years of meticulous direction by Baini had rendered the singers more reliant upon such external input. They had never had a director like that before, and no-one in the choir seemed to have the qualities necessary to take his place. During his final illness in 1844 the senior bass, Felice Patacchiola (da Cantalice), had briefly replaced him, but had not convinced. 'The gentlemen colleagues were very aware of the absence of our always praiseworthy director D. Giuseppe Baini.'[2] Given Nicolai's description of 'the exceptional obedience of the singers – who already know every movement of his finger and how to interpret it',[3] this sense of absence is perhaps unsurprising.

Against all the traditions of the College of Papal Singers, the possibility of appointing a director from outside, common practice for the other Vatican choirs at S. Pietro and S. Giovanni Laterano, may have been raised – even Liszt's name seems to have been mentioned! – so the singers moved quickly to make sure this did not happen. Within ten days of Baini's death they addressed a unanimous request to the Pope that the direction of the choir should continue as before, in the hands of the senior bass. They justified this by citing his important place in the singing of the chant in the particular way of the chapel ('colle moltiplici sue tradizioni, che cantansi esclusivamente nella Pontificia Cappella'), the fundamental role of the bass part in the music of Palestrina, and in the rather disingenuous assertion that Baini had been merely that – the senior bass who therefore directed.[4] This wish was granted. And so, after a hiatus of eighteen months from November 1848 to April 1850 (during the absence of Pius IX due to the revolutions in Rome and elsewhere),

---

[2] 'Li signori colleghi si sono accorti la mancanza del nostro sempre lodato direttore D. Giuseppe Baini', according to the *puntatore* after a less than satisfactory performance on 7 March (*DS* 260 (1844), fol. 17, quoted in Kantner and Pachovsky, *L'Ottocento*, 44).

[3] See p. 132.

[4] The document is reproduced in full from *DS* 260 (1844), fols. 82–4, in Kantner and Pachovsky, *L'Ottocento*, Appendix 2 (222–3).

the beat was once again given by the senior bass, no doubt still standing by the *finestrino* to keep an eye on the ceremonies at the altar, while the *maestro pro tempore* organised the repertoire and the discipline, and his assistant, the *puntatore*, noted the fines and kept the diary. It was all just as it had been for three hundred years. But the genie of 'conductor-led interpretation' was out of the bottle and, had they but known it, the successor to Baini was already amongst them.

Mustafà's life and career

Domenico Mustafà, born in April 1829, showed such a precocious talent as a boy that by the age of twelve he was already a *cantore onorario* in the *Cappella Giulia*, in which his teacher G.M. Tubilli sang.[5] In 1828 Tubilli had been rated the best soprano in Rome 'when power, abundance and freshness of the voice are taken into account'.[6] Soon afterwards, still aged twelve, Mustafà became a *beneficiato cantore* at Agnani Cathedral, where he studied with the *maestro*, the composer Giuseppe D'Addrizza. While there he taught music to a fellow pupil, and future colleague in the Papal Choir, Innocenzo Pasquali, receiving in return lessons in philosophy. He started composing, and may also have studied with Saverio Mercadante. He was admitted to the Papal Choir as a *soprannumerario* in March 1848, a month short of his nineteenth birthday. Confirmed as a *partecipante* just seventeen months later, he soon established a reputation both as a singer, specialising in the highest range, and as a conductor. Over the next twenty years 'the best choirs both in the city and around about competed to have him as director and singer'.[7]

---

[5] Most of what follows is taken from Kantner and Pachovsky, *L'Ottocento*, chapter 5 ('Schede biografiche dei Cantori'), biography of Mustafà (169–70). A letter from Tubilli the previous year, asking for Papal permission to keep him at S. Pietro as a pupil (reproduced in *L'Ottocento*, appendix 4), makes clear that Mustafà's career path had already been decided: he is described as *mutilato*.

[6] 'wenn von Stärke, Fülle und Frische der Stimme die Rede ist'. G.L.P. Sievers, 'Zustand der Kirchenmusic in Rom', *Cäcilia, eine Zeitschrift für die Musikalische Welt*, vol. 8, N°32 (1828), 217–18.

[7] 'le più accreditate cappelle della città e di fuori si contendevano il vanto di averlo come direttore e come cantore'. Alberto de Angelis, *La Musica a Roma nel secolo XIX* (Rome, 1935), 89. He is even said to have been Wagner's first choice for the role of Klingsor in *Parsifal* (1882). For more on his singing see p. 249. Mustafà also contributed to the repertoire of the Chapel as a composer: his *Miserere* a6 was performed for the first time in 1855 (the year it was copied into CS 371), followed by a *Benedictus* a5 in 1859 and a *Dies Irae* a7 in 1861.

Despite the re-installation of the *basso al finestrino* as director of performance, it seems to have quickly become clear that Baini was not to be replaced as easily as that, particularly on important occasions. In 1847 the first reference is found to a new role in the choir: *direzione dei concerti*. This referred not to concerts, but to small groups of soloists, and initially it was filled for short specific periods.[8] The most important moment in the choir's year – at least as far as its reputation was concerned – was Holy Week, so it is no surprise to find that the first holder of this post, the tenor Pietro Paolo Bovieri, was appointed for that period. Nor is it surprising that the small groups involved, on whom so much depended, were given special attention, and it may be that his appointment merely marked the acknowledgement of an established practice. Well before Baini instituted regular rehearsals, Burney had reported in 1770 that the choir devoted the whole of the Monday of Holy Week to 'repeating and polishing the performance'.[9] Bovieri appears to have made such a success of the role that from 1852 he was paid an extra 3 *scudi*.[10] But given their importance in so much of the Holy Week repertoire – especially the Miserere – the senior sopranos seem to have felt it should be their job, so Bovieri was succeeded in 1857 by the *castrato* Carlo Sintoni; when he was replaced in 1860 by a bass, Baldassare Mirri, there was once again friction. Finally in 1861 it was Mustafà who was chosen as *direttore dei concertisti*, 'coll'approvazione unanime di tutto il Collegio'.[11] In 1868 he was confirmed in that post and, even more importantly, named *direttore del coro*. His appointment as conductor of the whole choir was certainly helped by the extraordinary success he had in directing a performance of his own motet *Tu es Petrus* for the celebration in S. Pietro of the 1800th anniversary of the martyrdom of St Peter and St Paul the previous year. Conducting more than four hundred participants in three choirs, his triumph was generously applauded in the press.[12]

---

[8] The term *direzioni dei concertisti* is also found in the *DS* and other documents, seemingly without any significance being attached to the different word.

[9] See p. 41. Whether one of the singers took charge of these rehearsals is difficult to say, except to note that even in the most 'democratic' music-making, there is generally a preponderant voice which emerges.

[10] Nicolai was a great admirer of Bovieri, esteeming him as an excellent soloist ('the best tenor in the Sistine'), and often made music with him at home, in the presence of the German scholar and Palestrina enthusiast Karl von Bunsen.

[11] *DS* 276 (1861), fol. 6^r (and see Kantner and Pachovsky, *L'Ottocento*, 45).

[12] The importance of this post going to a *castrato* rather than a bass can hardly be over-estimated. Soon afterwards he became an even more important figure in the concert life of Rome with his nomination in 1874 as the first president (and director) of the Società Musicale Romana, which he conducted in performances of *La Vestale* and *Fernando Cortez* by Spontini, and Handel's *Messiah* and *Israel in Egypt*.

That the *coro* as well as the *concertisti* needed some more attentive direction in 1868 may perhaps be shown by the impressions of the German musicologist and critic August Wilhelm Ambros.

> In the College of singers of the Papal Chapel in Rome compositions in the Palestrina style have been preserved. On certain days pieces by Palestrina, Morales, Allegri, Biordi, Pitoni, etc. are heard. The Improperii on Good Friday and the Miserere are still amazing pieces in their way. But, incomprehensible contradiction, these same singers, whose purity of intonation and the finest nuances left nothing to be desired in soulful expression, scream their Palestrina in a manner so unbelievably raw and lacking in emotion in the not-so-spacious Sistine Chapel that one could not believe one's own ears and would rather keep them plugged. *Crier comme un aveugle* [cry out like a blind man] say the French, you could also say: *Crier comme un chanteur de la chapelle du pape* [shout like a papal singer].[13]

It is clear that Ambros already saw Baini's era as something of a golden age. He continued:

> While still under Baini's leadership, the performances of the Chapel were highly praised. Baini died on 21 May 1844, in Rome, and it needed less than a quarter of a century for the Chapel make us feel like this. And the famous Holy Week music of the Sistine has also recently received its critical attention. On Wednesday of Holy Week 1866, Allegri's Miserere was sung, on Good Friday Bai's, and on the Thursday a new Miserere by the Abbate Mustapha, the old soprano of the chapel – 'a prophet on the right, a prophet on the left, and Mustapha in the middle'. More serious friends of art shook their heads at the Sistine, and it was probably the fault of Rome, when a very familiar refrain from the *Italiani in Algeri* hummed in my ears.[14]

---

[13] 'In dem Sänger-Collegium der Päpstlichen Capelle zu Rom haben sich allerdings Compositionen des Palestrina-Styles erhalten, man hört an bestimmten Tagen gewisse Stücke von Palestrina, Morales, Allegri, Biordi, Pitoni u.s.w. Die Improperien am Charfreitag, das Miserere sind noch jetzt in ihrer Art erstaunliche Leistungen. Aber, unbegreiflicher Widerspruch, dieselben Sänger, welche hier an Reinheit der Intonation, an feinster Nuancierung, an seelenvollem Ausdruck nichts zu wünschen übrig ließen, schreien bei der nächsten *Cappella papale* in der nicht großräumigen Sixtinischen Capelle ihren Palestrina so unglaublich roh und seelenlos herunter, daß man den eigenen Ohren nicht traut und sie lieber zuhalten möchte. Crier comme un aveugle sagen die Franzosen, statt dessen könnte es auch heißen: *Crier comme un chanteur de la chapelle du pape*.' August Wilhelm Ambros, 'Musikalisches aus Italien', in *Bunte Blätter* (Leipzig, 1872), 31–2.

[14] 'Noch unter Baini's Leitung wurden die Leistungen der Capelle als ganz vorzüglich gerühmt. Baini starb am 21. Mai 1844 zu Rom, es hat von da kein

In 1878 Mustafà added the title *direttore perpetuo dei concertisti*, one of the last acts of the dying Pope Pius IX. Despite Ambros' doubts, Baini's successor had been found.

    Vierteljahrhundert gebraucht, um die Capelle zu dem zu machen, was man jetzt zu hören bekommt. Und schon hat auch die berühmte Charwoch-Musik der Sixtina in neuester Zeit ihren bedenklichen niß bekommen. Am Mittwoch der Charwoche 1866 wurde Allegri's, am Charfreitag Bai's Miserere gesungen, am Donnerstag ein neues Miserere von -Abbate Mustapha, dem alten Sopran der Kapelle. "Prophete rechts, Prophete links, Mustapha in der Mitten." Ernstere Kunstfreunde schüttelten über diese Bermustaphirung der Sixtina die Köpfe, und es mag wohl der Rom daran schuld sein, wenn mir für meine Berson ein jehr bekannter Refrain aus den *Italiani in Algeri* vor den Ohren summte.' Later in the same article, Ambros could not resist poking some fun at Mustafà who, always a fine figure of a man, had been gaining weight: 'It gives a tragicomic impression, this long glorious sequence of Palestrinas, a triumphal impression of the spirit and most noble beauty, a glorious sequence brought to a close in the tottering form of fat wobbly Mustapha.' ('Es macht einen tragikomischen Eindruck, die lange, glorreiche Reihe der Palestriner, einen wahren Triumphzug des Geistes und der edelsten Schönheit, durch die nach wackelnde Gestalt des alten dicken Mustapha beschlossen zu sehen!'). As noted above (n. 7) Mustafà's *Miserere* was not in fact new in 1866, and in that year 'the old soprano' was actually only thirty-seven.

12

Nineteenth-century sources 3 – The Vatican manuscript of Domenico Mustafà

✷ The final source

By 1892, when Mustafà created the final and most important source of knowledge of the 'Allegri Miserere' in the nineteenth century, circumstances in the Vatican had changed dramatically. In 1870 the Papal States had been annexed by the new Kingdom of Italy at the climax of the *Risorgimento*. Over the following decades expensive ceremonial at the Vatican would be greatly reduced, and part of the cost-cutting would eventually include the disbanding of the College of Papal Singers, whose members would be merged with those of the choirs of the Basilica of S. Pietro (the *Cappella Giulia*) and of the Cathedral of S. Giovanni Laterano (the *Cappella Pia*). The new choir would eventually be called the *Cappella Musicale Pontificia 'Sistina'* (popularly but mistakenly known in English as the Choir of the Sistine Chapel), which continued (and continues) to perform at important feasts, although hardly ever in the Chapel itself.

The seven years following the *Risorgimento*, which coincided with the end of the reign of Pius IX, were a disastrous period for the choir. In a fit of what some have described as pique, he declared himself 'prigioniero in Vaticano' and closed it entirely to visitors.[1] At the same time he suspended most of the choir's musical obligations. Holy Week offices remained, but were given in private. What is more, for seven years 'no disciplinary orders were issued, no voice searches undertaken … a general and clear abrogation of decrees, interest and tradition, accumulated little by little. A real disaster. Seven years were enough to destroy the work of centuries.'[2]

---

[1] His mood would not have been helped by the plebiscite conducted in the Papal States by the new authority on 2 October 1870 as to who should rule them. After hundreds of years of autocratic neglect, only a little over 1 per cent preferred to be ruled by the Pope rather than by King Vittorio Emmanuele, and in Rome itself, the figure was just over 0.1 per cent, which means that not even all the priests voted for him. Clapton, *Moreschi*, 66.

[2] Gabrielli, 'Riassunto delle conversazioni', 254, trans. in Clapton, *Moreschi*, 94. The choir contented itself with appearances at special events in other churches. The *Diario Sistina* indicates that, apart from these events and some of the

Fig. 20 Domenico Mustafà's gravestone in Montefalco, showing him leading his singers in the *Cantoria*

Only the death of Pius IX and the accession of Leo XIII in 1878 gave new hope and direction. The new Pope restored the choir's duties and re-established discipline. He also had to rapidly resolve Mustafà's status, whose title of *direttore perpetuo dei concertisti* was not definitive enough for some of the singers, notably Innocenzo Pasquali.[3] It was only after an attempted coup in 1881, and much argument, that Mustafà was finally given the title of *direttore generale perpetuo*, the only *castrato* to be so honoured.

Confronted by the increasingly influential 'Cecilian' movement (the *Cäcilianismus*), whose wish for a return to what they saw as 'first principles' in Gregorian plainchant and *stile antico* polyphony was allied to a desire to replace *castrati* with boys on the highest parts, Mustafà was not a man to give up lightly. Far from ceding any ground to the 'Cecilians', he saw his role as trying to restore the unique performing tradition of the College of Papal Singers. He also wished to set down that tradition for posterity, against the fervently wished-for day when the College regained its former glory. That this unique performing tradition involved direction in the expressive style of Baini, who 'often varies the tempo according to the meaning of the words, his own sensibility and the tradition that has come down to him; he lets *rallentando* and

---

major offices, the choir did not sing at all, although the singers were paid as normal. Many offered their services to other churches in Rome. For more detail see Kantner and Pachovsky, *L'Ottocento*, 46–54.

[3] The ex-student friends Pasquali and Mustafà had frequently quarrelled once they became colleagues about both interpretation and composition, Pasquali preferring a 'straighter' and less extravagant style than that which Mustafà espoused. See Clapton, *Moreschi*, 97–100 and Kantner and Pachovsky, *L'Ottocento*, 49–50.

stringendo and *crescendo* and *diminuendo* happen, where Baini's quite particular art ... really cannot be admired enough',[4] is clear from his publication in 1878 of Palestrina's motet *Peccavimus*, full of extravagant marks of expression – phrasing, dynamics and, for the first time in such detail, *portamenti*. The edition is headed 'with the "affects" according to the traditional execution of the Sistine Chapel, accurately notated by Maestro Cavaliere Domenico Mustafà, *Direttore perpetuo dei concerti* of the said chapel, and President for Music in the Musical Society of Rome'.[5] Mustafà's edition and execution of this motet became very famous – almost a *cause célèbre*. 'Who in Rome has not heard the *Peccavimus*?', wrote the critic of *L'Italia Reale* in 1894 after a concert in the Vatican marking the tercentenary of the death of Palestrina.[6]

It was the 'Allegri Miserere', however, which was the jewel in the choir's crown, and its revival and preservation were one of Mustafà's central aims, especially when he found a *castrato* capable of singing it well. The retirement from the choir of Evangelista Bocchini at the end of 1882 gave Mustafà the opportunity to recruit the leading soprano in Rome, Alessandro Moreschi (Fig. 21), who for the last ten years had been principal soloist in the choir of S. Giovanni Laterano.[7] In 1891 he was described as follows.

> Four years ago there were still fourteen sopranos in the Sistine 'and the one with the freshest and best trained voice is, as has been written recently, M. Moreschi of S. Giovanni in Laterano. The pen is not adequate to describe the penetrating sweetness of this powerful and agile voice, the timbre of which is purer than that of the best female voices, and with far superior fullness and strength. M. Moreschi's extraordinary talent means that he is the most

---

[4] Otto Nicolai: see p. 132; see also 'Dynamics' in Chapter 16 below.

[5] 'Cogli "affetti" secondo execuzione tradizionale della Cappella Sistina, notati ac. curatamente dal Ch. Maestro Cav. Domenico Mustafà, Direttore perpetuo dei concerti della Cappella medesima, e Presidente alla musica nella Società Musicale Romana.' Trans. mostly in Clapton, *Moreschi*, 111–12. The motet is reproduced in Kantner and Pachovsky, *L'Ottocento*, 70–3. *Peccavimus* is the *secunda pars* of *Tribulationes civitatum*, first printed in Palestrina's *Mottettorum quinque vocibus Liber V* (1584), No. 19.

[6] Clapton, *Moreschi*, 147–8.

[7] Most of Mustafà's energetic recruiting policy since 1878 had consisted of stealing singers already employed in the other papal choirs of S. Pietro and S. Giovanni (see Kantner and Pachovsky, *L'Ottocento*, 50). Moreschi is now famous for the recordings he made at the beginning of the twentieth century, the only *castrato* ever recorded. The story of his career is comprehensively told in Clapton, *Moreschi*, which is also generous in its examination of context. See also the most recent article on Wikipedia: https://en.wikipedia.org/wiki/Alessandro_Moreschi (accessed 2 February 2020).

Fig. 21 Alessandro Moreschi (drawing by Paul Renouard, 1891)

sought-after soprano. Sometimes some tiredness can change the wonderful timbre of his voice, but his sense of style remains incomparable.'[8]

Moreschi was officially accepted into the choir on 22 March 1883, just in time to sing the *Miserere* the following day, Good Friday. We can safely assume that Mustafà, who had sung it often himself, had rehearsed intensively with him

---

[8] 'Les soprani chantant à la Sixtine étaient encore, il y a quatre ans, au nombre de quatorze et "celui qui possède la voix la plus fraîche et la plus exercée, est, a-t-on écrit récemment, M. Moreschi, de Saint-Jean-de-Latran. La plume est impuissante à rendre la suavité pénétrante de cette voix puissante et souple, dont le timbre est plus pur que celui des belles voix féminines, avec une ampleur et une vigueur bien supérieures. Le talent extraordinaire de M. Moreschi en fait le soprano le plus recherché. Parfois un peu de fatigue altère le timbre admirable de son organe. Mais son style demeure incomparable."' Drawing (Fig. 21) and comments in Renouard, *Rome pendant la semaine sainte*, 92–5, with the quotation taken from the *Journal des Goncourt*, 58 (see also pp. 68–9). Note how 'the Sistine' is taken as a generic term for anything to do with papal music.

in the preceding weeks. The arrival of Moreschi must have given Mustafà's quest for a definitive version extra impetus, for early the following year he instructed his colleague Innocenzo Pasquali 'to write down the ornaments, in order to assure and guarantee the true tradition'. This version was rehearsed on 24 March 1884, in plenty of time for the *Tenebræ* services that year, which fell on 9–11 April.[9]

Further refinements were no doubt added over the following years, and it was 1892 before he was ready to write it down for posterity. A 1913 interview with Moreschi sheds some light on the story.

> Here is an interesting story: since 1870 the Pope had no longer presided at the Holy Week ceremonies, and the order came to no longer sing the famous Allegri 'Miserere' which was, as is well known, one of the most celebrated performances of the singers of the Sistine Chapel. In 1890 the wonderful singer Mustafà obtained permission from the late Pope, His Holiness Leo XIII, to perform this Miserere, but he had enormous difficulties with it because only the skeleton of the work is written down, the singers of the Sistine relying on tradition to supplying accidentals, decorations and other special aspects of the interpretation. After unrelenting work and more than forty rehearsals, Mustafà and his colleagues performed this 'Miserere', which is written for two choirs – one of four voices and one of five – in the Sistine Chapel, in the presence of the whole of the Roman musical world. When the performance was over, Mustafà put the score into a large envelope and hid it away, addressing it 'to His Holiness, with my humble prayer that this envelope be placed in the archives and only opened after my death'.[10]

---

[9] 'A scrivere le ornamentazioni per assicurare e garantirne la vera tradizione.' *DS* 290 (1883), fol. 79ᵛ (24 March) (Kantner and Pachovsky, *L'Ottocento*, 75). The strained relations between Pasquali and Mustafà, not to mention Pasquali's preference for a less extravagant performing style, must have added a certain piquancy to his role in this project.

[10] 'Une anecdote intéressante: depuis 1870 le Pape ne préside plus aux cérémonies de la Semaine Sainte et ordre fut donné de ne plus chanter le fameux "Miserere" d'Allegri, qui était, c'est connu, une des plus célèbres interprétations des chantres de la Chapelle Sixtine. En 1890, Mustafà, le magnifique chantre, obtint de feu Sa Sainteté Léon XIII la permission de faire exécuter une fois ce Miserere, mais il se trouva lui-même dans des graves difficultés, car c'est seulement le squelette musical du morceau qui est noté, les chantres de la Sixtine ayant des altérations, fioritures et autres interprétations spéciales, transmises seulement par tradition. Après un travail opiniâtre et plus que quarante répétitions, Mustafà et ses collègues, en présence de tout le monde musical romain assemblé à la Chapelle Sixtine, firent entendre ce "Miserere" qui est écrit pour deux chœurs, l'un à quatre et l'autre à cinq voix; quand l'audition prit fin, Mustafà renferma la partition dans une grande enveloppe qu'il cacheta et l'adressa ainsi "A Sa Sainteté, avec l'humble prière que cette enveloppe soit mise aux archives et ouverte seulement après ma mort".' Margharita Berio, 'Lettre de Rome',

While it may be true that the *Miserere* was not performed for some years after 1870, it is untrue that it was not reincorporated into the repertoire of the choir after 1878. Perhaps two stories have become confused here. Nor does the article make clear whether this anecdote comes from Moreschi or has been added by the writer, in the same way as she also added Burney's old story about the Emperor Leopold's attempt to procure a score.[11] But allowing for this, as well as a certain vagueness about dates and, as will be seen below, an inexact text of Mustafà's instructions on the envelope, it does at least corroborate both the difficulty that Mustafà must have had in making his score, and the evident importance of his having made it.

He finally presented manuscript CS 375 (hereinafter **M**) to the choir on 8 March 1892, just over six weeks after finishing it.[12] The *Diario Sistino* describes the moment.

> The Maestro Director presents his afore-mentioned Miserere, a work which has cost him many years of patient toil in order to transmit to posterity the manner in which it came to be executed; and modestly demands of his colleagues, turning particularly to those of some seniority who remember former performances, freely to disclose their opinion of the said work, saying that he was ready to remove those flaws and to make redress for those omissions into which he may have fallen. The senior members, and with them the whole College, approve of this valuable work by its illustrious Director; and the *maestro pro tempore* [suitably enough, Moreschi] speaks on behalf of the most reverend College as a whole in thanking him for this work of his given to the Chapel.[13]

Revue Musicale S.I.M., 12/12 (December 1913), 63–4. For more on the difficulties Mustafà must have faced in making his edition, see Chapters 7 and 10.

[11] Apparently unable or unwilling to believe its age, the writer applied it to 'Léopold I de Bavière', presumably thinking of either Prince Leopold of Bavaria (1846–1930) or his father Luitpold (1821–1912). The same temptation to update has been observed in Chapter 6, in the anonymous preface to the 1838 publication of Mesplet's manuscript.

[12] The full score is dated 22 January. The separate parts are not dated, but given the extra detail in them, it is clear that they were completed afterwards, perhaps during that six weeks.

[13] 'Il maestro direttore presenta su detto Miserere un suo lavoro costatogli molti anni di fatiche e di pazienza, per tramandare ai posteri le tradizioni sul modo col quale esso veniva eseguito; e modestamente domanda ai colleghi, rivolgendosi specialmente agli anziani che rammentano le passate esecuzioni, di esternare liberamente il loro parere su detto lavoro dicendosi pronto a togliere quelle mende e a riparare a quelle omissioni nelle quali fosse per avventure incorso. Gli anziani, e con essi tutto il Collegio fa plauso alla pregevole opera dell'illustre direttore; e il maestro pro-tempore si rende interprete del rev[erendissi]mo Collegio, ringraziando sentitamente per questo suo lavoro donato alla Cappella.' *DS* 294 (1892), fol. 9ᵛ–10ᵛ (8 March) (reproduced in Kantner

Mustafà dedicated the score to Pope Leo XIII, and wrote:

> Miserere by Bai and Allegri. In which is noted the work's traditional mode of performance in the Sistine by the Singers of the Papal Chapel. Owing to the unfortunate interruptions to the continuity of papal ceremonies in consequence of which much may be forgotten, I, the writer, after forty-five years passed amongst my dear colleagues in the service of God, the Supreme Pontiff and the Chapel, have thought to describe the above-mentioned traditions (in so far as I could), as much for those who must conduct as for the solo singers, so that after many years the effects which made the Sistine performance so renowned should not be lost.[14]

And he added on the envelope in which the manuscript was wrapped: 'On behalf of the College of Papal Singers I beg the Supreme Pontiff that he should not permit the making of copies.'[15]

The habit of secrecy, not to mention the ghost of Baini, died hard.

---

and Pachovsky, *L'Ottocento*, 246), trans. in Clapton, *Moreschi*, 130. Given the somewhat poisonous atmosphere which seems to have pervaded the Vatican in general and the choir in particular at this period, graphically described by Clapton, Mustafà's appeal for help from his senior colleagues, and their unconditional approval, may not have been entirely sincere.

[14] 'Miserere di Bai ed Allegri in cui sono state accennate le tradizioni come se eseguivano nella Sistina dai Cappellani Cantori Pontifici. Nella sventura in cui viviamo per la mancanza delle Funzioni Papali e per conseguenza molto si può dimenticare, la servente dopo quaranta cinque anni passati tra gli amati Colleghi, servendo Dio, il Sommo Pontefice e la Cappella, ha creduto di transcrivere le sud.te tradizioni (come ha potuto) tanto per chi dovrà dirigere che per i singoli Cantore, onde dopo tanti anni non andasse perduto quell'effetto che rese tanto celebri l'Esecuzioni nella Sistina.' (It is signed 'D. Mustafà perpetuo della Cap. Pont. Manu Dominici Mustafà scriptus Romae 23 ianuarii 1892'.) Trans. in Clapton, *Moreschi*, 131.

[15] 'Si supplica il S. Padre affinche non dia il permesso ad alcuno per farne copia.' DS 294 (1892), fol. 14^r (8 March). Mustafà's version was given a private performance on 16 March, a full month before Easter that year (Kantner and Pachovsky, *L'Ottocento*, 75), perhaps the performance referred to in the interview with Moreschi above as taking place 'in the Sistine Chapel, in the presence of the whole of the Roman musical world'. Mustafà's request does not, of course, exclude the possibility of his version being used during Holy Week either in that year or in subsequent ones.

What Mustafà's manuscript shows

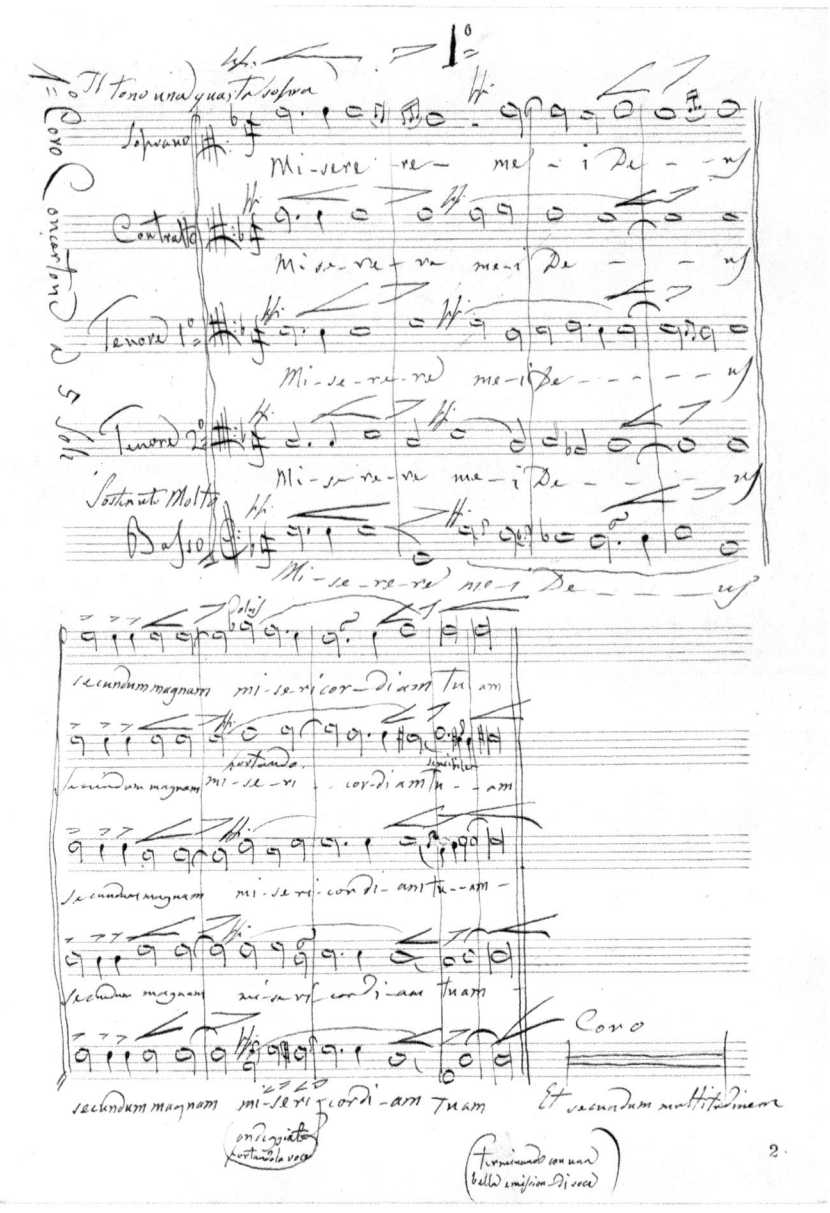

Fig. 22 CS 375: *Miserere di Bai ed Allegri,* in the hand of Domenico Mustafà, verse 1

Fig. 23 CS 375: *Miserere di Bai ed Allegri*, in the hand of Domenico Mustafà, verse 3

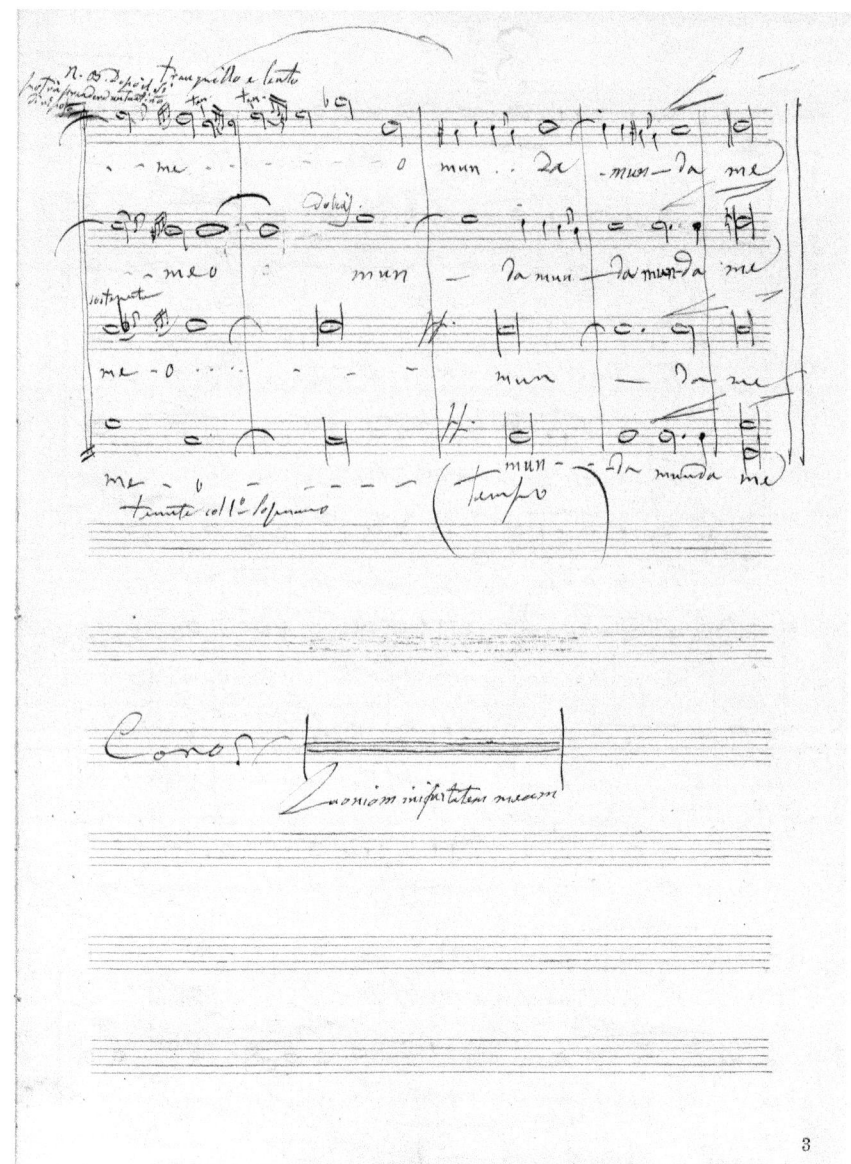

Fig. 23 (continued)

Fig. 24 CS 375: *Miserere di Bai ed Allegri*, in the hand of Domenico Mustafà, verse 20a

Fig. 25 CS 375: *Miserere di Bai ed Allegri*, in the hand of Domenico Mustafà, first page of the first soprano part in *Coro 2°*, showing verses 3 (Allegri) and 7 (Bai)

It is striking that Mustafà's choice of what he clearly considered to be the definitive version of the 'Allegri Miserere' consists predominantly of Bai's, the only Allegri being verse 3 (Figs. 23 and 25). It thus follows Alfieri's formula, outlined above, for a performance of the Bai, although Mustafà's title is *Miserere di Bai ed Allegri*. The presence of Allegri's music here is like a formal bow to the origin of this extraordinary piece – the verse which gave rise to the most extravagant *abbellimenti*, and which made the reputation of the *Miserere* and the Papal Choir – finally brought to perfection in the endless variety of Bai's setting. Because he knew that it was not the notes but the manner of its performance which set it apart from all other music, in his score and accompanying set of parts Mustafà recorded not only the *abbellimenti* and other ornaments, but also tempi and dynamics, phrasing and *portamenti* as he had in his edition of *Peccavimus*. Moreover he added copious instructions and advice addressed both to singers and future directors about expressive devices and special effects. It is as close as we can get on paper to an aural recording.

The last in the series of manuscripts begun more than a century before, it provides confirmation and extra detail about most performance questions. As will be seen from the extracts of CS 375 (Figs. 22–25) and the score reproduced in Appendix 13 (Edition 1), the *fioriture* have much in common with those found in earlier manuscripts: compare for example the end of verse 7 with the version given in Alfieri (Appendix 11) for that verse and marked **D**. Dynamic markings are much more precise and copious than those in the sources from the 1820s; for example, the indications *f* for the chanted sections and *p* for the polyphony discussed in Chapter 9, and further in Chapter 16, are greatly refined.

Regarding the chanted sections of the polyphonic verses, **M** also sheds extra light on their rhythmic interpretation. Not only are they written out metrically with great precision, as in the late eighteenth-century sources **Man**, **P** and **Mil**, but the use of the phrases *a piacere* and *col direttore* are supplemented by many written directions, such as *dolcissimo, ondeggiato, tranquillo, sostenuto* and *risoluto* – all the kinds of things normally transmitted to singers by a director. The filiation from Burney's 'certain customs, expressions, and graces of convention, (*certe espressioni e Gruppi*) which produce great effects; such as swelling and diminishing the sounds altogether; accelerating or retarding the measure at some particular words, and singing some entire verses quicker than others' (1770) through Baini's 'varying the pace... with *rallentandi* and *stringendi* and *crescendi* and *diminuendi*... Baini's quite particular art' (Nicolai, 1836) to this kind of micro-management of interpretation is clear. This continuity from the early practices to **M** shows clearly not only the resistance to change of the choir's traditions, but also the importance of this stylistic feature in performances of the *Miserere* from the eighteenth century onwards.

M includes examples of all the different kinds of embellishments already seen in earlier sources, notably short *appoggiature*, and the preliminary *gruppetto*, a kind of filled-in double *appoggiatura* resembling a turn. These are discussed more fully in Chapter 16. Most striking are the extraordinary number of indications of *portamento*, something found in no other source, if we except the 'parallel fifths' moments in **Man**, **P**, **Mil** and Mus. ms. Alfieri 1 that so shocked Spohr and others. There is no doubt that, writing his manuscript specifically for the attention of singers and directors rather than simply for the archive, and thinking of it as a manuscript prescribing a very particular interpretation rather than merely recording notes, Mustafà marked in it much of what was normally left out. The *portamenti* indicated are nearly all of the kind first discussed in the 1780s by Friedrich Rellstab and, particularly, Domenico Corri, where they are labelled 'the anticipation grace'.[16]

On the question of pitch, **M** gives its *imprimatur* to upward transposition of a fourth from the written key of G minor as the ideal, being marked 'Il tono una quarta sopra' at the beginning (see Fig. 22). There is thus a high C in the first half of the four-part verses. While the upper voices have most of the

---

[16] J.C. Friedrich Rellstab, *Versuch über die Vereinigung der musikalischen und oratorischen Declamation* (Berlin, 1786); Domenico Corri, *A Select Collection* (Edinburgh, c.1782) and *The Singer's Preceptor* of 1810. For a detailed discussion see Clive Brown, *Classical and Romantic Performing Practice 1750–1900* (Oxford, 1999), chapter 15, esp. 566–72. See also Chapter 16 below.

more expansive *abbellimenti*, as in the manuscripts of **A**, all the parts share the expressive devices. With the exception of the 'high C moment', there is little sense that the lower parts serve merely as accompaniment to the first soprano: notably, the two sopranos in the four-part verses often engage in a real dialogue of equals (for example, at the beginning of verse 19). The singers in the five-part verses are expected to be just as expressive as those in the four-part ones. Either the problems experienced earlier in the century with finding soloists of sufficient calibre had been resolved, or Mustafà preferred to record an ideal interpretation rather than a compromise.

Detailed discussion of all these aspects – with some remarks concerning their origins as well as their implications for modern performance – will be found in Chapters 15 and 16. Chapter 17 deals with questions of performing forces, as well as the manner of performing the 'plainsong' verses on a single note. CS 375 confirms that proposed in manuscripts 9, 10, 11 and 12 of **A** by printing one long breve (on d) for the first words of every even-numbered verse for the tenors and basses.

PART FOUR

PERFORMING THE *MISERERE* IN THE TWENTIETH CENTURY

13

The current 'popular' version of 'the Allegri': the 'English Miserere'

✴ The five-part verses

IN the version generally heard nowadays, verses 1, 5, 9, 13, 17 and the first part of 20 (for five voices) and the second part of 20 (for nine voices) come directly from Burney's 1711 publication (*La musica che si canta annualmente nelle Funzioni della Settimana Santa nella Cappella Pontificale*).[1] Although this is similar in many respects to the identical Sistine Chapel manuscripts CS 185 (of 1731) and CS 341 (of 1748), there are nonetheless important differences which merit discussion.

Burney seems to have been confused by the different versions he was shown in Rome.

> This composition used to be held so sacred, that it was imagined excommunication would be the consequence of an attempt to transcribe it. Padre Martini [whom Burney had seen at length in Bologna] told me there were never more than two copies of it made by authority, one of which was made for the late king of Portugal [no doubt João V (died 1750), whose dream was to recreate the Vatican and all its ceremonial in his royal chapel in Lisbon and his monastery-palace in Mafra], and the other for himself: this last he permitted me to transcribe at Bologna, and Signor Santarelli favoured me with another copy from the archives of the Pope's chapel: upon collating these two copies, I find them to agree pretty exactly, except in the first verse. I have seen several spurious copies of this composition in the possession of different persons, in which the melody of the soprano, or upper part, was tolerably correct, but the other parts differed very much; and this inclined me to suppose the upper part to have been written from memory, which, being so often repeated to different words in the performance, would not be difficult to do, and the other parts to have been made to it by some modern contra-puntist afterwards.[2]

---

[1] It is available online at imslp.org, incomplete except for the Allegri (but the 1809 German edition there is complete).

[2] *The Present State*, 277–8 (and see p. 43).

He wrote these lines after his return to London (they do not figure in his journal), and it is clear that he was puzzled by the various pieces of music he had brought back. One wonders, for example, how the different versions could 'agree pretty exactly' except in the first verse. In fact it is in verses 5 and 13 that his version differs most from Vatican manuscripts, which have an important variation in the second half created in the early eighteenth century by Biordi.[3] All Burney's verses are given to identical music, as if he had before him only verse 1, to which he slavishly adapted the others; it is noteworthy that he does not venture to give a rhythmic interpretation of the chanted parts of the later verses, preferring to leave the reciting chords in breves. It seems therefore likely that he had, from both Santarelli and Martini, only one verse to use as a model.[4]

It is arguable that the setting he published is superior, from the point of view of polyphonic device, to that given in CS 341. One only has to compare the alto and tenor parts in bars 2 and 3, and the bass and tenor parts in bars 7 and 8, to

---

[3] See pp. 41–2, particularly n. 11, and Appendix 2.

[4] No doubt Santarelli gave him verses from CS 341, the source in current use by the choir; CS 205 is so different that it would have stood out almost like a different work (which in effect it is). However, there seems to be no trace of such a manuscript in the catalogue for the sale at auction of his music collection on 8 August 1814; see *The late Dr. Burney's Musical Library. A Catalogue of the valuable and very fine collection of music, printed and MS* (London, 1814), facsimile edn with an introduction by A. Hyatt King in A. Hyatt King, *Catalogue of the Music Library of Charles Burney, Sold in London, 8 August 1814* (Amsterdam, 1973); and Graham Sadler, 'La Bibliothèque Musicale du Dr Charles Burney, in Catherine Massip et al. (eds.), *Collectionner la musique: érudits collectionneurs* (Turnhout, 2015), 99–115. All the other works printed in *La Musica* are present. The Allegri copied from Padre Martini was sold as Lot 225, described as 'Miserere, by Permission from P. Martini's copy. MS 1770. It fetched (together with Lot 226, Anerio's *Missa pro Defunctis*) 2s. 6d. Bai's *Miserere* and Palestrina's *Improperia* were sold together as Lot 240 for 3s. 6d., Palestrina's *Stabat mater* (Lot 282) fetched 2s. 6d., and *Fratres ego enim* 2s (Lot 283).

As for the Allegri, there is, however, one intriguing possibility. Lot 239, just before the Bai in the catalogue, is a 'Miserere della Cap. Pont. 4 Voc.', attributed to the otherwise unknown 'Balami (D.)'. It went for 3s. to the same buyer as the Bai. Could this have been it, with an original title written by Santarelli, such as 'D.B.' (for Dottore Burney) and some Italian (Guidonian?) shorthand misread by the auctioneer? In any case, the argument is academic, as none of these scores has so far been identified. There remains the possibility that Burney obtained other sources which fit the description he gives them of having been put together from memory and imagination (for example, Blainville's *Histoire* described in Chapter 5), but there are none such specifically identified in his diary.

see the better workmanship.[5] Burney's version of the four-part verses is also unique. Similar to CS 206 in general harmonic outline, it nevertheless doubles the length of the chord of E♭ just before the end of the first phrase which, with its 7–6 suspension, supports the most famous *abbellimento*. It also may be judged to be marginally superior polyphonically to that found in Allegri's original. One wonders then if the copies given him by Martini had been 'corrected' by the learned Padre, himself a very important 'modern contra-puntist'. Given that it was not destined for performance, there is no reason why he should have bothered to write down the other verses, and he would thus have left Burney with a template from which to work rather than a full score. This would explain his puzzlement at the first verses of the sources he was shown in the Vatican, the fact that all the verses in his version are identical, and the lack of rhythmic indications in the chanted parts of all subsequent verses. As noted above, he could not confront his doubts with a performance as his only visit to Rome was in the autumn. Having no means to evaluate the relative importance of his sources, one can easily understand why he chose to publish Martini's version, unaware that it had almost certainly never been heard in the Vatican. This would certainly account for the uniqueness of his readings, and add an amusing irony to the current ubiquity of the 'English Miserere'.[6]

※ The four-part verses

It is however in the verses for four voices (3, 7, 11, 15 and 19) that the real problems with the 'English Miserere' arise, those sung nowadays being nothing less than pure invention. They were put together from disparate sources (Burney, Alfieri and, crucially, the textless phrase with the top C (Ex. 6) in Mendelssohn's letter quoted in Chapter 9) by the English musicologist W.S. Rockstro (1823–95) for a long article on the *Miserere* published in the first edition of Grove's *Dictionary*.[7] One supposes that he didn't for a moment anticipate the use to which his reconstruction would be put, and to give him credit, having realised that Allegri's original (as reproduced by Burney) was so far from actual performance as to be irrelevant, he wanted to give his readers a flavour of the piece as it

---

[5] These examples, from verse 1, refer to the transcription of CS 341 in Appendix 3.
[6] Burney's version of Bai's *Miserere* is also unique, being notably more elaborate than all Vatican-related sources (CS 203–4, CS 340–1, Mustafà's CS 375 and Alfieri). This is particularly true in verse 7 (a4), and in verses 9, 13 and 17 (a5), all of which have been rewritten and considerably extended by a highly competent hand. Perhaps Padre Martini felt the need to 'improve' Bai as well.
[7] George Grove (ed.), *A Dictionary of Music and Musicians* 1st edn, vol. 2 (London, 1880), 335–8 (see Fig. 26). Rockstro's article also includes a transcription of Burney's verse 1.

could still be heard in the Chapel. Unfortunately, apart from 'improving' Mendelssohn's soprano phrase – turning the appoggiaturas into measured minims, shortening the top C, and relegating the f♮, which he described as 'undoubtedly due to the caprice of individual singers' (as if the whole tradition of the *abbellimenti* was not based on exactly that!) to parentheses – he misunderstood both its tonality and its placement. Mendelssohn wrote what he heard, transposed up a fourth from the original key, as his letters make clear. For Rockstro to use this phrase for an edition in G minor, he needed to transpose it back down a fourth. It is strange that he missed this, because he must have been aware of the considerable transposition that was normally practised.[8]

Even stranger is the fact that his reconstruction used Alfieri's *abbellimento* **A** for the end of the first phrase, but he somehow failed to notice that Alfieri's *abbellimento* **B** for the second phrase bore no resemblance – melodic or harmonic – to what he put in its place (see Appendix 11 and the discussion on p. 152). Nor is there any evidence that Rockstro had read Alfieri's commentary, which also indicated the use of transposition.[9] Mendelssohn's phrase, which is textless, is of course another version of *abbellimento* **A**, transposed a fourth higher and ending the first part of the verse on a major chord clearly functioning as a dominant. Either the considerable difference in the detail was sufficient to blind him to the harmonic similarity, or he simply decided that, against all the evidence, he preferred it. In that case, it was an obsession with providing the mythical top C that led him into error, as may be surmised by his note:

> In describing this beautiful passage, Mendelssohn says, 'The *Abellimenti* are certainly not of antient date; but they are composed with infinite talent, and taste, and their effect is admirable. This one, in particular [footnote: That is, the last shewn in our example], is often repeated, and makes so deep an impression, that, when it begins, an evident excitement prevades [sic] all present ... The Soprano intones the high C, in a pure soft voice, allowing it to vibrate for a time, and slowly gliding down, while the Alto holds its C steadily; so that, at first, I was under the delusion that the high C was still held by the Soprano. The skill, too, with which the harmony is gradually developed, is truly marvellous.'[10]

---

[8] Rockstro studied with Mendelssohn in his youth and later wrote his biography.

[9] At this time (1880) he was clearly unaware that Geminiani was Alfieri's *nom-de-plume*. He corrected this in his article on the 'Sistine Choir' (in volume 3 of the first edition, published three years later, 1883, 519–23) and in that on Alfieri in the appendix to volume 4 published in 1890 (there is no article on Alfieri in the first volume of the first edition). An emendation was also made (adding 'i.e. Alfieri' in brackets after Geminiani's name) in the second edition of the *Dictionary*.

[10] Rockstro, 'Miserere', 337. Rockstro's translation of the Mendelssohn quotation is curiously similar to Selden-Goth's much later one (Mendelssohn, *Letters*, 140–1, from the letter of 16 June 1831 addressed to Professor Zelter). The

Fig. 26 Rockstro's reconstruction of verse 3 as printed in the first three editions of Grove's *Dictionary* (1880, 1927 and 1929), showing its sources

footnote identifying Mendelssohn's phrase as 'the last shewn in our example', is the only clue that the reconstruction was not entirely based on Alfieri, a clue which, as will be seen below, was missed by the editors of the third edition of Grove. Rockstro's article 'Miserere' was reproduced virtually unchanged in the second edition (ed. J.A. Fuller-Maitland), vol. 3 (1927), 216–19.

The result is an impossible, but strangely exciting, harmonic sequence in which the bass ascends by a diminished fifth and the soprano leaps two successive fourths to a top C. The current *Wikipedia* article on the Miserere, while containing misconceptions in other ways, describes it well: 'The curious "trucker's gear change" from G minor to C minor is because the second half of the verse is the same as the first half, but transposed up a fourth. The original never had a Top C.'[11] The writer is correct about this phrase, but wrong about the top C. The *Miserere* was often heard with a top C (or perhaps a B♮, or even a D♭), but it came not as the result of an outlandish harmonic shift but, as we have seen, by the upward transposition of the whole work. Rockstro had the information to come to the right conclusions but, perhaps in a state of 'evident excitement', and by the fact that the phrase's final chord was G, he put it at the end of the verse, despite its 'dominant' feel. It is this moment that has made 'Allegri's Miserere' famous in the twentieth century. Rockstro would not be the last to be seduced by its strange beauty, but it was never heard in the Sistine Chapel before visits by modern English choirs.

※ Misereres in England 1 – early days

In the Anglican Church nowadays, the *Miserere* is most often sung on Ash Wednesday. In the Christian calendar, this marks the beginning of the forty days of Lent, the first day in the sequence of repentance leading to Easter Day, when all used to be required to take communion in a shriven state.[12] It was a particularly important office for the first Anglicans of the sixteenth century. The ashes were those with which, it was said, penitents had been required to cover themselves in the early Church (along with sackcloth) as a reminder both of their mortality and of their possible fate in the afterlife. It being thus the most penitential day of the church year, it is no surprise that in the first edition of *The Book of Common Prayer* (*BCP*) of 1549 all seven Penitential Psalms were appointed for it, as they had been in the old Sarum rite.[13] Psalms 6, 32 and 68

---

[11] *Wikipedia* article on Gregorio Allegri, https://en.wikipedia.org/wiki/Gregorio_Allegri (accessed 13 June 2019).

[12] 'The Church begins her Lent this day to supply the Sundays in Lent; upon which it was not the Church's custom to fast, Sundays being high festivals in memory of our Saviour's joyful resurrection. Now if you take out of the six weeks of Lent, six Sundays, there will remain but thirty-six fasting days; to which, these four of this week being added, make the just number of forty.' Commentary by Bishop Sparrow (*Rationale on the Book of Common Prayer*), in Richard Mant (ed.), *The Book of Common Prayer ... with Notes Explanatory, Practical, and Historical, from Approved Writers of the Church of England* (Oxford, 1825), 140.

[13] See H.A. Pearson (ed.), *The Sarum Missal, in English*, 2nd edn (London, 1884), 52–8.

were said (or sung) at Matins, and 102, 130 and 143 at Evensong. The seventh, *Miserere* (Psalm 51 in Anglican usage), always considered the most important, was incorporated into a new service to be said immediately after Matins, entitled "A declaracion of Scripture, with certain prayers to be used the firste daye of Lent, commonlye called Ash-wednesdaie".[14]

> In the ancient services there was nothing that corresponded at all nearly to the first part of this service, except the sentences of the greater excommunication, which were commonly read in parish churches three or four times a year. Some of the reformers were very anxious to restore the primitive practice of public penance in church, which was indeed occasionally practised, at least until the latter part of the eighteenth century, and they put forward this service as a sort of substitute. The *Miserere* and most of what follows were taken from the Sarum services for Ash Wednesday.[15]

Psalm 51 follows the vigorous cursing of sins and impressive harangue to incite repentance that opens the service, and itself is succeeded by a series of responses taken from the Sarum rite. The title of the service was modified more than once in subsequent editions of *BCP*, initially because of an enthusiasm among certain revisers, particularly the German theologian Martin Bucer, for its use as a general Act of Contrition at different times of the year. Its final title was 'A Commination, or Denouncing of God's anger and Judgements against sinners, With certain Prayers, to be used on the first Day of Lent, and at other times'.[16] Despite the misleading impression given by the random capitalisa-

---

[14] This is the title of chapter xii in the index; on the page itself it is simply entitled 'The firste daye of lente, commonly called Ashe-wednisdaye'. It can be consulted online at http://justus.anglican.org/resources/bcp/1549/BCP1549.pdf.

[15] J.H. Maude, *The History of the Book of Common Prayer* (New York, 1901), 110. As the Anglican office could not include an absolution, the language of condemnation was correspondingly more severe. In the words of Dean Comber, 'Of the lesser Litany, the Lord's prayer, and suffrages, which introduce these devotions, we have spoken before. The rest are three Collects, two of them to be repeated by the minister alone, the third by the priest and people together; but all of them are earnest petitions for pardon. We dare not here with the Roman Church, in a mixed assembly, pronounce a positive and formal absolution to all: yet we address ourselves to Almighty God, who best knows who needs a pardon, and who is fit for it; beseeching him importunately to grant it to all such.' (Mant (ed.), *Common Prayer*, 511.

[16] Mant (ed.), *Common Prayer*, esp. 505–7 and n. 2, based largely on Charles Wheatly's *Rational Illustration of the Book of Common Prayer*. Bucer was a Protestant reformer welcomed by Thomas Cranmer to assist with revisions to the first edition of *BCP*. Modifications in the Ash Wednesday service itself were restricted to phraseology.

tion and multiple commas, the office was apparently rarely used in its entirety except on the first day of Lent.

There is thus a certain logic in attaching the *Miserere* to Ash Wednesday, although this has become common practice only recently. During the nineteenth century, for example, Sir John Stainer performed a *Miserere* of his own composition (in English of course) at St Paul's Cathedral during his time as Organist there, 1872–88.[17] The version of it published in 1894 (recently reissued) includes settings of the responses which follow it in the Commination service, but this of itself does not seem to have meant to Stainer or the St Paul's authorities that it should be sung during that office. Instead it was given on Tuesday of Holy Week, followed by his own abbreviated and translated version of Bach's *St Matthew Passion*.[18]

As there was no question at this time of singing in Latin during Anglican offices, Allegri's *Miserere* was not available. However, in 1889 a new edition with English text was issued by Novello, assembled by the enthusiastic Tractarian H.A. Walker.[19] One wonders if he had been inspired by reading Rockstro's article in the first edition of Grove's *Dictionary* nine years earlier. If so, his inspiration did not spread so far as to adopt Rockstro's version of the four-part verses. Perhaps he thought that no choirboy in England would be able to sing the top Cs, and at the time probably no-one would have tried. He simply reproduced the music of Burney's publication, which was widely available, and

---

[17] J.C. Dibble, *John Stainer: A Life in Music* (Woodbridge, 2007), 172. Composed in 1873, it is a kind of *falsobordone* based on what Dibble calls a *tonus irregularis*: i.e. the reciting note of the second part is a tone lower than that of the first, as in the *tonus peregrinus*, but the endings are individual. I would like to thank Professor Dibble for his discussions with me on this subject, during which he suggested that Stainer could have become familiar with the Allegri during his time as Organist at St Michael's College, Tenbury (1857–9), with access to Sir F.A. Gore Ouseley's extraordinary library there (now mostly in the Bodleian Library, Oxford), which contained multiple manuscript copies of both the Allegri and the Bai. He suggests further that Stainer may have been influenced by the end of Bai's *Miserere* in his expansion of the Gloria of the psalm (included in the Commination service, in contrast to Catholic usage in Holy Week) into *cori spezzati* writing.

[18] Its published title is a masterpiece of vagueness: *Miserere &c., as used in St Paul's Cathedral at Special Lenten Services*. The Responses can only have been provided for those who wished to incorporate the *Miserere* into the Commination service, but I have yet to find anywhere where this was ever done.

[19] It appears in Novello's 1890 catalogue. The Rev. Henry Aston Walker (1834–1906) was curate and choirmaster of St Alban's Holborn from 1862 to 1879 and the author of guides to Gregorian chant such as *Holy Communion: As sung at St Alban the Martyr, Holborn* (n.d.) and *The Altar Service Book* (1867), and involved in the musical side of publications such as *The Sarum Missal, in English* (1868; see n.13 above).

adapted it to the *BCP* version of the psalm.[20] He may however have taken the musical text of the five-part verses from Rockstro's article, as he reproduces a 'correction' in that score that was previously unseen.[21] Apart from the first two verses, in which he adopted Burney's rhythms, the chanted parts of each verse were simply printed as breves, leaving choirmasters to decide whether, and if so how, they wished to rhythmicise them. Surprisingly for an avowed enthusiast and connoisseur of Gregorian chant, the music supplied for the *cantus planus* verses, to be sung by the congregation, is based on Tone VII; the organ accompaniment added (no doubt to encourage participation) thus necessitates a change of key signature to G major![22] While this provides a pleasant musical contrast and is reasonably practical in terms of the chord sequence from verse to verse, clearly it has no relationship with the *tonus peregrinus*, leaving one to wonder whether Walker had noticed its use as the basis of the *Miserere*.

Soon after Stainer left St Paul's in 1888, his successor Sir George Martin (1844–1916) adopted the Allegri for use there in Lent, no doubt using Walker's edition. However, he appears to have become dissatisfied with it and published a new one of his own in 1905, the music still based entirely on Burney.[23] In it, the plainchant verses are sung to Tone II, as Rockstro had suggested in his article in Grove's *Dictionary*, which is hardly closer to Allegri's *falsobordone* than Walker's Tone VII, but has unaccountably been widely used since.[24] The principal modification however was to provide detailed rhythms for the chanted sections of all the verses except the first halves of 15 and 20 (14 and 19

---

[20] Apart from Burney's original (1771) and multiple later reprints by English, German and French publishers, a non-exhaustive list of English reproductions includes those by Thomas Warren (c.1775); William Ayrton, in *The Harmonicon*, 3/35 (1825), 195–8; John William Parker, in *Sacred Minstrelsy* (1834), 133–5, (an identical copy of Ayrton's) and Vincent Novello (c.1840). Ayrton and Parker give verses 1, 3 and 20b only. Although the text is of course in Latin, the title used by both Ayrton and Parker is according to English usage, 'Psalm 51' (as in every subsequent English edition in either language), and for the same reason verse 20 is labelled as verse 19, because in *BCP* the Latin verse 2 is treated as the second part of verse 1.

[21] Three bars from the end, note 2 of the alto part is altered to a (in unison with the tenors) to avoid fleeting consecutive fifths with the first soprano which would otherwise occur between beats 2 and 3.

[22] He also gives the *Gloria patri* to the same music at the end, as required in the Commination service.

[23] It was printed as a supplement to *The Musical Times* of 1 April that year (46/746 (1888), 1–16), and then added to Novello's catalogue. Like Walker, he reproduced Rockstro's 'correction' of the alto part.

[24] The accompaniment he provides for the suggested congregational participation is perhaps even more bizarre than Walker's: in the second half the notes b♭–a–f–g are accompanied by chords on b♭, f, b♭ and e♭! The *Gloria patri* is not included.

in English usage). That this responded to the needs of choirmasters is shown in the fact that Martin's edition appears to have immediately replaced that of Walker, which was no longer listed in the Novello catalogue of 1907.

These English editions seem to have provoked the adoption of Allegri's *Miserere* in some places almost immediately. It was at least as interesting musically as Stainer's work, and most church musicians would have been aware of its reputation. In Worcester, for example, it had been the custom since 1895 to sing Joseph Barnby's anthem *Have Mercy Upon Me*, which sets only the first verse of the psalm, at every Friday Evensong in Lent. From 1906, the year after Martin's publication, the Allegri was heard on three of those Fridays, where it is marked 'at the close of service' in the music list. By 1909 the Barnby had been dropped entirely, and Allegri was heard on all six Fridays until 1917, when records become scarce.[25] At New College, Oxford, the Allegri was sung every Ash Wednesday from at least 1923 (when records begin) until 1956 with scarcely a break. Stainer's *Miserere* did not disappear entirely from English choir repertoire: for example, it was sung at Evensong on Ash Wednesday in King's College, Cambridge, from 1919 or earlier until 1929, after which the Allegri replaced it.[26] At Canterbury Cathedral it was still being performed as late as the years 1942 to 1945, when it was given twice, on both Ash Wednesday and Good Friday; in 1946 and 1947 the Allegri was heard on one of these days, and finally Stainer's work was entirely dropped.[27]

A *Miserere* attributed to Palestrina was also sometimes sung in Lent, notably at King's College, Cambridge, from at least 1937. It had been published by Novello in 1905, adapted into English by W. Barclay Squire. It is based on one found in Haberl's Palestrina *Werke*, which reproduced *Miserere* 9 from CS 205–6, described by Baini as a modification to Palestrina's original (*Miserere* 4 in the same source) by G.M. Nanino.[28] As in the Allegri, there are two choirs,

---

[25] During this time all the services on Ash Wednesday – Matins, Commination and Evensong – were sung to a monotone.

[26] In 1930, the Allegri was given at King's no fewer than three times: on Ash Wednesday, and twice as part of a 'Passion Devotion'. Perhaps this innovation shows the influence not only of the recently appointed organist Boris Ord, but also that of Eric Milner-White, creator of the 'Nine Lessons and Carols' service for Christmas 1928. No chapel bills earlier than 1919 survive, so Stainer's *Miserere* may well have been in use earlier. It had a brief and perhaps surprising comeback on Ash Wednesday of 1969 and was heard at King's again on the third Sunday of Lent in 1971.

[27] L. Saint, 'Choral Music in Canterbury Cathedral, 1873–1988: The Role of Service Settings and Anthems in the Regeneration, Preservation and Sustenance of Cathedral Worship' (PhD diss., Canterbury Christ Church University, 2011), 173–4.

[28] See Table 1 in Chapter 2, and p. 28, n. 22. It is attributed to Palestrina in a manuscript in the Biblioteca Vallicelliana. Haberl printed it in *Pierluigi da Palestrina Werke*, vol. 31 (1894), 28–34.

one of five voices and one of four, but the verses they sing are exchanged: it is the four-part choir which sings verse 1. The final half-verse is for both choirs together, a practice perhaps inaugurated by Nanino in this work. As there is no recognisable Tone on which the piece is based, Squire suggested that the *cantus planus* verses should be recited on a monotone, thus reflecting, no doubt unwittingly, Papal Choir practice from at least the eighteenth century onwards.

✳ Misereres in England 2 – Rockstro in the ascendant

From the 1930s onwards the Allegri increasingly became the preferred *Miserere* in a majority of British choral institutions, often given on Ash Wednesday (although never as part of the Commination service to which it belonged) and sometimes repeated later during Lent. It was always, even in Oxbridge colleges, sung in English, Anglican ecclesiastical authorities showing themselves much more concerned about the language in which it was sung than about the office to which it was attached.[29] The edition used was therefore Martin's, entirely based on Burney, and with no ornaments of any kind. Rockstro's 'creation' of the four-part verses for his article in Grove's *Dictionary*, being of course written out in Latin, became an option only in 1951 when Novello published an edition 'with the traditional *abbellimenti* sung in the Sistine Chapel, Rome. Adapted and arranged for English use by Ivor Atkins.'[30]

Atkins' version shows a clear debt to Martin in the wordy underlay – neither hesitated to repeat words or phrases, as if they were afraid to let the choir sing too many melismas. Maybe that was how they felt psalms should in principle be sung. The few textual amendments Atkins made involved placing important

---

[29] It could turn up at almost any service during Lent and, moreover, at almost any moment in that service. During Evensong it could be an Introit, replace the psalm, serve as the anthem or, as at Canterbury and Worcester, simply be tacked on 'at the close of the service'. In a Communion service it could be heard at the beginning or end (after the Agnus Dei, for example) or somewhere in the middle. All of these solutions were, and still are, found. Resistance to singing in anything other than English remained strong until the 1970s, when the pressure created by interest in 'historically informed performance' – in which the ideal of using the original language was seen as an essential part of recreating the composer's sound world – became irresistible.

[30] Sir Ivor Atkins (1869–1963, Fig. 27) also edited English-language versions of both Bach Passions and Brahms' *German Requiem*, so had experience in the exercise of language adaptation. He also had expertise in scholarly editing, having made many editions of music by Worcester composers of the sixteenth and seventeenth centuries.

Fig. 27 Sir Ivor Atkins

words ('truth', 'joy', 'clean', 'sacrifice') where the harmony changed, no doubt seeking to make them more telling. Like Martin, he proposed Tone II for the *cantus planus* verses (at the same time correcting a few of his solecisms of accentuation), but he abandoned entirely the idea of congregational participation and thus of organ accompaniment. The musical text of the five-part verses was all from Burney, with Rockstro's 'correction' of the alto part disappearing, as well as the variant which had crept into the final half-verse, discussed below.[31]

The title affirmed Atkins' belief that the *abbellimenti* were genuine, and acknowledged clearly his sources: 'the text of the Chorus verses is based upon Burney (1771), the *abbellimenti* upon Alfieri and Rockstro'. Presumably it did not occur to him to doubt the veracity of what he read in Grove's *Dictionary*. Even if it had, he could have found an impeccable musicological *imprimatur* in Robert Haas's monumental work on performance practice, *Aufführungspraxis der Musik*, published in Potsdam in 1931. There Rockstro's work was presented as entirely derived from Alfieri's publication of 1840.[32] While it is clear that

---

[31] See n. 39 and Appendix 13, n. 4.

[32] Haas, *Aufführungspraxis der Musik*, 157–60.

Haas did not check the original sources, it is also evident that he was misled by the third edition of Grove's *Dictionary* (1929). There the entry 'Miserere' as published in the first two editions was drastically shortened. Rockstro's version of verse 3 was transferred to the entry on Allegri, where, after reproducing most of E.F. Pember's original article (including information on the effect on listeners of performances of the *Miserere*), the following sentence was interpolated:

> An edition including these *abbellimenti* was published by ALFIERI (*q.v.*) in 1840. The example [footnote: Quoted by Rockstro under MISERERE in previous editions of the Dictionary] on [the] next page, in which the embellished cadences are printed in small type sufficiently shows their nature.[33]

The clear implication of the word 'quoted' (rather than, say, 'invented') is that the whole reconstruction is Alfieri's. Haas's note shows that he accepted this statement without question: 'The Diminutions the papal Chapel added to Allegri's Miserere were published in 1840 by Pietro Alfieri, under the secret name of Alessandro Geminiani, in Lugano, wherein we find the traditional Mendelssohn manner of singing.'[34] It is evident that he had noticed the inclusion of Mendelssohn's phrase, which he also reproduced, but he appears to have taken that as confirmation of the authenticity of both sources, as Atkins did twenty years later. Perhaps it never occurred to either of them that a musicologist would invent such a thing!

In 1951 Ivor Atkins had just retired after fifty-three years as Organist and Choirmaster of Worcester Cathedral. One would like to imagine that he tried out his edition with the choir towards the end of his time there, but that cannot be proven: the Allegri was not sung in 1947–8, and there is no record of the subsequent years. Neither are there any manuscript traces of Atkins' work there, as they were all apparently given to his family, and remain untraced. The only edition of the Allegri now in the Worcester archives from that time is Martin's.

Atkins' successor there was David Willcocks. The absence of service lists from the 1950s does not permit us to know whether he tried out Atkins' edition at Worcester, but it seems likely that proximity with its creator must have had some effect,[35] for when he moved to King's College, Cambridge, in 1957, it appears to have entered the repertoire almost immediately. By Easter 1959 he was confident enough to include it in the choir's broadcast for the BBC of

---

[33] *Grove's Dictionary*, 3rd edn, vol. 1 (1929), 68–9.

[34] 'Die Diminutionen der päpstlichen Kapelle zu Allegris Miserere hat dann 1840 Pietro Alfieri unter dem Hehlnamen Alessandro Geminiani in Lugano veröffentlicht, darin finden wir die von Mendelssohn überlieferte Singmanier.' *Aufführungspraxis*, 158.

[35] The Allegri was often programmed by his successor Douglas Guest, but it is impossible to know which edition was used.

Choral Evensong for Ash Wednesday, using Atkins' edition. This is no doubt the first time it was heard by a wider public, albeit incomplete.[36] At first the top Cs were done by three boys together, and it was also thus in 1961, when King's was again heard singing Choral Evensong on Ash Wednesday, this time using a modified edition by Willcocks himself. But the following year a treble named Roy Goodman (Fig. 28), who had arrived in the choir in 1960, was trusted to do it alone, and in 1963 his performance was captured on record, released the following year on an LP entitled *Evensong for Ash Wednesday*.[37]

There is little doubt that the current standing of the 'English Miserere' is almost entirely due to this recording, Goodman's top Cs being sung with an effortless grace that seems to defy gravity. Moreover, Willcocks' decision to use one entire take without edits gave it a unity and presence that more than make up for occasional imperfections of attack.[38]

[36] Verses 6–9 and 11–14 were omitted, no doubt for pressure of time (the BBC liked Choral Evensong to not exceed 45 minutes). It can be heard on the YouTube channel of Colin Brownlee's *Archive of Recorded Church Music* (http://www.recordedchurchmusic.org). The *Miserere* had also been performed by the choir of Wakefield Cathedral during Choral Evensong's Ash Wednesday broadcast of March 3, 1954, but apparently Martin's edition was used. John Holt, Head Boy at the time, is 'certain that we did not sing the full and proper version of the Allegri *Miserere* made famous by St John's Cambridge and performed by today's choir at Wakefield. I would remember the top C nightmares! I do however have a vague recollection of a comparatively simple version of the Miserere (probably the George Martin version) and I suspect that this is what was sung.' (My thanks to him, to John North, chair of the Old Choristers Association, and Tom Moore, the present Director of Music at Wakefield, for their prompt answers to my questions.) The 'top C' version was only introduced at Wakefield in 1970 by the new Director of Music Jonathan Bielby.

[37] Argo ZRG 5365 (1964). Roy only shares the honour of being the first to sing it as a solo in 1962, as Stephen Varcoe did so at Canterbury Cathedral in the same year. According to Stephen, this was largely due to the arrival of the new organist Allan Wicks: 'We did indeed sing the version with top Cs, and the thing which was life-changing for me was that until Allan arrived I could hardly reach the top of the treble stave. He released all those top notes, and without him I'd probably have become a lawyer' (personal communication).

[38] Roger Fiske wrote in *Gramophone* (review of 'Allegri: Miserere', reissued in 1964 as a single on Argo ZFA111, November 1965, 259) that 'the high Cs of the soloist are exquisite and unforgettable', and that he had 'never before heard such high notes from a boy'. Michael George, another good treble and later a fine baritone, was one of the two boys singing the second treble part in the quartet (the other was Paul Santer, later a professional trumpeter), and the other singers were Charles Brett, alto, and Peter Cairns, baritone. Mike recollects: 'I probably could have sung the main solo part with the top C, but Roy was an absolutely outstanding treble.' Roy recalls that 'I was able to sing

Fig. 28 Roy Goodman aged nine at King's College, Cambridge, c.1960
(photo by permission of the subject)

comfortably high F♯ ABOVE top C', which rather explains the lack of apparent effort!

The recording of the *Miserere* was re-released no fewer than eighteen times between 1964 and 2015 (for a full list, see Jacob Sagrans, 'Early Music and the Choir of King's College, Cambridge, 1958 to 2015' (PhD diss., McGill University, Montreal, 2016), 121), often with other repertoire. Only the most recent (Universal Eloquence 480-2075) includes the whole of the original *Evensong for Ash Wednesday*. Roy's note for it mentions a practical aspect of the recording which has since tickled many people's imaginations: 'On the day that we made the present recording, I had only just finished playing a rugby match an hour or so before the session. I had no time for a proper shower and still had muddy knees under my long trousers.' For a somewhat surprising reprise of this story, see p. 213.

Willcocks' 'written-in' modifications of Atkins' edition after 1959 concerned mostly the underlay of the English text. Whereas Atkins used almost exclusively one-syllable-per-note with free repetition of phrases (as Martin had done), Willcocks' aim was clearly to have as little text as possible in the melismatic sections of each verse, particularly those for the quartet, so he got through most of it in the chanted openings of each half-verse and did not repeat words. In this it was closer to the original Latin versions, although whether this was a conscious historical decision is unclear. It certainly allowed the singers to concentrate on vocalisation and beautiful sound.[39] According to Roy Goodman:

> I don't remember EVER rehearsing the Allegri – there was certainly no private coaching or voice training whatsoever. You just sang it – and for the recording we simply did 3 complete takes, and David chose one of them, with absolutely no editing![40]

The tradition was also established in this recording of placing the solo quartet at a distance, a practice which has no historical basis whatsoever because it was impossible in the *Cantoria* of the Sistine Chapel, but which has since become virtually the norm for the 'English Miserere'. Roy recalls:

> I don't remember any spatial separation normally, except for the recording. Then our solo group ... was placed on the Decani side about a quarter of the way between the choir stalls and the main altar. We didn't have any relayed beat and were just left to ourselves! In those days it was very dark (the old dark wood panelling has since all been removed) and just a few candles![41]

---

[39] It is thus rather a surprise when in the last verse, for no obvious reason, the last few words 'upon thine altar' are repeated, necessitating two syllables on the final chord. This may be a function of the musical text he chose, in which an extra semibreve is added to the antepenultimate chord of G minor. This had also been used by Walker and Martin. It is found in an edition edited by Schott by Frédéric Rochlitz in 1835, and also in Mesplet's manuscripts (**Man** and **P**), but the connection between these disparate sources is not clear (see Appendix 13, n. 4). Andrew Parker later made a fair manuscript copy of Willcocks' version – for the moment mislaid – for use by the choir in the early 1970s (personal communication from John Nixon, choral scholar from 1970 to 1973). A chorister from the time remembers Willcocks' original as being 'roneoed on foolscap paper with purple ink and a very strong smell of chlorine'.

[40] He did rather well out of it. 'I remember David read out some "fan mail" to us all in 1962 (after the radio broadcast) – from a kind generous Irish gentleman, who always enclosed three 10 shilling book tokens for the 'boys' (sic) who had sung the high C. David chuckled with amusement – and sent a reply back to say that there was just one boy that year – and so I did rather well for book tokens!!'

[41] Charles Brett, as senior choral scholar, provided some direction. Spatial separation has since become a constant feature of concerts also, although Roy remembers doing it thus just once, from the organ loft at Lincoln Cathedral.

Fig. 29 Reunion at King's College for the fiftieth Anniversary of Roy Goodman's recording, Saturday 16 February 2013). *Left to right*: Roy (aged sixty-two), Tom Pickard (the soloist that year), the Director of Music Sir Stephen Cleobury, and Sir David Willcocks

One wonders if the spatial effect, which has since become so much part of listeners' expectations, was not originally an idea of the producers. When Peter Phillips made his first recording of the *Miserere* in 1980 he not only 'placed the solo group at some distance from the remainder of the choir' but pointed this out in his sleeve note,[42] and from around that date critics would systematically complain when it was not done, and praise both the conductor and the sound engineers when it created the right mysterious effect.

> I still feel that more use could have been made of this space for the recording of Allegri's *Miserere*, in which the solo choir ... is placed uncomfortably close to the listener; a little extra distance would have produced a more magical result. (1985)[43]

Afterwards the soloists were made 'Free Men' of Lincoln, a reward well deserved in Roy's case as he was afterwards informed by his choirmaster that the pitch had risen by at least a semitone during the performance! This and Roy's other comments by personal communication.

[42] Classics for Pleasure CFP 40339 (1980).

[43] John Milsom, 'Music of Sixteenth-Century Rome', *Gramophone*, May 1985, referring to EMI 747065–2, Choir of King's College, Cambridge (Cleobury).

the semi-chorus, with its top C boy ... is considerably distanced. This takes away a good deal of anxiety and also emphasizes the robust nature of the plainsong when we return to it. (1986)[44]

As far as the showcased piece is concerned, there are certainly more involving performances (there is little or no spatial differentiation between the two choirs). (1996)[45]

The recording engineers cope well and find effective placing ... for the semi-chorus. (2011)[46]

The programme opens with a double-choir version of Allegri's justly famous *Miserere*, with the second group atmospherically recessed alongside the confident soprano soloist. (1999)[47]

Perhaps the strangest comment concerns a DVD recording of a live concert in S. Maria Maggiore.

The spatial effects of this music could not be rendered nearly so spectacularly in the Sistine (video will show you how: Choir 1 to the right of the chancel, the chant-intoning tenors to the left, Choir 2 magically distant, far away beyond the gates of the chapel of Paul V).[48]

The spatial separation has also become a constant feature of performance during the office. As early as 1964 in Canterbury the organist Allan Wicks placed the quartet

in the aisle above 'the Martyrdom' [the site which marks the murder of Thomas Becket] just outside the Quire ... That added to the atmosphere but the Dean and Chapter took exception to the 'theatricality' and sometime after, they asked Allan to stop such practices.[49]

---

[44] Anon, 'Sacred Choral Works', *Gramophone*, May 1986, referring to Archiv 415 517–1AH, Choir of Westminster Abbey (Preston).

[45] Fabrice Fitch, 'Miserere', *Gramophone*, July 1996, referring to Sony SK 66615, Choir of Westminster Abbey (Neary).

[46] John Steane, 'Hear my words', *Gramophone*, Jan 2011, referring to Chandos CHSA 5085, Choir of St John's College, Cambridge (Nethsingha).

[47] Ivan March, 'Sacred Voices – Music of the Renaissance', *Gramophone*, August 1999, referring to The Full Works 75605 57029–2, New Company (Bicket).

[48] Michael Oliver, 'The Tallis Scholars Live in Rome', *Gramophone*, September 1994, referring to Gimell 1585T–994, Tallis Scholars, (Phillips).

[49] Personal communication from Anthony Dawson, chorister at Canterbury and soloist in the *Miserere* there in 1964–5.

Not all chapters were as conservative, however, and finding an imaginative place for the quartet is an important aspect of modern performance. At St Paul's Cathedral, it is naturally found in the 'whispering gallery', even if the singers have been known to lose their way up to it during the service and find themselves outside the building on the roof! Perhaps the most extreme example was that at King's, following a scheme instituted by Philip Ledger when he succeeded David Willcocks in 1974:

> The piece commenced with the full choir at the west end of the chapel in rows, behind the seating in between the north and the south doors ... The solo quartet (conducted by the senior organ scholar) would start in the south side-chapel as near to the east end as possible. The first two semi-choruses were sung in the east-most available chapel. It then moved one side-chapel west between each portion. This meant that there were, in total, four locations from which it sang, and that it was never visible to the congregation in the chapel (or ante-chapel), other than when processing at the start of the piece, and joining the full choir at the end. During the singing of the third semi-chorus section the full choir would process east towards the organ screen, and remain in processional format with the Director of Music on the organ steps. After the fifth semi-chorus the plainsong singers would leave the men's vestry (now the full choir vestry, I believe) and join the main choir, simply inserting into their individual places. The last short chorus (*Tunc imponent*) was then sung in nine-part harmony rather than a full choir in five parts plus quartet.[50]

The fight against chapter reluctance for innovation took longer where language was concerned. Probably the first time the Allegri was heard in Latin was at Canterbury in 1963, at Allan Wicks' insistence, but the chapter was not content: 'Attention was drawn to the words of a Latin Anthem sung at Evensong on March 24th, 1963 [the fourth Sunday in Lent]. It was Allegri's Miserere.'[51] The following year it reverted to English. At King's it was sung in Latin from 1974, when Philip Ledger succeeded Willcocks. In the absence of a printed edition, Ledger 'cobbled together' one of his own.[52]

---

[50] My thanks to Colin Hawke (choral scholar 1974–7) for this detailed account. According to Ben Byram-Wigfield (chorister 1979–84) 'the sound would just come out of nowhere', but a more recent listener found it 'a bit disconcerting for listeners, like chasing moths'. Much of this scheme is preserved nowadays, except that the semi-chorus generally moves in one go from the easternmost end to the side-chapel by the organ screen, and the plainsong verses are sung by a solo cantor placed in the organ loft.

[51] Chapter meeting, quoted in Saint, 'Choral Music in Canterbury Cathedral', 273.

[52] It may be that Willcocks would not have approved: as late as 1978 he still thought it a good idea to record the Bach Choir singing the *St Matthew Passion* complete in English. According to Ben Byram-Wigfield, heavily involved

It was not until 1976 that an edition appeared in Latin, prepared by Sir George Guest, Organist and Choirmaster of St John's College, Cambridge, since 1951. It is not known exactly when he introduced the work into the choir's repertoire, but local rivalry meant that he was very keen that his choir should be chosen ahead of the one 'down the road' to sing it in the yearly BBC broadcast of the Ash Wednesday Evensong.[53] After 1967, the last of a sequence of seven by King's College, the chapel was closed for maintenance, and the Allegri was not programmed again there until 1970.[54] Despite the enthusiasm the King's recording had aroused, the BBC does not seem to have been in a hurry to find another choir to sing it on Ash Wednesday. It finally reappeared only in 1972, when St John's College took over the privilege that it has held virtually ever since. Although the published edition was still four years away, the choir was certainly singing in Latin from Guest's manuscript: the BBC's *Radio Times* described it as 'Psalm 51, Allegri, arr. Guest' (at St John's, the Allegri was always sung as the psalm). One wonders if this provoked problems within the Anglican hierarchy. Is it fanciful to detect a touch of unease in the *Radio Times*' description of the Allegri in 1975: 'Miserere, the Latin text of Psalm 51'? Had there been complaints from listeners? In sum, it is unclear whether the adoption of Latin by St John's accelerated or held back the achievement of Guest's aim to sing it for the BBC.[55]

---

not only as soloist but also as head chorister librarian, the choir used 'a home-made cut-and-paste edition, taken from Burney plus hand-written bits for the small choir. There's no clue as to who made it.' In 1980 Ledger conducted a performance of the *Miserere* in Latin for a video entitled *The Story of King's College Choir – The Boast of King's*, made in 1980 by Robert Chesterman for Prometheus Productions, a Canadian company, and since re-released on DVD. Rather than including the elaborate movements practised during Evensong, it is remarkable for being a rare occurrence of the solo quartet (in fact a quintet, because two boys shared the top line) singing their verses from the middle of the choir, with no spatial separation whatever.

[53] Roy Goodman does not remember any other choir singing it during his years at King's (1960–3), but ex-choristers from St John's remember it being new in the very early 1960s, when it was sung in English, presumably from Atkins' edition. One of them remembers Guest telling them that there was no Latin edition at that time with the *abbellimenti*, so perhaps he was already thinking about filling that gap (my thanks to Tim Brown, Nicolas Robertson and Jonathan Seers for their recollections).

[54] Since 1972 it has been sung twice each year – on Ash Wednesday and Good Friday – but it has been broadcast only once, on Wednesday of Holy Week 2005, as part of a series of programmes entitled 'Easter at King's'.

[55] This and other information about Choral Evensong broadcasts is from the BBC's *Genome* website, https://genome.ch.bbc.co.uk/ (accessed February–March 2017). Thanks are due to Canon Stephen Shipley of the BBC, and to Colin Brownlee (*Archive of Recorded Church Music*), who generously allowed me to hear certain archive recordings not yet on his website.

As Atkins had done, Guest took the notes of the five-part verses (and the nine-part half verse at the end) directly from Burney, and those of the four-part ones from Rockstro, identical in all aspects except that the 'capricious' f♯s were definitively silenced. There still remained many decisions to be made about underlay. As noted at the beginning of this chapter, Burney's edition was probably completed from a version which gave verses 1 and 3 only, and gives no hint of the Papal Choir's manner of singing the chanted sections of the other verses, in which the 'proportion of long and short syllables' was very important.[56] Guest's solution was to precisely notate the kind of chanting that would be found in an English psalm, in which 'all the notes are equal but some are more equal than others' (Fig. 30). While the liberal use of triplets, in particular, looks somewhat fussy on the page, when interpreted by Guest's choir at St John's with a supple speech rhythm, it worked well.

One effect of Guest's edition seems to have been to quell entirely any enthusiasm for recording, and soon even for performing, the *Miserere* in English.

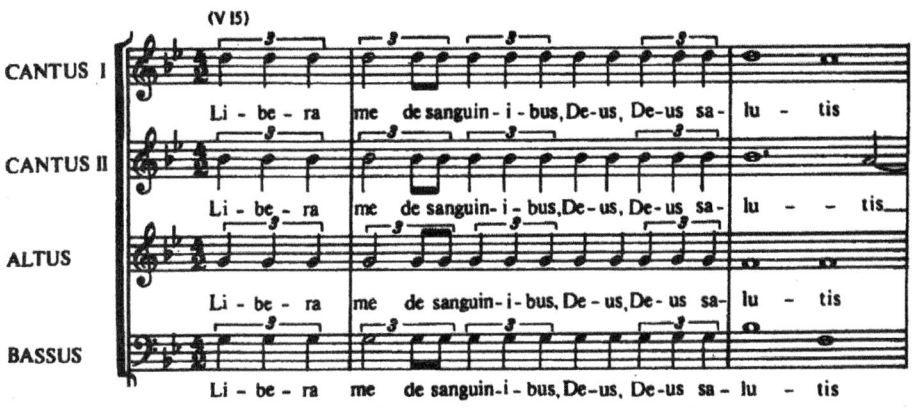

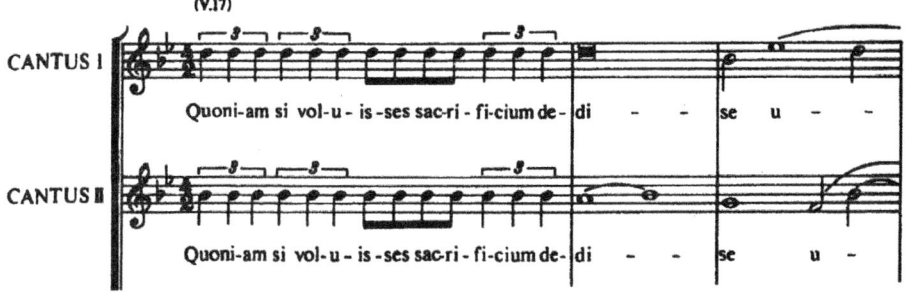

Fig. 30 Prosody given in George Guest's edition (1976) for verses 15 and 17

---

[56] See pp. 49–50 and 238–9.

It prompted a spate of recordings in Latin, firstly by Peter Phillips' Tallis Scholars in 1980, followed rapidly by St John's College itself in 1981.[57] The 'top C' sopranos in recordings by mixed choirs which followed – Alison Stamp, Deborah Roberts and others – were soon nearly as famous as Goodman had been, although few managed that note with the ridiculous ease that Roy had displayed. The following year saw the first recording by a Catholic choir, that of Westminster Cathedral directed by Stephen Cleobury (released in 1983), and he wasted little time in recording another one when he went to King's College and replaced Ledger's 'cobbled together' manuscript with Guest's edition. Two more followed in 1986, by the choir of Westminster Abbey, directed by Simon Preston, and Mark Brown's Pro Cantione Antiqua.

Suddenly every good choir in England wanted its own *Miserere* in the catalogue, and they all seemed happy to accept Guest's edition more or less as gospel, although they all were liable to treat the underlay of the chanted sections – and sometimes even the polyphonic ones – in their own ways.[58] All

---

[57] It was as well that the Tallis Scholars recording (released originally on the Classics for Pleasure label, CFP40339) specified that the soprano soloist was Alison Stamp; otherwise many would no doubt have taken her for a boy. This, of course, was the idea, picked up by John Milsom in a *Gramophone* review of an LP by King's College, Cambridge, 'Music of Sixteenth-Century Rome', December 1984, where he wrote of 'the spectral and wonderfully boyish singing of Alison Stamp' (repeated in a later version of this review (see n. 43), coinciding with the release of the EP). The Tallis Scholars have made three recordings of the 'English Miserere' over twenty-five years, and hold the record for the most performances of it to date – 476 (as at March 2017, out of a total of 2,106 concerts) – an achievement unlikely ever to be surpassed.

[58] For example, the Tallis Scholars have tended to sing them more rhythmically than The Sixteen (1989) and Pro Cantione Antiqua, both of which aimed for something closer to equality. Alfieri had proposed rhythmic solutions for most of the verses in his 1840 edition, nearly all of which coincide with those found in Bai's *Miserere*, but there is no evidence that anyone thought to look at it.

The Englishness of these performances has also been increased by a preference by some for Tudor-style syllable divisions. Pioneered by Willcocks' English version (af-*m*. ter*c* thy*c* great*cm*. good-*cm*[ness]), it was enthusiastically followed by Phillips among others in Latin (mi-*m*. se-*cc* ri-*c* cor- ; hu-*m*. mi-*cc* li-*c* a, etc.).

Guest's version has now generally been superseded by one edited by John Rutter (Oxford University Press, 1996), which suggests no reciting rhythms other than those in Burney. While less fussy on the page, it underlines a clear assumption of equality. Bizarrely, Rutter also suggests that at the end of the four-part verses, the transposed phrase of Mendelssohn (Fig. 26, Rockstro's reconstruction of verse 3) could·be sung a fourth lower. This makes sense as far as its transposition is concerned, but as it belongs at the end of the first part, this 'solution' makes the end of both parts of the verse harmonically identical.

these recordings were sung in the written key of G minor, with the five-part verses sung by the full choir and the four-part ones by a solo quartet. Many followed the lead of Willcocks' recording by placing the quartet at a distance, the exceptions being The Sixteen, Cleobury's two versions (although he did follow this practice in a later 1998 recording with King's College) and Pro Cantione Antiqua. A new work had been invented, and the public, it seemed, couldn't get enough of it.[59] There was not even any meaningful argument to be had as to whether the upper parts were better sung by boys or women. In the Sistine Chapel they had been sung by neither.

✺ Misereres in England 3 – other ideas

The performance of Rockstro's ornaments provoked varied reactions in the early years. Academics in various parts of Oxbridge were apparently heard muttering about them, on grounds not only of historical authenticity, but also

---

[59] ArkivMusik currently lists no fewer than 100 performances of the 'English Miserere' on CD, including arrangements, duplicates and re-releases (Sagrans, 'Early Music and the Choir of King's College', 123). Before 1980, the public could have been excused for thinking that no other versions of 'the Allegri' were possible, so little was there in the way of alternative recordings. I have heard only two, both, in their own way, unusual. That by the Coro Vallicelliano, released in 1962 as part of volume 2 of RCA Italiana's collection *Storia della musica italiana*, is typical of much Italian choral singing of the time – the big full voices more concerned with emotional gesture than blend or precision of attack. It is disappointing that whatever local knowledge might have survived the disbanding of the College of Papal Singers, and suggested by the name of the choir (after S. Maria in Vallicella, in many ways its parish church) seems to have been lost in the meantime. The plainsong verses are ignored entirely, and the systematic exaggerated *rallentandi* and *smorzandi* at every single cadence (an interpretative feature nowhere found in Mustafà's manuscript, or in any other) outstay their welcome well before the end. More interesting, if even more quirky, is a 1953 recording by the Harvard Glee Club. The music is arranged for men's voices in an edition by A.T. Davison (*Harvard University Glee Club Collection of Part Songs for Men's Voices*, vol. 1 (Boston, 1922), 37–42), and here only the first four polyphonic verses are sung. The chanted sections are particularly energetic – almost aggressive at times – and no two bars are ever at the same tempo. Technically, the singing is excellent: the singers are doing exactly what they wish to do. The basis of the interpretation is difficult to guess but in its sheer strangeness it seems to come closer to listeners' experiences in the Sistine Chapel than does the Coro Vallicelliano, or even some of the less imaginative modern English readings. I am indebted to Jacob Sagrans for letting me hear these recordings that he found with some difficulty and discussed in 'Early Music and the Choir of King's College', 119–20.

of taste. One of the first to reflect in depth about the many problems was Hugh Keyte. His earliest practical input came as a BBC producer, helping to organise a visit by Gavin Turner's William Byrd Choir to the Sistine Chapel in 1980, where it was allowed several nights to record. Thus the 'English Miserere' was performed in that space for the first time.[60] Keyte was not yet ready to seriously question its musicological basis, and the only differences to standard practice consisted of a few fairly anodyne ornaments by the 'top C' soprano, Kym Amps.[61] Perhaps the most interesting part of the project was to experience the acoustic space of the Chapel, which will be discussed more fully in Chapter 17.

It was only when requested by Andrew Parrott to prepare the music for a recording by the Taverner Consort in 1987 that Keyte went more deeply into the many problems with the 'English Miserere'. His extensive programme note, after showing the origins of Rockstro's various mistakes, expressed surprise

> that so glaring a series of errors could have been overlooked in the editing process for Grove's dictionary, but, rather than being weeded out, the error was compounded by Ivor Atkins' 1951 edition of the piece, which lifted the Choir I part from Burney's publication, and the Choir II from the erroneous example in Grove. Later editions continue to use this mismatched version, even in the knowledge that the piece has now moved very far from its origins.[62]

The resulting recording got many things right. It was sung a tone higher than written – not as extreme a modulation as that the Papal Choir sometimes managed, but a meaningful gesture towards the brighter colour cultivated there. The plainsong verses were sung, correctly, by men's voices in a somewhat aggressive monotone on the dominant, and the two groups of solo singers – the quintet and the quartet – were placed side by side in the foreground, as they would have been in the *Cantoria* of the Sistine Chapel. There was some use of dynamics, particularly a contrast between the fairly loud chanted sections and the softer 'composed' parts of each verse, often prepared by a *diminuendo* on a held chord just before them.

The actual notes sung, however, were something of a *potpourri*. Of the five-part verses, verse 1 was taken, plain, from Allegri's original, in CS 205 (Appendix 1), and verse 5 from CS 341 but without the variation for that specific verse

---

[60] More recently, the Tallis Scholars sang it there in a televised concert to mark the restoration of Michelangelo's ceiling paintings in 1994.

[61] The most refreshing reading among the recordings made there is that of Palestrina's *Stabat mater*, performed at low pitch and with most of the voices – especially the sopranos – contributing generous roulades and divisions, in the style of Conforti and Severi.

[62] *Musica della Cappella Sistina*, EMI Reflexe CDC 7 47699 2 (1987) and later reissues.

as shown in Appendix 3. Verse 9 followed Burney. Verse 13 was taken from what has been labelled here **A**, the 1820s series of manuscripts one of which Haas had printed, but again without the variation specific to that verse, and verse 17 reverted to Burney, but with embellishments. The first half of verse 20 again relied on **A** but with extra ornamentation. The four-part verses followed a similar pattern of increasing complexity during the course of the performance: verse 3 directly from CS 206 without ornaments, verse 7 from the same source, but with Mendelssohn's phrase added at its proper place at the end of the first half, and decorations elsewhere. Verse 11 followed the same pattern but with extra ornaments, while verse 15 broadly used **A** as its basis, as did verse 19, but with increased embellishment. While it is impossible that all these versions were ever heard in the same performance in the Vatican, at least most of them (with the exception of Burney, as explained above) had some historic credibility in their own right.[63]

That this was still a 'work-in-progress' for Keyte became clear with his 1995 project, discussed below. But before that was heard, a completely different approach was taken by the French ensemble A Sei Voci, directed by Bernard Fabre-Garrus.[64] Musicologist Jean Lionnet, an outstanding authority on Roman sacred music of the sixteenth and seventeenth centuries, produced a version full of ornamentation based on the treatises of the period, particularly the *Salmi passaggiati* (1615) of Francesco Severi. Naturally therefore CS 205–206 was taken as its basis except, curiously, for one verse (9) based on Burney.[65] The ornaments are more harmonically adventurous and less formalised than most of Severi's – for example, there is no example in his publication of a solo part holding a suspension over the final chord (Bovicelli did give some examples in 1594) – but in general the execution sounded convincingly improvised. A Sei Voci left most of them to its fine soprano, Ruth Holton, although Severi gave examples for all the parts, with the implication that the singers might have taken turns in ornamenting.[66] While its authenticity is unprovable, it remains until recently the only attempt so far to imagine how the *Miserere* might have sounded within the first fifty years of its existence. In this it has more than a

---

[63] The fact that many directors feel the need to vary the settings throughout the piece (a feature of some recent recordings discussed below) perhaps gives a clue as to why the Papal singers came to prefer Bai's *Miserere*, with its constant variation, over Allegri's.

[64] Astrée Auvidis E8524 (1994). The CD also includes a performance of the 'English Miserere'.

[65] See Appendix 1 for the five-part verses and Appendix 3 for the four-part ones. There is an odd variant in the version adopted at the end of the five-part verses, in which the suspension provoked by the first tenor part is resolved on the last chord instead of after it.

[66] The only example in Severi where all parts improvise at the same time is fully written out, almost composed (the last verse of a series of ornamentations based on Dentice's *Miserere*, found on page 75).

little in common with the performance of the Palestrina's *Stabat mater* by the William Byrd Choir discussed above.[67] Lionnet also innovated by using an unusual form of Tone I for the plainsong, which is at least more appropriate than Tone II.

A recent performance, by Le Poème Harmonique directed by Vincent Dumestre, adopts many of the same solutions.[68] In fact Dumestre acknowledges his debt to Lionnet and Fabre-Garrus in an accompanying note, and he adopts wholesale both the odd version of CS 205 for the five-part verses and the same form of Tone 1 for the *cantus planus*. The ornamentations are rewritten however, with fewer division-like roulades and more short 'graces'. This accords better with Zenobi's description of the art of singing 'plainly' (see p. 38), and with the praise of *sprezzatura* by Rognoni, Giustiniani and others. They are (beautifully) performed at just about every conceivable opportunity by all the singers, and the transposition down a tone into F minor, while slightly surprising, gives plenty of scope for invention in the highest reaches.

However, despite the enjoyment this version gives as a performance, it cannot be taken seriously as a re-creation. There is nothing in any seventeenth century text which justifies the liberties taken with the basic harmony, provoked by a series of seemingly random suspensions and anticipations. Nicolai's observation of 1835/6 comes to mind: 'it will be easy for you to understand that if different voices add passing notes to the harmony, each according to his caprice, the result must often be repulsive' (p. 115). The result is far from repulsive to a modern ear, but it would have been very surprising to a seventeenth century one. The commitment to fun is made clear at verse 19, in which Rockstro's outrageous 1880 modulation is introduced; and in the final 9-part verse (20b), the harmony is re-invented, giving not only a very special moment of portamento in its resolution, but also a very twentieth-century feeling of dodecaphony!

By 1995 Hugh Keyte had visited the Vatican library again and searched out sources dating from the period of the *Miserere*'s heyday in the eighteenth and nineteenth centuries. He came back with a copy of CS 375, Mustafa's extraordinary composite Bai-Allegri manuscript of 1892 described in Chapter 12, and it was immediately recorded by the Westminster Abbey Consort.[69]

---

[67] See n. 61.

[68] 'Anamorfosi' (Alpha 438), released in September 2019.

[69] Sony SK66615 (released in 1996).

It is important to underline that this was the first, and so far only, recording of the *Miserere* to use an authentic score without any reconstruction whatsoever, and this makes it unique. It was however a mixed success. It was sung in A minor, less than the transposition of a fourth marked on Mustafà's score (even allowing for low Roman pitch), and the omnipresent vibrato of the sopranos showed little sign of Spohr's 'beautiful 5-part chording, tender and pure, like a harmony from another world'[70] or Mendelssohn's 'soprano [who] intones the high C in a pure, soft voice, allowing it to vibrate for a time, then slowly glides down'.[71] Both these accounts imply a certain calmness in tempo and approach; indeed those who heard the *Miserere* habitually described a marked contrast between this sense of repose and the loud and aggressive chanting of the plainsong. Despite its many embellishments, such a sense of calm is amply present in the version by A Sei Voci, but here it is hidden by a strange and somewhat superfluous urgency. Perhaps as a result, the ornamentation sounds not like a decorative addition but part of a composed score, making the whole extremely busy and over-full of events. One had to wonder if all the singers really believed in the project.

I would like to think that things turned out better in Keyte's more recent realisation, in which he prepared a score transposed a fourth higher from Mustafà's manuscript for my Ensemble William Byrd, which was recorded in 2000.[72] It is more gentle and calm than the Westminster Abbey Consort (it lasts 15'37" as against 13'10"), there is much less vibrato, the ornaments sound, I think, more natural, and the *portamenti* considerably more audible. Certain drawbacks stem from my lack of knowledge at the time. Keyte adapted all the four-part verses to Allegri's which (as will be seen in Chapter 11) was the basis only for verse 3. While this was a formula that was sometimes heard in the Chapel, it meant that Bai's fine settings of the other four-part verses (7, 11, 15 and 19) were absent. During the next seven years, while performing the piece at least forty more times in concert, we restored Bai's original four-part verses, a move which met with universal approval from the singers. We also made the parallel *portamenti* on the reciting chords – almost absent on the recording – more evident (at the time I struggled to believe they could be true), restricted the unison recited verses to tenors and basses only (as specified in some of the manuscripts described in Chapter 9), and did away with the appoggiaturas at the beginnings of them, which revealed themselves to be merely cues (see Chapters 12 and 14). On a practical level, we became better at separating the highest voices, whose overtones fought each other painfully in some acoustics – another aspect that the papal singers no doubt became expert at managing. We were lucky to be blessed with a stupendous soprano, Catherine Greuillet,

---

[70] See p. 113.

[71] *Letters*, 141.

[72] Naive E 8846 (2000). The Ensemble William Byrd is no relation of Gavin Turner's William Byrd Choir.

whose top Cs never failed to provoke a frisson among the other singers, their director, and our listeners.

Performances of the 'English Miserere' are now part of Lenten ceremonies throughout Britain. A rapid count of Oxbridge colleges and Anglican cathedrals around the country on Ash Wednesday will usually reveal around thirty being given at more or less the same time, and many more will be heard during the forty days of Lent.[73] Recordings continue to appear with almost monotonous regularity, which is not to say that most of them are of anything other than the highest quality, and the work continues to inspire musicians of all kinds; instrumental arrangements for various groupings of strings, wind and brass regularly appear. There is even (a very interesting) one with much extra music composed for three choirs and an improvised solo saxophone.[74]

Over the last few years, directors have started to notice that Rockstro's creation has no historical merit, and put together compromises of their own. One of the earliest was *Ensemble Officium*, which proposed a potpourri of Burney and Alfieri in 2011.[75] Two years later Harry Christophers' The Sixteen went further in their 'Evolution' version.[76] Counselled by Ben Byram-Wigfield, this is similar in some ways to the Taverner Consort's performance of 1987, but with less variation.[77] The fact that the five-part verses are sung by the full choir, rather than soloists, automatically excludes any embellishment in them, although they are at least based on CS 341 rather than Burney, and include that source's important variant in the second part of verses 5 and 13. The four-part verses are similarly unadventurous, starting from CS 206 and adding

---

[73] It seems that there is no longer a problem in finding the necessary soloist for the top C, which is perhaps a measure of the progress made in the voice training boys now receive. As Edward Higginbottom expressed it to me in a private communication, 'there's always a boy who can do that'. The difficulties for him resided more in 'the tuning (e.g. that A flat in the bass) and pace'. His 1996 recording with the choir of New College, Oxford, slower than many, has an exceptional sense of calm and repose.

[74] *Chorus Sine Nomine*, directed by Johannes Hiemetsberger, arranged by Vladimir Ivanoff (Gramola GRAM 99027, 2012).

[75] Christophorus 77345. In the commentary of director Wilfried Rombach, 'for this recording, we have permitted ourselves the liberty of blending a variety of versions, particularly in the sections for the second choir, not only to demonstrate the work's history of reception, but also to achieve a climactic progression which is surely in keeping with the original intentions in the performance of this work.'

[76] COR 16118 (2013).

[77] More or less the same edition was recorded in 2016 by Suzi Digby's group ORA ('Refuge from the Flames', Harmonia Mundi HMW 906103). It brings a new approach to the question of spatialization by placing the quartet progressively further away with each verse it sings.

some (but by no means all) of the ornaments from **A** (although usually the version in Appendix 10 from British Library Add. 31525(1), which is different from all the other contemporary sources. All of these recordings return to the crowd-pleasing Rockstro-inspired top Cs for the final 4-part verses, no doubt in search of Rombach's 'climactic progression', a decision which means that they are necessarily performed in G minor.[78]

These are quintessentially English compromises for what is now a quintessentially English piece, almost entirely divorced from its Italian roots. Its use as a marker for typical Oxbridge choral singing in the films *Chariots of Fire* (1981) and *Maurice* (1987) starkly underlines its current status. This process arguably began with the 1964 recording: 'By including the *Miserere* sung in English as part of a recorded Anglican service where all other items are in English and by English composers, King's and Argo, the record company that issued the album, claimed Allegri's piece as an English and Anglican work (rather than an Italian and Catholic one)'[79]

Nor has singing it in Latin reduced its English aura, as the following story shows. A recent French novel, *Miserere* by Jean-Christophe Grangé (Paris, 2008, adapted in 2013 as a film with the title *La marque des anges – Miserere*), is a murder mystery which turns on the creation of a master race of boy soldiers by a combination of harsh discipline and choral singing, with the aim of creating a voice of a purity which kills! The debt not only to King's College, but even to Roy Goodman's story of his muddy knees (see n. 38 above), is made manifest in the programme note to a recording of the *Miserere* supposedly made by the first murder victim, the choir master, who writes,

> this almost divine recording was made one rainy afternoon in 1989 in most unpromising circumstances. A few minutes earlier, the choristers had been playing football in the gardens of the church of St Eustache in Saint-Germain-en-Laye, where the recording was to take place. The soloist, a lad by the name of Régis Mazoyer, nailed his solo in the first take, his knees still stained with mud. In the icy chapel, the miracle happened: his amazing voice resounding in the vault of the nave ...[80]

---

[78] In 1990 Tess Knighton could still write of the *Miserere* that 'of course, it's not quite so appealing without the top Cs'. ('Allegri/Lotti/Palestrina Sacred Choral Works', *Gramophone*, October 1990).

[79] Sagrans, 'Early Music and the Choir of King's College', 138.

[80] 'Lors d'un après-midi de pluie de 1989, il avait obtenu cet enregistrement quasi divin, alors que rien ne laissait prévoir. Quelques minutes plus tôt, les petits chanteurs jouaient encore au football dans les jardins de l'église Saint-Eustache de Saint-Germain-en-Laye où la prise de son devait avoir lieu. Puis l'enfant soliste, un gamin du nom de Régis Mazoyer, avait lancé sa mélodie dès la première prise, les genoux encore maculés de boue. Alors, dans la chapelle glacée, le miracle s'était produit. La voix stupéfiante s'était élevée sous les voûtes de la nef ...', Jean-Christophe Grangé, *Miserere*, (Paris, 2008), 53.

An interesting postscript is provided by a recent (2015) recording made by the *Cappella Musicale Pontificia 'Sistina'*.[81] The choir performs what is as far as we know the original version (as transmitted in CS 205–6) without ornamentation of any kind. Consisting of about twenty boys and twenty-four men, it brings a warm sound to the generous acoustic of the Sistine Chapel. The plainsong is unfortunately given to the inappropriate Tone II, but it is sung appropriately quickly. In fact the whole tempo is rapid, although it manages to sound not at all rushed.[82] The commentary lays much emphasis on 'injecting life, pulse and colour into the sacred music of the Renaissance, distancing it from the black-and-white vision typical of many northern European performances.'[83] The influence of English habits is none the less felt in the use of the *tutti* for the five part verses, and the placing of the soloists for the four-part ones (which include two falsettists) at a distance (in fact in the next room, the *Sala Regia*), even though that never happened during *Tenebræ* in the time of the College of Papal Singers.

---

[81] This name is translated in the booklet as 'Sistine Chapel Choir', but, as pointed out above, this term provokes too many false resonances with its predecessor of the fifteenth to nineteenth centuries to be an accurate term. The disc is entitled *Cantate Domino* (Deutsche Grammophon 479 5300, 2015).

[82] In this it is unlike some strangely aggressive performances which seem to be becoming fashionable. That by the Oxford Camerata (Naxos 8.553238, 1995), used to be the shortest on record at 10'10, but it was easily outstripped in 2017 by the *Saint Cecilia Choir* of St John Cantius, Chicago, directed by Daniel V. Robinson (Sony Classical 886446368931) which rushes through the Miserere in just 9'14!

[83] 'conferiscono vita, pulsazione, "colore" alla musica sacra del Rinascimento allontanadola decisamente da una visione in "bianco e nero" – tipica di molte esecuzioni del nord Europa.'

14

Introduction to the editions

MANY editions of Allegri's *Miserere* have been made and published, all of them, with the exception of the Paris publication of 1838 (and, to a certain extent, Alfieri's of 1840), misleading insofar as they pretend to represent the work as performed in the Sistine Chapel by the Papal Choir. The editions published in Appendix 13, and also available separately, propose solutions for a director who wishes to perform the work in the style which made it famous, used in the Chapel between the mid-eighteenth century (or earlier) and the end of the nineteenth. At the same time, for the interested listener, they offer a window into some of the more surprising techniques of the Papal Choir: paper representations of a style of performance which has almost entirely disappeared.

Edition 1 is a transcription of Mustafà's manuscript of 1892 (**M**) described in Chapter 12, which sought to include everything necessary to performing 'the Allegri'. As noted there, most of the music in it is in fact Bai's *Miserere* – a measure of the extent to which it had become the singers' 'Allegri Miserere' of choice or, as they might have put it, the *Miserere della nostra Cappella*. It is so complete that it would be superfluous to add any editorial input, so the only change which has been made is to transpose it a fourth higher, as instructed on the first page. A detailed textual commentary will be found after the score in Appendix 13.

Edition 2 is based on what is thought of today as Allegri's music, with the ornaments taken largely from the series of manuscripts dating from the 1820s described in Chapter 9, labelled collectively Source **A**. As these give only a limited number of performance indications, many more have been added following the example of **M**. The readings of the Manchester (**Man**), Paris (**P**) and Milan (**Mil**) manuscripts, which show that much of the tradition demonstrated by Mustafà stretched back at least a hundred years, have also been taken into account, as have the various *abbellimenti* performed by the lead soprano of the time Mariano Padroni, and transcribed by Mendelssohn and Nicolai, among others. The edition has also been transposed up a fourth, to conform to the custom of the Papal Choir. All other necessary information will be found after the edition in Appendix 13.

Unlike Edition 1, Edition 2 is not to be considered in any way an *Urtext* but rather as one option among many. On any particular day there would have been variations, as each group of singers – particularly the lead *castrato* – put their own personal stamp on its execution. One has only to compare the many different versions of the famous 'high C' phrase as sung by Mariano, all of which had currency in the same thirty years or so, to realise the possible extent of the differences. Every performance can – indeed should – be different; and while it is unlikely that the singers varied their *abbellimenti* drastically between different verses of the same performance, the overall effect of slight variations will alleviate some of the monotony that can be felt if all the verses are identical.

The aim of the following chapters is to summarise the information conductors need to make informed choices about their own interpretations, especially of Edition 2 and, for both performers and listeners, to delve a little more deeply into their application and possible origins.

15

Aspects of performance practice 1 – Performing pitch

WITHOUT doubt the single most surprising aspect of the Papal Choir's performance practice to be revealed by this research is its attitude to written pitch. As already noted in Chapters 9 and 10, there is no reason to suppose that the tradition of upward transposition of the *Miserere* by at least a third, widely reported from the end of the eighteenth century onwards, was not already well established rather earlier. It seems clear also that it was not only the *Miserere* which was so treated. Exactly when this started is however impossible to determine with any certainty. Was the choir already singing very high in 1700, or even earlier? If so, what catalysts could have provoked such a development?

Two important events stand out. Between them they determined the future of sacred music in Italy – in many ways in Europe as a whole – and their influence started to be felt in the early years of the seventeenth century. Until then, most Italian choirs did not have the means to sing in what we would now call the 'treble' range, as the highest parts were taken by either by *alti naturali* (male altos, as in the Papal Chapel) or by boys. In both cases, they would rarely sing higher than e″ – soprano falsettists have always been extremely rare, and in the sixteenth century only in England do boys appear to have been seriously trained to use their 'treble' range. Nor were the higher notes necessary in polyphonic music of the time when it was written in normal clefs, the *chiavi naturali*, the uppermost clef of c_1 defining precisely the upper limit of the range. However, music was often notated very much higher than this, using *chiavi alti* – high clefs – in which the upper clef was g_2, which implies a range rising to g″ and beyond. How then was it performed?

Confusion about performing pitch during the Renaissance is caused by our still imperfect understanding of the rationale and practice of *chiavette* – transposing clefs. Renaissance polyphony was based on the eight church modes used in Gregorian chant. To drastically simplify the situation,[1] in fact there

---

[1] The relevant *Grove Music Online* article currently runs to 42,000 words and countless examples (https://doi.org/10.1093/gmo/9781561592630.article.43718). For a concise summary of the principles, and much else, see Frans Wiering, *The Language of the Modes: Studies in the History of Polyphonic Modality* (London, 2001), esp. chapter 1.1.

were only four modes, but each existed in two forms, known as authentic and plagal, each pair being based on the same scale and *final* (cadence note) but with different *ambitus* (compass) and reciting note. In plainchant this different *ambitus* existed merely to offer the possibility of a different reciting note and/ or *final* relative to the rest of the melody. It was irrelevant to the actual pitch of performance, as a recent *Liber usualis* summarises clearly:

> It must be clearly understood that in Plainsong the notation is not, and was never meant to indicate the absolute but only the relative pitch of the melodic intervals. The two clefs of *Doh* and *Fa*, and their different positions, have no other aim than to make possible or easier the writing of the melodies on the stave ... It must therefore be well understood that the notes read on the stave are to be sung at the pitch which is within the compass of the singers, according to the size of the building, and the special character of the piece.[2]

Composed sacred music, all conceived within the modal system, was based on the same assumption. Those pieces based on the lower form of a chant (plagal, in which the *final* was in the middle of the *ambitus*) were written in *chiavi naturali*, and sung more or less at the written pitch. Those using the higher form (authentic, with the *final* at the lower end of the *ambitus*) were written in *chiavi alti*, but were necessarily sung lower than written, as there was no second choir, with higher voices, kept in reserve for performing music that happened to use these clefs. Just as plainsong had always been, those pieces were adapted in performance to the tessitura of the singers regardless of their written notes. This system was known as *chiavette* and was indicated by the use of *chiavi trasportati* – transposing clefs.[3]

This study is not the place to delve deeper into the origins and *raison d'être* of *chiavette*, of which much remains imperfectly understood.[4] Suffice it to say

---

[2] *Liber usualis*, reprint (Tournai, 1961), xix. The four scales were created by the use of white notes only, starting on D (known as the Dorian mode), E (Phrygian), F (Lydian, with the addition of a B♭) and G (Mixolydian). Later Glareanus (*Dodecachordon*, 1547) argued for the addition of two more modes, the Aeolian, starting on A, and the Ionian, on C (B was never used because of the problem of the tritone created by the interval B–F♮). As these two also existed in both authentic and plagal forms, that brought the total number of modes to twelve.

[3] The term *chiavette* came into use only in the eighteenth century.

[4] Among the abundant literature on *chiavi trasportati*, see A. Johnstone, '"High" Clefs in Composition and Performance', *Early Music*, 34/1 (February 2006), 29–53. This article makes clear the complicated history of pitch notation related to modes (which is much more complex than can be usefully discussed here), and notes that in certain modes, the same work could be written in two ways: his tables 2 and 3 give thirty-two such works in sources dating from the mid-sixteenth century, which are found a fourth or a fifth apart. Some light on

that by 1600 the system had been more or less formalised and, when the music was unaccompanied, worked perfectly well.[5] The first catalyst for change was the use of the organ and other instruments for the accompaniment of music in Italian churches. If pieces written in *chiavi alti* were to be accompanied at their performance pitch, the players had to transpose at sight. As Barbieri puts it: 'In the organ partbooks of some early seventeenth century editions, indications such as *alla quarta* – always against a section in high clefs – were added to remind the organist to transpose downwards.'[6]

For those who found such transposition difficult, help was soon at hand, initially for lutenists. Barbieri lists four publications of secular music published in Venice from 1586 in which transcriptions for the harpsichord and the lute are transposed, broadly according to the rules of *chiavette*.[7] Organists (and other accompanying instrumentalists) were already expected to be adept at transposition, either because of the pitch of some organs, or for other reasons.[8] The necessity of this skill for all organists was still being emphasised more than sixty years later:

---

the use of *chiavette* in a particular context is found in Jeffrey G. Kurtzmann, 'Tones, Modes and Clefs in Roman Cyclic Magnificats of the 16th Century', *Early Music*, 22/4 (November 1994), 641–64. This article begins with a detailed and useful summary of writings about the theory, practice and origins of *chiavette*.

[5] An excellent survey of the theory and practice of *chiavette* at that time, particularly in a Roman context, is Patrizio Barbieri's 'Chiavette and Modal Transposition in Italian Practice (c.1500–1837)', *Recercare*, 3 (1991), 5–79, available at http://www.patriziobarbieri.it/pdf/recercareiii.pdf. Barbieri points out that 'such transpositions ... had as their sole objective better adaptation of the works to the ranges of the singers or instruments for which they were intended' (51).

[6] Ibid., 52. Rudolf Rasch, in his valuable article 'Modes, Clefs and Transpositions in the Early Seventeenth Century' (in *Théorie et analyse musicales 1450–1650: Actes du Colloque International Louvain-la-Neuve, 23–25 septembre 1999*, Louvain-la-Neuve, 2001, 403–32), points out that it was only when instrumental accompaniments were written out that the transpositions generally used became visible.

[7] Barbieri, 'Chiavette and Modal Transposition in Italian Practice', 47–8. The rules of transposition also applied, at least theoretically, to secular music, although it seems clear that strict modal practice started to disappear there earlier than in sacred repertoire.

[8] 'Transpositions are useful and above all also necessary for every skilled organist who serves with choirs; and similarly for other players that play other sorts of instruments, to accommodate the pitch to that of the voices, which sometimes cannot ascend or descend far enough to reach the proper place of the modes.' Gioseffo Zarlino, *Le istitutioni harmoniche* (1558), 321, trans. in Laurie Stras, 'The Performance of Polyphony in Early 16th Century Italian Convents', *Early Music*, 45/2 (May 2017), 195–215.

'You must now understand another kind of transposition in order to answer the choir at a comfortable pitch both in figured music and in plainsong. Since the majority of organs are pitched high, beyond the range of the choir, the organist must accustom himself to playing a step or a 3rd lower.'[9]

Similarly, Asprilio Pacelli, *maestro di cappella* at the Collegium Germanicum, wrote in the introduction to his *Chorici psalmi et motecta* (1599) regarding singing motets to the organ that

'since not everyone will have voices appropriate for singing these works, the skilled organist should bear in mind that, according to the voices that are available, almost all of these compositions can be easily transposed downwards, or upwards in various modes as is judged convenient'.[10]

Lodovico Zacconi, like Zarlino, extended the need to transpose to all instruments:

'... instruments can play a composition sometimes in one key, sometimes in another because they are all without exception high compared to the voices. Thus, when it happens that instruments wish to accompany singers, most of the time, to oblige them, they play a 2d, 3d, 4th etc [lower].'[11]

For inexperienced keyboard players who had not yet mastered the art of transposition, there was soon similar assistance, firstly in Viadana's *Cento concerti ecclesiastici* (Venice, 1602), and perhaps most famously in Raverio's 1608 reprint of Palestrina's Fourth Book of Motets – the *Canticum canticorum* – with all the transpositions notated in the added organ part 'pro pulsatoris organi commoditate' according to the rules set out by Adriano Banchieri in his *Cartello overo Regole* of 1601.[12]

---

[9] Rules for a pupil organist in Girolamo Diruta, *Seconda parte del Transilvano*, book 3 (Venice, 1622), 4; trans. in M.C. Bradshaw and E.J. Soehnlen, *Girolamo Diruta: The Transylvanian* (Henryville, 1984), and quoted in Kurtzmann, 'Tones, Modes', n. 9. This reference perhaps refers to *alternatim* performance, in which the organ answered the choir, rather than simultaneous accompaniment, which would demand a higher level of skill.

[10] Trans. in O'Regan, 'The Performance of Palestrina', 150.

[11] *Prattica di musica utile et necessario* (Venice, 1592), trans. in Haynes, *Performing Pitch*, 65. There are many other accounts of singers and/or instruments being accompanied by the organ from the 1560s onwards (ibid., 57–8, 62–7), a practice which would almost always, for reasons he outlines there, involve transposition.

[12] The full title is *Cartello overo Regole utilissime à quella che desiderano imparare il canto figurato* (Venice, 1601). In general, those pieces with the lowest part in f_3 were to be transposed down a fourth, and those with a c_4 down a fifth,

This was obviously a lot of work for someone, but providentially what may have been a second catalyst for change was operating at almost exactly the same time: the arrival of *castrati*, which provided the possibility of extending the overall range of a group of singers upwards.[13] Was this one of the stimulants of the seventeenth-century passion for increasingly high voices? Rosselli posits that it may have been driven by its association with superiority in 'a society that was at once intensely hierarchical-minded and accustomed to displaying hierarchical order in forms readily perceived to the senses', citing as evidence the superior pay of singers with high voices in opera houses (both castrati and women) and in cathedrals, churches and private chapels.[14] In such places, as well as in convents, an obvious solution would have been to gently bend the 'rules' of *chiavette* in order to utilise the higher range of *castrati*: for example, by transposing pieces in *chiavi alti* down by only a third, or even a tone, which organists would have found easier to manage.[15] In any case, the

---

although a wish to avoid F♯s in the key signature, which would occur when a piece with no B♭ in the signature was transposed down a fourth, was also relevant. Banchieri was far from the first writer to deal with this question – the earliest was Silvestro Ganassi, in chapter 22 of his *Lettione seconda pur della prattica di sonare il violone d'arco* (Venice, 1543), and see Barbieri, 'Chiavette and Modal Transposition in Italian Practice', Kurtzmann, 'Tones, Modes', and Johnstone, '"High" Clefs in Composition and Performance', for others – but his publication gives a summary of current practice, a very useful tool at this precise time for publishers among others.

[13] Their effect is described in retrospect by Giuseppe Paolucci (*Arte pratica di contrappunto*, 1772, vol. 3, 173), who wrote that, with reference to a motet by Andrea Rota (1553–97), the reader 'will find that the parts are low in their position, and [such a composition] might appear to him not very well done if he were not to reflect that during this composer's lifetime there were no voices other than natural ones [of male singers], the use of castrati not having been introduced until well into the seventeenth century, so that composers could not use very high notes, since there would not have been any voices able to perform them.' trans. in Barbieri, 'Chiavette and Modal Transposition in Italian Practice', 37.

[14] 'The Castrati', 148–9. It must also be noted that there had been a market for suitable music in the many convents of central and northern Italy since the mid-sixteenth century. Stras ('The Performance of Polyphony', 196–7) gives a list of sixteen books of motets dedicated to nuns dating from the last twenty years of the century in Florence, Ferrara, Milan, Bergamo, etc.; historical records show that performances of polyphony by them were common in Venice, Rome and many other places; and two exceptional manuscripts, now in Verona and Brussels, show the wide repertoire sometimes sung there. Their performance would have necessitated various stratagems to bring them into the range of female voices.

[15] Barbieri, 'Chiavette and Modal Transposition in Italian Practice', shows that transposition by a third lower rather than a fourth was prescribed by more

regular use of instruments signalled the death knell of the practice of notating music according to the modal system, and by the end of the seventeenth century it was often only vaguely understood by many performers and even composers. When voices were accompanied by instruments it was obviously much simpler to write new compositions using the actual notes which would sound when they were played.[16]

It is also a matter of record that during the seventeenth century many organs in Rome were transposed downwards, perhaps the product of a desire to align organ and choir pitch.[17] It has been suggested, by Doni among others, that the singers may have been simply lazy or, surprisingly, that *castrati* were unable to sing as high as boys: 'And I have heard specialists discussing in a different way these matters related to the pitch in Rome: some attribute the lowness to the "softness" and work-shy nature of the singers; other put it down to the plethora of *castrati* who when they are adult do not reach the same height

---

    theorists as the seventeenth century advanced, and it seems quite likely that, as so often, the theory lagged behind the practice. Transposition down a third is much more simply achieved by both players and singers by pretending that the clef has been moved upwards by one line of the stave, with a little adjustment of semitones. It is also certain that as the century advanced, unequal tuning systems such as quarter-comma mean-tone were giving way to gentler ones, particularly in Italy, making transposition to harmonically more distant keys possible.

[16] Hence the fierce arguments about transposition in Monteverdi's *Vespers* of 1610, which stands right at the cusp of new practice: its notation is necessarily based on the modes of the psalm-tones, some of which inevitably pose problems for the instruments. In this it was one of the first, as well as one of the last, of its kind. It should be noted that transposition for other reasons did not end; see Haynes, *A History of Performing Pitch*, chapter 2, for a detailed discussion of the complications of *tuono corista* and *chormäßig*, *mezzo punto* and *tutto punto*, and various kinds of *Cornett-ton*, *Chorton* and *Cammerton*, not to mention the French *ton de chapelle* and English quire-pitch.

[17] Barbieri ('Chiavette and Modal Transposition in Italian Practice', 53–4) cites evidence that the organs of both S. Luigi dei Francesi and S. Lorenzo in Damaso were lowered by a semitone in 1617, and Giambattista Doni in 1640 stated that many organs had been half a tone higher at the beginning of the century (*Annotazioni sopra il Compendio de' Generi*, 182). Much later, in 1721, the organ of the cathedral in Orte (in the Papal States) was lowered by a whole tone (to about A=380–90, a large tone below 'normal' pitch of A=440) 'to match the pitch of Rome'. In 1751 the organ of the *Cappella Gregoriana* in S. Pietro was also transposed down a whole tone, and as late as 1883 the organ of the *Cappella Giulia*, also in S. Pietro, was still at around A=384, the pitch where the organs of S. Giovanni in Laterano and S. Maria Maggiore had always been.

that "complete" boys do.'[18] He also notes that in Rome there was a 'plethora of *bassi profundi*, of which there are more here than elsewhere'.[19] However, it may be that this downward transposition in performing pitch, which for the present argument may initially seem counter-intuitive, can be explained not by supposed weaknesses in singers but by the possibility that choirs wished to modify, or even to ignore entirely, the rules of *chiavette* and sing high-clef pieces more or less at written pitch. Anyone who has sung the soprano or tenor parts in this repertoire in mixed choirs knows how much easier they are a tone lower than written, and lowering the pitch of organs would make this possible without any transposition at all, thus making accompaniment simpler.

The singers of the Papal Chapel, who always sang unaccompanied, were touched only indirectly by the problem of accompanying instruments. Nevertheless they did not work in a vacuum. They too, with the arrival of *castrati*, had the possibility of transposing pieces in *chiavi alti* down less than before, or even not at all. And it can only have been a small step to start singing those in *chiavi naturali* higher than written, in order to use the possibilities of those *castrati*. After all, why employ them if their most outstanding quality – the ability to sing high with great skill – was unused?[20] Untroubled by instruments, the singers of the Papal Chapel had always had an open choice of pitch, and now they had a chance to show they were the best in town by singing higher than everyone else.[21] It could be that the process to the stratospheric heights

---

[18] 'Ho sentito poi discorrere diversamente da i periti di queste cose, circa il Tuono di Roma; et attribuirsi da altri la sua gravità alla mollitie, et insingardia de' cantori; da altri alla copia de' castrati; che quando sono provetti inetà, non arrivano all' acutezza di voce, che formano i fancuilli interi.' Doni, *Annotazione sopra il Compendio de' Generi*, 182. Presumably Doni is saying that some *castrati* turn out to be altos rather than sopranos, although whether he thinks that to be an unintended result of 'the operation' is not clear. Perhaps, like Tosi in the following century, he is complaining that the singers are badly taught: "Many masters put their Scholars to sing the *Contr' Alto*, not knowing how to help them to the *Falsetto*, or to avoid the trouble of finding it." ('Molti Maeftri fanno cantare il Contralto al loro Difcepoli per non sapere in essi trovar il falsetto, o per isfuggire la fatica di cercarlo.') Tosi, *Opinioni de' cantori*, 14, trans. J.E. Galliard as *Observations on the Florid Song* (London, 1742), 23. By 'falsetto' Tosi here means the head register.

[19] 'copia maggiore de' Bassi profondi, ch più qui, che altrove, si trovano'.

[20] They would also have been aware of such practices by their colleagues; for example Girolamo Chiti, *maestro di cappella* at S. Giovanni Laterano, added a continuo part in 1753 to Palestrina's *Missa Laudate Dominum* a8 (notated in *chiavi naturali*) with the instruction to transpose it up a third ('Per cantarla in giusto tono l'organo va trasportato alla 3a sopra', quoted in Barbieri, 'Chiavette and Modal Transposition in Italian Practice', 55 and n. 126).

[21] The setting of pitch in the Chapel seems always to have been a rather hit-and-miss affair. Sherr explains that it was the responsibility of the senior singer of the part that began the piece or, when the voices began together or in chant,

of a *Miserere* in C minor began soon after Allegri set down the work on paper, and proceeded relatively quickly towards fulfilment by the early eighteenth century. Indeed, we cannot be sure that it was ever sung in what we would recognise as G minor.

When Alfieri wrote that 'it is necessary to know that in the Chapel the note G is sung as B' he stated this as a general rule, not specific to the *Miserere*.[22] It has been shown above that the use of upward transposition was not restricted to that work, as Mendelssohn also transcribed Palestrina's *Improperia* directly from a performance in 1831 a fourth higher than the standard score, and his sister in 1840 noted it a semitone higher again.[23] What is unsaid, no doubt because the whole concept of *chiavette* had been largely forgotten by 1840, is that this rule must apply only to pieces in *chiavi naturali*. Those in *chiavi alti* were sung in the written key, or very close to it. Another of the choir's favourite Lenten works, Palestrina's *Stabat mater*, written in *chiavi alti*, could easily have been sung more or less as written but could only with the greatest difficulty have been transposed upwards by a third! It should be noted also that in Mesplet's 1798 concert in the Vatican (see Chapter 6) the *Benedictus* of Palestrina's *Missa Assumpta est Maria* was sung by two sopranos, an alto and a tenor, the voices required if it is sung at the written (high) pitch without transposition.

Ignorance of the existence of transposing clefs may also account for Sievers' muddle-headed comments on the performing pitch of the choir and of the *Miserere* in his long essay of 1825. He begins by praising the singers' impeccable intonation.

---

the senior bass ('Performance Practice in the Papal Chapel', 454–6). Numerous accidents are recorded throughout the seventeenth century in the *DS*, to the point where in 1718 it was decreed that it was better to recommence a piece than persist with an unsuitable pitch (see also Kari Turunen, 'Performing Palestrina from Historical Evidence to Twenty-First Century Performance', DocMus diss., University of the Arts Helsinki, 2014, 118–19). It is clear in any case that from earliest times it was comfort and habit which determined the pitch rather than the actual notes on the page.

[22] See Chapter 10.

[23] When Mariano Padroni attempted to retire from the choir in 1815, his colleagues resisted his request, pleading their need for his 'acutezza rarissima' to sing not only the *Miserere* but also the *Improperia* (see CS 681, fol. 164^v, reproduced in Kantner and Pachovsky, *L'Ottocento*, 172). He could clearly have sung it higher than the g″ required in the *Coro 2°* when it is transposed up a fourth. It should also be noted that the choir's performance of Baini's *Miserere*, which is notated in G minor, conformed to Alfieri's rule, at least in 1831: 'On the first day ... the Miserere of Baini, in the key of B minor was given. See Mendelssohn, *Letters*, 139 and pp. 156–7 above.

The most admirable quality of the performance is the intonation, which is hair – I might say 'atom-sharp' [sharp in the sense of 'precise'], so that even dissonances become harmony. This perfection is the result of the secure tuning with which the singers have sung for centuries, so that they are so sure of every single note – as I witnessed both with my ears and my eyes – as if it were pitched for them by an instrument. This tuning is approximately, as far as I could tell from my own ears without a tuning-fork, that used in Paris; however, all old scores are sung a tone lower than they are written, for example the *Miserere*, which is written in G minor, is sung in F minor.[24]

This is an interesting conflation of diverse information. Sievers appears to be asserting that recently composed music (Ciciliani, Fazzini, Baini himself) was performed at 'Paris pitch', which he is probably thinking of as around A=440, whereas that of Palestrina and other old music was transposed down a tone.[25] To say such a thing, he must have heard – or at least verified with the score in front of him – only old pieces written in high clefs, and imagined that they were the norm, hence his statement about the *Miserere*. Like Burney in 1770, he never had the chance to verify his assertion about it by experience, as his interview with Baini took place in July 1824. Much work remains to be done on the evolution of performing pitch in the everyday polyphony of the Chapel, but in general the evidence for a gradual move upwards, and the parallel abandonment of the system of *chiavette*, seems incontrovertible.

With the upward transposition used in these editions of about a fourth taken as a starting point, directors should nevertheless feel free to decide the pitch of performance according to the capacities of the singers in front of them, just as the *maestro* of the Papal Chapel did. There is nothing sacred about

---

[24] 'Als bewundernswürdigste Eigenschaft der Ausführung steht die Intonation da, welche haar ich möchte sagen, atomscharf ist, so, dass selbst Dissonanzen zu Harmonie werden. Diese Vollkommenheit ist Folge der unverrückten Stimmung, in welcher die Sänger seit Jahrhunderten gesungen haben, so, dass sie jedes einzelnen Tons, wie ich davon einstens selbst Ohren – und Augenzeuge gewesen bin, so sicher sind, als würde er ihnen durch ein Instrument angegeben. Diese Stimmung ist ungefähr, so viel ich ohne Gabel und nach dem blossen Gehöre habe vernehmen können, die Pariser; doch werden alle alten Partituren einen Ton tiefer, als sie geschrieben stehen, zum Beispiel, das Miserere, welches in g-moll steht, in f-moll gesungen.' Sievers, 'Das Miserere von Allegri', 75–6.

[25] There was no one standard of pitch at this time in Paris, reports varying from A=392 to 460 according to context (see p. 158, n. 22). It could equally of course be the case that Palestrina was performed at low Roman pitch (around a tone lower than 440) and the 'modern' music was transposed up a tone from that. For a useful summary of the evidence of Roman pitch, see Haynes, *A History of Performing Pitch*, 69–73, Turunen, 'Performing Palestrina', 120–1, and n. 17.

A=440, especially in a Roman context, and upward transposition of a fourth at A=415 still feels very high! Singing the Misereres in B♭, a tone lower than these editions, should perhaps be thought of as the minimum necessary to conform to the voicing and texture of the piece.

16

Aspects of performance practice 2 – Expression

✳ Dynamics

THE dynamics found in **A** necessitate much filling out, even after applying them in strictly parallel places. They are also sometimes puzzling, as noted in Chapter 9, because the chanted sections are always marked *f* and the polyphony *p*, which hardly accords with contemporary descriptions of the variations possible. Mendelssohn, speaking of the performances in 1831, is perhaps the most eloquent:

> The best voices are reserved for the *Miserere*, which is sung with the greatest variety of effect, the voices swelling and dying away and rising again from the quietest piano to the full strength of the choir. No wonder that it excites deep emotion in every listener.[1]

Herold, sixteen years earlier, had also observed this, and added some technical detail.

> The effect of this music really is a function of its execution; the pianos and the fortes are very important for this effect; the swelling sounds, either held for a long time or suddenly cut off, are also very fine.[2]

Nor could Spohr's description (in Chapter 8) of the very first chord as 'a beautiful 5-part chording, tender and pure, like a harmony from another world' be indicated by *f* in its normal sense.

No doubt *f* often simply meant louder than *p* rather than simply loud, and *p* not necessarily soft, but in any case softer than *f*. But it may be even more subtle than that. It was suggested in Chapter 9 that these indications are roughly equivalent to *a piacere* and *a misura*, which are found in the earliest

---

[1] *Letters*, 138.
[2] 'L'effet de cette musique dépend vraiment de l'exécution ; les p. et les f. entrent pour beaucoup dans l'effet; les sons enflés, soutenus longtems, ou coupés, sont aussi fort bien.' *Lettres d'Italie*, 218.

manuscripts (**Man** and **P**) and which reappear in **M**. Historically the relation is made explicit by **Mil**, which replaces the *a piacere* and *a misura* indications of **Man** and **P** with *for*[*te*] and *dol*[*ce*], while retaining a very large part of the earlier readings. The real meaning of *forte* in this context is therefore dramatic, i.e. following the meaning of the text (*a piacere* – occasionally *col direttore* in **M**); while *dolce* implies regularly and calmly following the written notes, i.e. *a misura*. In the first the sense of the words predominates, in the second the musical composition.³

In this connection, the 1705 description by Sébastien de Brossard of the term *a battuta* is illuminating.

> *Battuta* means the movement of the hand up and down to indicate the length of sounds, which we call *mesure*. In Italy we often find the words *A battuta*, which means *mesured*, with each beat indicated equally. It normally follows what they call *Recitativo*, which is a kind of singing which is declaimed rather than sung, and in which the beat is hardly observed. *A battuta* therefore indicates the moment when it is necessary to recommence marking each beat equally and well.⁴

Despite the difference of context, the equivalence of *a piacere* to *recitativo*, and of *a misura* to *a battuta*, seems clear.

Also curious in **A** is the *f* marked for the top C in nearly every verse, which accords neither with Mustafà's recommendation to approach it *pianissimo* from the c below with *un filo di voce*, nor with Mendelssohn's description of Mariano intoning it 'in a pure soft voice' (see Chapter 9), nor with received wisdom about the capacity of *castrati* to float high notes quietly. Perhaps here too it simply meant 'with emotion'. It is also true that the manuscripts which make up **A** and give the *Miserere* complete tend to reproduce slavishly the dynamics of the first two verses in later ones, so are to be taken with some reserve.

Generous use of *crescendi* and *diminuendi* was part of the choir's style. Otto Nicolai's testimony concerning the freedom of tempo and dynamics exercised in the whole repertoire under Baini's direction has been cited in Chapter 8, and no doubt the effect Herold describes, suddenly cutting off the notes – a way of 'playing to the acoustic' – also had its place. Berlioz described the feeling provoked by listening to the choir as being like

---

³ See also the discussion about *portamento*, below, particularly p. 237.

⁴ 'BATTUTA, veut dire, ce mouvement de la main en baissant & en levant, qui sert à marquer la durée des Sons, & que nous apellons MESURE. On trouve souvent chez les Italiens ces mots A battuta, qui veulent dire de Mesure, ou en battant également chaque temps. Ce qu'ils mettent ordinairement après, ce qu'ils apellent Recitativo, qui est un chant où l'on déclame plûtôt qu'on ne chante, & dans lequel on n'observe presque point la mesure. A battuta veut donc dire pour lors qu'il faut recommencer à marquer ou à battre également & juste tous les temps de la mesure.' Sébastien de Brossard, *Dictionaire de Musique* (Paris, 1705), s.v. 'Battuta'.

the fantastic harmonies of an æolian harp hung from the top of a leafless tree, and I defy you not to experience a profound feeling of isolation and abandonment, a vague and infinite desire for another life allied with an immense disgust with this one; in a word, a powerful access of spleen combined with an inclination to suicide.[5]

He was by no means the only writer to make this unexpected comparison with an æolian harp, even if few others mention suicide in the same breath! He was commenting here about what he perceived as the utter randomness of harmonic change in the music of Palestrina, an idea also picked up by the painter and art critic Etienne Delécluze:

> When we listen, in either Rome or Paris, to some of Palestrina's works, for example his *Stabat mater*, his Lamentations and his madrigal *Alla riva del Tebro*, it has to be said that we, who have been used since our childhood to modern tonality and melodies which are rhythmic and clearly divided into intelligible phrases, have trouble coping with their continuous modulation, whose sequence, even if doubtless governed by profound learning, remind me of the strange chords which the wind produces in an æolian harp.[6]

However, the sound of the æolian harp was also characterised by generous changes in volume. For Moritz Hauptmann, that was the most striking aspect of the Papal Choir's interpretations, and it was worthy of note when it was not used; during Vespers, for example, he found that the choir sang 'without the slightest sentimentality ... there was not the slightest trace of the famous *crescendo* and *diminuendo* effects which people compare to Æolian harps'.[7]

---

[5] Hector Berlioz, 'Voyage musical', his contribution to *Italie pittoresque* (Paris, 1836), 5–6: '... la fantastique harmonie d'une harpe éolienne balancée au sommet d'un arbre dépouillé de verdure, et je vous défie de ne pas éprouver un sentiment profond d'isolement, d'abandon, un désir vague et infini d'une autre existence, un dégoût immense de celle-ci; en un mot, une forte atteinte de spleen joint à une tentation de suicide.' English trans. from Boursy, 'The Mystique', 315.

[6] 'En entendant, soit à Rome, soit à Paris, un certain nombre de morceaux de Palestrina, entre autres son Stabat Mater, ses Lamentations et son madrigal : Alla riva del Tebro, etc.; habitué comme nous le sommes tous dès l'enfance à la tonalité moderne, ainsi qu'à la mélodie rythmée et disposée en phrases claires et courtes; je dois l'avouer, je n'ai pu me faire qu'avec quelque difficulté à cette suite non interrompue de modulations, dont la succession, bien que dirigée par une science profonde, me rappela ces accords étranges que le vent produit en frisant les cordes d'une harpe éolienne.' Etienne-Jean Delécluze, 'Palestrina', *Revue de Paris*, 4th ser., 10 (October 1842), 326.

[7] Moritz Hauptmann, *The Letters of a Leipzig Cantor: Being the Letters of Moritz Hauptmann to Franz Hauser, Ludwig Spohr and other musicians*, trans. and ed. A.D. Coleridge (London, 1892), vol. 1, 42.

The most famous dynamic effect was that described by Burney for the last verse of the Allegri *Miserere*. '... the last verse of this psalm is terminated by the two choirs; the *Maestro di Capella* beating time slower and slower, and the singers diminishing or rather *extinguishing* the harmony, by little and little, to a perfect point'.[8] Burney gives us the original Italian taken from Adami, which allows us to amend his somewhat poetic translation as follows: 'Also the choirmaster must remember that the last verse of the psalm ends with two choirs, and so the beat should be slow, so as to finish the music *piano*, with a gradual *smorzando*'.[9] This at least does not give the impression of the singers stopping one by one to finish on a unison, as could be inferred from Burney's somewhat fanciful translation. In any case, the effect is confirmed by all manuscript sources with any dynamics at this point.

The choir was certainly capable of sustained but dramatic soft singing, as shown in Mendelssohn's comments about the choir's interpretation of Palestrina's *Improperia*.

> I have only once heard this composition, but it seems to me to be one of Palestrina's finest works, and they sing it with remarkable enthusiasm. There is surprising delicacy and harmony in its execution by the choir; and they are careful to place every passage in its proper light, and to render it sufficiently prominent without making it too conspicuous – one chord blending softly with the other ... They sing the oft-recurring Greek 'Holy' in the most admirable manner, each time with the same smoothness and expression. You will be not a little surprised, however, when you see it written down.[10]

Cardinal Wiseman agreed:

> In the chorus and semi-chorus of the Trisagion, each voice has actually only two notes, and those of the most obvious harmony. And yet to hear those sung, slow yet bold, full yet soft, with the melting modulation which that choir alone can give, produces a feeling of sweet devotional melancholy, a mildened emotion, which not even the more artful and far-famed Miserere can excite.[11]

For dynamics in general, our best guide is **M**, which contains so many performance indications that it is sometimes difficult to see the notes! I have taken

---

[8] *The Present State*, 277.

[9] Burney's Italian reads: 'Averta [Avverta in Adami] pure il Signor Maestro che l'ultimo verso del Salmo termina a due Cori, e però sarà la Battuta Adagio, per finirlo Piano, smorzando a poco, a poco l'Armonia.' Adami, *Osservationi*, 36. I take 'l'Armonia' to mean simply 'the music'.

[10] *Letters*, 147–8. His transcription (Ex. 3) is given on p. 114 and that of his sister Fanny (Ex. 7) on p. 146.

[11] *Four Lectures*, 78.

its readings for the different verses as my model for the dynamics of Edition 2 – the 'Allegri'. The best preparation for singing it is to work first on Edition 1 – Mustafà's version of the Bai. Directors can best use their own imagination and musicality once they and their singers have entered into this world. As far as the top Cs are concerned, it is certain that a soprano who can sing them both softly and loudly, with both *crescendi* and *diminuendi*, is preferable to one who can only sing them loudly.

✳ Rubato

The writings of Burney ('accelerating or retarding the measure at some particular words, and singing some entire verses quicker than others'), Nicolai ('varying the pace, with *rallentandi* and *stringendi*') and others make clear that a certain amount of tempo variation between verses, and of *rubato* within them, was expected and habitual. The use of a fluid approach was so important to the scribe of **Mil** that he felt the need to draw attention to it on the title page: 'in executing this Miserere, do not use a fixed tempo'. Likewise one of Baini's reproaches to Alfieri's printed *abbellimenti* was that they were 'impoverished by the limits of a constant tempo' ('impoverite dai limiti del tempo sempre equale'). Mustafà's edition of Palestrina's *Peccavimus* (see Chapter 12), shows that the practice of *rubato* was not confined to the *Miserere*. Instructions in **M** relating to tempo include *lento, tempo sostenuto, dolcissimo, risoluto* and *trattenuto* ('drawn out'), and there are frequent *ritardandi*. These kinds of instructions have not been applied to the edition of the Allegri, but directors should not hesitate to add the effects they indicate for their own performances, as I do for mine. In any case, the basic tempo is a slow and flexible four-minims-to-the-bar: 'The *Miserere*, which is the show piece, is sung very slowly, in long-drawn chords, which swell and die away in almost total darkness.'[12] 'What gives this way of singing a very particular character is, I believe, that there seems to be no regularity. Everything goes very slowly, without rhythm and without much sense of direction' (Herold).[13]

The 'high C' moment is a special case of the use of *rubato*, where in **M** the accompanying parts are instructed 'si tenga fine alla resoluzione del 1° soprano', or 'tenuta finchi risolvi il 1° soprano'. It was clearly the first soprano, no doubt in synergy with the director, who determined the amount of *rubato*

---

[12] '[Miserere] in höchst langsamer Bewegung in langaustönenden Accorden, anschwellend und abnehmend in der Stärke, fast in völliger Dunkelheit gesungen.' Hauptmann, *The Letters*, letter of 1871, quoted in Amann, *Allegris Miserere*, 39 n. 4.

[13] 'Ce qui donne je crois un caractère tout particulier à ce chant, c'est qu'il n'y a point de mesure. Tout va très lentement, sans rythme, sans cadences bien déterminées.' Herold, *Lettres d'Italie*, 217.

to be applied at this point; it is worth remembering that when Mustafà sang the *Miserere*, as he did, the first soprano and the director were the same person. British Library Add. 31525(1) (see Appendix 10) gives *slent*[*ando*] in the highest part at this point and a strange notation resembling a large *fermata* in the others. There is little doubt that the same effect is intended. I have inserted a pause in all the parts at this point in the edition of the Allegri; the soprano should try to hold the top note as long as possible.

Ornamentation

The use of embellishments, the famous *abbellimenti*, was the most publicised aspect of the Papal Choir's unique way of singing the *Miserere*, although for the hearers, it seems to have been the expressive aspects that made the most impression; Burney's description of the great effects of the *Miserere* only mentions 'graces' in passing. Mendelssohn, in calling the decorations used by the choir 'little ornaments and trills such as were popular at the beginning of the last century',[14] gave some examples which are worth reproducing in their entirety (Ex. 10).

Ex. 10 Papal Choir gracing in polyphonic music according to Mendelssohn

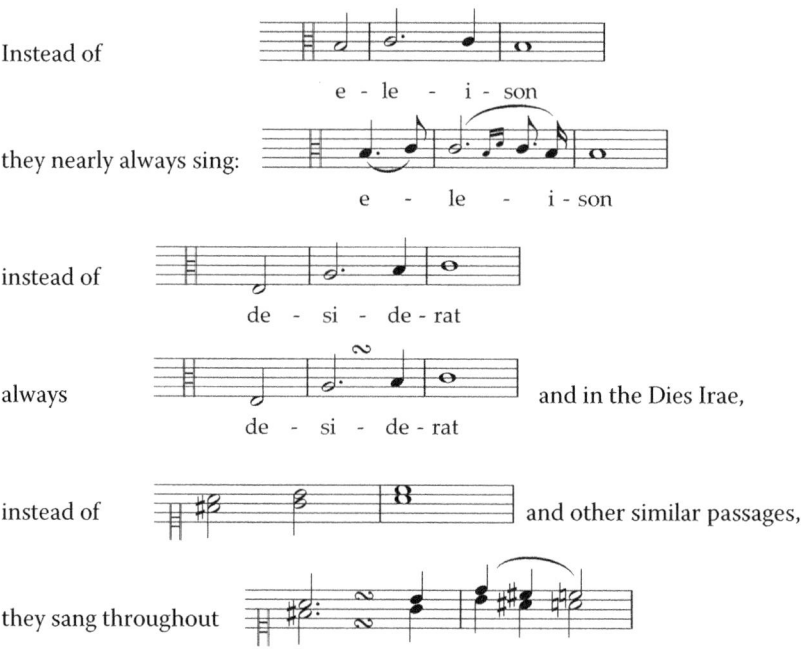

[14] Letter to Zelter, 1 December 1830, in *Letters*, 95–6.

You can imagine what a singular effect it has when it is sung consistently by all the inner voices through the whole Mass. Incidentally this style of singing:

instead of 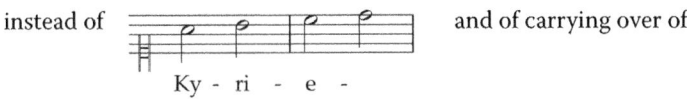 and of carrying over of

each note into the next, is at times justified, and gives the whole thing a beautiful, smooth tone; and if now and again very peculiar dissonances result, the effect in the music they sing is not at all bad.

This style of gracing, briefly discussed in Chapter 3, derives clearly from writers such as Bovicelli (1594), Viadana (1602), Caccini (1602), Rognoni (1620), Giustiniani (1628) and Doni (1640), refined by eighteenth-century taste as found in the writings of Tosi (1723) and Mancini (1774). The 'graces' are exactly what Mendelssohn wrote: flourishes, spiced up with a certain amount of chromatic adventurousness. They are ubiquitous in **M**. Two should be singled out.

Gruppetti

Very few ornaments are written with standardised ornament signs; there are a few trills (*tr*) and in **M** an occasional turn.[15] All the others are written out in full. The one most often found is a kind of *gruppetto* preceding the note. It is the most characteristic stylised ornament of both **A** and **M**: for example, it occurs ten times in verse 3 alone (*Amplius lava me*) in **M**, if we count the bass ornament on the word 'peccato' as the same thing, imperfectly written out (it is in fact in this form that it occurs in Mendelssohn's second phrase in Ex. 10, at the word 'eleison'). It is a standard Italian vocal ornament, found in most nineteenth-century singing methods – Garaudé (1779–1852), Duprez (1806–96), Concone (1801–61), etc. – all of which, of course, are derived from Italian models, although the systematic use of it by the papal singers to decorate a *portamento* is unusual.[16] There is a wide range of variations in the notation of

---

[15] Even there Mustafà sometimes supplied in the separate parts the notes of the turns that he indicated by a sign in the full score, which not only emphasises the pedagogical nature of the whole enterprise but perhaps also shows the level of ignorance of such things he expected in the singers!

[16] Alexis de Garaudé, *Méthode complet de chant* (Paris, 1809), 57–62; Duprez, *L'Art du Chant*, 42–7; Giuseppe Concone, *Introduction à l'Art de bien chanter* (Paris, c.1845), 39–40. It is also mentioned by Corri (*The Singer's Preceptor*, 32), who describes it as the 'turn grace'.

these *gruppetti*. The differences between different notations of *gruppetti* in manuscript **M**

Ex. 11 The different notations of *gruppetti* in manuscript **M**

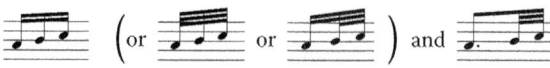

are perhaps the result of the amount of time available for its execution, the last two profiting from extra time to lean longer on the first note. In the edition I have for the sake of simplicity always used the third of the options above (*sq dsq dsq*). The important thing is to get to the essence of the vocal gesture implied.

Portamento

One thing that makes **M** unique is its generous indications of *portamento*. To avoid all doubt, the word *portando* is sometimes added to the slurs used, for example in bar 6 of the bass part in verse 1, or in bars 2–3 of verse 7. Is there any difference between the execution implied by this notation and Mendelssohn's slurred dotted crotchet–quaver figure in his 'Kyrie' phrase (the last example of Ex. 10)? Almost certainly not. Mendelssohn's description, 'die noten ganz ineinander herüberzuziehen' – 'carrying over each note into the next' (as in Selden-Goth's translation) or perhaps, more literally, 'drawing the notes completely into one another' – is an exact description of *portamento*, which enables singers to join notes in different registers of the voice or on different syllables to make a perfect legato. This is the basis of what came to be known as *bel canto*.

Although rarely indicated in composers' scores, there is little doubt that *portamento* was widely used in all kinds of music from at least the seventeenth century onwards. Tosi wrote about it in some detail in 1723, and one of the earliest references to it in a theoretical work is found as early as 1620 in Francesco Rognoni's *Selva di vari passaggi*.[17] It did not necessarily entail an audible slide. In the words of Nicola Vaccai:

---

[17] Published in Milan. The relevant page (fol. 1ʳ) is reproduced in Feldman, *The Castrati*, 119. There may be a reference to it also in Luigi Zenobi's letter of c.1600 (Blackburn and Lowinsky, 'Luigi Zenobi', see p. 38, n. 2). Among his recommendations for tenors is the following: 'I should recommend that these middle parts use embellishments rarely and content themselves with knowing how to ascend and descend with a delicate wavy motion *(ondeggiando)* and at times use a few gentle *trilli* or *tremoli*.' The term *ondeggiando* is used again to describe 'simple' singing: 'He must know how to sing the piece in its simple form, that is, without any *passaggio*, but only with grace, *trillo, tremolo, ondeggiamento*, and *esclamatione*.' As Blackburn and Lowinsky point out ('Luigi Zenobi', 93), Zenobi uses a different term for *crescendo* and *diminuendo* ('cominciare con voce gagliarda, e lasciarla a poco a poco morire'), so it is hard to

> It is not to be understood that by 'portamento of the voice' that incorrect practice of dragging the voice from one interval to the other through the intermediate steps, is meant, but, that the one tone be completely and fully bound with the tone following.

This was achieved as follows.

> In the first manner one should ... anticipate almost imperceptibly the following tone with the vowel of the previous syllable, by means of which a graceful melody or one where an intense expression is required becomes especially effective. The rendering must however not be overladen with consequence and must be free from mannerism and monotony.[18]

By the expressions 'overladen with consequence' and 'mannerism and monotony' Vaccai was no doubt showing his dislike for exaggerated sliding, a view expressed by many writers.[19] By the mid-nineteenth century, Manuel Garcia no doubt reflected general opinion when he separated the meanings: *port de voix* and *con portamento* interchangeably implied a slide, while *vocalisation liée* described simple *legato*.

> To slur [*porter la voix*] is to conduct the voice from one note to another through all the intermediate sounds. The time occupied by the slur should be taken from the last portion of the note quitted; and its rapidity will depend on the kind of expression required by any passage in which it occurs. This dragging of notes will assist in equalising the registers, timbres and the power of the voice.[20]

> imagine to what other technique of ascending and descending it may refer. For other references to the use of *portamento* in the seventeenth and eighteenth centuries see Ellen Harris, 'Portamento' in *Grove Music Online*.

[18] Nicola Vaccai, *Metodo pratico di canto italiano per camera* (London, 1832), lesson xiii, trans. from a multilingual reprint by Edition Steingraber (Leipzig, n.d.).

[19] To a man they insisted on the student listening to its use by their teacher and other masters before daring to incorporate it into their own performances (see Brown, *Performing Practice*, 558–73). In an interesting modern study, 'Beggar at the Door – the Rise and Fall of Portamento', *Music & Letters*, 87/4 (2006), 523–50, John Potter complements the theoretical background with detailed listening and comparison of early recordings, and brings the story up to date with a consideration of the unpopularity of *portamento* nowadays – a trend he dates to the years around World War II. Also relevant is Daniel Leech-Wilkinson, 'Portamento and Musical Meaning', *Journal of Musicological Research*, 25 (2006), 233–61.

[20] Manuel Garcia, *Traité complet de l'Art du Chant* (Paris, 1847), 30; trans. from *Garcia's Treatise on the Art of Singing*, trans. and ed. Albert Garcia (London, 1924), 8.

Domenico Corri, who described this gesture as 'the anticipation grace', was clearly not worried by a bit of sliding.

> *Portamento di voce* is the perfection of vocal music; it consists in the swell and dying of the voice, the sliding and blending one note into another with delicacy and expression – and expression comprehends every charm which music can produce; the Portamento di voce may justly be compared to the highest degree of refinement in elegant pronunciation in speaking.[21]

The papal singers would no doubt have echoed these sentiments. They seem to have used *portamento* in abundance. It is indicated throughout Mustafà's score, although the expansion of the anticipatory note into a *gruppetto* is a usage not generally found in contemporary singing methods. *Portamento* is also present, if hidden, in **A** (Appendix 9). For example, if in bar 3 of verse 1 a *portamento* slur was added between the third and fourth notes of the first soprano part, at the same time reducing the d" to a grace note, we would have exactly the same ornament as in bar 17 (verse 3) of Mustafà's first soprano (complete with following *gruppetto*), and in Mendelssohn's examples of the *Kyrie*. Similarly, the g' at the end of the alto part in bar 2 of **A** can be considered the end of a *portamento* preparing the first note in the following bar, itself preceded by a *gruppetto* abbreviated to an *appoggiatura*. Mustafà was essentially transcribing the same tradition as the other sources but with more precision for the benefit of singers of the future.

The painter Ingres was particularly sensitive to its effect in the Chapel when sung by a solo voice: 'Imagine a celestial voice, all alone, as piercing as a glass harmonica in the way it slips and passes imperceptibly from one tone to the next.'[22] However, what set the Papal Choir apart was its extensive use of *portamento* in a choral context. Stendhal, while confirming the tradition, would not have believed it possible to transcribe it on the page. 'Tradition has taught the Papal singers certain effects of portamento which are indescribably beautiful, yet which it is impossible to convey in the written score.'[23] Samuel Morse, painter and inventor of the eponymous code, also noticed this in 1830.

---

[21] *The Singer's Preceptor*, 3–4.

[22] 'Figurez-vous une voix céleste, toute seule, et qui fait mal comme l'harmonica, tant elle file et passe insensiblement d'un ton à l'autre.' Letter to M. Forestier, 7 April 1807, in *Lettres de France et d'Italie*, 155. Ingres is here commenting on the performance by a solo *castrato* of one of the Lamentations, which he found even more striking than the *Miserere* (a performance by Moreschi of an extract from the Lamentations is available on 'The Last Castrato' (see Introduction, n. 6)).

[23] Stendhal, 'Life of Mozart', in *Lives of Haydn, Mozart and Metastasio*, first published 1815, trans. and ed. Richard N. Coe (London, 1972), 174–5, quoted in Boursy, 'The Mystique', 299. Although much of Stendhal's writing on the Papal

The *Miserere* is the composition of the celebrated Allegri, and for giving the effect of wailing and lamentation, without injury to harmony, it is one of the most perfect of compositions. The manner of sustaining a strain of concord by new voices, now swelling high, now gradually dying away, now sliding imperceptibly into discord and suddenly breaking into harmony, is admirable.[24]

Spohr (1817) noticed particularly 'the delicate attack on a new chord while the previous one is still fading away [which] is something so unique and individual that one is irresistibly drawn to it'.[25]

In **M**, there are even indications of *portamento* between two notes which are the same, for example the second alto part between bars 50 and 51, soprani 1 and 2 and alto 1 between 54 and 55, soprano 2 and alto 1 between 103 and 104, and alto 2 at 126 (part names as transposed), which can only mean that the voice is supposed to leave the note momentarily and re-attack it with the others that have *portamenti* at this point, thus 'sliding imperceptibly into discord and suddenly breaking into harmony'. Moreover, the famous 'parallel portamento' on reciting chords, which so appalled Spohr and others (see Chapter 7) is found throughout **M**, as well as clearly indicated in certain manuscripts of **A**, and in **P**, **Man**, **Mil** and Alfieri 1.

To returning again to the question of the meaning of *a piacere* and *a misura* and their relationship to markings of *forte* and *dolce*, it seems likely that the 'polyphonic' sections were generally sung in a softer, less dramatic manner than the 'recited' ones. Once the parts started to move, the effect of the use of *portamento* was to make the notes, particularly the shorter ones, became part of a kind of moving flux, rather than having fixed pitches with ornaments added. Perhaps herein lies another clue to understanding the seemingly stilted dynamic indications in **A**. As the *portamenti* work best when they are treated as gentle slides rather than accented swoops, it follows that the general dynamic is *piano*. There are, however, exceptions. The extraordinary effect indicated in the middle of verse 20 (bar 130) of **M** (Fig. 24), where the singers are required to make a kind of 'collective swoop' at the end of the word *holocausta*, no doubt onto an anticipation of the C minor chord which launches the eight-part section at *Tunc imponent*, is clearly an element of *crescendo*, and is so marked.

In order to apply the practices shown in **M** in Edition 2, I have freely added slurs, all of which indicate *portamenti*. Singers and directors are free to study Mustafà's use of them and modify their application if they wish. A

Choir and the *Miserere* was plagiarised from Burney, this phrase either comes from another, so far unidentified, source, or is original.

[24] *Samuel Morse: His Letters and Journals*, ed. Edward Lind Morse (Boston, 1914), vol. 1, 345–6, quoted in Boursy, 'The Mystique', 320.

[25] *The Musical Journeys of Louis Spohr*, 190, quoted in Boursy, 'The Mystique', 306.

portamento-free interpretation would be as inappropriate as the performance of a French baroque dance (or a piece of traditional jazz for that matter) without *notes inégales*. Modern consort singers, usually trained to see 'cleanness' as a virtue, may be resistant to their use at first, but usually take to them with alacrity in the end!

Appoggiature

Vocally, the *appoggiatura* is without doubt the hardest aspect of the style to come to terms with, as even Mendelssohn found (see p. 112). Corri, contrasting it with 'the anticipation grace' of *portamento*, called it 'the leaping grace', a more rapid *portamento* – almost a hiccup – anticipating the syllable of the following note. Its very rapidity however makes Mendelssohn's characterisation of it as more a vocal tic than a true ornament, perhaps related to an audible change of registers, completely understandable. Its use seems to have decreased during the century, although it can still be heard in Moreschi's recordings and, less frequently, in those of his contemporaries, particularly Adelina Patti (who of course was older than most of the other singers recorded). This decreasing frequency is echoed in manuscripts of the *Miserere*. The earliest manuscripts, **P**, **Man** and **Mil**, have the most, with varying levels of precision regarding their pitch. Mendelssohn transcribed them with a cross-stroke, but **A** rarely does so (although there are more cross-strokes in Add. 31525(1)).

In **M** *appoggiature* often seem to have acquired a different function and become more integrated into the vocal phrase (e.g. the last few bars of the four-part verses). Mustafà adds the cross-stroke mostly in the parts, for the singers' benefit. Occasionally they are indicated by a crotchet rather than a quaver. In these cases one wonders if they have not become real *appoggiature*.

✷ Prosody

Every writer makes clear that conveying the meaning of the text was vitally important, and the first step to perfection was careful prosody in the chanted sections. As shown in Chapter 2, the Misereres preserved in CS 205–6 include rhythmic indications for these parts of each verse from around 1600. Whether this notation indicates a new kind of more expressive interpretation, or merely codified what the singers of the Papal Choir were already doing, is impossible to say. It is arguable that the new expressivity of the *seconda prattica* around the beginning of the seventeenth century may have been an influence, but it may equally be the case that, as so often, the notation took a while to catch up with performance practice; the earliest Misereres (and *falsobordoni* in general) may well have been sung more rhythmically than this source suggests.

Bai's *Miserere* was considered in this, as in many other ways, the culmination of Papal Choir practice in the singing of the Miserere, as Burney's comments upon it make clear.[26] In CS 340–1, every verse – with the exception of the second half of verse 7 and both halves of verse 9 – is given with precise rhythms throughout. Alfieri's edition of the Bai reproduces them all, and adds rhythmic indications for those two verses as well. Moreover he appears to have used them as models for Allegri's *Miserere* in all the verses except those (the second part of verse 5, verse 15, the first part of verse 17 and verse 19) with a particularly long text. In Bai's setting these verses are very close to being through-composed – effectively no longer *falsobordone* at all but choral recitation with considerable harmonic change. Bai handles them particularly carefully and successfully, but of course this makes them less useful as models for the Allegri. In any case, there seems little doubt that for Alfieri they were an essential part of the performance.

Man, **P** and **Mil** give even more precise rhythmic indications for these sections, as does **M**, which has not only the rhythmic indications, based largely on Bai's original, but detailed interpretative directions as well. The fact that the indications in **A** are minimal – consisting merely of the different *appoggiatura* signs – perhaps reflects the overriding interest in the *abbellimenti*, rather than in the prosody, of the German and English collectors who sought out these copies. In any case, in this edition of the Allegri, I have primarily followed Mustafà's model. While precise rhythmicisation of the chanted sections is both important and obligatory, the marking *col direttore* also means what it says: the conductor has a duty to add something of his own even to the precisely written rhythms, and to 'interpret' them in such a way as to illustrate their meaning.

---

[26] See p. 49.

17

Aspects of performance practice 3 – Performing forces

 Soloists

THE tradition in the Papal Choir was that the polyphonic verses were sung by soloists, and it is clear from the gracing found in all the verses that this is not 'choral' music. Apart from this evidence, the genesis outlined in Chapter 8 of Baini's *Miserere* – written in response to the perception that the five-part verses had become 'almost monotonous, because ... there are no variations' – is very telling. Baini's solution, to make sure that 'every verse is treated with faithfulness to the meaning that the specific words of this psalm deserve', created a work which can fairly be described as 'choral' in spirit. The simple performance of the notes on the page would suffice, with no embellishing skills required. And yet it too was performed by soloists, as Mendelssohn's testimony of 1831 makes clear.

> On the first day, when the Miserere of Baini, in the key of B minor was given, they sang thus: 'Miserere mei Deus' to 'misericordiam tuam' according to the score with solo voices, 2 choirs with the maximum possible use of the vocal capacity.[1]

The problem of monotony in 1820 was clearly due to a lack of soloists capable of embellishing in an interesting way, and Kantner and Pachovsky are surely mistaken when they attempt to argue that this monotony was due to choral performance of those verses.[2] It is therefore all the more surprising that Alfieri, alone of all witnesses, marked the five-part verses *tutti*. Either there really was at least one year around 1840 when the *Miserere* was performed thus, or else he was misinformed.[3]

---

[1] I have lightly amended the translation in *Letters* (139). The original phrase reads 'Miserere mei Deus bis misericordiam tuam nach den Noten mit Solostimmen, 2 Chören, und allem möglichen Aufwand der Mittel ihrer Stimmen.'

[2] *L'Ottocento*, 114.

[3] Given that he had no access to the archive of the Papal Choir and so was obliged to find his sources elsewhere, it could be that this information came

In the Sistine Chapel the Miserere was always sung entirely from the *Cantoria*, the modern English practice of placing the *concertino* choir at a distance being impossible, especially during the overcrowded offices of Holy Week. All the singers were thus crowded together in a relatively small space, and one might imagine that there would hardly be room in the *Cantoria* for all of them. Burney clearly struggled with this, making a point of visiting it to see for himself when he returned to Rome from Naples in November 1770.

> I went into the orchestra [sic] with respectful curiosity, to see the place sacred to the works of Palestrina. It seems hardly large enough to contain thirty performers, the ordinary number of singers in the pope's service; and yet, on great festivals, supernumeraries are added to these.[4]

It seems that he misunderstood the information he had been given, because while it is true that the choir was twice as big as usual on major festivals, that was because on ferial days the choir was organised on a rota basis, with only half the choir – no more than sixteen – present at any one time.[5]

Despite the cramped conditions, the singers seem to have been relatively content with their performing space, although when in 1615 Pope Paul V ordered the construction in the Quirinale palace of a chapel of identical size to the Sistine (which became the *Cappella Paolina*), they took advantage of the opportunity to ask for some practical modifications.

> May 3, 1615. Before mass there was a meeting. Signor Paolo Facchonio, *Maestro di Cappella*, told us that there will be built in the new chapel in Monte Cavallo (the Quirinale) a cantoria [*un coro*] just like the one in *S. Pietro*, (and because) that *coro* is far away both from His Holiness and the celebrant, also, because of the noise of the congregation, it is extremely difficult to make responses since they can barely be heard, it was decided by

---

from, say, a member of the *Cappella Giulia*, and reflected practice in S. Pietro (as suggested on pp. 152–3). On the other hand his two manuscripts of *abbellimenti* in MS Alfieri 1 clearly give sufficient graces to show that verse 1 was destined for soloists. He seems to have made a conscious decision to ignore this information.

[4] *The Present State*, 367.

[5] See Chapter 1, n. 5. This misunderstanding led Burney to note that 'There is likewise a number of supernumeraries ready to supply the places of those occasionally absent, so that the singers are never fewer than thirty-two, on common days, but on great festivals they are nearly doubled.' He was even more wrong when he wrote that 'Besides the supernumerary *expectants* of this chapel, many of the capital opera singers from other parts of Italy, are employed in Passion week' (*The Present State*, 271–2). This may have happened occasionally in the *Cappella Giulia*, but would have been unthinkable in the choir that sang in the Papal Chapel.

unanimous consent that *il signor maestro* will negotiate with the *Congregatione* (of prelates overseeing the construction) to see that it is placed 12 or 16 *palmi* closer to the altar, that it is made larger, that the balustrade is pushed farther out and is larger, and that the ceiling is smooth without any carvings [*senza lavoro alcuno*], so that the music can make good effect.[6]

Their requests were granted in every particular, a slight increase in size coming about as a result of the balustrade encroaching further into the chapel.

When Gavin Turner's William Byrd Choir recorded in the Sistine in 1980, the singers found it difficult.

We sang the Palestrina Hexachord Mass from the Cantoria, and how we ever crammed 21 singers into that cramped space I cannot imagine. ... From within [it] one just sings out into the vast space almost as if from a very small and claustrophobic anechoic chamber, with no idea of how well the sound was projecting or what the balance as heard down on the floor of the chapel would be.[7]

However, a recently retired member of the *Cappella Pontificia Musicale* expresses a contrary view.

I've sung so many times in the *Cantoria* (I like to sing there), it's not difficult, it's a bit uncomfortable when you sing in a large group because today we have the music in hand and there is the director to watch, but in ancient times that was not so. They all read the music from the big book on the lectern and there was no director, so less space was taken [by that]. From the acoustic point of view it is good to sing in the *Cantoria*, the singers are close and the sound blends well ... In ancient times there were many tapestries on the walls and this absorbed much of the sound, and today when you sing in the Sistine Chapel there is a great 'rumble' that once was not there.[8]

---

[6] *DS* 34, fol. 18ʳ, trans. (with slight amendments) from Sherr, 'Speculations on Repertory', 117, which also gives the original Italian. Clearly the name 'S. Pietro' is an error, perhaps referring to the Vatican in general, and hence to the Sistine.

[7] Private communication.

[8] 'Io ho cantato tante volte in Cantoria (I like to sing there), non è difficile, è un po' scomodo quando si canta in tanti perché oggi abbiamo la musica in mano e c'è il direttore da guardare, ma nei tempi antichi non avevano lo spartito, tutti leggevano sul grande libre che stava sul leggio e non c'era il direttore, quindi serviva meno posto. dal punto di vista acustico è bello cantare in Cantoria, i cantori sono vicini e il suono si fonde (verbo fondere) bene. ... Nei tempi antichi c'erano alle pareti molti arazzi e questo assorbiva molto il suono, infatti oggi quando si canta in Cappella sistina c'è un grande "rimbombo" che una volta non c'era.' Private communication from Luciano Luciani (see p. 12,

There are clearly two very different experiences being described here. Gavin also picked out the desirability of using solo voices.

> The acoustic tends to pick up the top line (whether the falsettists or the sopranos) and leaves the lower voices and the harmony a bit of a blur much of the time. It also has the effect of very quickly magnifying the sound ... I suspect that in that acoustic if we had used solo voices throughout, we could have achieved much greater clarity and a better balance ... the acoustic certainly amplifies solo voices quite enough to make a good impact down below.[9]

What is particularly desirable in a modern performance of the *Miserere* is to place the whole group out of sight of the public, as the choir was to almost everyone in the Chapel. The effect of the music coming from somewhere unknown in a darkened space was one of the most appealing parts of the experience to many nineteenth-century visitors, steeped as many of them were in the German Romantic traditions established by E.T.A. Hoffmann and Jean Paul Richter in which 'darkness and the invisible performer were linked to sublimity and transcendence'.[10]

※ The *cantus planus* verses

As noted above (Chapters 9 and 12) these verses were sung to a monotone, and the use of any psalm-tone is inappropriate. It is difficult to know when this practice was instituted. The Miserere, when it was sung at the end of *Tenebræ*, was in a sense extra-liturgical: perhaps it was felt that this precluded the use of a psalm-tone. More importantly, as noted in Chapter 2 (p. 35), from the second half of the sixteenth century, although the style and form of the *falsobordone* remained intact, composers began to treat the Tone increasingly loosely, sometimes abandoning it completely. The use of a monotone may date from as early as this, as few of the Mistereres in CS 205–206, apart from the first one, are clearly composed around a recognisable Tone. Even when one is recognisable, the endings are often varied. It is noteworthy that in the only manuscript now in the choir archive devoted entirely to *falsobordoni* (CS 343, copied in 1735) the final is given at the beginning of each setting, and within

---

n. 12). See the front cover for a picture of the Chapel with Raphael's tapestries in place.

[9] My thanks to Gavin, and also to Sally Dunkley, for their conversations with me about this experience.

[10] Ellis, *Interpreting the Musical Past*, 193.

the harmony the *cantus firmus* is carefully distinguished from the rest by being in written in black notes. If this was thought necessary for simple *falsobordoni* such as these, it is difficult to see how the singers could have been expected to find the right tone and the first note in the *cantus planus* verses of the Misereres, the parts of which give no such indications.

The manuscripts of **A** give either 'il populo risponde l'altro verso' or 'in coro' for these verses, although only manuscripts **9–12** actually give one long breve on d (g when transposed up a fourth) for the first words of every even-numbered verse, with the rubric 'Tutti i Tenori e Bassi'.[11] **M** gives 'Coro' before the d, and an elaborate series of cues in the separate parts (see Figs 22 and 23, discussed in Appendix 13) for the lower voices of both choirs. Clearly, all the other tenors and basses, already present for the considerable plainsong of the lengthy office, joined in. This is all corroborated by Mendelssohn.

> On the first day, when the Miserere of Baini, in the key of B minor was given, they sang thus 'Miserere mei Deus' to 'misericordiam tuam' according to the score with solo voices, ... then all the bass singers commenced tutti forte on F-sharp, chanting on that note 'et secundum multitudinem' to 'iniquitatem meam' which is immediately succeeded by a soft chord in B minor, and so on, to the last verse of all, which they sing with their entire strength.[12]

In his 'explanations', Alfieri did not even deign to call these verses music: 'Finally it should be noted that the verse of the psalm which is not sung should be read [*leggesi*] *sotto voce* by the whole choir on the tone the singers end on',[13] although it is clearly the kind of 'reading', more like chanting, that needs the pitch of a note. The use of a monotone, clearly established by 1708, must certainly have simplified matters, although even that did not guarantee perfection in more harmonically complex music.[14]

---

[11] Manuscript **9** gives octave ds.

[12] *Letters*, 139. In the previous paragraph, Mendelssohn wrote 'all the male voices in unison' (see below). It would have been almost impossible for Mendelssohn to tell whether or not the tenors joined in with the basses in the unison *cantus planus* verses.

[13] 'Finalemente è da avvertirsi che il versetto del Salmo che non si canta, leggesi sottovoce da tutto il Coro nel tono che si lascia da cantori.' Preface to Alfieri, *Il Salmo Misere posto in musica da Gregorio Allegri e da Tommaso Bai*, 1840.

[14] In 1708, during what was possibly the first performance of Alessandro Scarlatti's *Miserere*, the singers of the plainsong choir were all fined for singing verse 2 a tone too low. 'In the Miserere of Sig. Scarlatti the voice in the verse was taken a tone lower by the *cantus firmus* choir, for which each of the following gentlemen were fined 20 *baiocchi*: Perrini, Sauli, ... [17 names in all]. And because in the second polyphonic *choro* the tenor and altus, entering together,

Evidence that the *sotto voce* described in Alfieri does not mean *pianissimo* comes from Germaine de Staël in her novel *Corinne*. She devotes a whole chapter to Holy Week in Rome, which she visited in 1805.

> The *miserere* ... is a psalm composed of verses sung antiphonally in very different styles. Heavenly music is heard alternating with recitative murmured in muffled, almost harsh, tones; it would seem to be the response of hard nature to sensitive hearts, life's reality come to blight and deny the wishes of generous souls. When the sweet chorus resumes, we take heart again. But when the recited verse resumes, a cold sensation seizes us once more, not from terror but from the discouraging of enthusiasm.[15]

This description accords with Mendelssohn's.

> They do not neglect the power of contrast; verse after verse is chanted by all the male voices in unison, *forte*, and harshly. At the beginning of the subsequent verses, one hears the lovely, rich, soft sounds of the other voices; they last only for a short space, and are again succeeded by the male chorus. During the verses sung in a monotone, every one knows how beautiful the softer choir is going to sound ... [16]

It also accords with Mendelssohn's description of Sistine psalm-singing in general: 'they sing with the accent of a number of men quarrelling violently, and it sounds as if they were shouting the same thing furiously at each other'.[17]

---

the latter before the tenor in the lowered tone of the choir, and the tenor did not enter until the bass was heard to enter, also the *puntatore* was fined 20 *baiocchi*. The others who sang in the polyphonic choir are not fined, not even Sig. Carli, who by the resolution of the college is excluded from the fines. *DS* 128, fols. 44ʳ–45ʳ, trans. in Della Libera, introduction to *Selected Sacred Music by Alessandro Scarlatti*, viii, with the original text in a footnote. In the first verse (a4) of this *Miserere* (in G minor, like all Misereres) the composer, by a clever harmonic sequence, manages to give the G major chord at the end of verse 1 (a4) a dominant feel. It is thus easy to understand why the plainsong choir might instinctively sing C instead of D, which would surprise the three voices (S2, A and T – not ATB as the *DS* says) trying to begin verse 3 (a5) in B♭.

[15] Anne-Louise Germaine Necker, baronne de Staël-Holstein, *Corinne, ou l'Italie* (1807), trans. Avriel Goldberger (New Brunswick, NJ, 1987), 178, quoted in Boursy, 'The Mystique', 302.

[16] *Letters*, 139. As in Alfieri's marking the five-part verses as *tutti*, perhaps his *sotto voce* comes from a different tradition, for example that of the *Cappella Giulia*.

[17] *Letters*, 135. This was still the case in 1890: 'The voices are magnificent and the music is performed with great perfection, but the plainsong is hammered out, with a heavy beat, and shouted; one would not believe that these are the

Many listeners were shocked by the way the choir chanted in general, and some of this manner no doubt found its way into the even-numbered verses of the *Miserere*. The aim seems to have been to create as much contrast as possible with the ethereal polyphonic verses. As Mustafà gives no indications of interpretation in these verses, I have suggested in both editions occasional changes to a general loud dynamic and rapid speed, with the usual proviso that directors are free to vary or ignore them if they wish.

 Castrati

The use of *castrati* is self-evidently one aspect of the performance practice of the Papal Choir which it is impossible to reproduce; all the more reason then to take into account their unique qualities when performing the *Miserere*. The sound of the *castrato* was very particular: words commonly used to describe the best of them include 'flexible', 'sweet', 'pure', 'angelic', 'powerful', 'metallic' (in the sense of 'ringing'), 'golden' and 'silvery'.[18] Mendelssohn described one singer as having 'a pure, soft voice', and another's performance of a psalm as being 'executed with the purest, cleanest and most even intonation', although he found the sound of them in the choir 'sometimes repulsively shrill'.[19] Fanny Hensel heard a soprano who was both 'very powerful [and] particularly sweet in tone'.[20] Both were probably describing the singing of Mariano Padroni, who was also praised for his 'art of swelling and diminishing the tones by almost imperceptible gradations'.[21] He shared this outstanding quality with Alessandro Moreschi, 'whose *messa di voce* had never been equalled'.[22] That this was not a new virtue for *castrati* is shown by John Evelyn's description of Siface nearly two centuries before: 'his holding out and delicatenesse in extending & loosing a note with that incomparable softnesse & sweetenesse,

---

same artists.' Dom André Mocquereau from Solemnes, quoted in Dom Pierre Combe, *Histoire de la restauration du chant Grégorien d'après des documents inédits* (Solemnes, 1969), 150, trans. T.N. Marier and W. Skinner, *The Restoration of Gregorian Chant*, (Washington, 2003), 128.

[18] For a comprehensive survey of opinion, as well as an analysis of the means *castrati* used to produce such voices, see Feldman, *The Castrato*, particularly chapter 3, 'Red hot voice'.

[19] *Letters*, 95, 141 and 146.

[20] *The Mendelssohn Family*, Vol. 2, 98.

[21] *The Harmonicon* (1826), 151.

[22] Franz Haböck, *Die Gesangskunst der Kastraten* (Vienna, 1923), quoted in Clapton, *Moreschi*, 185–6.

was admirable'.[23] In a sacred context it was above all this flexibility which was prized, rather than the virtuosic coloratura display for which *castrati* had been famous on the operatic stage. Burney wrote of 'those minute occasional temperaments, for which the language of sound has no characters, and which the flexibility of voices alone can express' as the 'refinements' which were not 'hidden or corrupted' by the accompaniment of instruments 'whose tones are unalterably fixed'.[24] If this was the ideal of the whole choir, it was nevertheless the *castrati* who influenced most its realisation, because it was for them that the early writers on the voice – Tosi (1723) and Mancini (1774) – directed their advice and instruction. The rules and techniques of *bel canto*, as it later came to be called, were invented for them.

The virility that the *castrati* contributed to the overall sound and style of the choir made a great impression on Charles Gounod.

> I went ... as often as possible to the Sistine Chapel. The music there – severe, ascetic, horizontal, and calm as the line of the ocean, monotonous by reason of serenity, ante-sensuous, and, nevertheless, possessing an intensity of contemplation that sometimes amounts to ecstasy – produced at first a strange, almost unpleasant, effect upon me. Whether it was the character of the composition itself, entirely new to me, or the especial sonority of those particular voices, heard for the first time, or, indeed, that attack, firm to harshness, that forcible hammering that gives such strong relief to the various entrances of the voices into a web so full and close, I can not say, but, at any rate, this impression, however strange it might have been, did not displease me. I went the second time, and still again, and finished by not being able to do without it.[25]

It is clear that in the music of Palestrina, the subject of Gounod's impressions here, ethereal sweet sounds were not the priority. Moritz Hauptmann had noted the same things when he remarked that during Vespers the choir sang 'without the slightest sentimentality' (see p. 229).

What set *castrati* apart from both boys and women was their lung-power, which was due to the particular way in which their bodies developed at puberty following castration.[26] To make the most of their particular physique, not only their larger than average chest cavity but also their facial shape, they practised for several hours a day for many years to develop an often extraordinary control over the highest notes, notably the ability to sing them softly and for

---

[23] *Diary and Correspondence of John Evelyn, F.R.S.* (London, 1859), vol. 2, 276 (19 April 1687), and see p. 17, n. 25.

[24] *La musica*, iv.

[25] Charles Gounod, *Memoirs of an Artist*, trans. Annette E. Crocker (Chicago, 1895), 95–6.

[26] Feldman, *The Castrato*, esp. 95–106.

a long time if necessary: the top Cs in Mustafà's manuscript of the *Miserere* are all attacked softly and held as long as possible. In 1891 the French singer Emma Calvé was so impressed by Mustafà's top notes, which she described as 'strange, sexless tones, superhuman, uncanny', that she asked him for singing lessons. His reply was 'It's quite easy ... you only have to practise with your mouth tight shut for two hours a day. At the end of ten years, you may possibly be able to do something with them.' In the event she was able to add these disembodied tones, called by Mustafà his 'fourth voice', to her vocal armoury in only three. But she never managed to teach these 'flute tones', as she called them, to any of her pupils.[27] Many singers can produce such notes simply by humming. But these 'whistle notes', sometime labelled 'suprafalsetto', seem to have taken on a special colour when sung by *castrati*, producing a sound Calvé described as 'angelic, neither masculine nor yet feminine'.[28]

One can hear these notes occasionally in the recordings by late nineteenth-century female singers such as Adelina Patti, Nellie Melba, Emma Eames and Eugenia Burzio. Even in the opera house, it was rarely necessary to sing high notes loudly to be heard – they passed easily over the orchestra.[29] In the Sistine Chapel, unaccompanied and with a generous acoustic that favours the higher voices, the softest sound could be relied upon to have a magical effect, and while Moreschi does not appear to use a 'fourth voice' to any extent in his recordings, the indications in **M** to approach the top Cs with 'un filo di voce' would seem to be an instruction by Mustafà for its use.

If it took Mustafà ten years to acquire the control of this skill, it is unlikely that any boy would have time to do so before puberty, so female singers are generally better replacements for *castrati* than all but the most exceptional boys. However, if such a boy can be found, the experience of the twentieth-century papal falsettist Domenico Mancini (1891–1984) is telling. In a radio interview given in 1967, he recounted his lessons from Moreschi from the age of thirteen.

> I came under the spell of his outstandingly beautiful voice ... I began my studies with Moreschi by imitating his voice with my own, since, as it hadn't yet changed, I just sang as he did, in chest voice, passing from there into head voice. But then, at around fourteen, well, my voice became that of a

---

[27] Ibid., 123–5.

[28] Ibid., 124.

[29] Comparison of their recordings with those by Moreschi shows many qualities in common, to the extent that in a 'blind' listening it is not always easy to immediately identify which is the *castrato*. See Feldman (ibid., 82–9) for a detailed comparison of these five singers' versions of Gounod's *Ave Maria*.

man, and so singing with the falsettists, I began to use the type of head voice which normal adult men have.[30]

Feldman also quotes this passage in order to make a point about the use of chest voice by *castrati* in general, summarising it thus: 'the crucial point is that the boy Mancini "imitated" Moreschi's singing using his chest voice but the man Mancini could not'.[31] It is often noted that boy sopranos, especially those who mature late, have a kind of vocal 'swan-song' in the six months or so before their voices finally change, owing to early hormonal effects. Such a boy, if sufficiently skilled, may be the closest it is possible to get nowadays to the sound of the *castrato*. Unfortunately in the English system such late developers have generally left the choir school well before.

Apart from the skill of singing softly but tellingly, the lead soprano will need a sure control over vibrato, knowing how to turn it on and, even more importantly, turn it off. It has been noted above (p. 236) that Ingres compared the effect of the *castrato* voice to the sound made by a glass harmonica; it is worth underlining that the sound of a glass harmonica is almost entirely without vibrato.

---

[30] Trans. in Clapton, *Moreschi*, 181 and n. 193, which reproduces almost entirely the translation by Robert Buning.

[31] *The Castrato*, 95. Recordings of Moreschi seem to indicate that the transition from chest to head voice occurred around or slightly above c″, and it is interesting to note that Mendelssohn's examples of *appoggiatura* (Ex. 1, p. 112) all occur between that C and the notes above it. The different vocal production Mancini describes was not enough to persuade Mustafà's successor, the arch-Cecilian Lorenzo Perosi, that Mancini was in fact a falsettist. 'Because I had studied with Moreschi, Perosi thought I was a castrato and didn't want me, since he had rooted out the castrato voices from all the choirs … Perosi got it into his head, since I sang in Moreschi's way, that I was one of "those" voices.' (Clapton, 181). Mancini became a double-bass player, but eventually found his way into the Papal Choir as a falsettist for twenty-four years from 1935 and was highly esteemed there.

18

Conclusion

The manuscripts presented in this book, most of them published for the first time, served different functions. The Vatican sources of the Allegri, CS 205–6 and 340–1 (the latter also containing Bai's *Miserere*), were fair copies in choirbook format, made for the use of the Papal Choir. Biordi's manuscript, CS 263, shows a composer at work, as he completely re-imagines Allegri's composition. All these give the *Miserere* unadorned, although it is interesting to see that Biordi added some decorations to the cadences when, having worked on later verses (see verse 13 in Appendix 2), he further modified verse 1.

The earliest source with some decoration, printed in 1767 by Blainville (**B**), is hard to place. Certain phrases show that its maker must have at least heard the *Miserere* being sung, although other ornaments hardly even seem Italian. Its purpose as much as its provenance remains for the moment a mystery. However, all subsequent sources with performance indications clearly have their origins in the Vatican, although only Mustafà's extraordinary manuscript (**M**) is still there. The earliest, the Manchester manuscript (**Man**), was put together by members of the Papal Choir for a valued friend, possibly to be used in a private performance. The Paris manuscript (**P**) was the presentation copy made from it. Although these give only three verses of the *Miserere*, the exhaustive detail they present gives us a good idea of what Mozart heard in 1770. The manuscript in Milan (**Mil**) shares the same qualities and also seems to have been a private affair, presented by a papal singer to a friend or acquaintance. The series of manuscripts from the 1820s, now in the British Library and various parts in German-speaking Europe (collectively Source **A**), must have been created for interested collectors. While we do not know their ultimate source, nothing in them suggests anything other than a close relationship with the Papal Choir. They open a window into certain of its practices but, being focused on the famous *abbellimenti*, lack much important practical detail. Some of that necessary information was published in 1840 by Alfieri in his introduction, but the music in his edition adds little new information, despite his being an official Vatican publisher.

The most precious information comes from Domenico Mustafà, who made his copy in 1892 not for outsiders but for the singers of a future generation, so that they might re-create what he considered to be the miracle of the *Miserere*.

The essence of this miracle was the emotion it aroused in the listener, not only through the exotic sound of the *castrati*, but also because of its unique way of communicating an important part of one of the most sacred offices of the year in a highly theatrical setting. He thus noted down 'ways and means': vocal practices which had perhaps previously been taken for granted, and in the process allowed us to understand something of how this 'miracle' worked. The existence of his manuscript also permits us to use the series of 1820s sources as a basis for an edition of the *Miserere* based wholly on the adaptation of Allegri's original by then in use.

As a singer himself, Mustafà understood what future singers would need to know. When we compare these 'ways and means' with those found in the many published methods of the day, and with early recordings, we find that they are recognisably in the mainstream of the aims and techniques of nineteenth-century singing in general – especially those involving slow, 'pathetic' music. The *castrato*'s singing world was not greatly different from that of singers such as Patti and Melba, and perhaps even closer to that of *verismo* singers like Burzio. So despite its very particular provenance, the manuscript opens a small window onto the generality of vocal expression and technique in the second half of the nineteenth century.

What is less clear is how much we can extrapolate these techniques of expression into former periods. It is interesting, for example, that Mustafà felt the need to mark the *portamenti* so lavishly and clearly. He was certainly aware of the influence of new currents of thinking – of the Cecilians, for example – who were championing a new, 'cleaner' and more sober kind of interpretation. Did he feel that the general use of *portamento*, and of some of the other more extreme expressive devices, needed to be specifically noted because it was dying out? Do we see in this manuscript not a flourishing tradition of extreme expressiveness, but its swansong? Or was it the Papal Choir's unique way of using it which needed emphasis?[1]

None of the writers – Spohr, Mendelssohn *frère* and *soeur*, Nicolai – who expressed amazement at the 'parallel *portamento*' moments were amazed because they heard *portamento*; clearly, in their own performance tradition its use was normal, or at least common. What seems to have shocked them was the parallel movement, and the fact that there was so much of it in a choral context. Spohr gave detailed instructions for the use of *portamento* in his V*iolinschule* (1832), as had Friedrich Dotzauer in his *Méthode de Violoncelle* of about 1825 and Pierre Baillot in his *Méthode de Violon* of 1803. Fingerings marked in Mendelssohn's music by close associates imply it, as do indications

---

[1] John Potter, in 'Beggar at the Door', has shown that its use carried on uninterrupted in most genres of music until the 1940s, although there were grumbles about it, as there had always been.

in music as early as Haydn.[2] However, it is clear that it was considered a practice suitable for soloists only, and many writers, including Spohr and Dotzauer, strongly condemned its use by orchestral players. The Papal singers all seem to have wanted to join in, and sometimes the effect was less than happy. As Nicolai said, 'it will be easy for you to understand that if different voices add passing notes to the harmony, each according to his caprice, the result must often be repulsive'.[3]

The parallel *portamento* was in fact the opposite of this kind of anarchy. All the singers did the same ornament at the same time. It was part of what we would now call a 'consort' performance of extreme expressivity. Mustafà's manuscript shows this expressivity in very fine detail. Nothing is left to chance. He does not write the *portamenti* to show that singers should do some – he writes them to show exactly where and how, and the same is true of all the other copious expressive indications. In 1770 Burney heard the same kind of performance, the singers 'swelling and diminishing the sounds altogether; accelerating or retarding the measure at some particular words, and singing some entire verses quicker than others'.[4] We cannot know how much detailed difference there was between what Mozart heard and Mustafà's score, but it is quite possible that there wasn't very much. Certainly the parallel *portamento* was part of both, as is shown by its presence in **Man** and **P**. And given the normal rate of evolution of anything in the Vatican, what Mozart heard may not have changed much in the fifty preceding years.

The question which therefore presents itself is: how exceptional was the Papal Choir's method of performance in 1770? How far was it outside the 'mainstream'? Even more intriguing, was it a throwback or a precursor? Received opinion is that Romantic expressivity in performance was a practice still to come. But given the tendency in the Vatican to look backwards and resist change, perhaps it was the opposite – the last remnants of a particular kind of extravagant and extravert 'Baroque' expression, such as that found in the writings of Bovicelli and Rognoni, that subsequently, somehow, missed out any semblance of 'Classical' refinement before embracing a thoroughly 'Romantic' exaggeration. Whatever the answers to these questions turn out to be, we can at least conclude with some certainty that much of Mustafà's manner of performance reflected practices which have their origins in the eighteenth century and probably earlier.

---

[2] For many examples and comparisons for both orchestral and vocal music see Brown, *Performing Practice*, chapter 15. For specific questions concerning the cello, on which, because of its particular physical characteristics, *portamento* is difficult to avoid, see chapter 4 of George Kennaway, *Playing the Cello, 1780–1930* (London, 2014).

[3] 'Italienische Studien', in Kruse, *Musikalische Aufsätze*, 73–4. See p. 115.

[4] *The Present State*, 275–6. Whether 'altogether' means 'completely', or 'all together' is a moot point.

This manner concerns not primarily individual vocal technique, but the interpretation of polyphony. Many general questions about choral practice in the eighteenth and nineteenth centuries are provoked by what this study has shown, and one conclusion that can be drawn is that current 'one size fits all' choral technique, with its emphasis on unanimity rather than colour, regularity rather than fantasy and precision rather than expressiveness, is not always the most appropriate manner to approach its re-creation, especially of a work like 'the Allegri'. To do that, we are obliged to enter the world of style shown in Mustafà's manuscript and believe in it, just as he did.

PART FIVE

APPENDICES, EDITIONS AND NOTES

APPENDICES

1	Allegri's 'original' version of verse 1 a5, Cappella Sistina 205 (1661)	258
2	Biordi's rewriting of Allegri's five-part verses in Cappella Sistina 263 (c.1715)	259
3	'Allegri's Miserere' from Cappella Sistina 340–1 (1748)	261
4	Bai's *Miserere* from Cappella Sistina 340–1 (1748)	270
5	*Miserere del Sgr Allegri* in Blainville's *Histoire Générale* (1767)	281
6	The Paris and Manchester manuscripts *come si deve eseguire* (1798)	283
7	The Milan manuscript (c.1815)	286
8	Source **A** (1820s manuscripts): a summary of the sources	288
9	Source **A**: verses 1, 3 and 5, with variants	293
10	Source **A**: Verse 3 from British Library Add. MS 31525/1	298
11	Alfieri's published *abbellimenti* (1840)	300
12	Alfieri's manuscript – Berlin Staatsbibliothek Mus. ms. Alfieri 1	302
13	The Performing editions	306
	EDITION 1: Bai/Allegri as notated by Mustafà in 1892	306
	Commentary	324
	EDITION 2: 'Allegri's Miserere' based on Source **A**	328
	Commentary	349

✳ Notes on the editions

Variants in the appendices are noted as follows:
3 iii 1: *appoggiatura* in 2 only = bar 3, third part (reading from the top), note 1 (excluding ornaments, counting tied notes as 2, including rests): the *appoggiatura* in the edited score is only found in Source 2.

Pitch is given using Helmholtz notation (octaves reading upwards from eight-foot pitch (changing on c) are C, c, c' (middle c), c", c"').

Note values (in italics): *b* = breve, *s* = semibreve (whole note), *m* = minim (half-note), *c* = crotchet (quarter-note), *q* = quaver (eighth-note), *sq* = semiquaver (sixteenth-note), *d* = demisemiquaver (thirty-second-note). A dot is given as . (e.g. *q.sq* = dotted quaver–semiquaver).

Appendix 1

Allegri's 'original' version of verse 1 a5, Cappella Sistina 205 (1661)

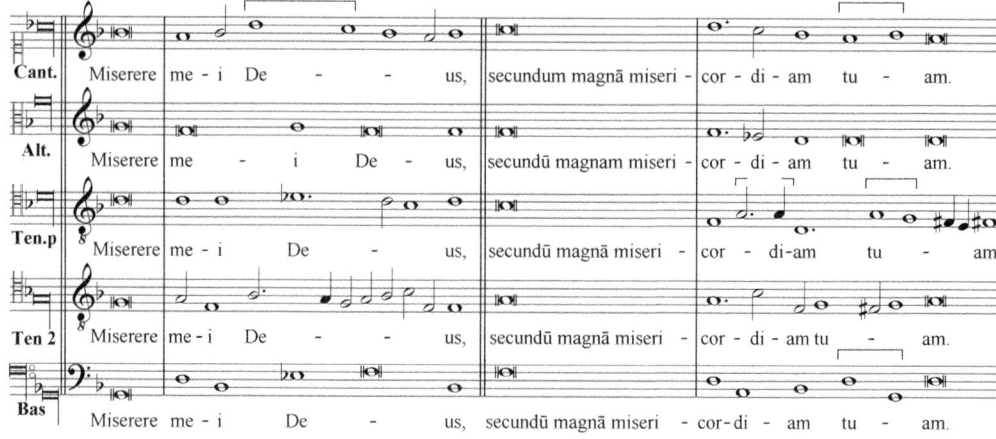

✳ Appendix 2

Biordi's rewriting of Allegri's five-part verses in
Cappella Sistina 263 (c.1715)

Verse 1

Notes

2 i 3–9: altered from *m*b(♭)' *m*b(♭)' *s*e♭'' *m*d'' (see v. 13)
2 ii 4–10: altered from *s*c'' *s*b(♭)' *m*a' (see v. 13)
4 i 1–2: altered from *b*c''
4 i 12 – 5 i 4: altered from *s*c'' *c*b(♭)' *c*a'

259

Verse 13

Showing early version (fewer passing notes) of the opening phrase, and the variation of the second phrase used in verses 5 and 13 only

✵ Appendix 3

'Allegri's Miserere' from Cappella Sistina 340–1 (1748)

CS 341: Coro Primo (fols. 3ᵛ–10ʳ), 340; Coro secondo (fols. 3ᵛ–9ʳ)

Verse 1

Variants in Paris and Manchester MSS 'come l'originale'

(All variants apply to both **Man** and **P**). **Man** gives text in i and v only.
2 i 5: *m*.e♭″ *cd*″
2 ii 4: *m.c*′ *cb*(♭)
[2 iv 1–3: note unique variant (*sd*′ *sd*′) in decorated version of **Man** and **P** (see Appendix 6)]
2 v 2: c for B(♭) in both. **Man** has a correction in pencil
4 i 9–10: *cd*′
4 ii 8–14: underlay -di- on n. 11, -am on n. 12, tu- on n. 14
4 iii 5–7: *se*♭′*cor*- *sd*′ -*diam*; 13–16: *se*♭′ *cor*- ('diam' between notes), *bd*′ *tu*-
4 iv 5 – 5 iv 2: *sb*(♭) *cor*- *sb*(♭) -*di mg* -*am sa* -*tu*
5 iv 5–9: *cb*(♭) *cc*′ *md*′ *sd*′ *sd*

Verse 3

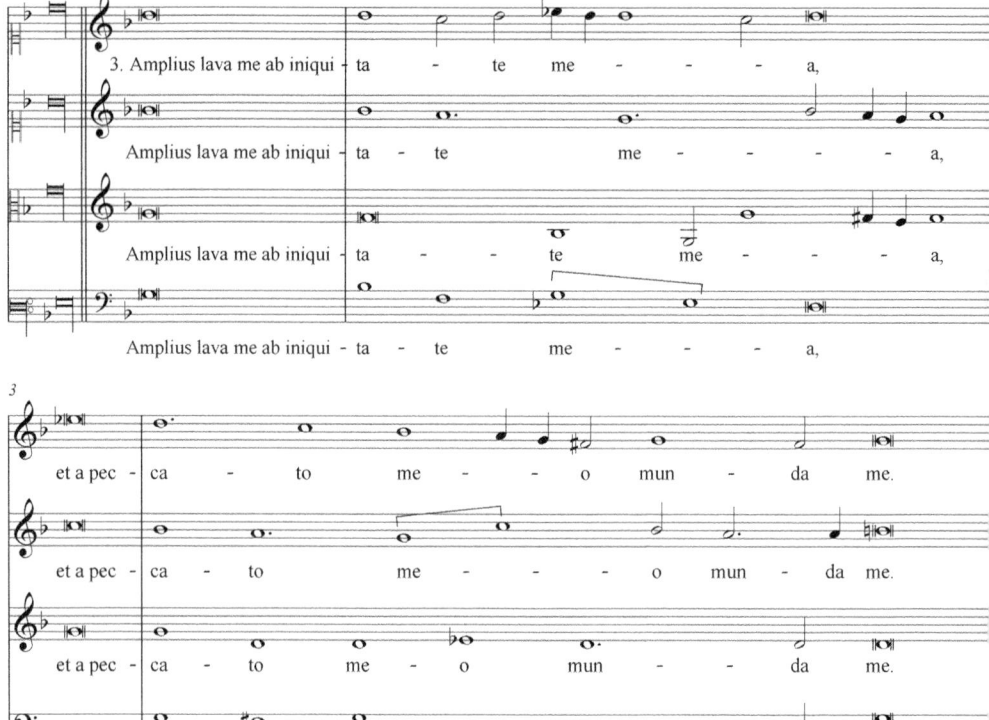

Variants in Paris and Manchester MSS 'come l'originale'

All variants apply to both **Man** and **P** except where marked. **Man** gives text in i and iv only.

2 i 2–4: **P** underlay -to on n. 2, me on n. 3; **Man** underlay -to on n. 2, me on n. 4
2 ii 1–4: *s s s.s*
2 iii 1–2: *sf'* -ta- *sf'* –te *sb*♭ me- in **P**. **Man** has same rhythm without the text
2 iii 4: *m* for *s* in **Man** only
4 i 4–7: underlay -o on n. 4, mun- on n. 6
4 ii 1–2: *s.s*
4 ii 3–5: underlay meo on n. 3, mun- on n. 5 in **P**
4 ii 6–7: *s*
4 iii 5–6: ♭ munda in **P**. **Man** has same rhythm without the text
4 iv 5–6: ♭ munda

Appendices   263

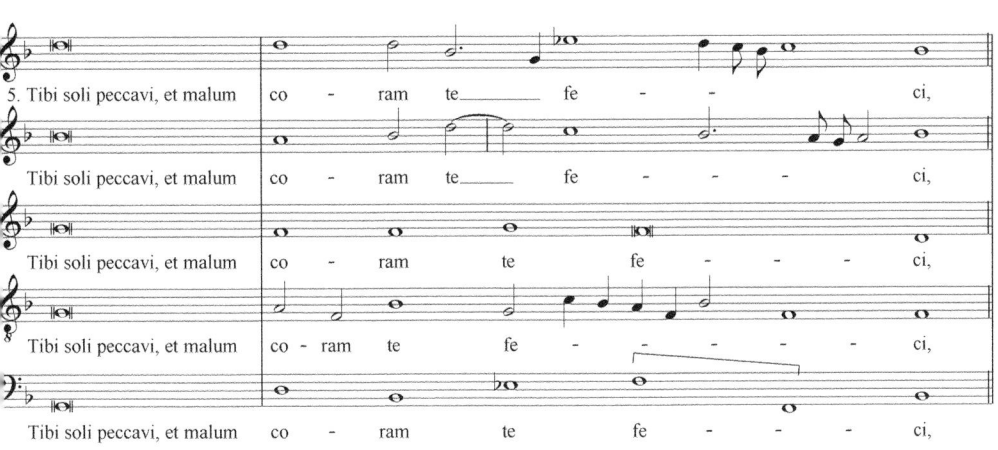

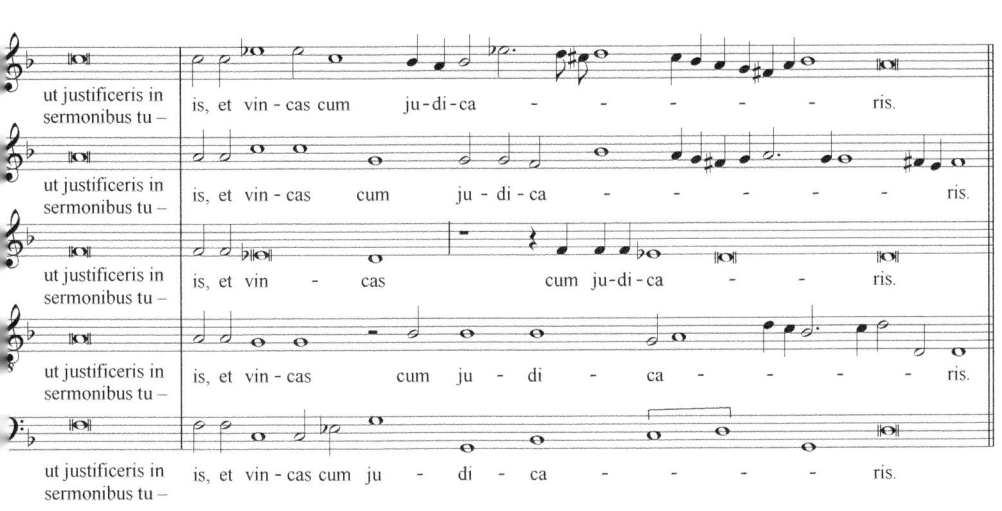

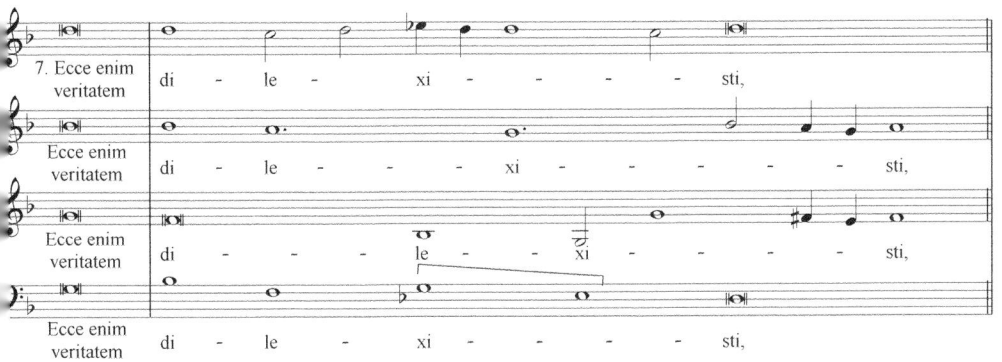

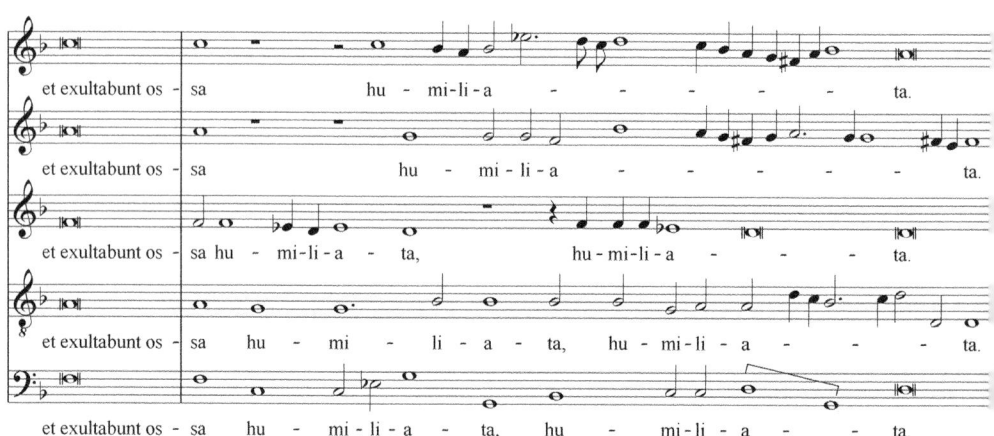

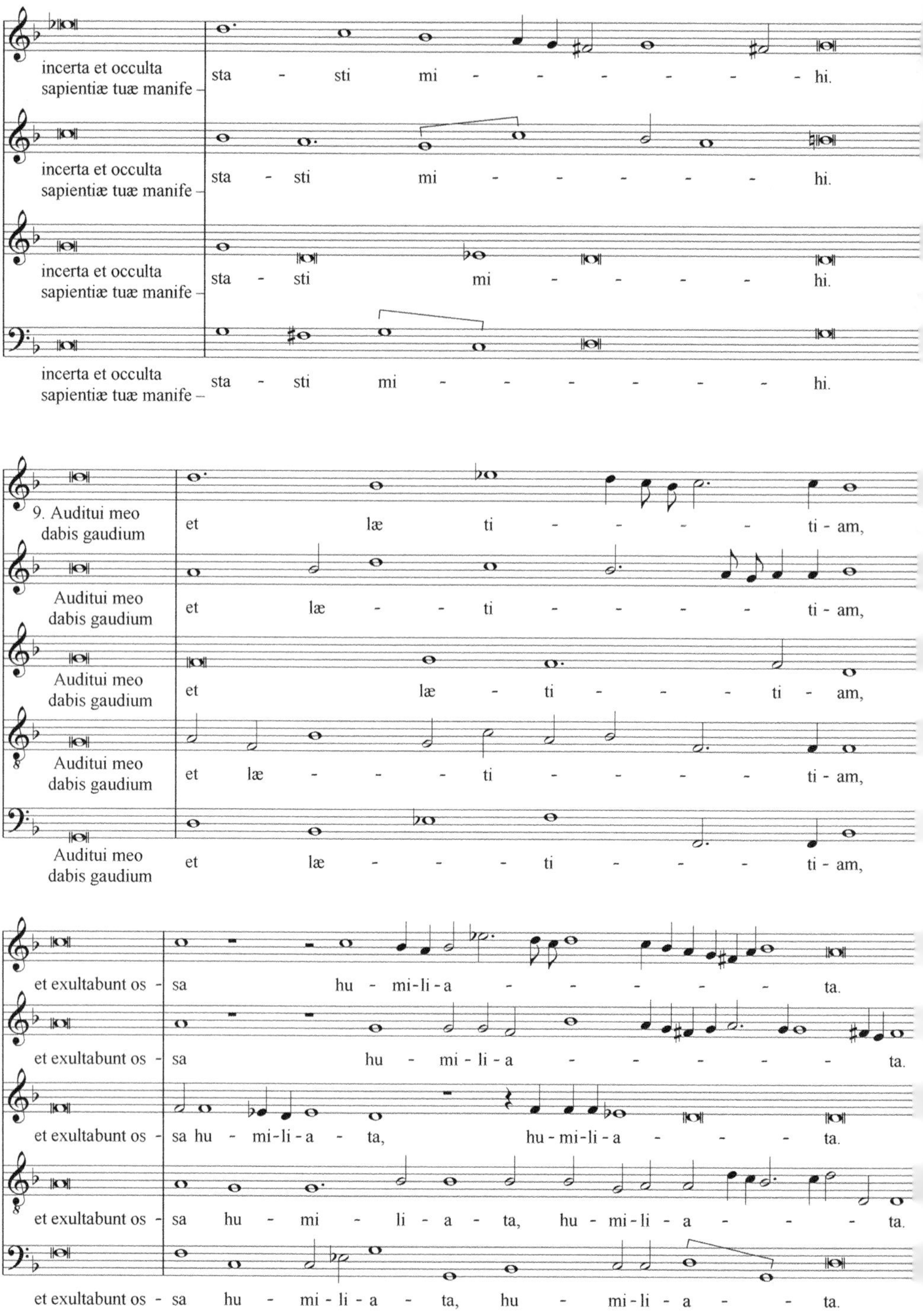
incerta et occulta sapientiæ tuæ manife –
sta - sti mi - - - - - - hi.
incerta et occulta sapientiæ tuæ manife –
sta - sti mi - - - - - hi.
incerta et occulta sapientiæ tuæ manife –
sta - sti mi - - - - hi.
incerta et occulta sapientiæ tuæ manife –
sta - sti mi - - - - - - - hi.
9. Auditui meo dabis gaudium
et læ ti - - - - ti - am,
Auditui meo dabis gaudium
et læ - - ti - - - - ti - am,
Auditui meo dabis gaudium
et læ - ti - - - ti - am,
Auditui meo dabis gaudium
et læ - - - ti - - - - ti - am,
Auditui meo dabis gaudium
et læ - - - ti - - - ti - am,
et exultabunt os - sa hu - mi-li-a - - - - - ta.
et exultabunt os - sa hu - mi - li - a - - - - - ta.
et exultabunt os - sa hu - mi-li-a - ta, hu-mi-li-a - - - ta.
et exultabunt os - sa hu - mi - li - a - ta, hu - mi-li - a - - - ta.
et exultabunt os - sa hu - mi-li-a - ta, hu - mi-li - a - - ta.

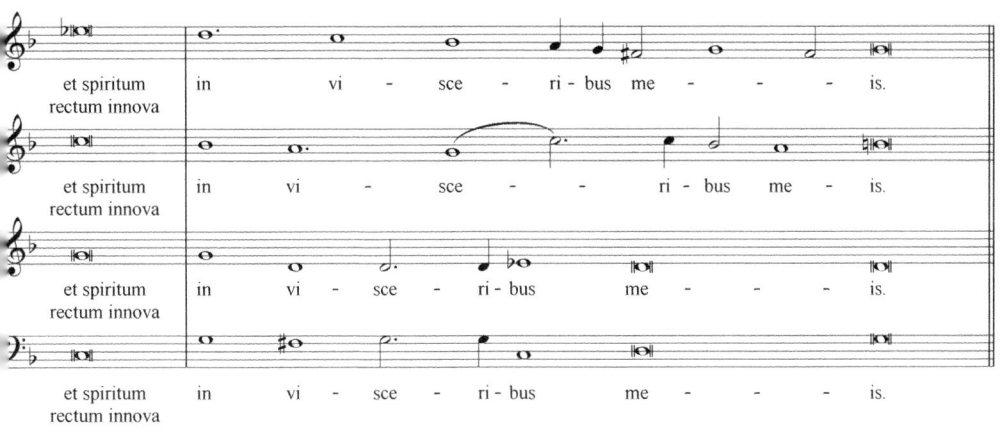
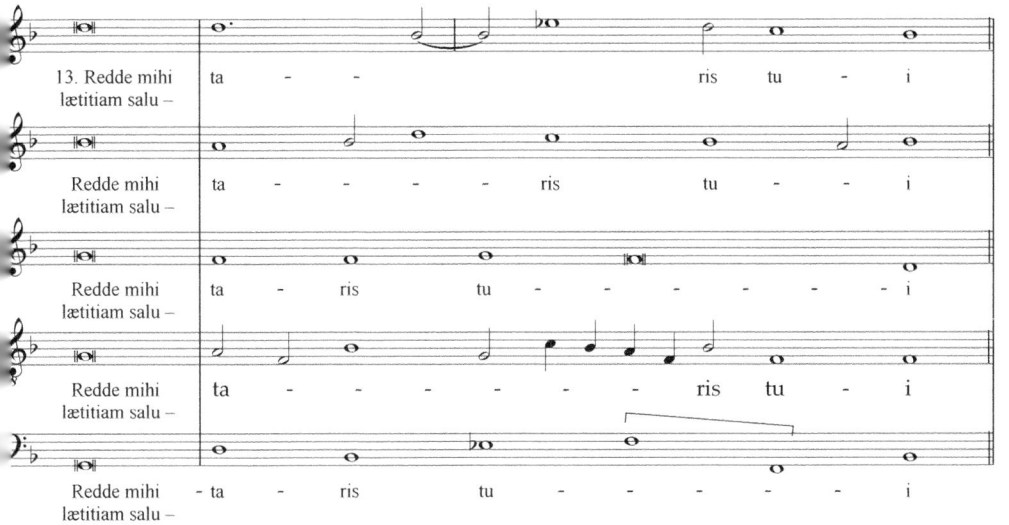

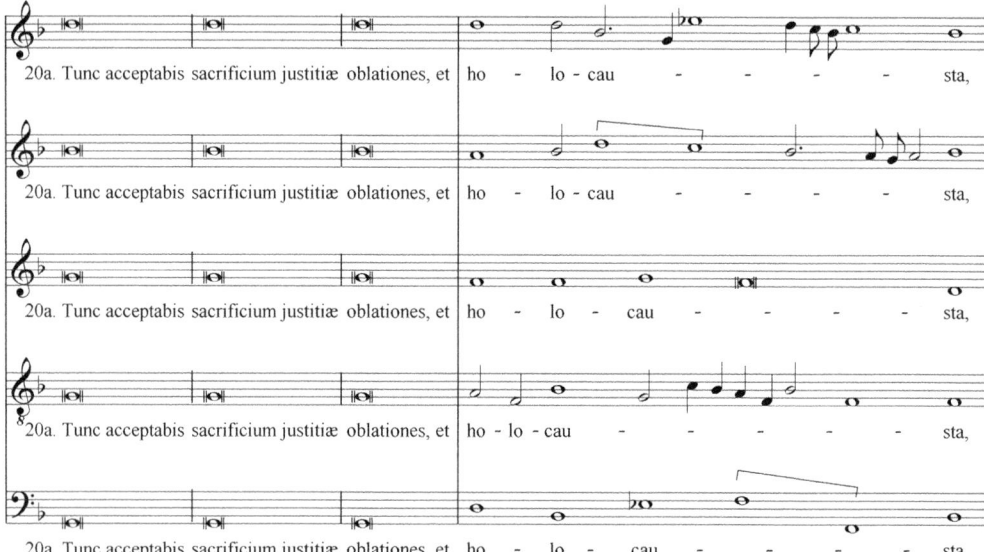

✳ Appendix 4

Bai's Miserere *from Cappella Sistina 340–1 (1748)*

CS 341: *Coro 1° (fols. 11ᵛ–18ʳ)*, CS 340: *Coro 2° (fols. 10ᵛ–16ʳ)*

Appendices 271

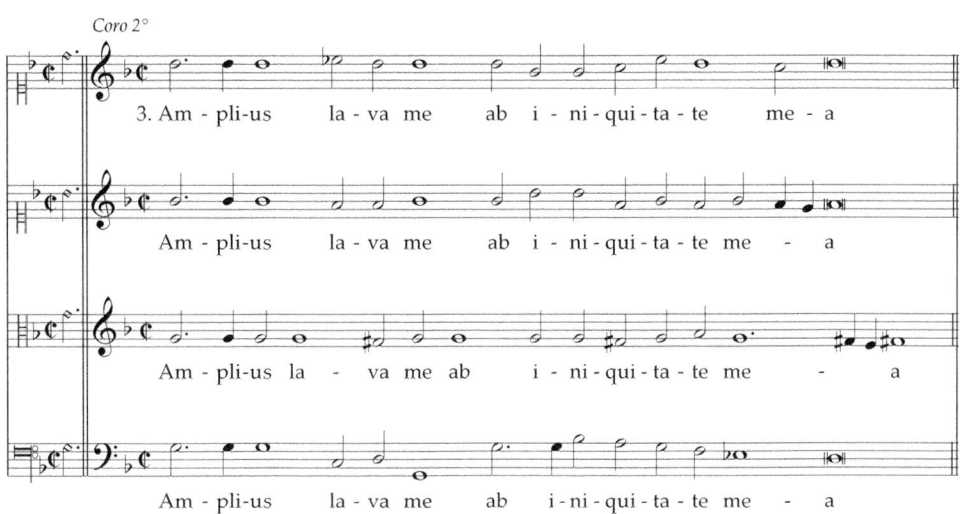

Appendices 273

Coro 2°

Coro 1°

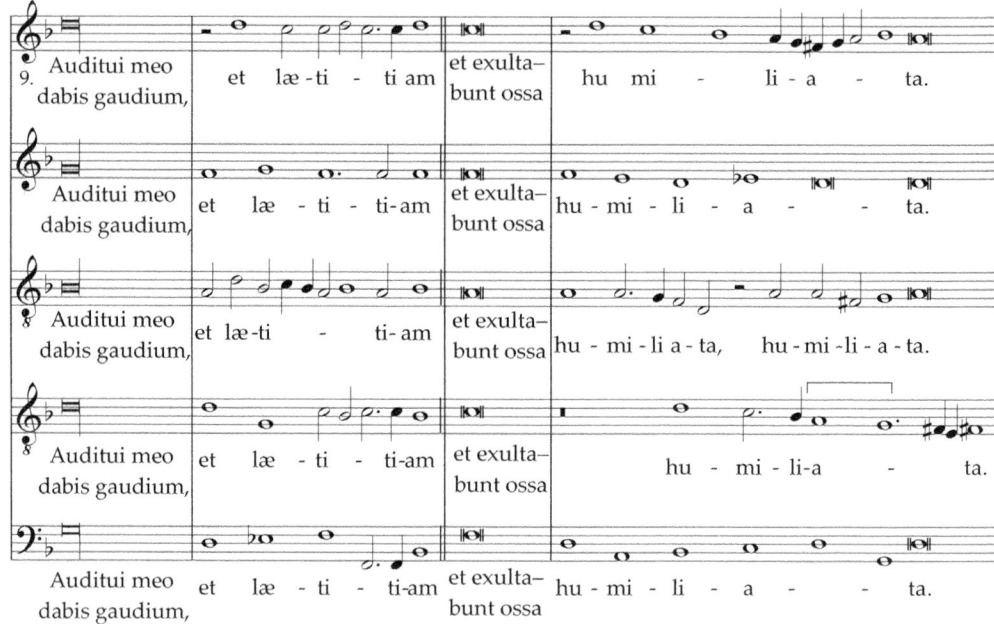

Coro 2°

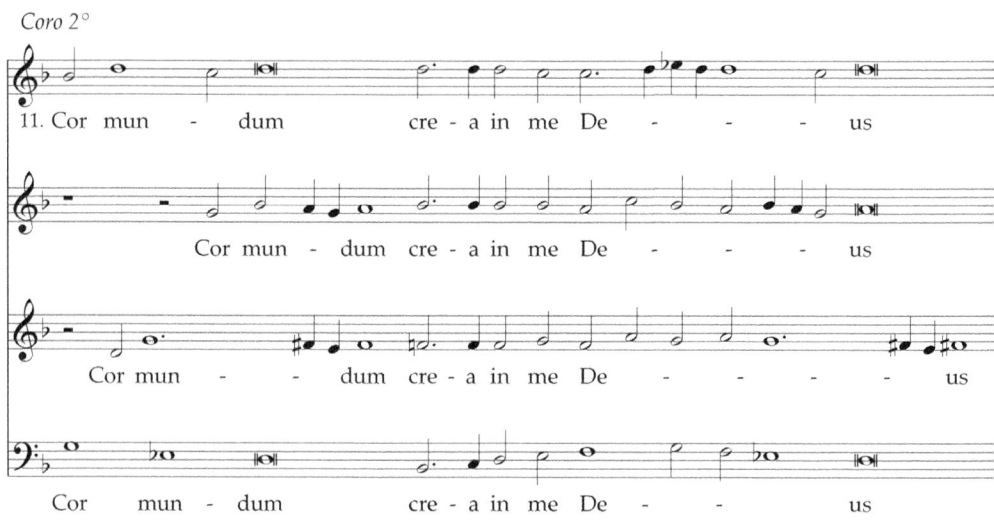

Coro 1°

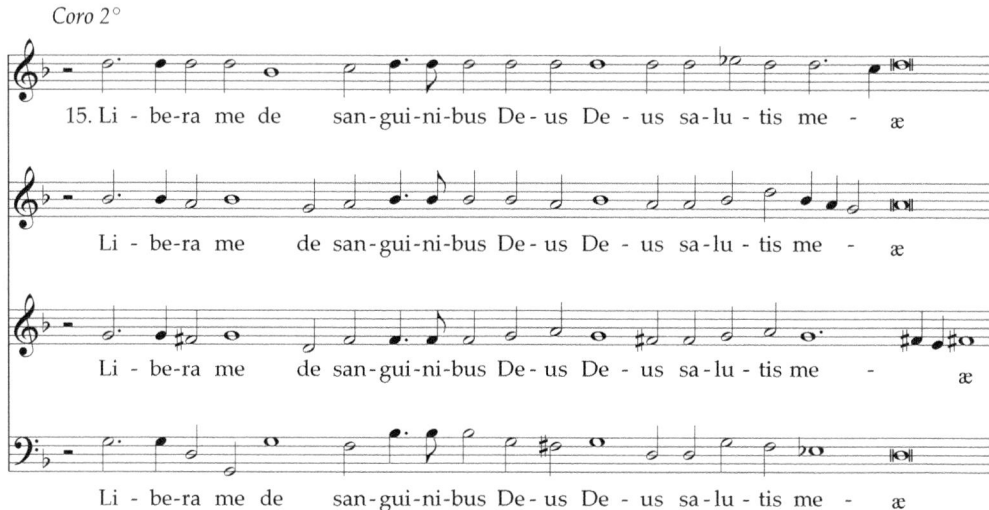

Appendices 277

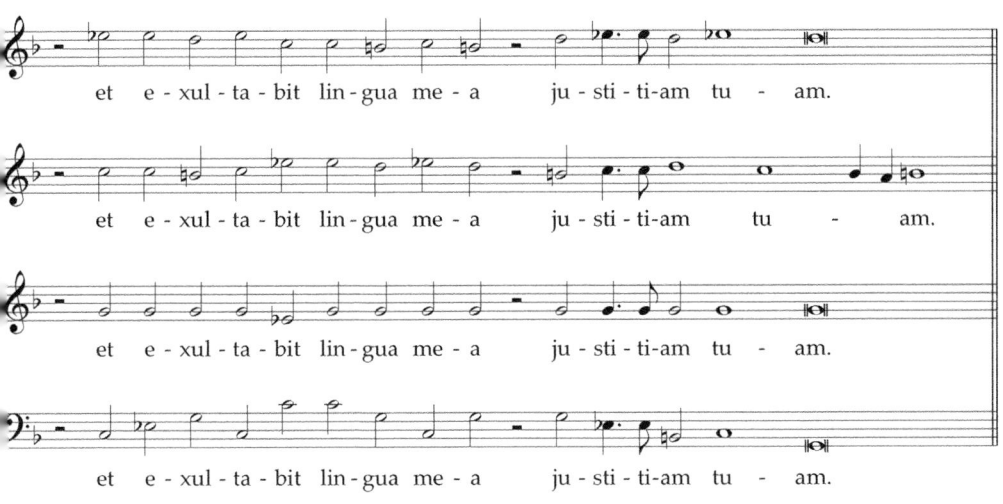

Coro 1°

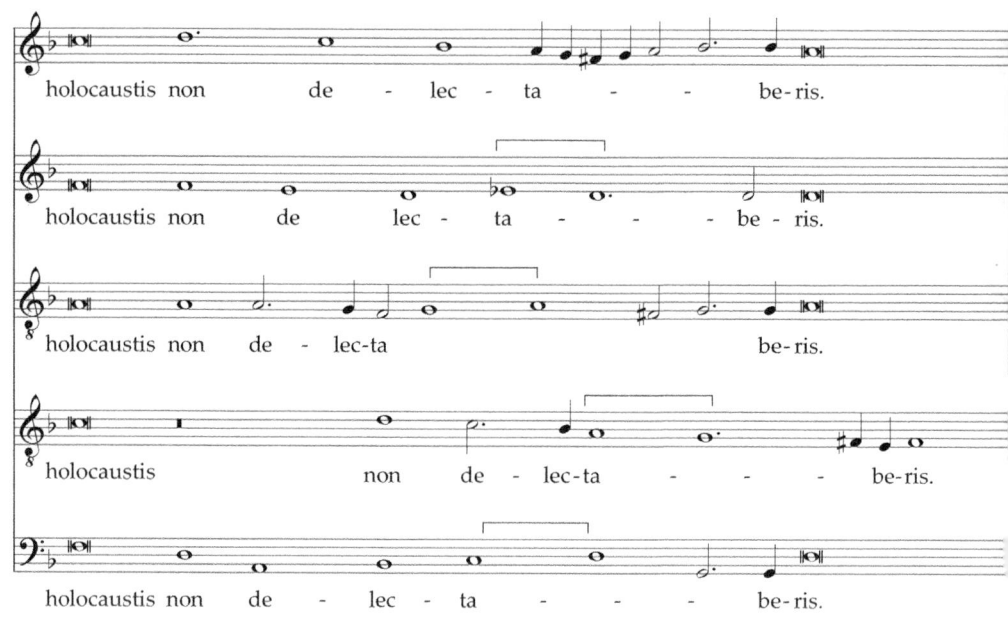

Appendices

Coro 1°

Segue subito

Appendix 5

Miserere del Sgr Allegri *in Blainville's* Histoire Générale, Critique et Philologique de la Musique *(1767), plates XXII–XXIII (B)*

Verse 1

v. 1 11 iv: f is probably a mistake for d

Verse 3

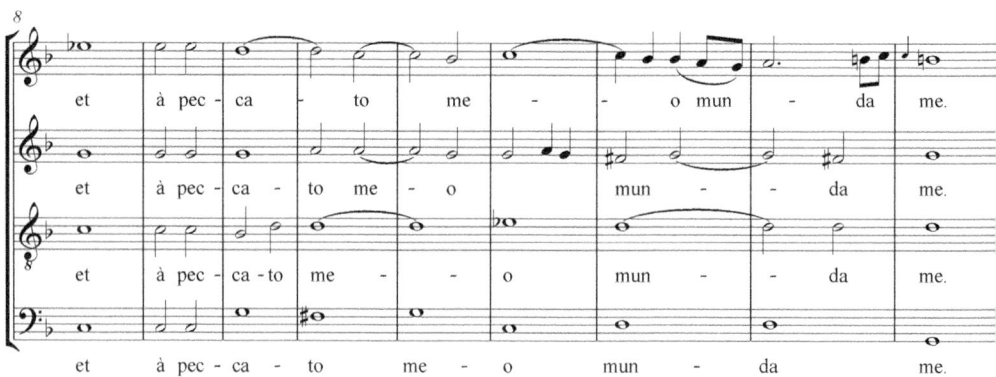

✵ Appendix 6

The Paris and Manchester manuscripts come si deve eseguire *(1798)*

The Manchester manuscript (**Man**) is virtually identical to **P**, as is the printed version of 1838 (variants are noted). All three also include the last verse a9, with two interesting dynamics for the final word *vitulos*: *p* at *vi-* and *f* at *-tu-*, the better perhaps to prepare the long *decrescendo* on the final chord described by Adami and Burney.

284   Appendices

Verse 1

Unique variant

3–4 iv: These are the only sources to give *sd' sd'* instead of the usual *ma mf* sb(♭)

Verse 3

Variants in the printed edition (1838) and **Man**

Appoggiature in **Man** have note heads and are generally one note higher than the note following.

The print slavishly follows **P**.

Verse 1

5 i: *appoggiatura* missing in print
6, 7 15 i: *Appoggatura* printed with a stroke through the tail, one note higher than following note
9 v: sf
20 i: **Man** gives sb(♭)' (not tied to 19), with final syllable on *sa'* in following bar

Verse 3

Crossed slurs are from the print only
7 i beat 2: *q sq sq* in print
18 i 1–2: no slur in **Man**
19 ii beat 2: *sq sq* in print
20 i: *tr* missing in print
Alternative version not given in **Man**

Appendix 7

The Milan manuscript (c.1815)

Verse 1

NB 4 iv: f (instead of normal reading of b(♭), gives octaves with alto 4–5.

Verse 3

# Appendix 8

Source A (1820s manuscripts): a summary of the sources

Complete sources

The transcriptions of verses 1 and 5 in Appendix 9 have been made from a collation of sources **1**, **2**, **3** and **4**. Verse 3 is based on **2**, **3** and **4**. **1** provides a unique reading for verse 3, so has been transcribed separately in Appendix 10.

1 and 2 *London, British Library Add. MS 31525 (1) and (2) (not mentioned in Amann,* Allegris Miserere*)*
Two manuscripts, both of ornamented versions of the Allegri *Miserere*; complete, including verse 20b a9. Acquired by the British Museum in 1881 from the English collector Julian Marshall, who himself bought it from Joseph Warren, organist, musicologist, collector and teacher, whose name is found in pencil at the top of the title page. Perhaps bought by Warren in Rome between 1822 and 1826. Pencil annotations (apparently in Warren's hand) in **2** as follows. On the title page: 'It ought to be sung 4 tones higher, in C'; on the first page of the score: 'Misura largo assai' ('speed very slow and broad'), and 'bisogna alzare qua una nota e poi tornare negli soli voci de due soprano' ['you have to rise one note here and then return in the solo voices of the two sopranos']. Presumably this refers to the rise and fall of the parallel *portamento* on the word *Miserere*, and suggests that Warren is commenting on a live performance in which either the other voices did not execute the ornament, or he did not hear it. In later verses he supplies some missing text in the bass part, as well as notes about pronunciation.

The two manuscripts are in different hands, and both are mistakenly attributed to Bai. **1** – Add. 31525(1) – has the following title page, in the same hand as the score.

> *Miserere/del Sig. Mro Baj./Come si eseguisce nella Cappella Pontificia/Di Roma/In Roma presso Bened Morganti Via de Crociferi N°119*

The title page of **2** – Add. 31525(2) – has simply '*Miserere*' in the same hand as **1**, indicating that they were bought at the same time and place. Probably bound together later: the pages of **1** have been trimmed, then pasted at the spine to give dimensions of 28cm × 21cm, whereas **2** is bound as found (29.5cm × 22cm). **1** uses pages of eight staves until fol. 18, then takes ten stave pages in preparation for the final verse. **2** uses ten stave pages throughout. Both use space lavishly. **2** is more hastily written than **1** but shows evidence of the musicality of its scribe, who clearly hears what he is writing. This is not always the case with the scribes of **3** and **4**, who give the impression of copying slavishly from another source. For this reason **2** has been preferred when in doubt.

3 *Vienna, Österreichische Nationalbibliothek Mus. Hs. 15604, Version 2 (Amann, Allegris Miserere, 118–19)*
15604 gives three different versions of the *Miserere*. Version 1 (without ornaments, after Burney) and Version 2 (fols. 1^r–12^v) are copied on facing pages by the same hand some time before 1836, when the MS was acquired by the library. Readings are virtually identical to **4** and very similar to **1** and **2**.

Version 1 is on fols. 1^v, 2^v, 3^v, 4^v, 5^v, 6^v, 7^v, 8^v, 9^v, 10^v, 11^v, 12^r and 12^v (vv. 1–20).

Version 2 is on fols. 2^r, 3^r, 4^r, 5^r, 6^r, 7^r, 8^r, 9^r, 10^r and 11^r (vv. 1–19), and is marked 'von einem päbstlichen Sänger, mit allen Verzierungen und Andeutungen des Vortrags aufgesetzt, wie es in der Sixtinischen Capelle gesungen wird (d.h. seit 1824)' ('notated by a papal singer, with all ornaments and indications, as it is sung in the Sistine Chapel (that is, since 1824)'). Verses 1 and 3 of Version 2 are given in Haas, *Aufführungspraxis der Musik*, 159.

Version 3 (fols. 13^r–18^r, all verses except 20a) is of Allegri's original version as found in CS 205–6, supplied with a figured bass 'Wie es in Salzburg in der Domkirche gesungen wird'(which was sung in Salzburg in the Cathedral). The manuscript also gives eleven works by Benevolo, Bartolomeo Cordans, Foggia, Morales, Palestrina and G.A. Bernabei, all in the same hand. The text of 20a is given, indicating that it should be sung in *cantus planus*.

4 *Munich, Bayerische Staatsbibliothek Mus. ms. 671 (Amann, Allegris Miserere, 114)*.
Contains verses 1–19. Readings are virtually identical to **3** and very similar to **1** (for the 5-part verses only) and **2**. Copied by, or for, Anton Friedrich Justus Thibaut (died 1840), a friend of Bernhard Klein (see sources **5** and **6**), who gave him scores for his collection.

The score is marked: 'von einem päbstlichen Sänger, mit allen Verzierungen und Andeutungen des Vortrags aufgesetzt, wie es in der Sixtinischen Capelle gesungen wird (d.h. seit 1824), – auch bey dem Anhören revidiert' ('notated by a Papal singer, with all ornaments and indications, as it is sung in the Sistine Chapel (that is, since 1824) and revised after listening').

5 *Warsaw, Biblioteka Uniwersytecka RM 6027 (Amann, Allegris Miserere, 109)*
Contains verses 1–19. Probably copied from **4** by Emil Bohn (1839–1909). Formerly Musikalisches Institut bei des Universität Breslau (= Wrocław) Mf. 5132.

The manuscript consists of twenty-two pieces by Allegri, Bai, Anerio, Festa, Palestrina and Biordi, all copied from Munich sources, some printed, some manuscript. The *Miserere* is at the end. Used by Amann in his *Allegris Miserere* as the basis of his list of variants between most of these sources (58–65).

Sources **1–5** use * in the reciting sections of each verse, the meaning of which is revealed by sources **6–9**.

✷ Partial sources – first group

6 *Berlin, Staatsbibiothek Sammlung Teschner 119, fols. 10ʳ–13ʳ (Amann,* Allegris Miserere, *114)*

Verses 1, 3, 5, 7 and (incomplete) 20.

Title page: *Miserere von Allegri (Mit allen Verzierungen; so wie es in der heiligen Woche zu Rom in der Capella Sixtina gesungen wird ---)* ('with all the decorations, as it is sung in Holy Week in Rome in the Sistine Chapel').

Bottom right corner, in a different hand from the rest: 'G.W. Teschner'. Teschner (1800–83) was a singing teacher, editor and musicologist, pupil of Klein (and of Professor Carl Friedrich Zelter) in 1824–8. The library acquired the manuscript, together with others, from Teschner in 1879.

At the end of v. 1: 'Il populo rispondo unisono l'altro verzo.'

After v. 7 (bottom of p. 7): 'Also werden die übrigen Versette mit Abwechselung des Coro I° und II° und den Risp. nach der nämlichen Musik abgesungen. I auditui meo II cor mundum I Redde mihi II libera me II [sic] quoniam I [sic] Benigne fac' ('Thus the remaining verses are alternated between *Coro I* and *II* and the unison responses, sung to the same music. I auditui meo etc.'). V. 20a: reciting chord for the five voices, then Canto 1 only. Note: 'Nach der Musik der ersten Coro folgt das Übrigen des Versettes' ('after the first choir's music, the rest of the verse follows').

V. 20b: First two chords only of each choir to the words *Gloria patri et filio*.

Final page (8): 'So weit führte das Exemplar, nach welchem diese Copie gemacht [This is as much as was in the exemplar from which this copy was made], Rom im Februar 1825, Bernh. Klein.'

Under *Coro I*, v. 20: 'Soll das C.moll/dur Drejklang s[ingen?]', which appears to be simply harmonic analysis.

Underlay largely complete in vv. 1, 3 and 5 (i.e. more than in 7); v. 7: in soprano 1 only.

7 *Dresden, Sächsische Landesbibliothek Mus. 1474-E-3 (Amann,* Allegris Miserere, *110)*

Contents and title as **6**. Almost identical but with less underlay.

In pencil in a different hand: 'Handschrift Bernhard Klein, a[usgabe] letzter Hand' ('In the hand of Bernhard Klein, final definitive edition'), but a library note by Arno Reichert on final page denies this.

p. 2: a long extract from Part 1 (pp. 12–16) of Wilhelm Heinse's *Hildegard von Hohenthal* (1795), containing a description of the *Miserere*.

Notes at the end of v. 1, after v. 7 and v. 20a, and on final page (p. 7) as **6**.

Underlay: v.1: all parts but incomplete, vv. 3 and 5: soprano 1 nearly complete, others very little, v. 7: soprano 1 only.

8 *Munich, Bayerische Staatsbibliothek Mus. ms. 3268 (Amann,* Allegris Miserere, *107)*
Two Misereres in score in the same hand; the first one (fols. 1ʳ–5ᵛ) is Burney's version of vv. 1–19, without ornaments, the second (fols. 6ʳ–8ʳ) reproduces the contents of **6** (same underlay, less dynamics) but no commentary of any kind.

9 *Cologne, Hochschule für Musik und Tanz Bibliothek R1038/2 pp. 6–9 (not in Amann,* Allegris Miserere*)*
Contents as **6** but without verse 20. Readings and underlay almost identical to **6**.
Presented to the library on 4 October 1878 by Nikolaus Joseph Hompesch (1830–1902), who was one of the first graduates from the Conservatorium der Musik in Cologne and who taught piano there from 1854 to his death.
Title page as **6**. Bottom right corner: 'Erhalten im Jahr 1830 | von Bernhard Klein | welcher dieselben von dem | Capellmeister der päpstlichen | Capelle bei seiner Anwesen- | heit in Rom empfing.' ('Obtained in the year 1830 from Bernhard Klein, who received it from the Kapellmeister of the Papal Chapel during his presence in Rome.')
At the end of v. 1, 'Il populo risponde quasi parlante l'altro Verzo come segue' followed by verse 2 in octaves (d/d' on a stave with a c_3 clef) and rhythmicised.
On final page: 'Also werden die übrigen Versette mit Abwechselung des Coro I° und II° / und den Risposten, in einem Tone nach dem Versmaaße abgesungen Coro I auditui meo … (So weit führte das Exemplar, nach welchem diese Copietur gemacht.)' ('Thus the remaining verses are alternated between Coro I and II and the responses, the music according to the verse … (This is as much as was in the exemplar from which this copy was made).'
R1038/1 is *Giov. Batt. Casati Motetto a 4* (pp. 1–5).

NB Sources **6**–**9** give a symbol like a dumb-bell marked 'segno di Appoggiatura' in largely the same places as sources **1**–**4** give *. All four sources give the same serious error in verse 3 (bar 4, soprano 2).

✳ Partial sources – second group

10 *Basel, Universtäts-Bibliothek kk XII 22:3 (Amann,* Allegris Miserere, *107)*
Verses 1, 3 and 20a with ornaments, 20b without ornaments (same version as Alfieri).

Title page: *Miserere di Gregorio Allegri, con tutti quelli ornamenti come si canta nella capella sistina nel giorni Mercoldi* [sic] *Giovedi e Venerdi della Settimana santa.*
After v. 1 'Il popolo risponde l'altro verso : (tutti i Tenori e Bassi) "Et secundum multitudinem" etc.' With a bass clef and note d.
After v. 3 'Coro 1mo "tibi soli peccavi" risposta del popolo "Ecce enim"' [etc. for all the verses].
At the end, 'Roma, di 30 Ottobre [18]29.'

11 *Leipzig, Stadtbibliothek – Musikbibliothek PM 5618, fols. 24^r–26^r (not in Amann,* Allegris Miserere*)*
Contents as **10** but without verse 20b. Title page, notes after verses 1 (p. 48) and 3 (p. 49) and readings identical to **10**.
Verses 1, 3 and 20a only. Possibly in the hand of Moritz Hauptmann. Previously part of the collection Bernhard Friedrich Richter (1850–1931), who may have acquired it from his father Ernest Friedrich Richter (1808–79), composer, editor, teacher at Leipzig Conservatoire & Thomaskantor. Later owned by Kurt Taut (1888–1939), director of Edition Peters in Leipzig, and presented to the Leipzig public library after his death.
Also contains *Miserere* by Leonardo Leo.

12 *Oxford, Bodleian Libraries, MS M. Deneke Mendelssohn d.70 (not in Amann,* Allegris Miserere*)*
Verses 1, 3, 20a and 20b (without ornaments, after Alfieri). Copied by Franz Xaver Gleichauf (1801–56), and subsequently owned by Fritz Schlemmer and finally Helena Deneke, who presented it to the Bodleian Library in 1973 with many other Mendelssohn manuscripts.
Title page and notes after v. 1 (no note given) and 3 as **10** and **11**.
Readings identical to **10** and **11**, but adds rhythms (incompetently) in small notes on reciting chords.
Also contains Lamentations for the Papal Chapel by Allegri and Palestrina also found in Bibliothèque nationale D.14499 (**P**; see Chapter 6), and music by Lotti.

Sources **10**–**12** give neither * nor the *segno di Appoggiatura* (but in v. 20a of **10** and **11** the same places have a superscript x). They all label *Coro 1°* as *Coro maggiore* and *Coro 2°* as *Coro minore.*

Appendix 9

Source A: verses 1, 3 and 5, with variants

Verse 1

Variants *(largely sources 2, 3 and 4 only)*

2, 3 and 4 label the five-part verses *Secondo coro* and the four-part ones *Primo coro*, the opposite of all Vatican sources (and of **6–9**); **10–12** use the terms *coro maggiore* for the five-part ones, *coro minore* for the four-part ones; **1** has no labels. Clefs are given at the beginning only of each verse.

Underlay: **1** gives S1 and T1 only until bar 6. **2** gives soprano 1 and alto only until bar 6. **3** and **4** give all parts nearly everywhere except in bar 1. For underlay in **6–9** see pp.290–91. Underlay complete in **10–12**.

Dynamics: **1** gives very little, **2**, **3** and **4** give in all parts. **3** and **4** have the most *crescendo* and *diminuendo* signs

3 i 2–4: slur from 2–3, 3 marked *f*, 4 marked *p* in **1**

3 i 5: NB: in v. 5 (below) the first note has a ♯

3 ii 1–2: *mm* in **3** and **4**. Later verses adopt reading here

3 iii 1: *appoggiatura* in **1** only

3 iv 2–6: **2** reading is corrected (for some reason) from *qc' qb(♭) ma cf*, the reading in **3** and **4**

1 gives *cc' qb(♭) qa ca cf*, a reading adopted from verse 5 onwards by the other sources, sometimes with a *gruppetto* before n. 5 (e.g. v. 5 in **3** and **4**), which probably indicates that it should at least be re-attacked rather than tied

4 i 1: appoggiatura in **1** and **2** only (c in **2**)

4 iii 2: flat in **3** and **4** only

6 iii 2–3: slur in **3** and **4** only

6 iii 4–5 and 6–7: slurs in **2** only

7 i 2–3: slur in **3** and **4** only
7 iii 1: no ♭ in any source
9 iii 2–3: underlay in **1**: -diam tu-. 3 is tied to 10 n. 1
9 iv 2–4: underlay in **1**: -diam tu- on 3–4. 3–4 slurred in **2**. **3** and **4** clearly give -diam on 3–4, but in the absence of a slur, it is not clear whether -diam is one syllable on two notes, or two syllables, each with a note (cf. (am)-plius, and (gau)-dium in Bai)
10–11: barring as here in all sources

Verse 3

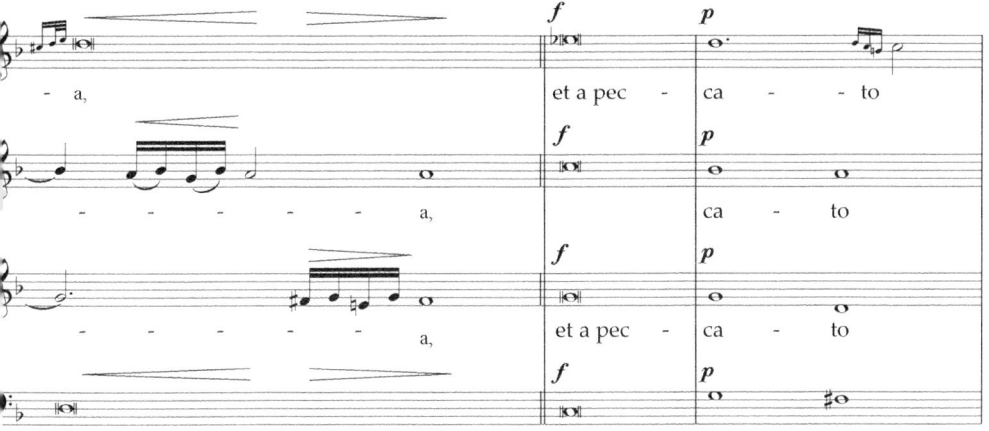

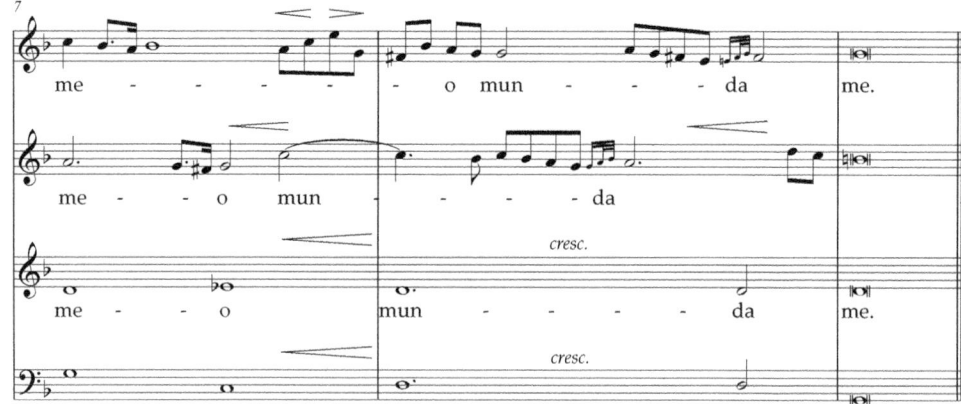

Variants (*including some comments on the other 4-part verses 7, 11, 15 and 19*)
Underlay: **2** gives i and iii only, **3** and **4** give all parts in 2–4, and most thereafter
2 i 5: *appoggiatura* in **2** only. **3** and **4** give it in vv. 15 and 19
3 i 1: *appoggiatura* in **2** only added in pencil by later hand. **3** and **4** give it in vv. 11, 15 and 19
3 i 9–12: c″d″c″e(♭)″ **2** and **3** ; corrected to version given here in later verses (ditto in sources **6–12, 6–9** make same correction in v. 5)
3 iii 5–6: No tie in **3** and **4**. Nor in most later 4-part verses. In v. 19 all sources add a *gruppetto* f♯ga before n. 6
4 ii 2–5: slurs in this verse only in **2** only
4 ii 6: preceded by a *gruppetto* g′a′b(♭)′ in v. 7 in all sources
4 ii 2–5 and iii 2–5: from v. 11 all sources simplify into qa′ qg′ (in ii) and qf♯′ qe (in iii).
7–8 ii: tie missing haphazardly in different verses in all sources
8 i 5: *gruppetto* f♯′g′a′ added in all sources in vv. 15 and 19
8 i 10: in **3** and **4** the *gruppetto* is a tone too low, corrected in v. 7, absent in vv. 11 and 19, and a tone too high in v. 15. **2** omits it, but adds a trill, in v. 11 and 19, v. 15 has both *gruppetto* and trill

Verse 5

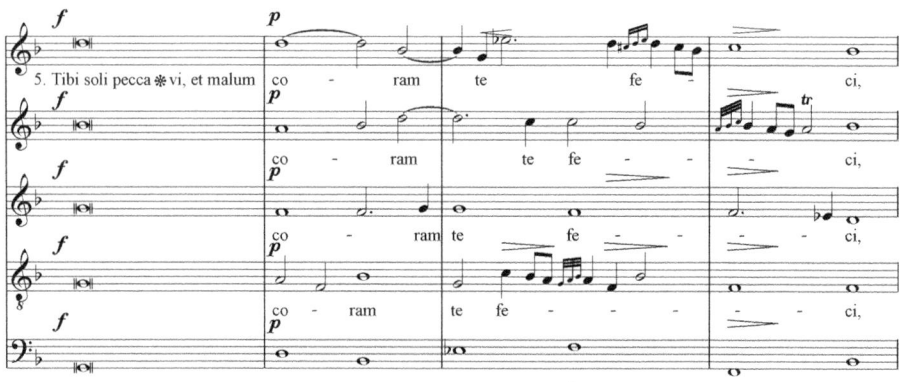

Variants

For most commentary on bars 1–4, see v. 1; it is 5–10 which is different from v. 1, in common with v. 13

- 3 i 5: the sharp in the *gruppetto* occurs also in vv. 13, 17 and 20a in **1**, in vv. 13 and 17 in **2**, and in v. 17 only in **3** and **4**
- 7 ii 1–2: tie missing in **3** and **4**
- 7 iv 1–3: **3** and **4** give *c*rest *ce m*b(♭) *c*b(♭), *c*d' corrected in v. 13 (*m*rest *s*b(♭) *m*b(♭), as is **2** there
- 10 i 1: *gruppetto* a tone too high in **2** and **3**

Verse 13 has less ornamentation in general

✳ Appendix 10

Source A: verse 3 from British Library Add. MS 31525/1

The four-part verses in **1** are sufficiently different to warrant printing one of them in its entirety. The text seems corrupt in bar 3: the E♭ in the bass part, on which the 'high g' ornament should be founded, does not arrive until the ornament is virtually finished. Note the long slur with the dot over bar 3, no doubt an indication of a kind of pause.

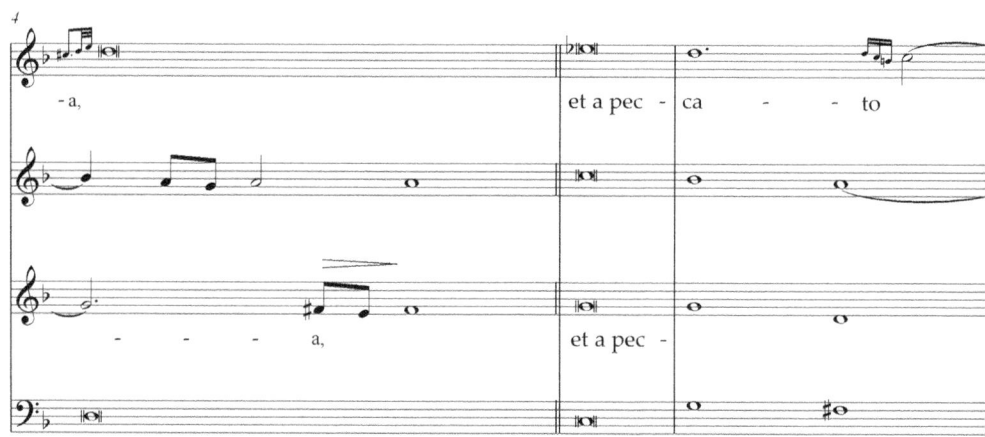

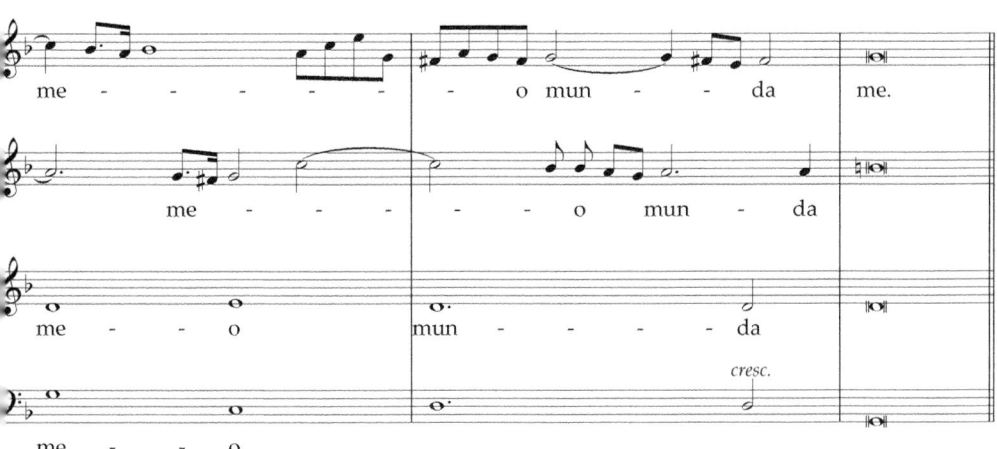

Appendix 11

Alfieri's published abbellimenti *(1840)*

✳ Appendix 12

Alfieri's manuscript – Berlin, Staatsbibliothek Mus. ms. Alfieri 1
(see also Chapter 10)

Berlin Staatsbibliothek Mus. Ms. Alfieri 1, pp.63–70
(Amann, Allegris Miserere, 108).

One of a group of Alfieri MSS acquired by the library in 1874.

63–6: 'Miserere di Gregorio Allegri con abbellimenti' (**a**)
67–70: 'Il medesimo Miserere di Allegri con altri abbellimenti' (**b**)

A conflation of the two similar versions of vv. 1 and 3 in Alfieri's hand. Clearly based on Mus. ms. 550/2, the basis of his printed score of 1840, it gives ornaments related to **P** (e.g. the duo for the sopranos at the end of v. 3). It also gives many *appoggiature* and *gruppetti* similar to **A** (e.g. 6–7 i, ii, iv; 13 iii), as well as features of other manuscripts (e.g. the parallel fifths on the reciting notes, as **P**, **Man** and **M**), and a few dynamics.

Appendices 303

Verse 1 a5

[Coro] P<u>mo</u>

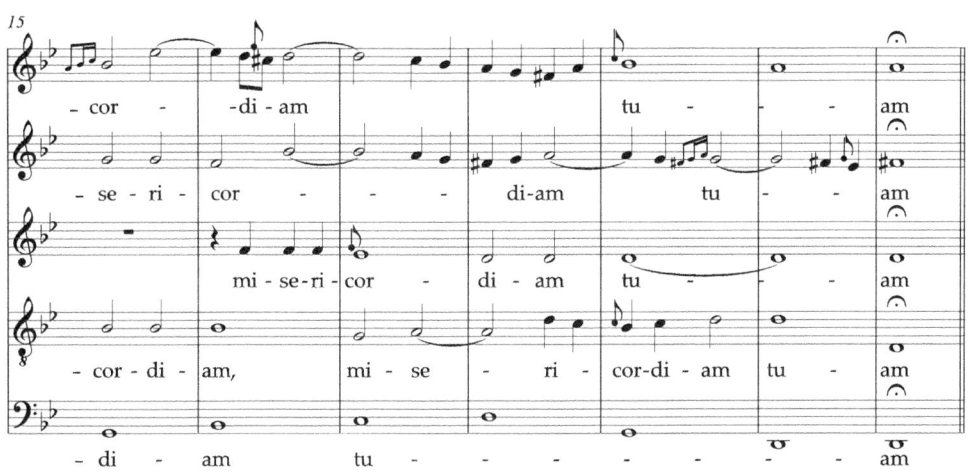

Appendices

Verse 3 a4

In general, **a** (63–6) gives more detail, especially of *appoggiaturas* and *gruppetti* (which are given here if they appear in either source) but **b** (67–70) has some interesting variants. Important variants as follows.

Variants

Verse 1 a5

5 i 2–3: *c*g' in **a**
6 i : *m*e♭ *appoggiatura f'* preceding *q*e♭" *q*d" *q*c" *q*b♭' in **b**
6 ii 1–2: *m*c in **b**
6 iv 2–3: *c*f in **a**
7 ii 1–3: *q*c" *q*b♭' *q*a' *q*g' in **b**
7 iii: *s*f' with *c appoggiatura* e♭' in **a**
15 iv: *m*.b♭ *c*b♭ in **b**
16–17 iii: *c*r *c*f' *c*f' *q*g' *q*f' / *appoggiatura f m*.e♭' *c*e♭' in **b**
19 –20 iv: *appoggiatura c m*.b♭ -*c*or *c*c' -di- / *m*d' -am *m*d *t*u- in **b**

Verse 3 a4

9 n. 2–10 ii: *m*g me- /tied to *c*g' *c*b♭' *m*b♭' in **a**
10 i 1: *m*e♭" -te in **a**
20–1 iii: *s*d' followed by *appoggiatura q*e♭' *q*f' / *s*e' (without *appoggiatura*)
21–2: Version from **b**: cf. M

Appendix 13: The performing editions

✳ EDITION 1: Bai/Allegri as notated by Mustafà in 1892

Miserere di Bai ed Allegri

ed. Graham O'Reilly

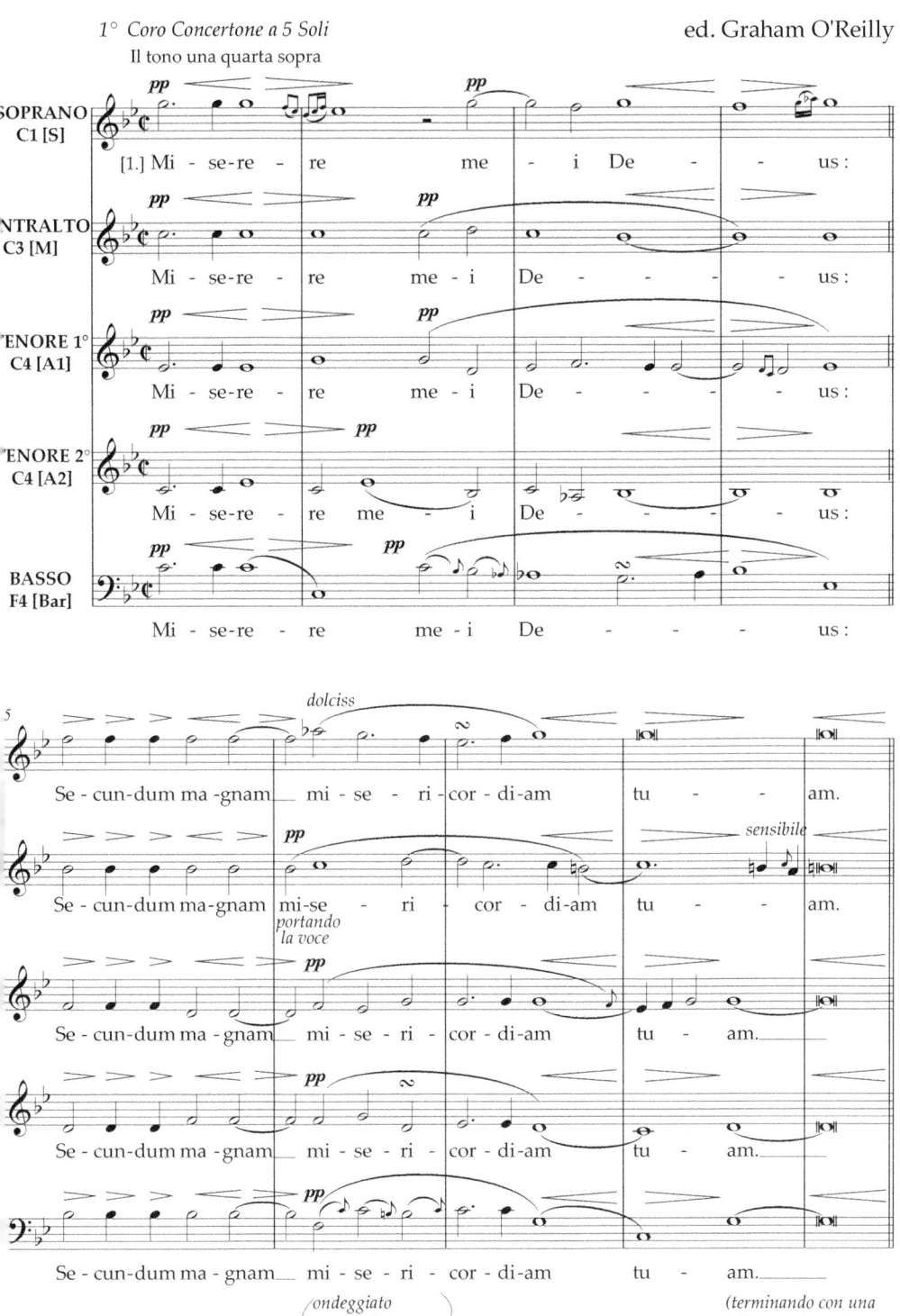

Coro
f
[2.] Et secundum multitudinem [miserationum tuarum : dele iniquitatem meam]
NB Se al 1° Soprano convenisse meglio di appoggiare il sol [=c'''] acuto potra prendere me prima il sol [=c''] medio
me -
un filo di voce
2° Coro a Quattro Soli
10
dolciss
a piacer
SOPRANO 1° C1 [S1]
[3.] Am - plius la-va me ab in - i - qui - ta - te me -
tempo
SOPRANO 2° C1 [S2]
dolciss
pp
Am - plius la-va me ab in - i - qui - ta - - - te me -
tempo
CONTRALTO C3 [M]
dolciss
pp
Am - plius la-va me ab in - i - qui - ta - - te me -
non troppo lento
tempo
respiro
BASSO F4 [T]
dolciss
Am - plius la-va me ab in - i - qui - ta - te me - -
13
tr
tempo
- - - - a :
tempo
- - - - - - - a :
tenuta fino alla risoluzione dal 1° Soprano
tempo
- - - - - - - - - a :
tempo
- - - - - a :
si tenga fino alla risoluzione dal 1° Soprano
(a tempo)

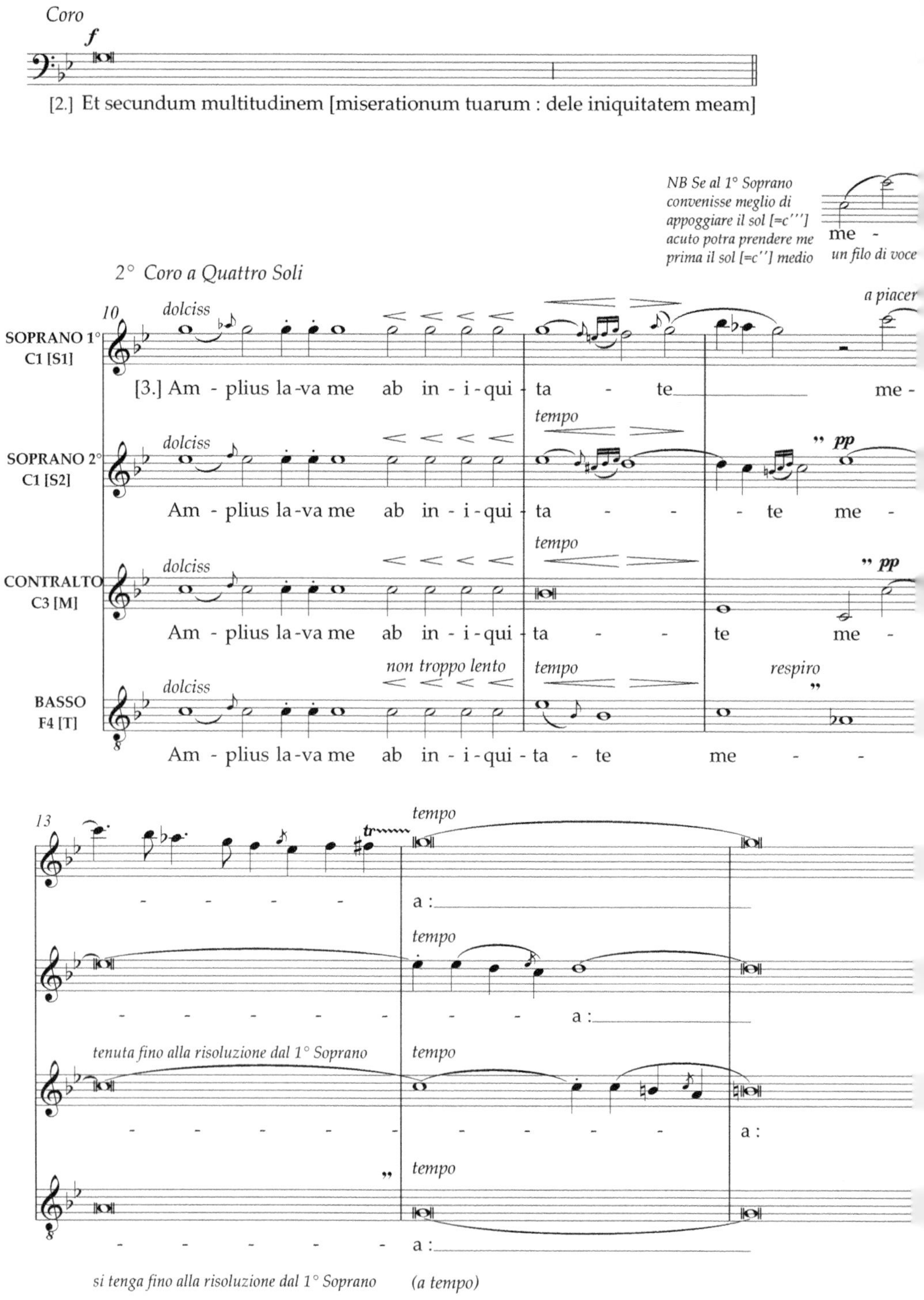

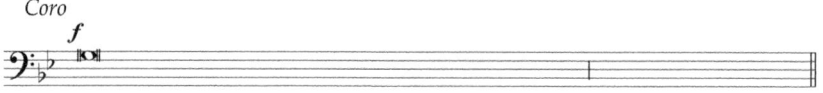

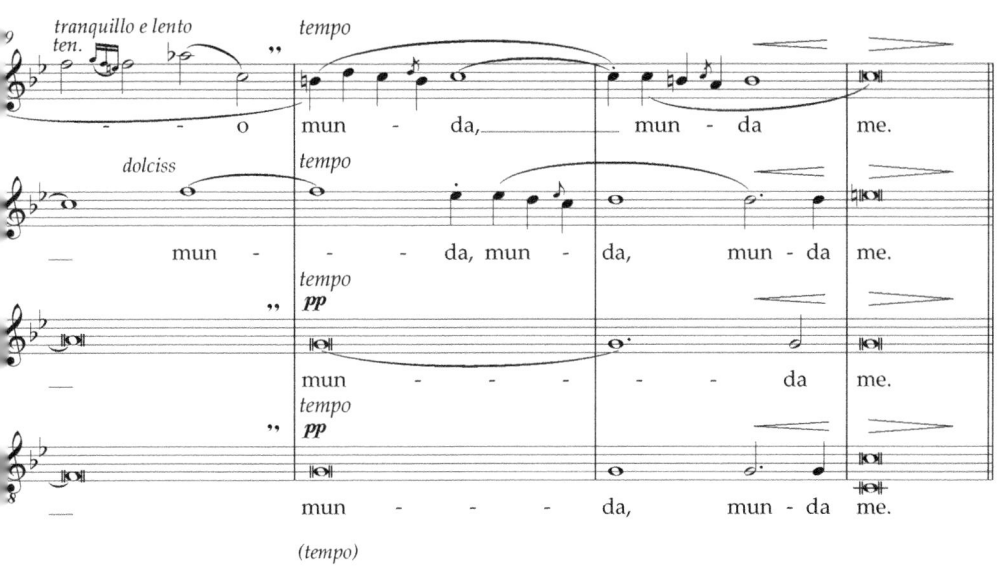
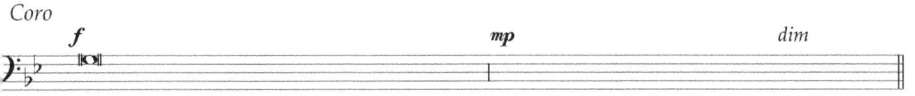

[4.] Quoniam iniquitatem meam [ego cognosco : et peccatum meum contra me est semper.]

1° *Coro Concertone a 5 Soli*

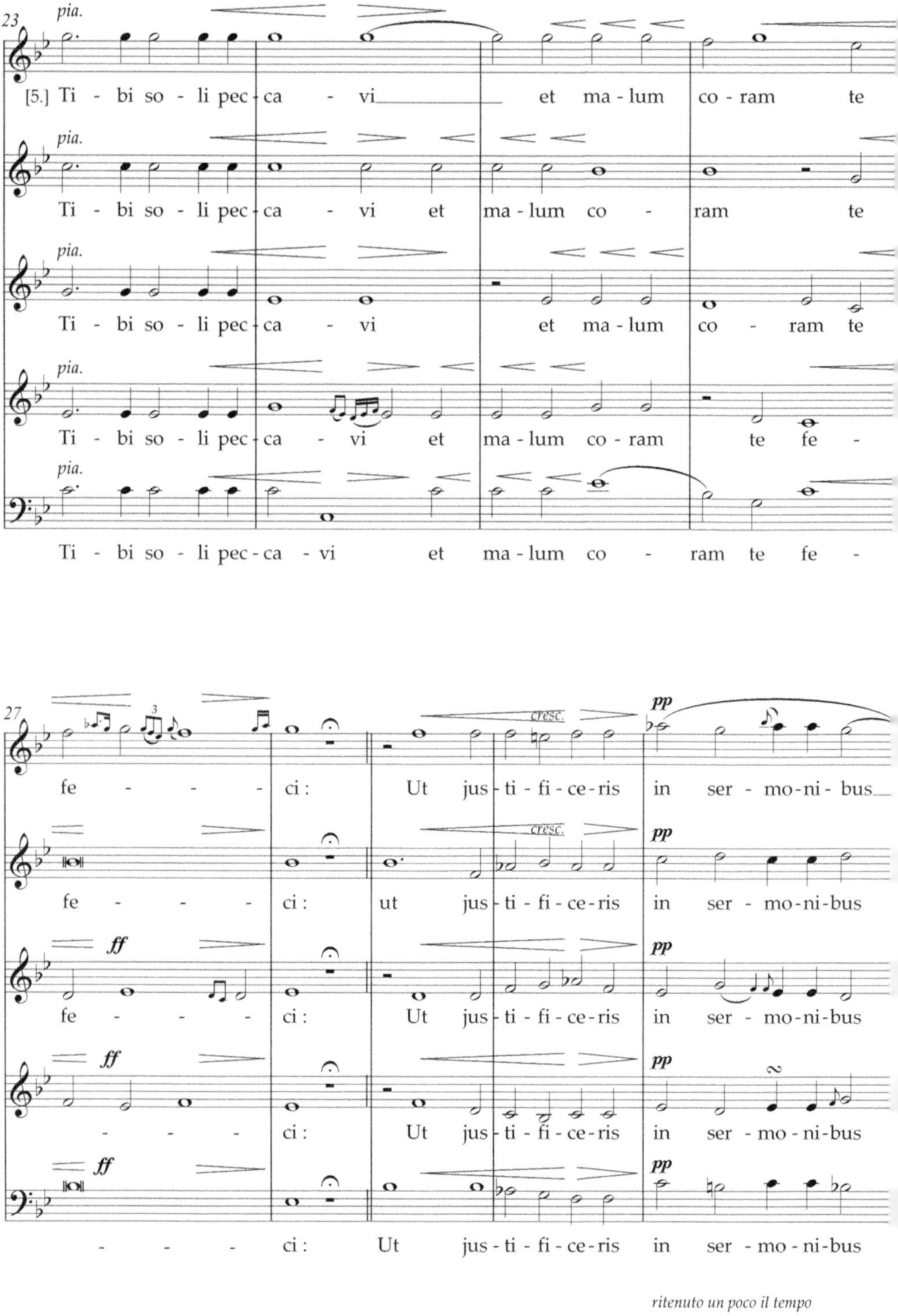
23
pia.
[5.] Ti - bi so - li pec - ca - vi et ma - lum co - ram te
Ti - bi so - li pec - ca - vi et ma - lum co - ram te
Ti - bi so - li pec - ca - vi et ma - lum co - ram te
Ti - bi so - li pec - ca - vi et ma - lum co - ram te fe -
Ti - bi so - li pec - ca - vi et ma - lum co - ram te fe -
27
cresc.
ff
pp
fe - - - ci : Ut jus - ti - fi - ce - ris in ser - mo - ni - bus
fe - - - ci : ut jus - ti - fi - ce - ris in ser - mo - ni - bus
fe - - - ci : Ut jus - ti - fi - ce - ris in ser - mo - ni - bus
- - - ci : Ut jus - ti - fi - ce - ris in ser - mo - ni - bus
- - - ci : Ut jus - ti - fi - ce - ris in ser - mo - ni - bus
ritenuto un poco il tempo

6. Ecce enim in iniquitatibus [conceptus sum : et in peccatis concepit me mater mea.]

2° Coro a 4 Soli concertino

[7.] Ec - ce e - nim ve - ri - ta - tem di - le - xi - sti:

[8.] Asperges me hyssopo [et mundabor : lavabis me, et super nivem dealbabor.]

1° Coro Concertone a 5 Soli

Coro

[10.] Averte faciem tuam [a peccatis meis : et omnes iniquitates meas dele.]

2° Coro a 4 Soli concertino

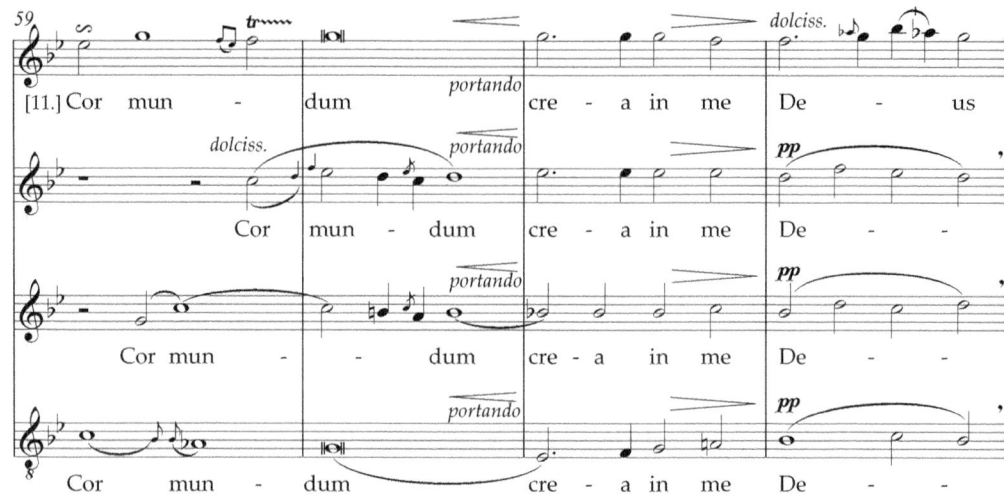

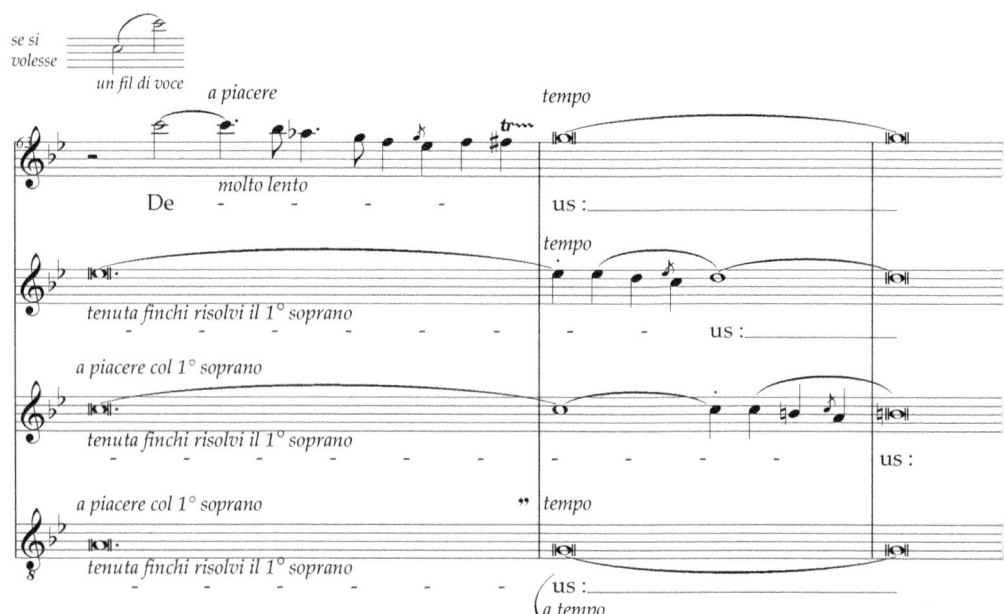

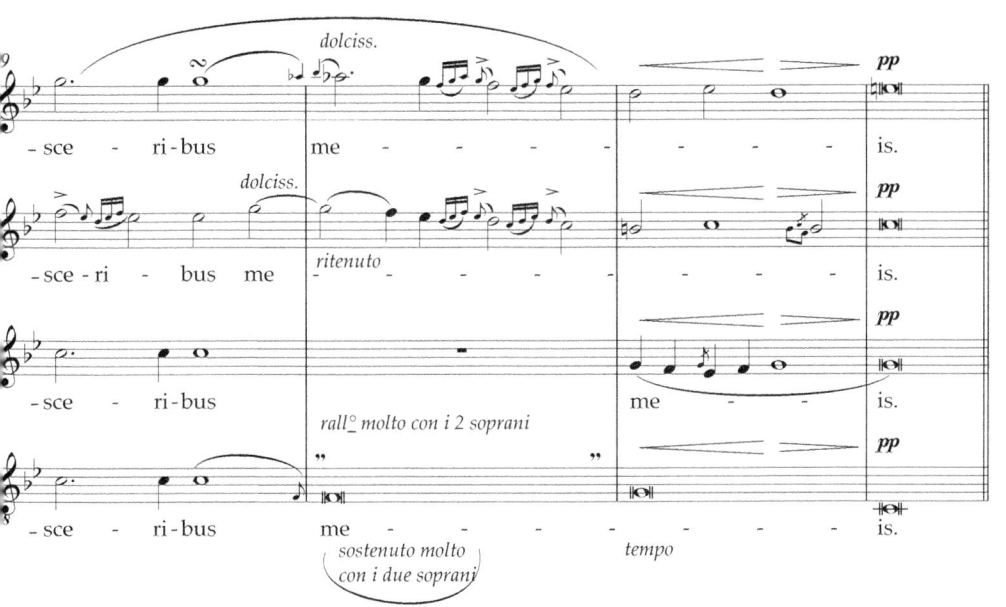

[12.] Ne projicias me [a facie tua : et spiritum sanctum tuum ne auferas a me.]

1° Coro Concertone a 5 Soli

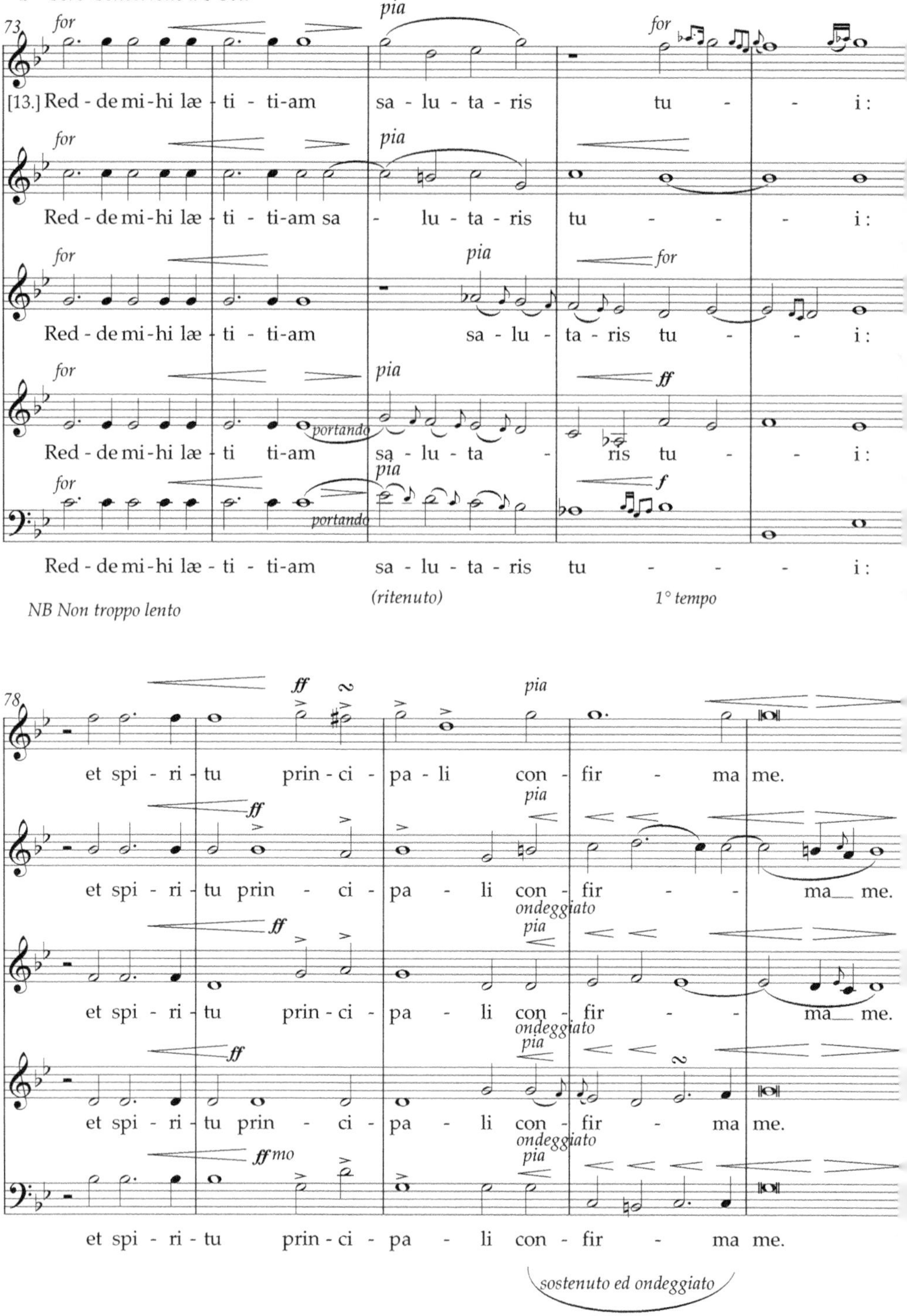

[13.] Red-de mi-hi læ-ti-ti-am sa-lu-ta-ris tu — — i:
Red-de mi-hi læ-ti-ti-am sa - lu-ta-ris tu — — i:
Red-de mi-hi læ-ti-ti-am sa-lu-ta-ris tu — — i:
Red-de mi-hi læ-ti ti-am sa-lu-ta - ris tu — — i:
Red-de mi-hi læ-ti-ti-am sa-lu-ta-ris tu — — i:

NB *Non troppo lento*   *(ritenuto)*   *1° tempo*

et spi-ri-tu prin-ci-pa-li con-fir — ma me.
et spi-ri-tu prin - ci-pa-li con-fir — ma— me.
et spi-ri-tu prin-ci-pa - li con-fir — ma— me.
et spi-ri-tu prin - ci-pa-li con-fir — ma me.
et spi-ri-tu prin-ci-pa - li con-fir — ma me.

sostenuto ed ondeggiato

Coro

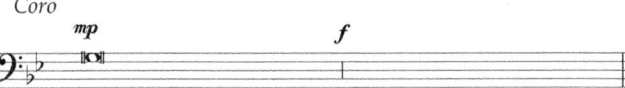

[14.] Docebo iniquos vias tuas : [et impii ad te convertentur.]

2° Coro Concertino a quattro soli

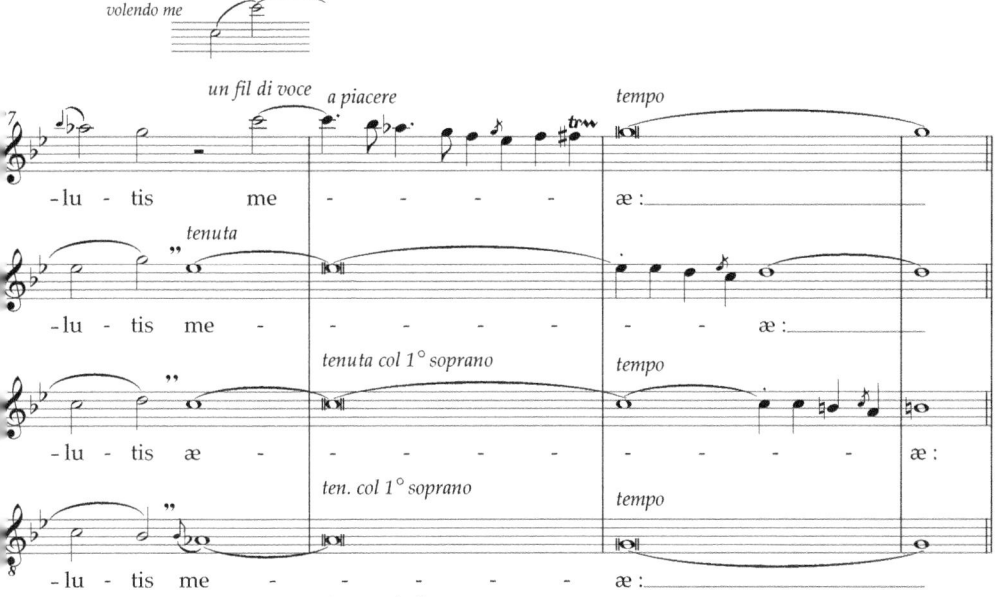

[16.] Domine labia mea aperies : [et os meum annunciabit laudem tuam.]

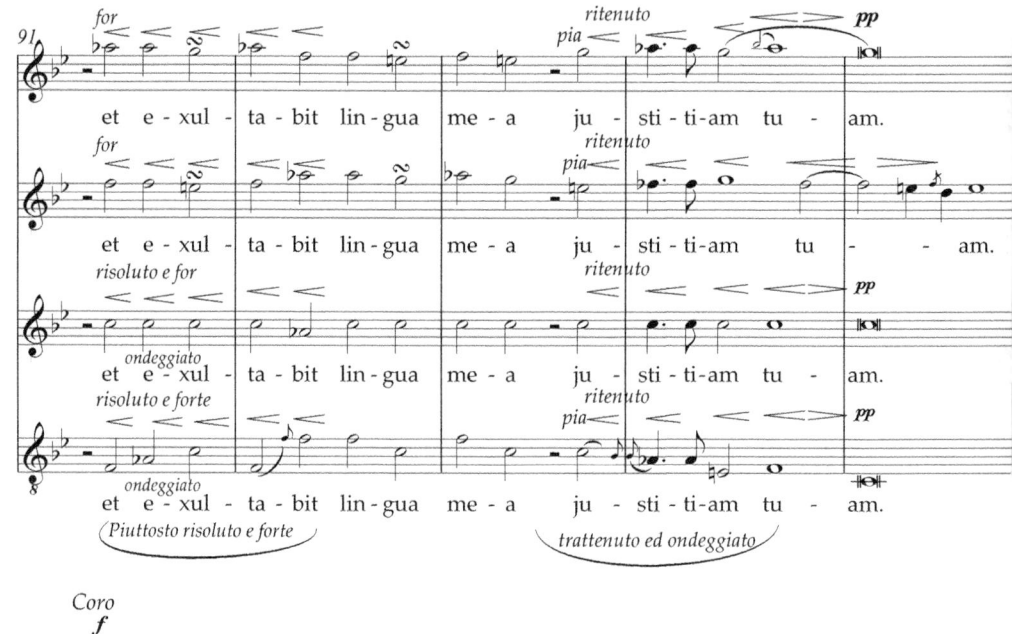

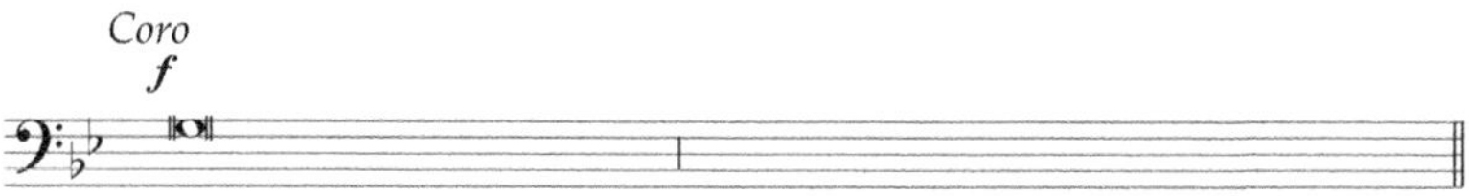

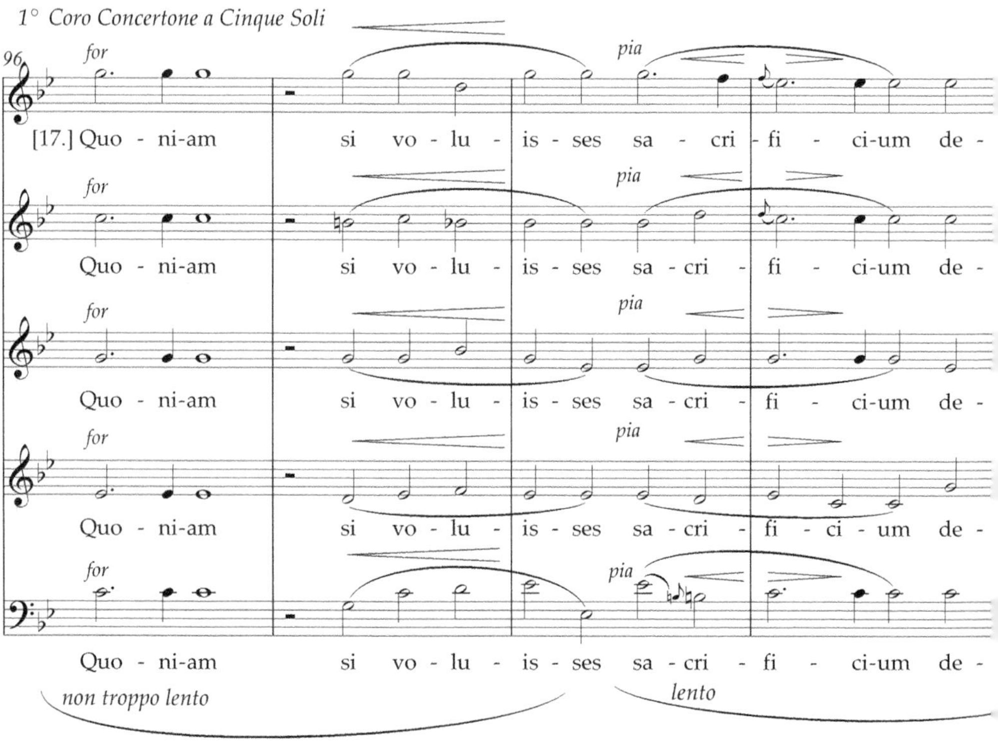

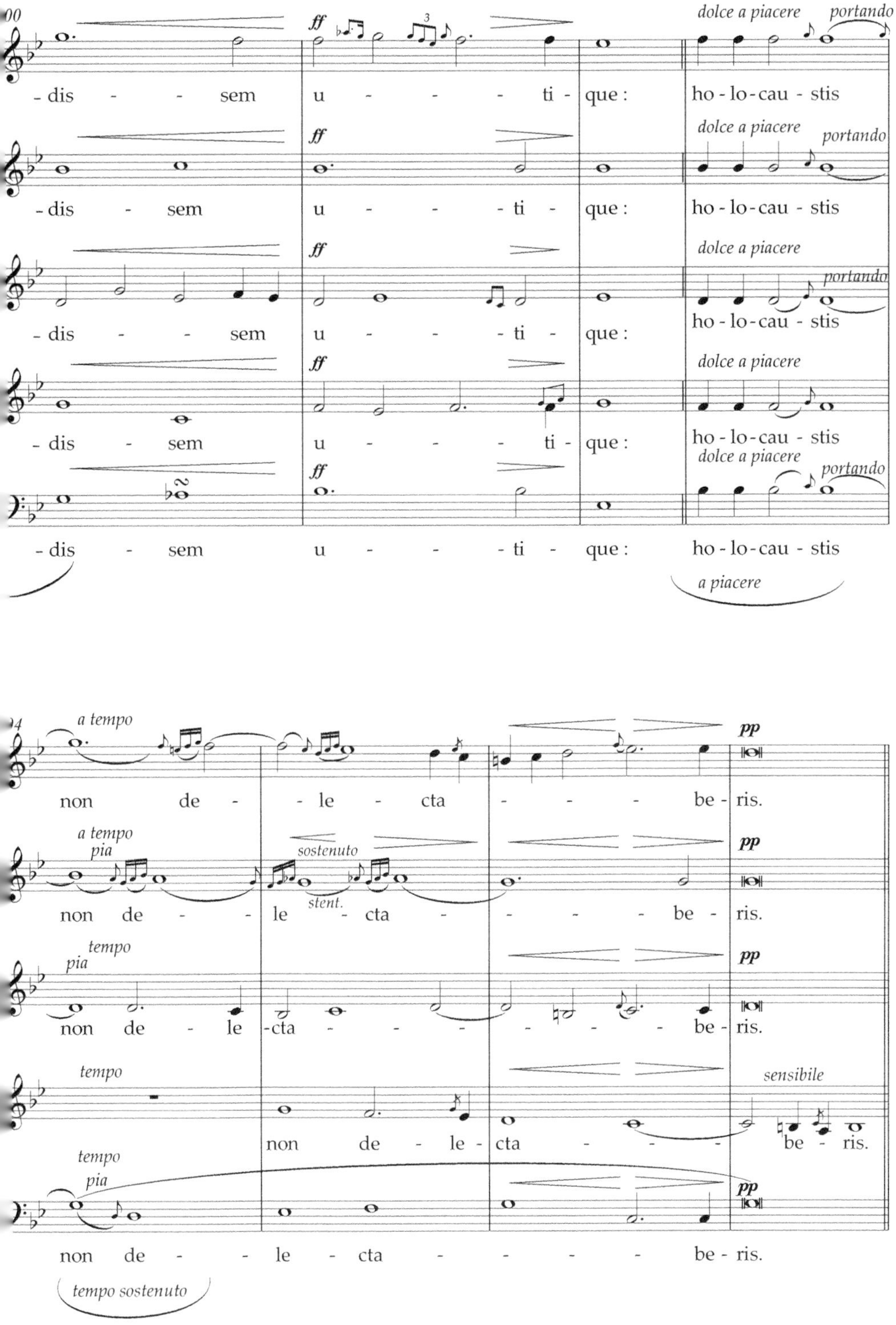
dolce a piacere
portando
ff
- dis - - sem u - - - ti - que : ho - lo - cau - stis
- dis - sem u - - - ti - que : ho - lo - cau - stis
- dis - - sem u - - - ti - que : ho - lo - cau - stis
- dis - sem u - - - ti - que : ho - lo - cau - stis
- dis - sem u - - - ti - que : ho - lo - cau - stis
a piacere
a tempo
pia
sostenuto
stent.
tempo
sensibile
pp
non de - - le - cta - - - be - ris.
non de - - le - cta - - - - be - ris.
non de - le -cta - - - - - - be - ris.
non de - le - cta - - - be - ris.
non de - - le - cta - - - - be - ris.
tempo sostenuto

Coro

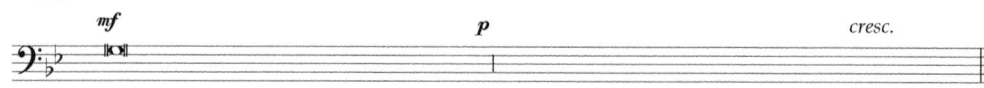

[18.] Sacrificium Deo [spiritus contribulatus : cor contritum et humiliatum, Deus, non despicies.]

2° Coro Concertino a quattro soli

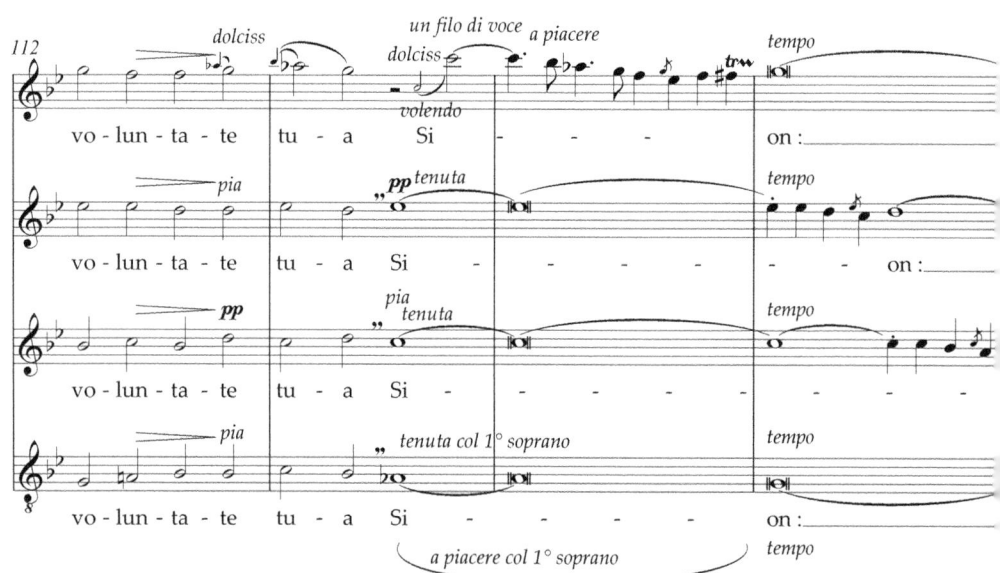

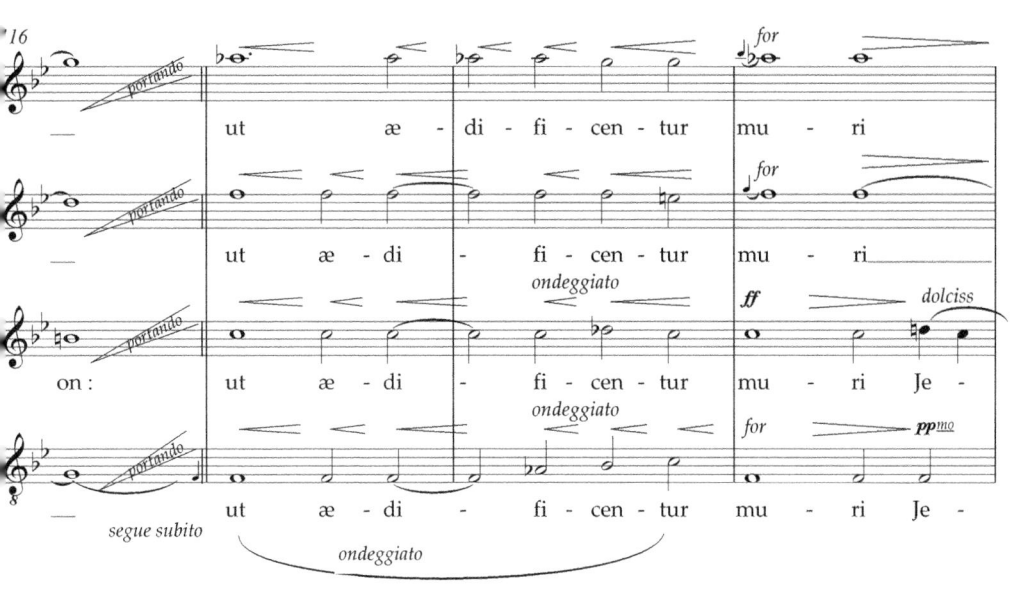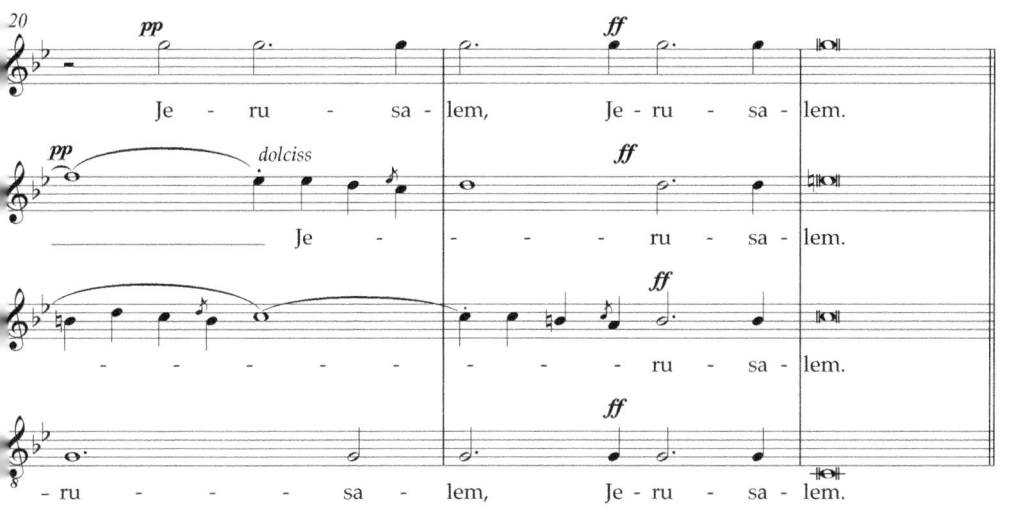

"NB Nota <u>Tunc imponent</u> è stata scritta la parte dol Tenore del 2° Coro perchè notendosi provare il Miserere a 9 sole voci sarebbe mancata una parte"["Ten 2°"]

✳ Commentary

Source **M**: *Biblioteca Apostolica Vaticana Cappella Sistina 375. Bai ed Allegri Psalmus 50*

The manuscript score, dated 22 January 1892, is accompanied by a full set of parts doubtless prepared subsequently, which often provide a gloss on the information contained in the full score (for example, writing out in full an ornament indicated there by a sign, and putting cross-strokes through the tails of *appoggiature*). Indications from the parts have been incorporated into the edition as much as possible, with important variants noted. All the indications from both score and parts have been included, even when they say virtually the same thing in different words. Mustafà's version is of course based on Bai's original *Miserere* as found in Vatican sources (Appendix 4) and Alfieri, not on the rewritten one published by Burney. An important difference however is the exchange of the choirs for verse 20b a8, something found in no other source, and which necessitated some rearrangement of the parts (see below).

Unlike the Allegri edition, this transcription of CS 375 is definitive, being an exact record of how we suppose Domenico Mustafà would wish to perform this work in the Sistine Chapel if he could come back to life to direct it, insofar as a manuscript can show that. The instruction to transpose it up a fourth has of course been obeyed.

Some specificities of the notation

Cross-strokes for appoggiature

The use or otherwise of a cross-stroke for a quaver *appoggiatura* seems to have had no significance for Mustafà. Nearly all the examples of its use appear in the parts – no doubt to make the execution clearer for the singers – and they have been reproduced in these places, even if they correspond to *appoggiature* without the cross-stroke in the score (e.g. 14 ii iii, 20 i ii and 21 i). Towards the end of the work, crotchet *appoggiature* appear (e.g. 60 ii, 112–13 i, and even a minim *appoggiatura* at 94 i) which may be considered to approach more the current sense of an *appoggiatura* as a melodic ornament as opposed to a somewhat strange 'leaping grace'.

Dynamics

Mustafà notes indifferently *f, ff* and *for* to mean 'loud' in the score and the parts; likewise *p, pp,* and *pia* for 'soft'. Again, for him, the differences seem not to have been important. I have followed the parts when they differ.

Cues for the cantus planus

In the separate parts of the three lower voices of each choir, the reciting note d is given for the even-numbered *cantus planus* verses, as it had been in manuscripts 10–12 of Source **A** (it becomes g when transposed in this edition). When it follows a verse which a choir has not sung (e.g. after verse 3 in the parts of *Coro 1°*) the final bass note of the other choir is indicated by a cue resembling a grace note, generally slurred to the note to be chanted. Thus those parts in *Coro 1°* are provided with a g (G for the bass), the final note of verses 3, 7, 11, 15 and 19, preceding the reciting d to be sung for verses 4, 8, 12 and 16. In *Coro 2°* a d (the final note of verses 1, 5, 9, 13 and 17) is given before the reciting d for verses 2, 6, 10, 14 and 18. This shows that the singers of these lower parts were expected to sing all the even-numbered verses. It is surprising that these cues are present in the soprano 2 part of *Coro 2°*,[1] and it should be noted that in the part of tenor 1 in *Coro 1°*, the cue is missing for verse 8. There is also a superfluous cue in the full score before verse 4. It is clear in any case that these small notes are merely cues, and are not to be sung.

It is also puzzling that these cues are present in the tenor parts which, when transposed up a fourth, would probably have been sung by altos. The third line in the four-part verses, as transposed, rises regularly to c″; and while the third and fourth parts in the five-part verses could be sung by tenors, they are certainly more comfortable for altos. Perhaps the altos participated in the reciting verses at tenor pitch. It is also not impossible that there were still in the choir altos who were high tenors rather than falsettists. How else to explain the case of Giuseppe Bernadini (1856–1918), who joined the choir in 1883, and five years later changed 'dalla parte dei contralti a quella dei tenori'?[2]

Breath marks

Breath marks (″) have been reproduced, mostly from the parts, and some editorial suggestions have been added in the *cantus planus* verses.

Underlay

New syllables should always start on the *appoggiatura*, despite Mustafà sometimes forgetting to slur them to the main note. *Portamenti* keep the syllable of the preceding note (e.g. 10). When the ornament is a pair of notes (e.g. 4 i, 27 i, 110 i) the syllable should change afterwards on the main note. After each of the *crescendi portamenti* (116 to 117, 130 to 131) a quick dramatic breath can be taken after arriving at the pitch of the subsequent note before attacking it (my thanks to John Potter for this suggestion).

Variants

Verse 3 (a4)

12 i: the part gives the same instruction as the score, but in slightly different words: 'se convenisse meglio appoggiare il sol acuto si farà prima …' (the lower c)

Verse 5 (a5)

24 v. 3 – 25 v. 2: dynamics >>> in part. Same mistake in iii but there corrected to <<<
27 iii iv v: *ff* in parts only

---

[1] Could it be that Mustafà prepared this part for himself to sing? As director, perhaps he wanted to have it as a reminder.

[2] *DS* 291, fol. 84r, quoted in Kantner and Pachovsky, *L'Ottocento*, 144.

Verse 7 (a4)

39 ii 4 ornament: the sign is in the score, the notes in the part (also see 67 iv)
48–49 iv: < and > missing in both score and parts

Verse 9 (a5)

50 5 and 9 all parts: No slurs between these notes and the following grace notes in either score or parts, but the following syllables should clearly come on the following notes
52 i last note: both score and part give both c and (smaller) $2q$ (cf. 101 iv)
54 6–7: slurs missing on grace note in i (part), ii and iii (score and parts), and iv and v (score)

Verse 11 (a4)

62 i: *m*.f" (grace note $qa\flat$") cg" (grace note $qb\flat$") $ca\flat$" cg" (si toglie) *mg*" in score. Ditto in part except the second grace note (b♭) is written as a c and slurred to the following note. Clearly 3–4 have been corrected from a♭" g" to b♭" a♭" after the parts were copied from the score, making 5 (g") superfluous (*si toglie* = to be crossed out)
67 iv ornament: The sign is in the score, both the notes and the sign in the part
70 i 3: Score (only) gives ♮ for first note of following *gruppetto*

Verse 13 (a5)

79 iv 2–3: > missing in both score and parts

Verse 15 (a4)

92 iii and iv 1–2: < missing in both score and parts
94 i 4: the *m appoggiatura* is in both score and parts

Verse 17 (a5)

98 iii 3–4 and 99: slur 98 3–4 in part, long slur missing in both score and parts
98 iv 3–4 and 99: long slur in part only, slur 98 3–4 in score
101 iv last note: both score and part give both c and (smaller) $2q$ (cf. 52 i)
105 i 1: no ♭ on third note of *gruppetto* preceding

Verse 19 (a4)

109 iv 3 – 110 iv 1: both grace notes c in part
118 i 3–4: score gives < <
121 ii 1–2 underlay: ru- in part with 1 tied to 2

Verse 20a (a5)

125 v ornament: The sign is in the score, the notes in the part
127 i 4: < over note in score but not in part

129 ii and iv underlay: ho-lo-ca-u-sta' is treated as a five-syllable word in both score and parts   (also in BL Add. 31525, both **(1)** and **(2)** in all the parts with text)

Verse 20b (a8)

Bai's *Tunc imponent* a8 is written for two *cori* of SATB. As noted above, the two choirs exchange parts compared to the Vatican original (perhaps Mustafà preferred the dramatic transition to the eight-part texture achieved by the extraordinary communal swoop of the singers of *Coro 1°*). So whereas in the original the two tenor parts of *Coro 1°* simply sang the same notes (see Appendix 4), in **M** the second tenor of *Coro 1°* is obliged to change choir. A note in the part reads: '*Nel Tunc imponent è stata scritta la parte del tenore del 2° Coro perchè volendosi provare il Miserere a 9 voci sole sarebbe mancato una parte*' ('In the *Tunc imponent* the tenor part was written for the second choir because if you wanted to perform the *Miserere* for 9 unaccompanied voices one part would have been missing'). Mustafà preferred to double the top line of *Coro 2°*, which the two sopranos sing in unison; the alto sings the second line, and the tenor from *Coro 1°* has to change choir to sing the third line (the *portando* indication given for him in the score – not in the part – is no doubt an error).

One supposes therefore that the '9' is a slip. It is however possible that he was thinking of Allegri's nine-voice *Miserere*, whose last verse may or may not have been sung after that of Bai's; it seems clear from the striking *portando* between 130 and 131 that even if both were sung, that of Bai was sung first. There is also a superfluous instruction for the Bass of *Coro 1°* at this point (in the score only): to immediately carry on singing his own voice ('subito col 1° coro') – perhaps a reminder not to change choir as the tenor does, or a hangover from the changing of choirs in **M**.

134 v–viii (*Coro 2°*) 1–3: score has < over 1 (and also 2–3 in viii). In the parts, v (soprano 1°) has none, v (soprano 2°, but singing the same part) has all 3, vi and vii have 1 but not 2–3, viii has none. These wave-like effects (*ondeggiato*) are probably best applied only to the minims, i.e. to 1 but not 2 or 3.

138 i 2: score and parts have >, different from iv, vi, vii and viii; iii 2 has neither in either score or parts.

In performance, the editor suggests that after Bai's v.20b (*Tunc imponent*), the verse be repeated in Allegri's setting, as found at the end of Edition 2, following the rather unclear indications of Alfieri. As it is not in Mustafà's manuscript, its use must be considered optional, although it certainly works very well in practice. The version in Edition 2 is based on CS 340-1, to which editorial suggestions of *portamento* etc. have been added.

✳ EDITION 2: 'Allegri's Miserere' based on Source A

Miserere Mei Deus (Psalm 50)

Gregorio ALLEGRI
Edition and reconstruction Graham O'REILLY

© Graham O'Reilly & Shorter House 2018. All rights reserved. Reproduced by Permission.

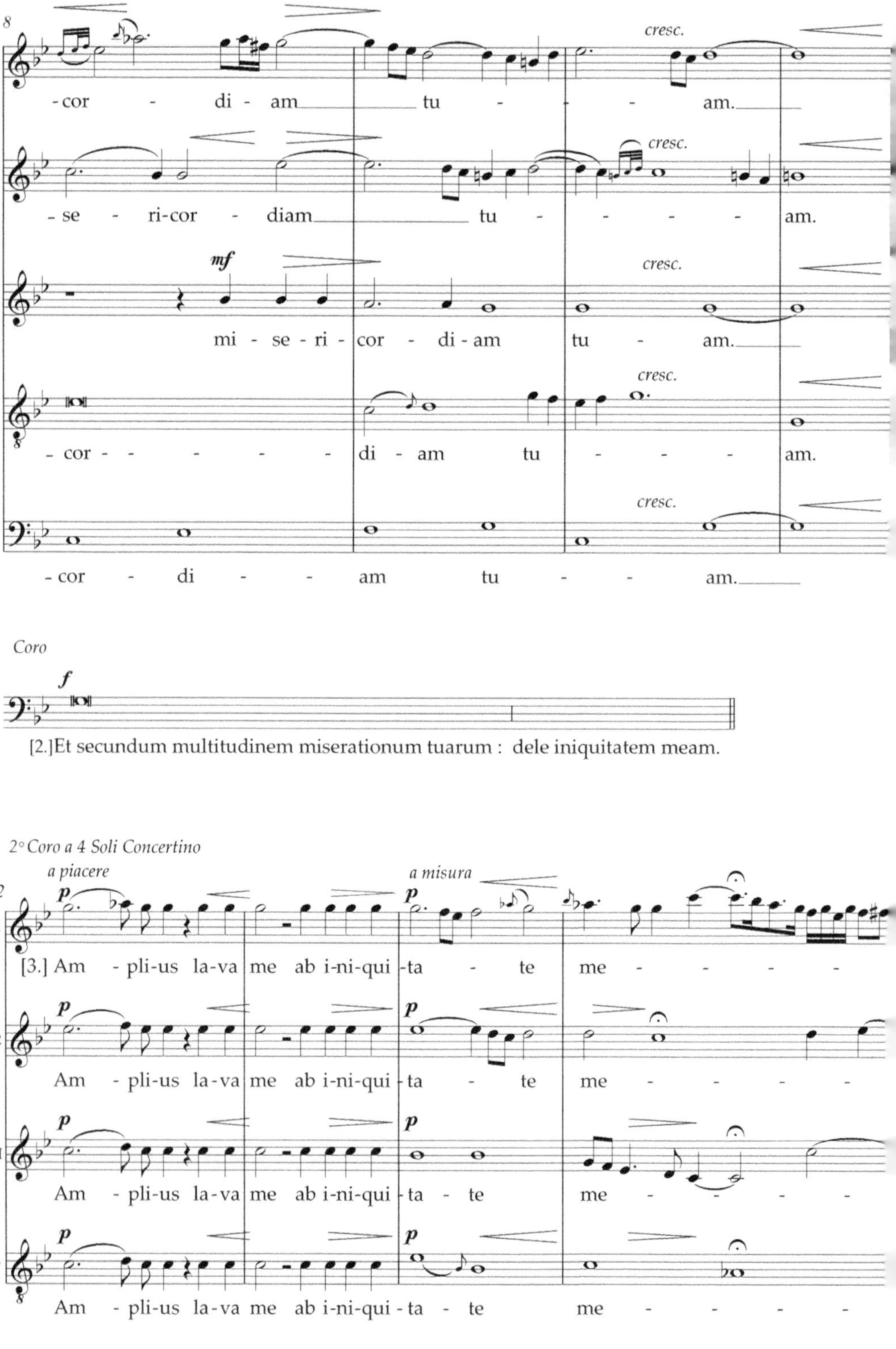

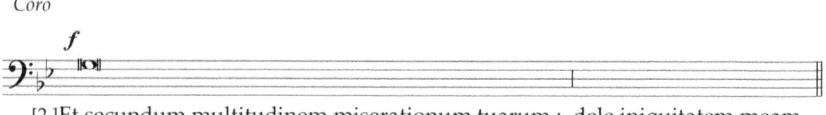

[2.] Et secundum multitudinem miserationum tuarum : dele iniquitatem meam.

2° Coro a 4 Soli Concertino

[3.] Am - pli-us la-va me ab i-ni-qui-ta - te me - - - -

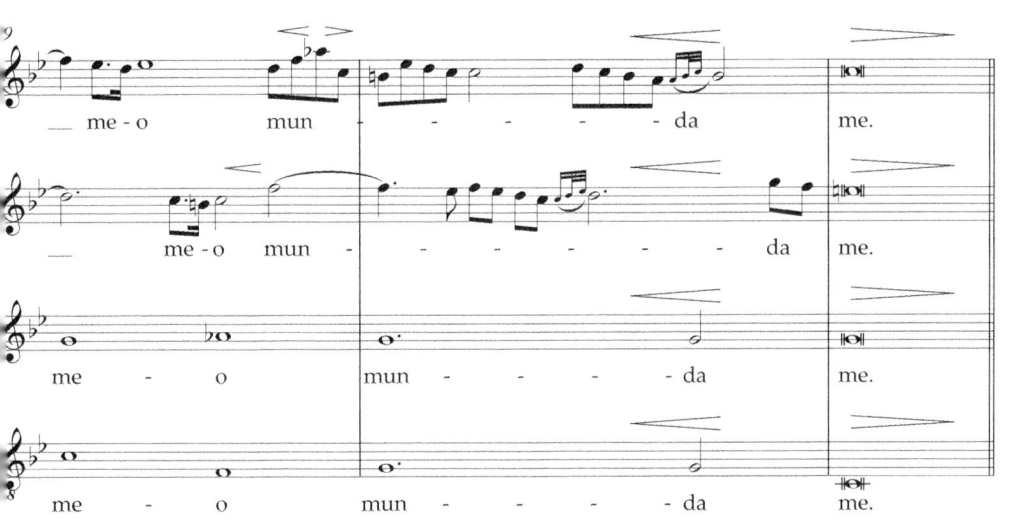

[4.] Quoniam iniquitatem meam ego cognosco : et peccatum meum contra me est semper.

27
f a misura
et vin-cas cum ju - di - ca - - - - - - -
et vin-cas cum ju - - - di - ca - - -
p
et vin - cas cum ju-di - ca -
et vin - cas cum ju-di - ca - - -
et vin-cas cum ju - - di - - - ca - - -
cresc.
- - - - - - ris.
- - - - - - - - ris.
- - - - - - ris.
- - - - - - - - - ris.
- - - - - - ris.

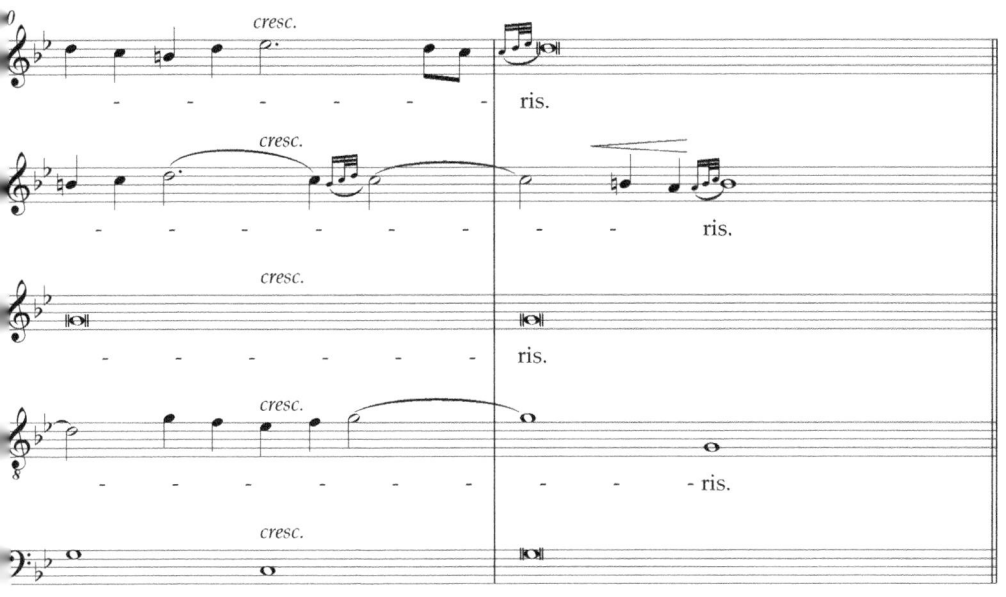

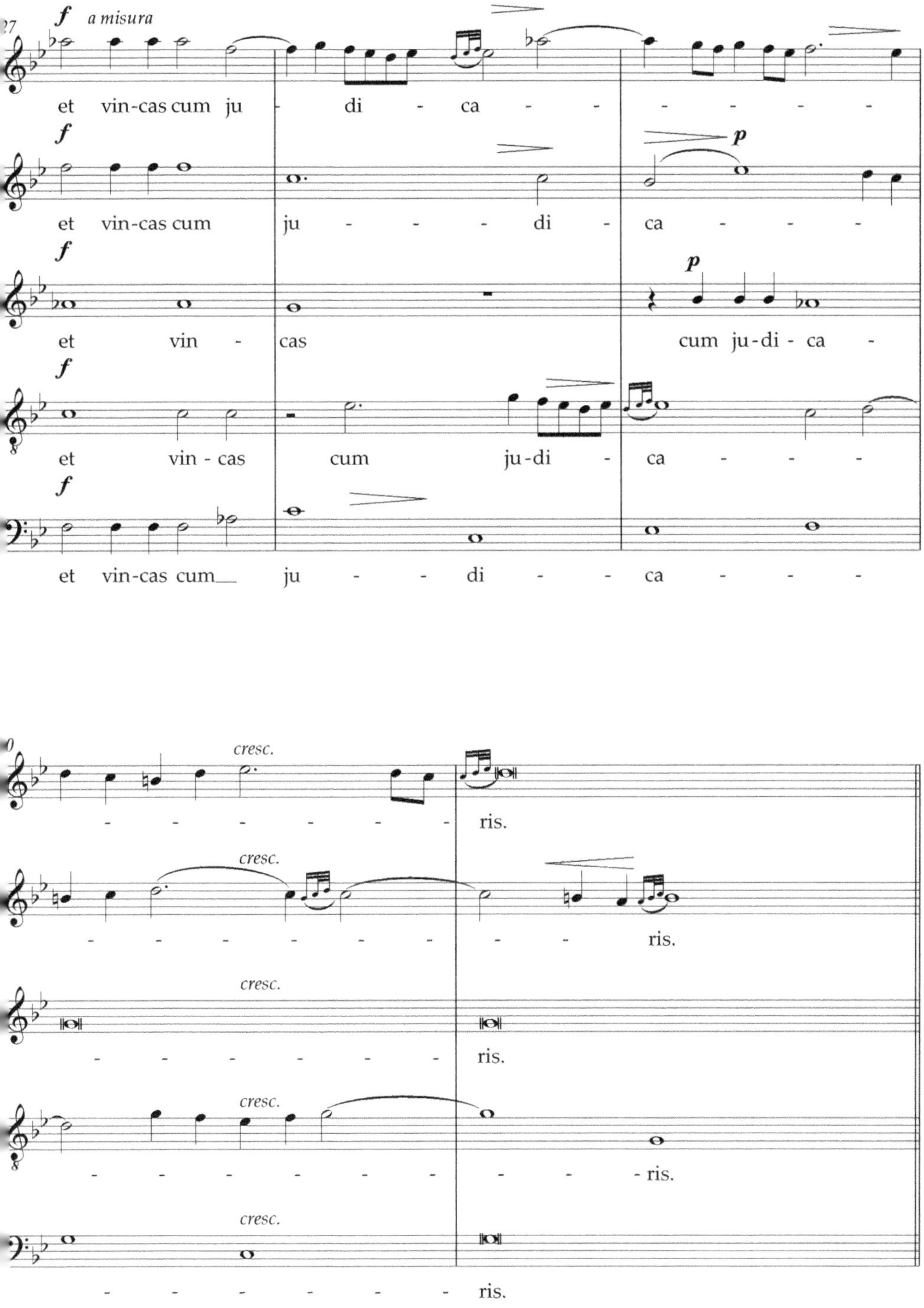

Coro

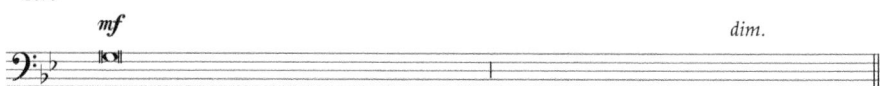

[6.] Ecce enim in iniquitatibus conceptus sum : et in peccatis concepit me mater mea.

2° Coro

[7.] Ec - ce e - nim ve-ri - ta - tem di - le - - - -

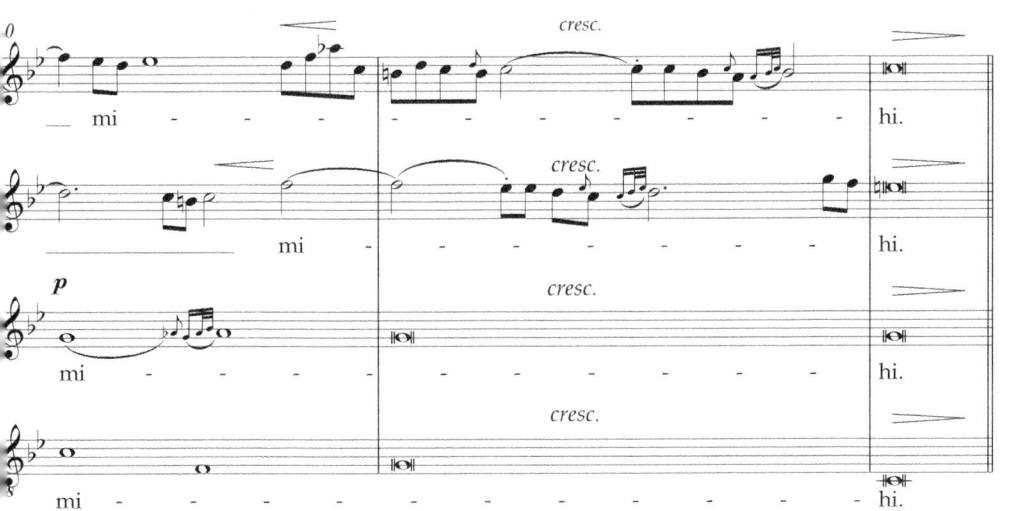

[8.] Asperges me hyssopo et mundabor : lavabis me, et super nivem dealbabor.

1° Coro

a piacere ... *a misura*

[9.] Au - di - tu - i me - o da - bis gau - dium et læ - ti - - -

Au - di - tu - i me - o da - bis gau - dium et læ - ti - -

Au - di - tu - i me - o da - bis gau - dium et læ - ti - - -

Au - di - tu - i me - o da - bis gau - dium et læ - - - ti -

Au - di - tu - i me - o da - bis gau - dium et læ - - ti - -

a piacere ... *a misura*

- - ti - am : et ex - ul - ta - bunt os - sa

- - ti - am : et ex - ul - ta - bunt os - sa

- - ti - am : et ex - ul - ta - bunt os - sa hu - mi - li

- - ti - am : et ex - ul - ta - bunt os - sa hu -

- - ti - am : et ex - ul - ta - bunt os - sa hu -

Coro

f

[10.] Averte faciem tuam a peccatis meis : et omnes iniquitates meas dele.

2° Coro

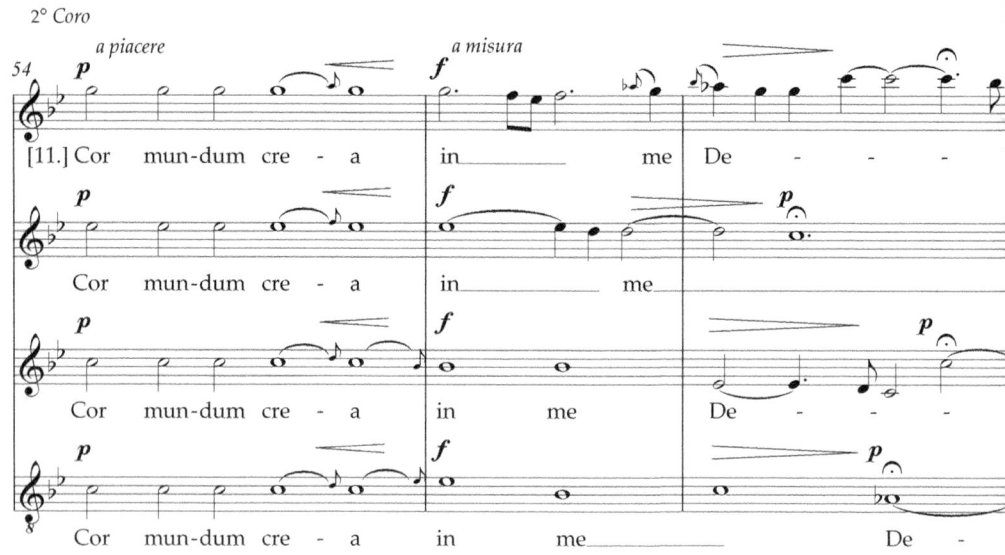

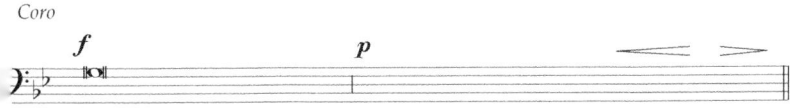

[12.] Ne projicias me a facie tua : et spiritum sanctum tuum ne auferas a me.

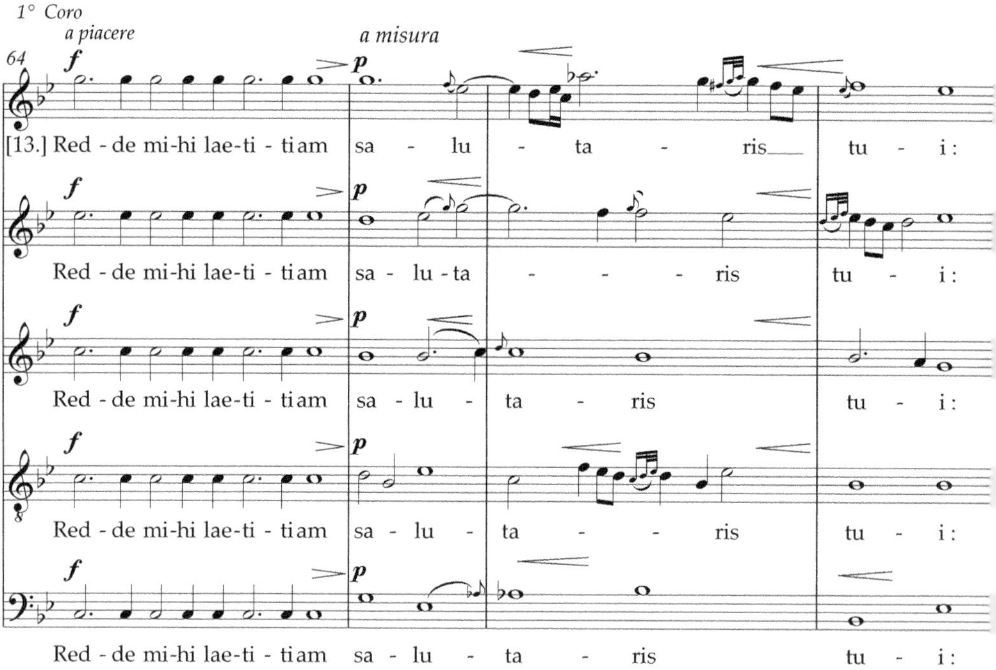
1° Coro
a piacere
a misura
64
f
p
[13.] Red - de mi-hi lae-ti - tiam sa - lu - ta - ris tu - i:
Red - de mi-hi lae-ti - tiam sa - lu - ta - - - ris tu - i:
Red - de mi-hi lae-ti - tiam sa - lu - ta - ris tu - i:
Red - de mi-hi lae-ti - tiam sa - lu - ta - - ris tu - i:
Red - de mi-hi lae-ti - tiam sa - lu - ta - ris tu - i:

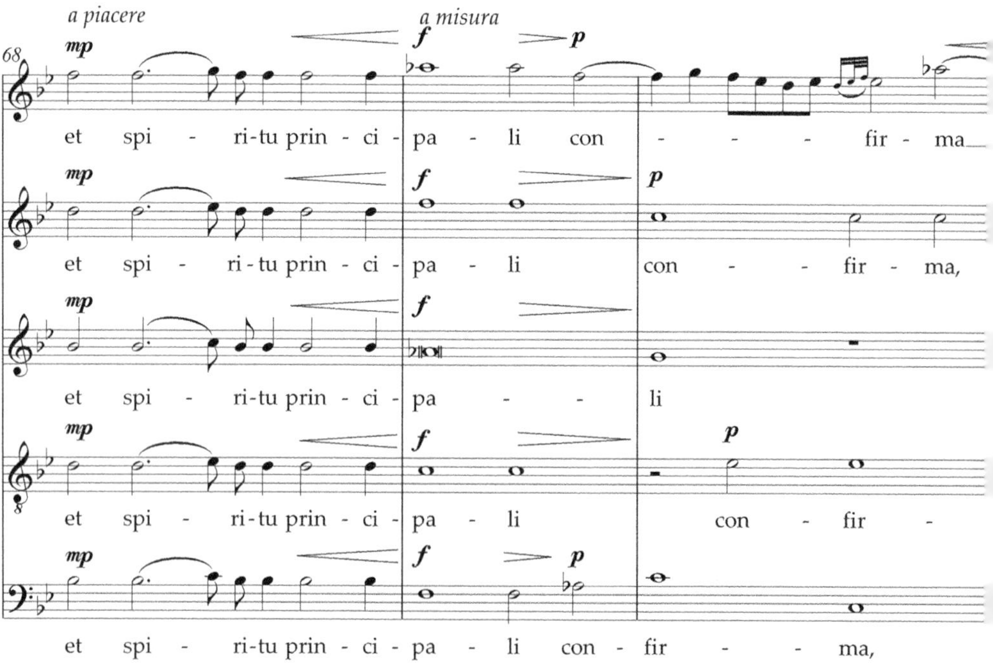
a piacere
a misura
68
mp
f
p
et spi - ri-tu prin - ci - pa - li con - - - fir - ma
et spi - ri-tu prin - ci - pa - li con - - fir - ma,
et spi - ri-tu prin - ci - pa - - li
et spi - ri-tu prin - ci - pa - li con - fir -
et spi - ri-tu prin - ci - pa - li con - fir - - ma,

Coro

[14.] Docebo iniquos vias tuas : et impii ad te convertentur.

2° Coro

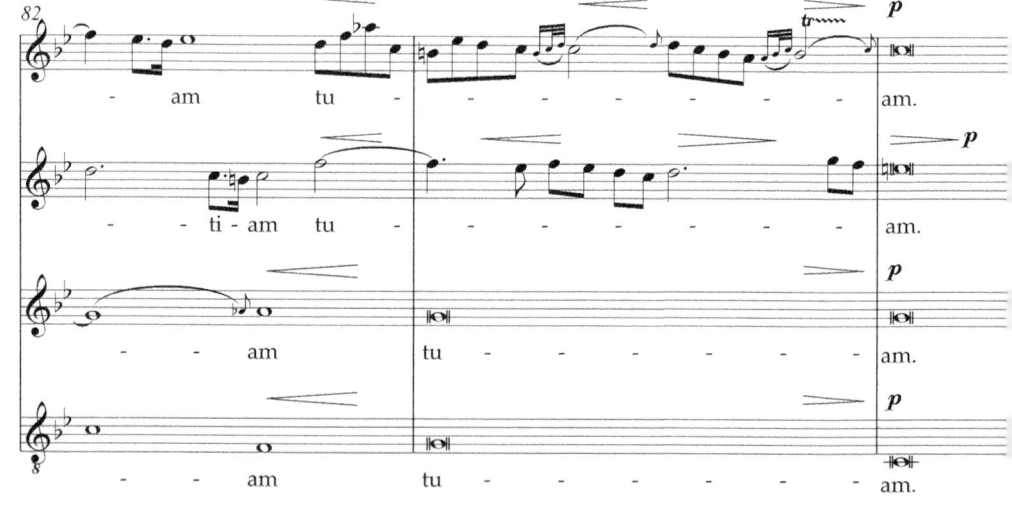

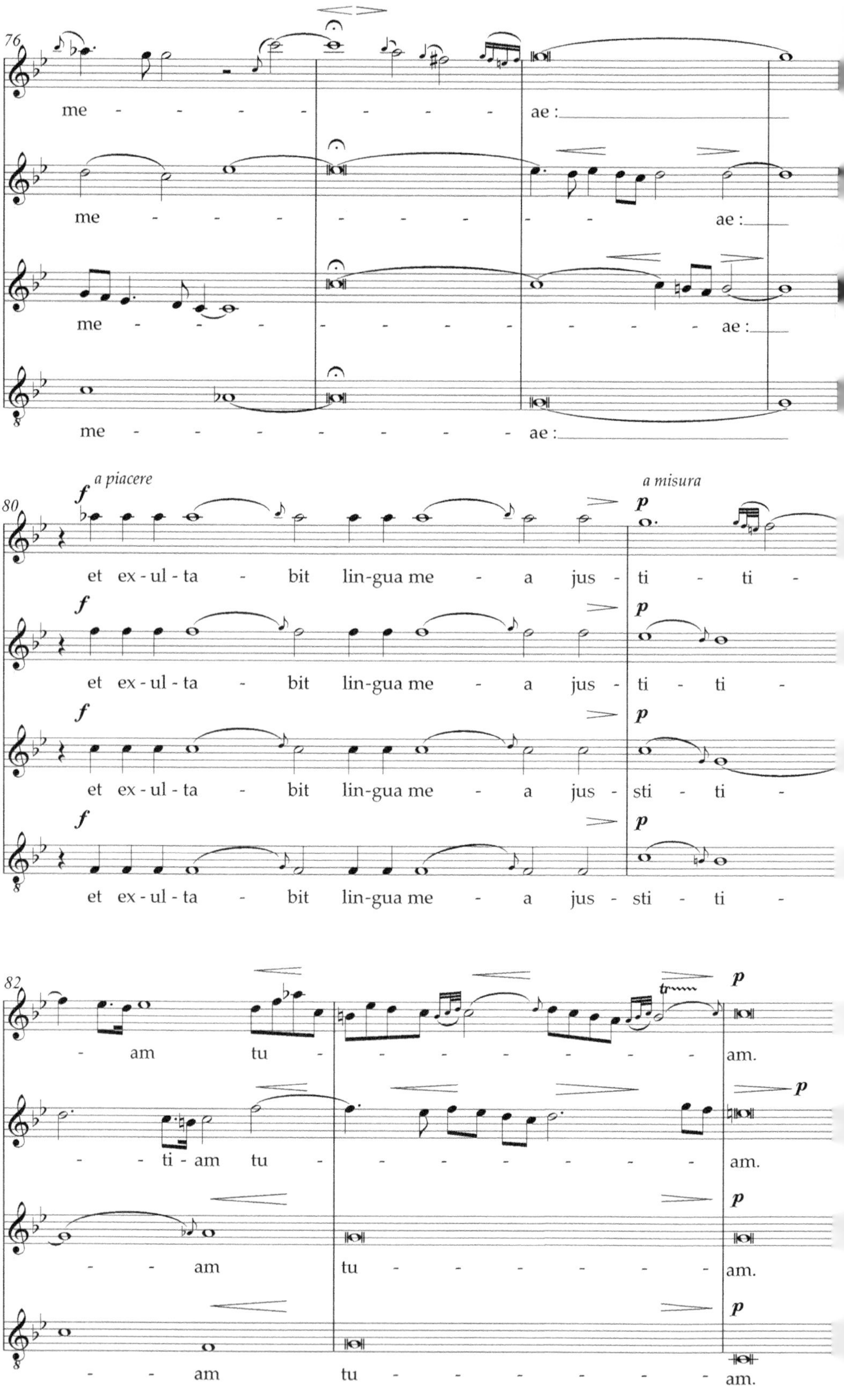
76
me - - - - - - - ae :
me - - - - - - - - - ae :
me - - - - - - - - - ae :
me - - - - - - - ae :
80
a piacere
a misura
et ex - ul - ta - bit lin-gua me - a jus - ti - ti -
et ex - ul - ta - bit lin-gua me - a jus - ti - ti -
et ex - ul - ta - bit lin-gua me - a jus - sti - ti -
et ex - ul - ta - bit lin-gua me - a jus - sti - ti -
82
- am tu - - - - - - - - - am.
- - ti - am tu - - - - - - - - am.
- - am tu - - - - - - - - am.
- - am tu - - - - - - - - am.

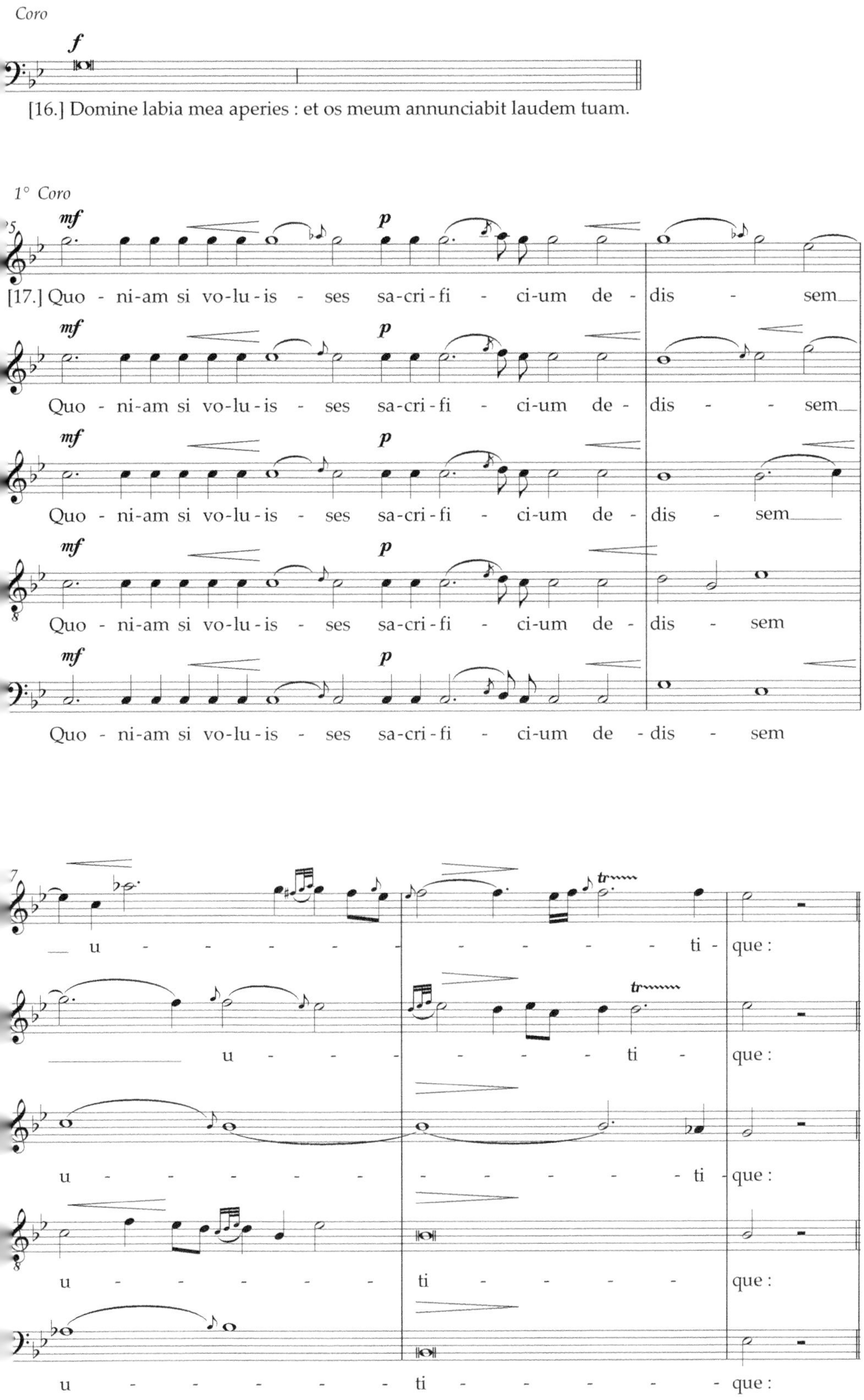
Coro
f
[16.] Domine labia mea aperies : et os meum annunciabit laudem tuam.
1° Coro
5
mf p
[17.] Quo - ni-am si vo-lu-is - ses sa-cri-fi - ci-um de - dis - sem
Quo - ni-am si vo-lu-is - ses sa-cri-fi - ci-um de - dis - - sem
Quo - ni-am si vo-lu-is - ses sa-cri-fi - ci-um de - dis - sem
Quo - ni-am si vo-lu-is - ses sa-cri-fi - ci-um de - dis - sem
Quo - ni-am si vo-lu-is - ses sa-cri-fi - ci-um de - dis - sem
7
tr
u - - - - - - - - ti - que :
u - - - - - - ti - que :
u - - - - - - - - - - - ti - que :
u - - - - - - ti - - - - - que :
u - - - - - - ti - - - - - - que :

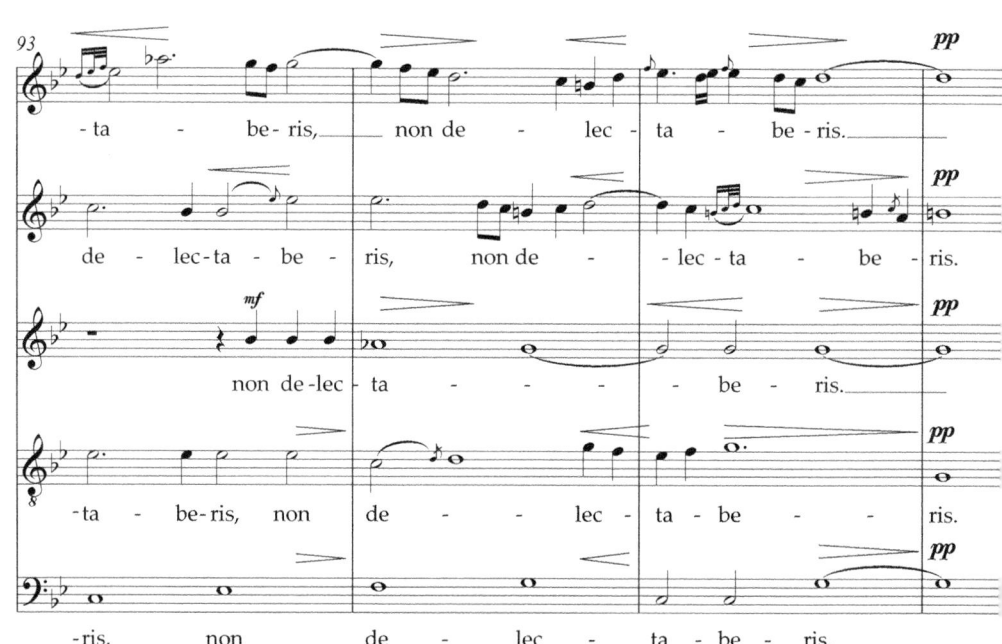

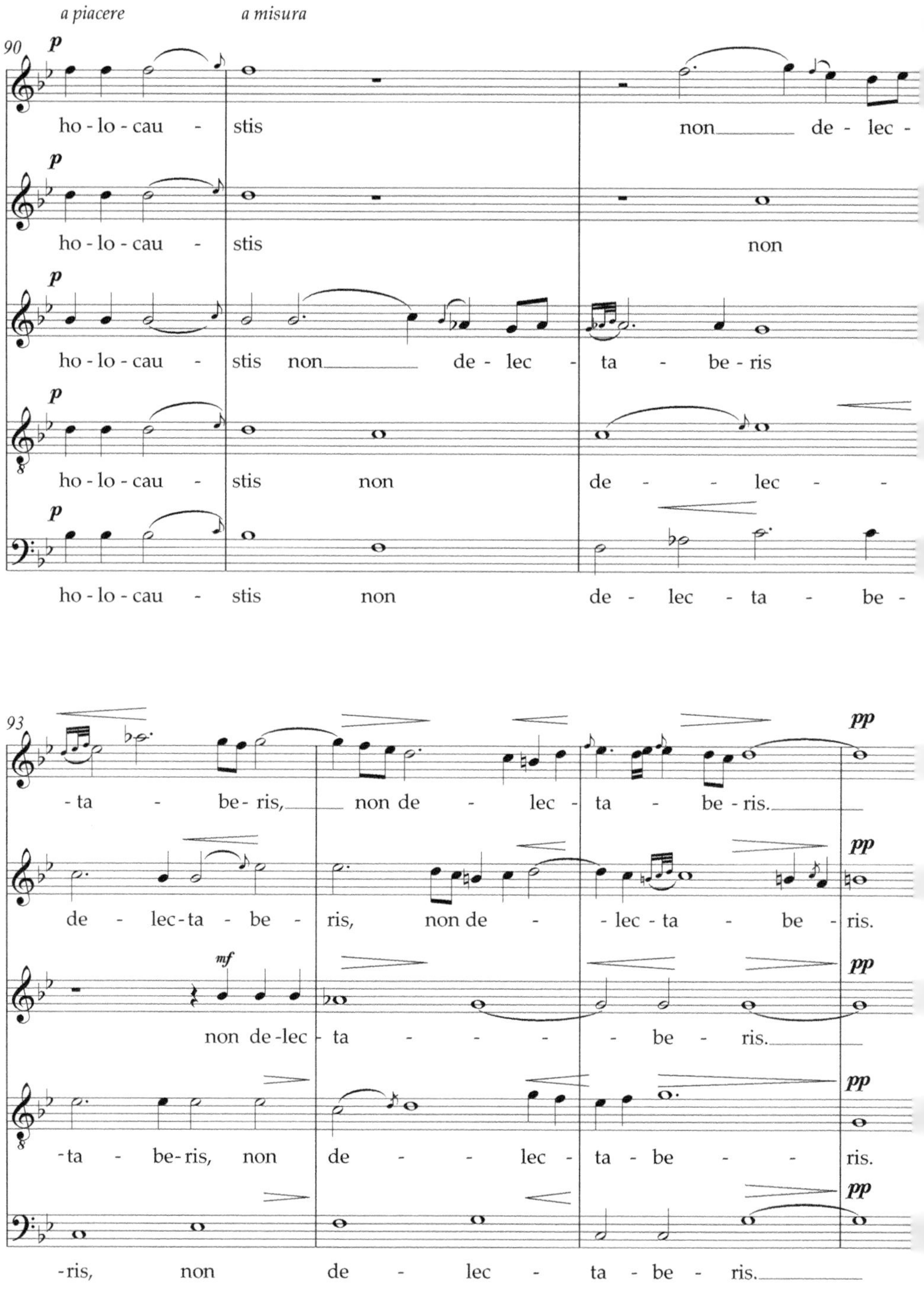
a piacere
a misura
90
p
ho - lo - cau - stis
non de - lec -
ho - lo - cau - stis
non
ho - lo - cau - stis non de - lec - ta - be - ris
ho - lo - cau - stis non
de - - lec - -
ho - lo - cau - stis non
de - lec - ta - be -
93
pp
- ta - be - ris, non de - lec - ta - be - ris.
de - lec - ta - be - ris, non de - - lec - ta - be - ris.
mf
non de - lec - ta - - - - be - ris.
- ta - be - ris, non de - - lec - ta - be - - ris.
- ris, non de - lec - ta - be - ris.

Coro

[18.] Sacrificium Deo spiritus contribulatus : cor contritum et humiliatum, Deus, non despicies.

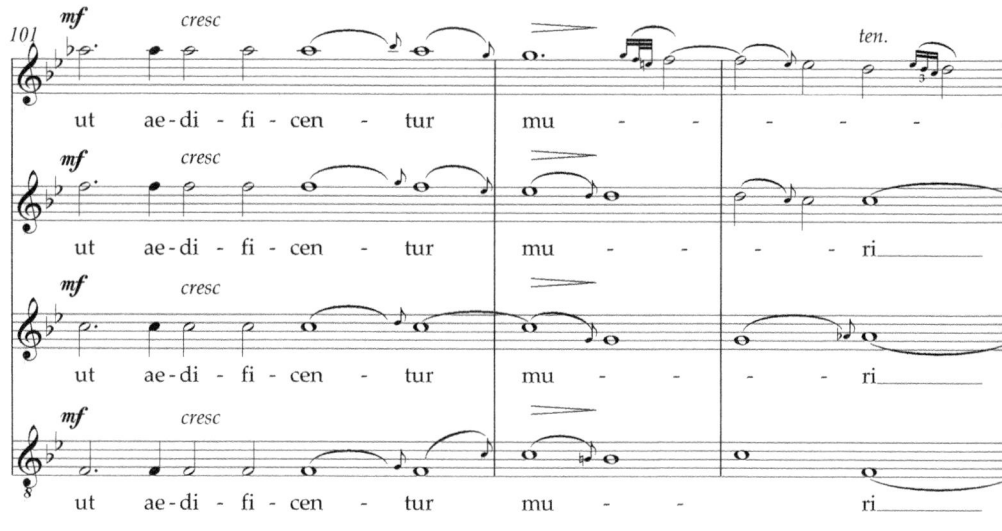

✴ Commentary

Time signatures and note values are as in the models, and the edition has been barred in four minims, as in **M**. Editorial accidentals are placed above the notes concerned and apply only to those notes. It has been transposed up a fourth into C minor and numerous suggestions of interpretation added. In particular, all the prosody of the reciting sections is the result of an editorial decision, as are the dynamics applied to them. The five-part verses have been labelled *Coro Primo* and the four-part ones *Coro Secondo*, following the practice of all Vatican sources, although those from the 1820s reverse this nomenclature.

Using Source **A** as the basis for the edition, I have incorporated some slight variations from verse to verse following hints from other sources. So for the *Primo coro*, verse 1 incorporates features from **P** (and **Man**) as well as **A**, and verses 13 and 17 some features from **Mil**. Similarly for the first part of the *Secondo coro*, verse 7 is reliant on both **M** and the phrase noted by Nicolai (Ex. 9 in Chapter 10), verse 11 incorporates features from **Mil** in the first half and **P** in the second, in verse 15 the simple phrase sung by Mariano in 1831 and noted by Mendelssohn is heard, and verse 19 is Mariano at his most extravagant, with his *galant* ornament from 1824 (Fig. 18 in Chapter 9) which takes the soprano part up to E♭.[3] The second half of 19 follows the end of verse 3 in **M**, the only verse there derived from Allegri. It will be noted that these variations sometimes vary the speed of harmonic movement, especially during the 'top C' moment. In practice, however, the length of the pause while the soprano looks down on the world from on high has a greater effect on the harmonic rhythm than changes in note values.

Underlay generally follows **A**, but **P**, **Man** and **Mil** have also been taken into account. It is rare that one reading is noticeably better than another and, especially in the lower parts, versions given there tend to be haphazard when they are present at all. As in **M** (Edition 1), both *appoggiature* and *gruppetti* are to be sung to the syllable of the note which they precede, something which is only rarely clearly indicated in the manuscripts. *Portamenti* are always sung to the syllable of the preceding note.

The *gruppetti* show much variation between sources, and appear to be of two types: even (*sq sq sq* or *ddd*) and with a longer first note (*sq dd*, *q.dd* as often in **2**, and even *sq.dd*, the latter systematic in the German sources such as **3** and **4**, see Ex. 11 (p. 234)). Given that there is little consistency in the sources, I have used only *sq dd* in this edition, in order to avoid indicating differences which are probably insignificant. In all cases, the first note should be 'leant on' as much as

---

[3] It must be remembered that when he sang it, the *Miserere* was performed in B♭, so the note was only (!) a D♭. Moreover, Roman pitch standards meant that it was at least a large semitone lower than that. If it is found to be too high, the *abbellimento* from verse 3 can be substituted.

the context allows. *Gruppetti* should be sung more or less on the beat, and the score has been prepared to show this. Even if an effort can be made occasionally to precede it (e.g. b. 18, canto 1) – usually there is not time (e.g. b. 7, alto). This may seem untidy, but it may be that the imprecision thus produced is part of the style.

I have suggested very sparingly the extra *acciaccatura* in the parallel *portamento* which so annoyed Nicolai (see Chapter 7), and which is sporadically present in **M**. Directors are free to use it as and when they wish.

The final half-verse a9 Tunc imponent

The voicing of this verse can raise questions because it was not brought into line with the modifications made to the other *Primo coro* (five-part) verses by Biordi in the early eighteenth century. Those changes recast the voicing as SSATB, but in this place uniquely, all the sources in the Vatican library still give the original version for SATTB. In CS 341, the final papal choirbook dating from 1748, not a single note has changed from the earliest manuscript, CS 205, copied in 1661 (except, curiously, that the verse is labelled a8 instead of a9 – perhaps the final verse of Bai's *Miserere* has confused the scribe). Neither do the manuscripts from the 1820s show any changes.

There seems to have been some awareness of the problem. Burney's edition proposes the solution which is generally performed today, which consists of simply transposing the first tenor part of the five-part choir an octave higher. One would be tempted to suggest that Burney may have obtained it from the same source as the other five-part verses he printed (possibly Padre Martini) were it not for the fact that the same solution is found in the manuscripts **P** and **Man**, both of which originate in the Papal Choir, so maybe he had it from Santarelli.[4] Another solution is that proposed by Alfieri in his publication of 1840, which moves the parts around a bit without changing the octaves. Although the second soprano and, especially, the alto of the four-part choir have to sing rather lower than in the rest of the piece, it has the virtue of preserving the original spacing of the chords. This version is found in a certain number of nineteenth-century manuscripts, but nearly all of them post-date Alfieri's publication; exceptions are two partial sources of **A**, **10** (Basel, dated 1829), and **12**.

No changes at all are necessary, however, when the *Miserere* is sung in C minor. In the five-part choir the alto part falls perfectly within the range of the second soprano, as does the first tenor part of the alto. The second tenor part is higher than before, but goes no higher than g'. This may be why no changes were made: singing in the keys they did, the papal singers had no need of them.

---

[4] **P** and **Man** also give a curious variant from other versions, in which the chord of G minor before the final dominant D ('vitulos') is held for an extra breve. This is not simply an error, as the underlay is carefully adapted in preceding bars to fit, and musically it is certainly satisfactory and arguably superior. It turns up in the early English editions by H.A. Walker and George Martin, and was used by Willcocks for his famous recording in 1963 (see also p. 200, n. 39).

Bibliography

✴ Primary sources unpublished

Italy

Biblioteca Apostolica Vaticana
    Armadio XII, Nos 17–21,
    Ott. Lat. 3388
    MS Barberini 4418
    MSS Cappella Sistina: (Referred to as CS): Choirbooks: 38, 72, 76, 100, 132, 137, 185, 188–9, 192, 203–4, 205–6, 212, 247, 263, 279, 280, 286, 302, 331, 340–1, 342, 343
    Scorebooks: 354, 371, 375 (score and parts, referred to as **M**), 450, 483
    Extracts from documents: 658, 681
    Diario della Cappella Sistina (referred to as *DS*): *Capp. Sist. Diari* 58 (1638), 70 (1652), 103 (1684), 128 (1708), 131 (1711), 208 (1785), 221 (1798–1800), 224 (1803), 226 (1805), 228 (1807), 229 (1808), 230 (1809–14), 231 (1815), 236 (1820), 237 (1821), 238 (1822), 248 (1832), 290 (1883–6), 294 (1892)
Biblioteca Vallicelliana, Rome, MS R. 45
Conservatorio della Santa Cecilia, Rome, G.Ms. 44
S. Giovanni Laterano, Rome, MS 59
Archivio della Congregazione dell'Oratorio di S. Filippo Neri, Rome, MS F.III.4
Biblioteca del Conservatorio G. Verdi, Milan, MUSA MS 2–2 (Referred to as **Mil**)
Conservatorio Luigi Cherubini, Florence, E.I.76
Conservatorio di San Pietro a Majella, Naples, MS 21.6.4
Biblioteca Nazionale Marciana, Venice, Cod.It.IV,1339

France

Bibliotheque nationale, Paris, D.670, D.14499 (Referred to as **P**)
    Vm⁷ 1121187
    Vm¹ 561/1
Archives Nationales, Paris, A537/71/2, MC/ET/XVI/1052

United Kingdom

British Library, London
  Egerton MSS 2450, 2468 & 2470
  Add. MSS 19939, 24291, 31395, 31525, 65482
  MSS R.M.23.f.20, R.M.24.c.3
John Rylands Library, University of Manchester, MS Italian 45 (Referred to as **Man**)
Oxford, Bodleian Library
  MS M. Deneke Mendelssohn d.70 & d.13, Ms Mus. d.293
Oxford, New College, Chapel Service Lists 1923–1987
Cambridge, King's College, Chapel Service Lists 1919–1987
Worcester, Cathedral, Service Lists 1895–1950

Germany

Berlin Staatsbibliothek, Mus. Ms 550/2, Mus. Ms. Alfieri 1, Sammlung Teschner 119
Cologne, Hochschule für Musik und Tanz Bibliothek, MS R1038/2
Dresden, Sächsische Landesbibliothek, Mus. 1474-E-1, Mus. 1474-E-3, Mus. 1474-E-4, Mus. 1474-E-500, Mus. 2-E-12
Leipzig, Stadtbibliothek – Musikbibliothek, PM 5618
Munich, Bayerische Staatsbibliothek Mus. Ms. 3268, Mus. Ms. 671

Austria

Vienna, Österreichische Nationalbibliothek, Mus. Hs. 15604

Switzerland

Basel, Universtäts-Bibliothek, MS kk XII 22:3
Basel, Sammlung Rudolf Grumbacher, Mendelssohn letter Nr. 487

Poland

Warsaw, Biblioteka Uniwersytecka, MS RM 6027

✳ Published

Adami di Bolsena, Andrea. *Osservazioni per ben regolare il coro de i Cantori della Cappella pontificia*. Rome, 1711, facsimile with introduction by Giancarlo Rostirolla. Lucca, 1988.

Alfieri, Pietro. *Il Salmo Miserere posto in musica da Gregorio Allegri e da Tommaso Bai, Publicato cogli Abbellimenti per la prima volta*. Lugano, 1840 (under the name of Alessandro Geminiani).

———. *Raccolta di Musica Sacra*. Rome, 1843.

———. 'Biografia di Monsignor Giuseppe Baini'. *Gazzetta Musicale di Milano*, 14 (1856), 8 parts, in every second issue from 18 May to 24 August.

Ambros, August Wilhelm. 'Musikalisches aus Italien'. *Bunte Blätter* (Leipzig, 1872), 25–36.

Angelis, Alberto de. *La Musica a Roma nel secolo XIX*. Rome, 1935.

Anon. 'Soprano singers', *The Parthenon, a magazine of Art and Literature* N°2 (18 June 1826), 29.

Anon. 'Nachrichten über Italien aus dem Briefe eines Reisenden', in Carl Friedrich Cramer (ed.), *Magazin der Musik*, 1/2 (Hamburg, 1783), 989–90.

Baggs, Charles Michael. *The Ceremonies of Holy-Week at the Vatican and S. John Lateran's*. Rome, 1839.

Baini, Giuseppe. *Memorie Storico-Critiche della Vita et delle Opere di Giovanni Pierluigi da Palestrina*, 2 vols. Rome, 1828.

Banchieri, Adriano. *Cartello overo Regole utilissime à quella che desiderano imparare il canto figurato*. Venice, 1601.

Benoist, Philippe et Félix. *Rome dans sa grandeur …, deuxième volume – Rome chrétienne*, Paris, 1869.

Berio, Margharita. 'Lettre de Rome'. *Revue Musicale S.I.M.*, 12/12 (December 1913), 63–4.

Berlioz, Hector. 'Voyage musical', in *Italie pittoresque*. Paris, 1836.

Blainville, Charles-Henri de. *Histoire Générale, Critique et Philologique de la Musique*. Paris, 1767.

Bovicelli, Giovanni Battista. *Regole, passaggi di musica, madrigali et mottetti passaggiati*, Venice, 1594, ed. Gawain Glenton, trans. Oliver Webber. London, 2018.

Brossard, Sébastien de. *Dictionaire de Musique*. Paris, 1705.

Burney, Charles. *La musica che si canta annualmente nelle Funzioni della Settimana Santa nella Cappella Pontificale*. London, 1771.

———. *The Present State of Music in France and Italy*, 1st edn. London, 1771.

———. *Tagebuch einer Musikalischenreise durch Frankreich und Italien* (trans. of *The Present State of Music in France and Italy*, by Christoph-Daniel Eberlin). Hamburg, 1772.

———. *De l'Etat présent de la Musique en France et en Italie* (trans. of *The Present State of Music in France and Italy*, by Charles Brack). Genoa, 1809.

———. *Musica Sacra quæ Cantatur Quotannis per Hebdomamam Sanctam Romæ in Sacello Pontificio* (trans. of *La musica che si canta annualmente nelle Funzioni della Settimana Santa nella Cappella Pontificale*). Leipzig, n.d. [1809].

———. *Continental Travels 1770–1772*, comp. C.E. Glover. London, 1927.

———. *An Eighteenth-Century Musical Tour in France and Italy*, ed. Percy Scholes. Oxford, 1959.

———. *Music, Men, and Manners in France and Italy 1770, being the Journal Written by Charles Burney, Mus. D. ... Transcribed from the Original Manuscript in the British Museum*, ed. H.E. Poole. London, 1969.

———. *The Letters of Dr Charles Burney*, ed. Alvaro Ribeiro, vol. 1: *1751–1784*. Oxford, 1991.

Caccini, Giulio. *Le Nuove Musiche*, Florence, 1602.

Celani, Enrico. 'I cantori della Cappella Pontificia nei secoli XVI–XVIII'. *Rivista Musicale Italiana*, 14 (1907), 83–104 and 752–90; 16 (1909), 55–112.

Celler, Ludovic [*nom de plume* of Ludovic Leclerc]. *La Semaine Sainte au Vatican; Etude musicale et pittoresque*. Paris, 1867.

Chateaubriand. *The Memoirs of François René Vicomte de Chateaubriand*, vol. 5, trans. Alexander Teixeira de Mattos. London, 1902.

Concone, Giuseppe. *Introduction à l'Art de bien chanter*. Paris, c.1845.

Corri, Domenico. *A Select Collection*. Edinburgh, c.1782.

———. *The Singer's Preceptor*. London, 1810.

Delécluze, Etienne-Jean. 'Palestrina'. *Revue de Paris*, 4th series, 10 (October 1842), 311–31.

———. *Louis David, son école et son temps*. Paris, 1855.

Deutsch, Otto. *Mozart: A Documentary Biography*, trans. Eric Blom, Peter Branscombe and Jeremy Noble. Stanford, 1965.

Dickens, Charles. *Pictures from Italy*, ed. David Paroissien. New York, 1974.

Diruta, Girolamo. *Seconda parte del Transilvano*, book 3. Venice, 1622..

Doni, Giambattista. *Annotazioni sopra il Compendio de' Generi, e de' Modi della Musica*. Rome, 1640.

Duprez, Gilbert. *L'Art du Chant*, Paris, 1845.

Emerson, Ralph Waldo, *Journals of Ralph Waldo Emerson*, vol. 3. London, 1910.

Evelyn, John. *Diary and Correspondence of John Evelyn, F.R.S.* London, 1859.

Fétis, François-Joseph. *Biographie universelle des Musiciens*. Paris, 1837.

Galliard, J.E. *Observations on the Florid Song* (trans. of Tosi's *Opinioni de' cantori antichi e moderni*). London, 1742.

Garaudé, Alexis de. *Méthode complet de chant*. Paris, 1809.

Garcia, Manuel. *Traité complet de l'Art du Chant*, Paris, 1847.

———. *Garcia's Treatise on the Art of Singing*, trans. and ed. Albert Garcia. London, 1924.

Giustiniani, Vincenzo. *Discorso sopra la musica de' suoi tempi*. Lucca, c.1628.

Gounod, Charles. *Memoirs of an Artist*, trans. Annette E. Crocker. Chicago, 1895.

Grassi, Paride de. *Il diario di Leone X di Paride Grassi* (from Biblioteca Apostolica Vaticana, Miscellanea, Armadio XII, Nos. 17–21), ed. Mariano Armellini. Rome, 1884.

Hauptmann, Moritz. *The Letters of a Leipzig Cantor: Being the Letters of Moritz Hauptmann to Franz Hauser, Ludwig Spohr and other musicians*, trans. and ed. A.D.Coleridge. London, 1892.

Hautcoeur, Edouard. *Histoire de l'église collégiale et du chapitre de Saint-Pierre de Lille*, vol. 3. Lille, 1899.

Hawkins, Sir John. *A General History of the Science and Practice of Music.* London, 1776.

Hensel, Sebastian. *The Mendelssohn Family (1729–1847) from Letters and Journals*, trans. Carl Klingemann, (2 vols.). New York, 1882.

Herold, Louis-Joseph-Ferdinand. *Lettres d'Italie, suivies du journal et autres écrits 1804–1833*, ed. Hervé Audéon. Weinsberg, 2008.

Hugo, Victor. *Les Misérables* (Brussels, 1862), trans. Isabel F. Hapgood. New York, 1887.

Ingres, Jean-Auguste-Dominique. *Lettres de France et d'Italie 1804–1841*, ed. Daniel Ternois. Paris, 2011.

——. *Ingres raconté par lui-même et par ses amis*, ed. Pierre Cailler. Geneva, 1947.

Jarves, James Jackson. *Italian Sights and Papal Principles Seen through American Spectacles.* New York, 1856.

Junker, Carl Ludwig. *Musikalisches Taschenbuch auf das Jahr 1784.* Freyburg, 1784.

Kandler, Franz. 'Present State of Music in Rome'. *The Harmonicon* (1828), 147–51, 198–200, 218–8.

Kemble, Fanny (Mrs Butler). *A Year of Consolation*, vol. 1. New York, 1847.

La Fage, Adrien de. *Essais de diphthérographie musical.* Paris, 1864.

Lassabathie, Théodore. *Histoire du Conservatoire impérial de musique et de déclamation.* Paris, 1860.

The late Dr. Burney's Musical Library. A Catalogue of the valuable and very fine collection of music, printed and MS, facs. edn. London, 1814, in A. Hyatt King, *Catalogue of the Music Library of Charles Burney, Sold in London, 8 August 1814.* Amsterdam, 1973.

Lefebvre, Léon (ed.). *Histoire du Théâtre de Lille*, vol. 3. Lille, 1907.

Liber usualis, reprint. Tournai, 1961.

Mainzer, Joseph. 'La Chapelle Sixtine à Rome', in 4 weekly instalments. *Gazette Musicale de Paris* 1834, Nos. 2–5 (12 January–2 February), 11–40.

Mancini, Giambattista. *Pensieri e riflessioni pratiche sopra il canto figurato.* Vienna, 1774.

Mant, Richard (ed.). *The Book of Common Prayer ... with Notes Explanatory, Practical, and Historical, from Approved Writers of the Church of England.* Oxford, 1825.

Martini, Padre Giovanni-Battista. *Esemplare, o sia Saggio fondamentale pratico di contrappunto*, 2 vols. Bologna, 1774 and 1776.

Maude, J.H. *The History of the Book of Common Prayer.* New York, 1901.

Mendelssohn Bartholdy, Felix. *Sämtliche Briefe*, vol. 2. Kassel, 2009.
——. *Letters*, ed. and trans. G. Selden-Goth. London, 1946.
——. *Voyages de Jeunesse, Lettres européennes (1830–1832)*, reprinted with a preface by Rémi Jacobs. Paris, 1980.
——. *Mendelssohn: A Life in Letters*. ed. Rudolf Ewers, trans. Craig Tomlinson. New York, 1986.
Morse, Samuel. *Samuel Morse: His Letters and Journals*, ed. Edward Lind Morse. Boston, 1914.
Mozart, W.A. *The Letters of Mozart & his Family*, trans. and ed. Emily Anderson. London, 1938.
Necker, Anne-Louise Germaine, baronne de Staël-Holstein. *Corinne, ou l'Italie*, trans. Avriel Goldberger. New Brunswick, 1987.
Nicolai, Otto. 'Italienische Studien: Über die Sixtinische Capelle in Rom', *Neue Zeitschrift für Musik*, 6 (1837), modern edn in G.R. Kruse, *Musikalische Aufsätze*, Regensburg, 1960.
——. *Otto Nicolais Tagebücher*, ed. Wilhelm Altmann. Regensburg, 1937.
——. 'Italienische Studien: Über die Sixtinische Capelle in Rom'. *Neue Zeitschrift für Musik*, 6 (1837).
Pacelli, Asprilio. *Chorici psalmi et motecta*. Rome, 1599.
Peale, Rembrandt. *Notes on Italy*. Philadelphia, 1831.
Pearson, H.A. (ed.). *The Sarum Missal, in English*, 2nd edn. London, 1886.
Reichardt, J.F. (ed.), 'Briefe aus Rom'. *Musikalisches Wochenblatt*, 1/5, 1/9, 1/11. Reprinted in *Studien für Tonkünstler und Musikfreunde, Eine historisch-kritische Zeitschrifte ... fürs Jahre 1792*, Berlin, 1793.
Rellstab, J.C. Friedrich. *Versuch über die Vereinigung der musikalischen und oratorischen Declamation*. Berlin, 1786.
Renouard, Paul. *Rome pendant la semaine sainte*. Paris, 1891.
Rognoni, Francesco. *Selve du vari Passaggi*, vol. 1. Milan, 1620.
Russell, John. *A Tour in Germany and some of the Southern Provinces of the Austrian Empire in 1820, 1821, and 1822*. Edinburgh, 1824.
Shelley, Mary. *Rambles in Germany and Italy in 1840, 1842 and 1843*. London, 1844.
Sievers, G.L.P. 'Die päpstliche Kapelle zu Rom' in 7 weekly instalments. *Allgemeine Musikalische Zeitung* (1825), Nos. 19–25 (May–June).
——. 'Das Miserere von Allegri in der Sixtinischen Capelle in Rom'. *Cäcilia, eine Zeitschrift für die Musikalische Welt*, N°5 (1825), 66–82.
——. 'Zustand der Kirchenmusik in Rom'. *Cäcilia, eine Zeitschrift für die Musikalische Welt*, N°32 (1828), 213–24.
Skene, James. *Italian Journey: Being Excerpts from the Pre-Victorian Diary of James Skene of Rubislaw*. London, 1937.
Spohr, Ludwig. *The Musical Journeys of Louis Spohr*, trans. and ed. Henry Pleasants. Norman, OK, 1961.
Spohr, Ludwig. *Louis Spohr's Biography* (anonymous trans. of his *Selbst-biographie*). London, 1878.
Stendhal (Henry Beyle). *Rome, Naples et Florence*. Paris, 1854.

——. *Life of Mozart*, in *Lives of Haydn, Mozart and Metastasio*, trans. and ed. Richard N. Coe. London, 1972.

Stowe, Harriet Beecher. *Agnes of Sorrento*. Boston, 1862.

Tosi, Pier-Francesco. *Opinioni de' cantori antichi e moderni*. Bologna, 1723.

Vaccai, Nicola. *Metodo pratico di canto italiano per camera*, London, 1832. Trans. anon, Leipzig, n.d.

Viadana, Lodovico. *Cento concerti ecclesiastici*. Venice, 1602.

Wiseman, (Cardinal) Nicholas. *Four Lectures on the Offices and Ceremonies of Holy Week as Performed in the Papal Chapels, delivered in Rome in the Lent of MDCCCXXXVI*. London, 1839.

Zarlini, Gioseffo. *Le istitutioni harmoniche*. Venice, 1558.

✳ Secondary sources

Amann, Julius. *Allegris Miserere und die Aufführungspraxis in der Sixtina*. Regensburg, 1935.

Annibaldi, Claudio. *Storia della cappella musicale pontificia nel Seicento, Da Urbano VII a Urbano VIII (1590–1644)*, vol. 4/1 of *Storia della Cappella Musicale Pontificia*. Rome, 2011.

——. '"The Singers of the said chapel are chaplains of the pope": Some Remarks on the Papal Chapel in Early Modern Times'. *Early Music*, 39/1 (February 2011), 15–24.

Barbieri, Patrizio. 'Chiavette and Modal Transposition in Italian Practice (c.1500–1837)'. *Recercare*, 3 (1991), 5–79.

Bignami-Odier, Jeanne. 'Christiniana'. *Mélanges d'archéologie et d'histoire*, 80 (1968), 705–47.

Bianchini, Luca. *Wolfgang Amadé Mozart*, trans. Robert Newman, 2011, www.italianopera.org.

Blackburn, Bonnie and Lowinsky, Edward. 'Luigi Zenobi and his Letter on the Perfect Musician'. *Studi Musicali*, 22 (1993), 61–114.

Boursy, Richard. 'The Mystique of the Sistine Chapel Choir in the Romantic Era'. *Journal of Musicology*, 11/3 (Summer 1993), 277–329.

——. 'Historicism and Composition: Giuseppe Baini, the Sistine Chapel Choir, and Stile Antico Music in the First Half of the 19th Century'. PhD diss., Yale University, 1994.

Bradshaw, Murray C. 'Performance Practice and the Falsobordone'. *Performance Practice Review*, 10/2 (Fall 1997), 224–47.

——. '*Falsobordone*'. *Grove Music Online*, https://www.oxfordmusiconline.com/grovemusic/.

——and E.J. Soehnlen, *Girolamo Diruta: The Transylvanian*. Henryville, 1984.

Brown, Clive. *Classical and Romantic Performing Practice, 1750–1900*. Oxford, 1999.

Byram-Wigfield, Ben. *A Quest for the Holy Grail?* 2012 and subsequent revisions, http://www.ancientgroove.co.uk/essays/sources.html.

Chen, Jen-yen. 'The Tradition and Ideal of the Stile Antico in Viennese Sacred Music, 1740–1800'. PhD diss., Harvard University, 2000.

Chrissocoidis, Ilias. 'London Mozartiana: Wolfgang's Disputed Age & Early Performances of Allegri's *Miserere*'. *Musical Times*, 151 (Summer 2010), 83–9.

Clapton, Nicholas. *Moreschi and the Voice of the Castrato*. London, 2008.

Combe, Dom Pierre. *Histoire de la restauration du chant Grégorien d'après des documents inédits*. Solemnes, 1969. Translated by Marier, T.N. and Skinner W. *The Restoration of Gregorian Chant*, Washington, 2003.

Cooper, Barry. 'Catalogue of Pre-1900 Music Manuscripts in the John Rylands University Library of Manchester'. *Bulletin of the John Rylands University Library of Manchester*, 79/2 (1997), 27–101.

Della Libera, Luca. Introduction to *Selected Sacred Music by Alessandro Scarlatti*, Recent Researches in the Music of the Baroque Era. Middleton, WI, 2012.

Dibble, J.C. *John Stainer: A Life in Music*. Woodbridge, 2007.

Dole, Nathan Haskell. *Famous Composers*. New York, 1891, repr. 1902.

Dower, C.A. 'Cappella Sistina Codexes in the Catholic University of America Library'. *Notes*, 36/3 (1980), 615–23.

Ellis, Katharine. *Interpreting the Musical Past: Early Music in Nineteenth Century France*. New York, 2005.

Feldman, Martha. *The Castrato: Reflections on Natures and Kinds*. Oakland, CA, 2015.

Finucci, Valeria, *The Manly Masquerade: Masculinity, Paternity, and Castration in the Italian Renaissance*. Durham, NC, 2003.

Fiske, Roger. 'Allegri: Miserere', review of performance by King's College, Cambridge, Argo ZFA111, *Gramophone*, (November 1965), 259.

Gabrielli, Alessandro. 'Riassunto delle conversazioni sulla storia delle cappelle musicali romane'. *Rassegna Dorica*, 10 (1938–9).

Garratt, James. *Palestrina and the German Romantic Imagination*. Cambridge, 2002.

Geay, Gérard. *Le troisième mode de Blainville*, Cahiers Philidor 32. Versailles, 2005.

Grangé, Jean-Christophe. *Miserere*. Paris, 2008.

Green, Richard D. 'Klein, Bernhard'. *Grove Music Online*, https://www.oxfordmusiconline.com/grovemusic/.

Haar, James. 'Festa, Costanzo'. *Grove Music Online*, https://www.oxfordmusiconline.com/grovemusic/.

Haas, Robert. *Aufführungspraxis der Musik*. Potsdam, 1931.

Haböck, Franz. *Die Gesangskunst der Kastraten*. Vienna, 1923.

Harris, Ellen. 'Portamento'. *Grove Music Online*, https://www.oxfordmusiconline.com/grovemusic/.

Haynes, Bruce. *A History of Performing Pitch: The Story of 'A'*. Lanham, MD, and Oxford, 2002.

Hutchings, Arthur. *Mozart: The Man, the Musician*. New York, 1976.

Janz, Bernhard. *Der Fondo Cappella Sistina der Biblioteca Apostolica Vaticana: Studien zur Geschichte des Bestandes*. Paderborn, 2000.

Johnstone, Andrew. '"High" Clefs in Composition and Performance'. *Early Music*, 34/1 (February 2006), 29–53.

Johnstone, H. Diack. 'Westminster Abbey and the Academy of Ancient Music: A Library Once Lost and Now Partially Recovered'. *Music & Letters*, 95/3 (August 2014), 329–73.

Kantner, Leopold and Pachovsky, Angela. *L'Ottocento*. Storia della Cappella Musicale Pontificia, 6. Rome, 1998.

Kennaway, George. *Playing the Cello, 1780–1930*. London, 2104.

Kirkpatrick, Ralph. *Domenico Scarlatti*. Princeton, 1953.

Konrad, Ulrich. 'Otto Nicolai und die Palestrina-Renaissance', in *Palestrina und die Idee des klassischen Vokalpolyphonie in 19. Jahrhundert: Zur Geschichte eines kirchenmusikalischen Stilideals*, ed. Winfried Kirsch, Palestrina und die Kirchenmusik im 19. Jahrhundert, 1. Regensburg, 1989, 117–42.

Kurtzmann, Jeffrey G. 'Tones, Modes and Clefs in Roman cyclic Magnificats of the 16th Century'. *Early Music*, 22/4 (November 1994), 641–64.

Lattes, Sergio. 'Baini, Giuseppe'. *Grove Music Online*, https://www.oxfordmusiconline.com/grovemusic/.

Leech-Wilkinson, Daniel. 'Portamento and Musical Meaning'. *Journal of Musicological Research*, 25 (2006), 233–61.

Lionnet, Jean. 'Quelques aspects de la vie musicale à Saint-Louis-des-Français: de Giovanni Bernardino Nanino à Alessandro Melani (1591–1698)', in *Les fondations nationales dans la Rome pontificale. Actes du colloque de Rome (16–19 mai 1978)*. Rome, 1981, 333–75.

———. 'Performance Practice in the Papal Chapel during the 17th Century'. *Early Music*, 15/1 (February 1987), 4–15.

———. Notes to A Sei Voci, *Miserere*, CD Astrée-Audivis E8524.

Llorens, Josef. 'Cristobal de Morales, cantor en la Capilla Pontificia de Paolo III (1535–1545)'. *Anuario Musical*, 8 (1953), 39–69.

———. *Capellae Sixtinae Codices musicis notis instructi sive manu scripti sive praelo excussi*, Città del Vaticano, 1969.

Lockwood, Lewis. Introduction to an edition of Palestrina's *Pope Marcellus Mass*, Norton Critical Scores. New York, 1975.

———, with Noel O'Regan and Jessie-Ann Owens. 'Palestrina, Giovanni Pierluigi da', *Grove Music Online*. https://www.oxfordmusiconline.com/grovemusic/.

Luciani, Luciano. *Sussidio per la consultazione dei cataloghi Boezi e Llorens dei fondi Cappella Giulia e Cappella Sistina della Biblioteca Vaticana*. Rome, 2014.

Lundberg, Mattias. 'The *Tonus Peregrinus* in the Polyphony of the Western Church'. PhD diss., Liverpool University, 2007.

———. *Tonus Peregrinus: The History of a Psalm-Tone and its Use in Polyphonic Music*. Farnham, 2011.

Lütteken, Laurenz. 'Perpetuierung des Einzigartigen: Gregorio Allegris "Miserere" und das Ritual der päpstlichen Kappele', in *Barocke Inszenierung: Akten des Internationalen Forschungscolloquiums an der Technischen Universität Berlin, 20.–22. Juni 1996*, ed. Joseph Imorde, Fritz Neumeyer and Tristan Weddigen. Emsdetten, 1999, 137–45.

Marx-Weber, Magda. 'Die Tradition der Miserere-Vertonungen in der Cappella Pontificia', in *Collectanea II: Studien zur Geschichte der päpstlichen Kapelle: Tagungsbericht Heidelberg, 1989*, ed. Bernhard Janz. Vatican City, 1994, 266–88.

Matošec, Matjaž. '"Female Voices in Male Bodies": Castrati, Onnagata, and the Performance of Gender through Ambiguous Bodies and Vocal Acts'. MA thesis, Utrecht University, 2008.

Milsom, John. 'Sixteenth- and Seventeenth-Century Choral Works', *Gramophone*, (December 1984), 790.

Montagnier, Jean-Paul. *The Polyphonic Mass in France 1600–1780: The Evidence of the Printed Choirbooks*. Cambridge, 2017.

O'Brien, David. *After the Revolution: Antoine-Jean Gros, Painting and Propoganda under Napoleon Bonaparte*. University Park, PA, 2004. In French as *Jean-Antoine Gros, peintre de Napoléon*, Paris, 2006.

O'Regan, Noel. 'The Performance of Palestrina: Some Further Observations'. *Early Music*, 24/1 (February 1996), 145–54.

O'Reilly, Graham. '"Per divertimento del Cittadino Mesplet, amatore et conoscitore della vera Musica": Two Early Sources of the *abbellimenti* used in Allegri's *Miserere*'. *Early Music*, 44/1 (February 2016), 21–44.

Partridge, Eric. *Origins: A Short Etymological Dictionary of Modern English*, 4th edn. London, 1966.

Pastor, Ludwig. *History of the Popes*, vol. 7, trans. and ed. R.F. Kerr. London, 1908.

Pember, E.F. 'Allegri, Gregorio', in *Grove's Dictionary of Music*, (1880), 3rd edn, ed. J.A. Fuller Maitland, vol. 1 (1929), 68–9.

Potter, John. 'Beggar at the Door – the Rise and Fall of Portamento', *Music & Letters*, 87/4 (2006), 523–50.

Rasch, Rudolf. 'Modes, Clefs and Transpositions in the Early Seventeenth Century', in *Théorie et analyse musicales 1450–1650: Actes du Colloque International Louvain-la-Neuve, 23–25 septembre 1999*. Louvain-la-Neuve, 2001, 403–32.

Ravens, Simon. *The Supernatural Voice: A History of High Male Singing*. Woodbridge, 2014.

Rodin, Jesse. *Josquin's Rome, Hearing and Composing in the Sistine Chapel*. New York, 2012.

Roche, Jerome, rev. Noel O'Regan. 'Allegri, Gregorio'. *Grove Music Online*, https://www.oxfordmusiconline.com/grovemusic/.

Rockstro, William Smith. 'Miserere' in George Grove (ed.), *Dictionary of Music and Musicians*, 1st edn, vol 2 (London, 1880), 335–8; 2nd edn, ed. J.A. Fuller-Maitland, vol. 3 (1907), 216–19.

——. 'Sistine Choir', in George Grove (ed.), *A Dictionary of Music and Musicians*, 1st edn, vol. 2., London, 1883, 519–23.

Rosselli, John. 'The Castrati as a Professional Group and a Social Phenomenon, 1550–1850'. *Acta Musicologia*, 60/2 (May–August 1988), 143–79.

——. *Singers of Italian Opera*. Cambridge, 1992.

Rostirolla, Giancarlo. *Musica e musicisti nella Basilica di San Pietro*. Rome, 2014.

Rostirolla, Giancarlo and Luciani, Luciano (eds.). *Il codice 59, autografo di Giovanni Pierluigi da Palestrina*. Palestrina, 1996.

Rutter, John. Introduction to an edition of Allegri's *Miserere*. Oxford, 1996.

Sadler, Graham. 'La Bibliothèque Musicale du Dr Charles Burney', in Catherine Massip *et al.* (eds.), *Collectionner la musique: érudits collectionneurs*. Turnhout, Brepols, 2015, 99–115.

Sagrans, Jacob. 'Early Music and the Choir of King's College, Cambridge, 1958 to 2015'. PhD diss., McGill University, Montreal, 2016.

Saint, L. 'Choral Music in Canterbury Cathedral, 1873–1988: The Role of Service Settings and Anthems in the Regeneration, Preservation and Sustenance of Cathedral Worship'. PhD diss., Canterbury Christ Church University, 2011.

Sherr, Richard. 'The Papal Chapel ca. 1492–1515 and its Polyphonic Sources'. PhD diss., Princeton, 1975.

——. 'From the Diary of a 16th Century Papal Singer'. *Current Musicology*, 25 (1978), 83–98. Reprinted in *Music and Musicians in Renaissance Rome and Other Courts*, Farnham, 1999, article IV.

——. 'Gugliemo Gonzaga and the Castrati'. *Renaissance Quarterly*, 33 (1980), 33–56. Reprinted in *Music and Musicians in Renaissance Rome and Other Courts*, Farnham, 1999, article XVI.

——. 'The Singers of the Papal Chapel and Liturgical Ceremonies in the Early Sixteenth Century: Some Documentary Evidence', in *Rome in the Renaissance: The City and the Myth*, papers of the 13th Annual Conference of the Center for Medieval and Early Renaissance Studies, ed. P.A. Ramsey, Medieval and Renaissance Texts and Studies, 18, Binghamton, NY, 1982, 249–64. Reprinted in *Music and Musicians in Renaissance Rome and Other Courts*, Farnham, 1999, article XI.

——. 'Performance Practice in the Papal Chapel during the 16th Century'. *Early Music*, 15/4 (November 1987), 452–62. Reprinted in *Music and Musicians in Renaissance Rome and Other Courts*, Farnham, 1999, article XIII.

——. 'Competence and Incompetence in the Papal Choir in the Age of Palestrina'. *Early Music*, 22/4 (November 1994), 607–28. Reprinted in *Music and Musicians in Renaissance Rome and Other Courts*, Farnham, 1999, article XIV.

——. 'Speculations on Repertory, Performance Practice, and Ceremony in the Papal Chapel in the early Sixteenth Century', in *Studien zur Geschichte der papstlichen Kapelle: Tagungsbericht Heidelberg 1989*, Cappellae Apostolicae Sixtinaeque Collectanea Acta Monumenta, Collectanea 2, ed. Bernhard Janz. Vatican City, 1994, 103–22. Reprinted in *Music and Musicians in Renaissance Rome and Other Courts*, Farnham, 1999, article XII.

——. 'Ceremonies for Holy Week, Papal Commissions and Madness (?) in Early Sixteenth-Century Rome', in *Music in Renaissance Cities and Courts: Studies in Honor of Lewis Lockwood*, ed. Jesse Ann Owens and Anthony M. Cummings, Detroit Monographs in Musicology/Studies in Music, 18 (Warren, 1997), 391–403. Reprinted in *Music and Musicians in Renaissance Rome, and Other Courts*, Farnham, 1999, article X.

——. *Music and Musicians in Renaissance Rome and Other Courts*. Farnham, 1999.

——with Noel O'Regan and Jessie-Ann Owens, 'Rome', 2: 'The Renaissance'. *Grove Music Online*, https://www.oxfordmusiconline.com/grovemusic/.

Solomon, Maynard. 'Mozart: The Myth of the Eternal Child'. *19th Century Music*, 15 (1991–2), 95–106.

Stras, Laurie. 'The Performance of Polyphony in Early 16th Century Italian Convents'. *Early Music*, 45/2 (May 2017), 195–215.

Ternois, Marie-Jeanne. 'Ingres et Montauban'. Diss., Ecole du Louvre, 1955.

Tinterow, Gary and Conisbee, Philip (eds.). *Portraits by Ingres: Image of an Epoch*. New York, 1999.

Turunen, Kari. 'Performing Palestrina: From Historical Evidence to Twenty-First Century Performance'. DocMus diss., University of the Arts Helsinki, 2014.

Vigne, Georges. '"Un ami de Mesplet": le Portrait d'Albert-Auguste Androt par Ingres'. *Bulletin du Musée Ingres*, 85 (Montauban, April 2013). 17–34.

Wiering, Frans. *The Language of the Modes: Studies in the History of Polyphonic Modality*. London, 2001.

Wistreich, Richard. *Warrior, Courtier, Singer: Giulio Cesare Brancaccio and the Performance of Identity in the Late Renaissance*. Farnham, 2007.

Zaluski, I. and P. *Mozart in Italy*. London, 1999.

Index

Abbellimento (–ti) (Adornamenti, Embellimenti) 43 n.15, 77 n.1, 98, 116, 130, 143–4, 147–55, 158, 180, 182, 187–8, 195–7, 204 n.53, 215–6, 231–2, 239, 241 n.3, 251, 349 n.3. *Apps. 11, 12; Ex. 6 & 9*
Adami, Andrea 22–3, 31–3, 43, 45 n.18, 94, 161, 230, 283. *Figs. 1, 5, 6*
Agostini, Paolo 34 n.38, 94
Albinoni, Tomaso 2 n.4
Alexander VI, Pope 7–8
Alfieri, Pietro 34, 45 n.17, 50–1, 97 n.41, 98, 101 n.56, 111 n.1, 123 n.7, 124 n.10, 131, 140–2, 145–56, 159–60, 162, 180–1, 187–8, 196–7, 206 n.58, 212, 215, 224, 231, 239, 241, 245–6, 251, 256, 292, 324, 350. *Apps. 11, 12*
Allegri, Domenico 29–30
Allegri, Gregorio 1, 10, 43, 46, 61 n.14, 100–2, 122 n.4, 167
  Life 29–31. *Figs 5 & 6*
  Lamentations 30, 41, 97, 101–2. *Table 2*
  Miserere 1–3, 23 n.12, 34, 42, 45, 49, 72, 77–80, 95–6, 98, 121, 167
    composition and first performances 18, 28 n.24, 29, 31–5. *Table 1*
    mode 35–6, 48–9. *Fig. 7*
    manuscript sources (*and see* Manuscripts) 43 n.15, 49–51, 71–2, 77–80, 95–100, 106, 108–9, 111, 116–17, 135–42, 152–6, 169, 171–5, 180–2, 210, 215–16, 237–8, 249, 251–3, 324, 327, 349–50. *Tables 1, 2; Apps 1–3, 5–12; Figs. 22–5*
    early manner of performance 37 n.1, 39–41
    re-composition by Biordi 41–2, 50
    publications 42–3, 50, 71–3, 95–9, 147–54, 202–5
    relationship to Bai's *Miserere* 3, 36 n.45, 45–6, 48–51, 127, 148–51, 156, 159–62, 180, 192 n.17. *App. 11, Fig. 8*
    accounts of performance 55–61, 63–5, 70–2, 107–8, 128–30, 132, 142–5, 156–9, 167. *Ex. 1, 6, 9*
    copying by Mozart 73–6
    later manner of performance 111–17, 126–7, 224, 230–2, 237–9, 244–7
    pitch of performance 144–6, 156–9, 224–6
  'English Miserere':
    sources 185–90. *Fig. 26*
    early editions without ornamentation 192–5
    performances 197–201, 207–11
    editions 195–8, 205–6. *Fig. 30*
    recordings 198–202, 205–11, 214
    language 192–4, 203–4, 213
    alternative recordings 37 n.1, 208–14,
Altemps library 28 n.24, 29 n.28
Alto (contralto) naturale 13, 16–17, 67 n.31, 126 n.17, 133, 217, 233 n.18
Altus 14, 16, 46, 245 n.14
Amelot, Antoine, marquis de Chaillou 81
Ambros, August Wilhelm 167–8
Amps, Kym 208
Anerio, Felice 27, 28 nn.22 & 24, 32, 34, 35 n.41, 45–6, 138 n.10, 186 n.4, 289. *Table 1*
Anerio, Giovanni Francesco 27. *Table 1*
Antonelli, Abundio 94

Index

Androt, Albert-Auguste 87 n.18
appoggiatura (*–e*, *–as*) 72, 95, 108,
    111–12, 140, 153–4, 181, 188, 211,
    236, 238–9, 250 n.31, 285, 291,
    302, 305, 324–5, 349. *Ex.1*
A Sei Voci (Ensemble) 29 n.26, 37 n.1,
    209–11
Astolfi, Mariano 164
Atkins, Sir Ivor 195–8, 200, 204 n.53,
    205, 208. *Fig. 27*
Ayrton, William 193 n.20

Baccellieri, Giovanni Battista 22 n.11,
    161
Baggs, Charles Michael 56
Bai (Baj), Tommaso 8, 51, 138 n.10, 130
    n.26, 289
  Life 46–8. *Fig. 8*
  Miserere 2–3, 49–50, 96, 111, 124,
      127, 130, 136, 142, 162, 167, 175,
      192 n.17, 206 n.58, 209 n.63, 215,
      231, 239, 244 n.13, 288, 295, 350.
      App. 13/1, *Figs. 22–5*
    composition and first
        performances 45–6, 48–51
    Mode 36 nn.44–5, 48–9
    Publications 43, 50–1, 98 n.45, 147,
        149–50, 152–3, 154 n.14, 187 n.6
    combination with Allegri's
        Miserere 50–1, 71–2, 74, 136,
        142, 152, 156, 159–62, 180,
        209–11, 215, *Ex.6*, *App. 11*
    manuscript sources 46 n.20, 47
        n.23, 50, 107 n.64, 175, 180, 186
        n.4, 187 n.6, 239, 251, 324–7.
        App. 4
    recordings 210–12
Baillot, Pierre 92 n.30, 252
Baini, Giuseppe 4, 13, 21–2, 25–9,
    32, 34, 40–2, 45–6, 45 n.18, 48,
    82, 85–6, 91, 94, 96–9, 101–2,
    107, 117, 131–2, 141, 151 n.6, 152,
    155–6, 160, 163–8, 170–1, 175,
    181, 194, 225, 228, 231. *Table 1*,
    Figs. 12, 16
  life and career 121–7, 131–3
  dispute with Alfieri 148–50, 154,
  Miserere 127–31, 157, 159, 161, 162
      n.37, 224 n.23, 241, 245. *Ex.8*
Baini, Lorenzo 121

Banchieri, Adriano 220
Barnby, Joseph 194
Barsanti, Benedetto 90
Benedict XIII, Pope 41
Benedictus 20, 21 n.7, 23, 36 n.44, 84–5,
    100–1, 165 n.7, 224. *Table 1*
Benevolo, Orazio 46, 289
Bernabei, Ercole 46
Bernabei, Giuseppe Antonio 80, 101,
    289. *Table 1*
Beretta, Francesco 46
Berlioz, Hector 56, 228–9
Berthier, Général Louis-Alexandre
    81
Bertozzi, Domenico 126 n.18
Bianchini, Luca 74
Bianchini, Saverio (Xavier) 84, 121
Biblioteca Casanatense, Rome 124
    n.14
*Biblioteca Communale di
    Crevalcore* 47 n.23
Biblioteca del Liceo Musicale,
    Bologna 36 n.45
Biblioteca Lindesiana,
    Manchester 77–8
Biblioteca Vallicelliana, Rome 28 n.22,
    29 n.28, 38 n.2, 194 n.28. *Table 1*
Bielby, Jonathan 198 n.36
Binder, Don Niccola Lamberto 84, 90,
    106–9, 116. *Fig. 14*
Biondini, Giovanni Domenico 50 n.30
Biordi, Giovanni 36, 41–2, 43 n.15, 50,
    72, 138 n.10, 167, 186, 251, 289,
    350. *Table 2*, *App. 2*
Blainville, Charles-Henri de 3, 71–3,
    79 n.6, 112, 251. *App. 5*
Bocchini, Evangelista 171
Bohn, Emil 138, 289
Bontempi, Giovanni Battista 43
Book of Common Prayer (BCP) 2 n.3,
    190–3
Bovieri, Pietro Paolo 166
Bovicelli, Giovanni-Battista 37, 40 n.6,
    111, 209, 233, 253
Boyce, William 135 n.1
Brett, Charles 198 n.38, 200 n.41
Brossard, Sébastien de 228
Brown, Mark 206
Bucer, Martin 191
Bunsen, Karl von 166 n.10

Burney, Charles 1, 23 n.12, 32–3,
    39–46, 47 n.23, 49–50, 56, 65–6,
    74–6, 79 n.7, 80 n.9, 94–9, 114
    n.6, 116, 133, 137, 147–8, 152, 156,
    159, 164, 166, 174, 181, 185–7,
    192–6, 204–5, 206 n.58, 208–9,
    212, 225, 230–2, 236 n.23, 239,
    242, 248, 253, 283, 289, 291, 324,
    350. *Table 2. Fig.1*
Burzio, Eugenia 249, 252
Busnois, Antoine 17
Buttaoni, Padre Domenico 45 n.17,
    148–9, 151
Byram-Wigfield, Ben 136 n.2, 203 n.50,
    212

Caccini, Giulio 2 n.4, 39, 40 n.6, 233
Cairns, Peter 198 n.38
Calvé, Emma 249
Camerlengo 12–13, 90, 124
Canterbury Cathedral 194–5, 198 n.37,
    202–3
Cantoria 1 n1, 10, 12, 27, 50 n.30, 117,
    200, 208, 242–3. *Front cover,
    back cover, Figs 1, 2, 3, 20*
Cantus planus 2, 17–18, 20 n.4, 25–7,
    36, 41, 137 n.8, 140, 193, 195–6,
    210, 244–5, 289, 324–5
Cappella Giulia 7 n.2, 16, 28, 34 n.38,
    46, 122 n.2, 153, 165, 169, 222
    n.17, 241 n.3, 242 n.5, 246 n.16
Cappella Magna 7
Cappella Paolina (Pauline Chapel, in
    the Quirinale) 7 n.1, 86, 242
Cappella Pia 7 n.2, 169, 171
*Cappella Pontificia, Collegio dei
    Cappellani Cantori della See*
    Papal Choir
Capucines, Couvent des (Paris) 87, 89
Caramici, Domenico Cesare 106
Carpentras (Eleazar Genet) 11 n.10, 19
    n.3
Castrato (-ti, castrat) 1, 3, 10, 14–17, 22
    n.11, 25, 65–8, 74–5, 112, 126–7,
    142–3, 145 n.27, 148, 166, 166
    n.12, 170–1, 216, 221–3, 228, 236
    n.22, 247–50, 252. *Fig. 4*
Celler, Ludovic 2, 21 n.7, 24 n.13, 62–4,
    67, 128 n.23, 162
Censi, Giuseppe 86, 90, 124

Cesare, Giovanni *Fig. 4*
Chariots of Fire (film) 213
Charles V, Emperor 23
Chateaubriand, François René,
    Vicomte de 56, 58
Cherubini, Luigi 94
Chiavi alti 217–19, 221, 223–4
Chiavi naturali 217–18, 223–4
Chiavi trasportati 218
Chiavette 217–19, 221, 223–5
Choron, Alexandre-Etienne 123
Christus factus est 21, 23–4, 42 n.11
Christoforo (Cristoforo, Christofori)
    da Novara, Carlo Domenico
    de 74–5
Christophers, Harry 212
Cianchetti, Bernardino 124 n.12
Ciciliani (Siciliani), Filippo 80, 84, 102,
    106–7, 116, 225. *Table 2*
Chiti, Girolamo 223 n.20
Clement XIII, Pope 148
Clement XIV, Pope 75
Cleobury, Sir Stephen 201 n.43, 206–7.
    Fig. 29
*Collegio dei Cappellani Cantori della
    Cappella Pontificia See* Papal
    Choir
Collegio Inglese 121
Collegio Germanicum 220
Collegio Romano 121
*Collegio Urbano di Propaganda
    Fide* 124 n.13
Comber, Dean Thomas 191 n.15
Comines 86
Commination Service 191–2, 193 n.22,
    194 n.25, 195
Compère, Loyset 17
Concone, Giuseppe 233
Conforti, Luca 37, 208 n.61
Coro Vallicelliano 207 n.59
Corri, Domenico 112 n.4, 181, 233 n.16,
    236, 238
Cramer, Carl Friedrich 55 n.1, 56
Cranmer, Archbishop Thomas 191 n.16
Cummings, William Hayman 135 n.1

D'Addrizza, Giuseppe 165
Dawson, Anthony 202 n.49
Decano 12, 106 n.62
Delécluze, Etienne 229

366   Index

Denon, Vivant 96
Dentice, Fabrizio 28 n.23, 37 n.1, 49, 209 n.66. *Table 1*
Dentice, Luigi 27, 37 n.1, 49, 209 n.66. *Table 1*
Devillers, Jean-Albert 80 n.9
Dickens, Charles 63
Digby, Suzi 212 n.77
Diruta, Girolamo 220 n.9
Dominici, Feliciano 127 n.20
Doni, Giambattista 14 n.16, 39, 222, 233
Donizetti, Gaetano 164
Dotzauer, Friedrich 252–3
Du Fay, Guillaume 16–17
Dumestre, Vincent 210
Duprez, Gilbert 112 n.4, 233

Eames, Emma 249
Emerson, Ralph Waldo 69
Ensemble Officium 212
Ensemble William Byrd 211
Eugene IV, Pope 7
Evelyn, John 247–8

Fabre-Garrus, Bernard 209–10
Falsetto (-tist) 10, 13, 15, 16, 67–8, 214, 217, 223 n.18, 244, 249–50, 325. And *see Alto naturale*
Falsobordone (-ni, Falso Bordone) 17–18, 21–2, 25, 28 n.24, 35, 37–8, 40, 46, 49 n.27, 50, 71, 111, 130, 192–3, 238–9, 244–5
Fauxbourdon 17, 72
Fazzini, Giovanni Battista 86, 100, 225. *Table 2*
Festa, Costanzo 25, 27, 34, 138 n.10, 289. *Table 1*
Fétis, François-Joseph 94, 96, 97 n.42, 98–9, 107 n.64, 144 n.24
Finestrino, basso al 12, 23, 165–6. *Back cover*
Forestier, Pierre 57 n.9, 87n.18, 89
Fornari, Matteo 16 n.23
Friedrich Wilhelm III, King of Prussia 160

Ganassi, Silvestro 220 n.12
Garaudé, Alexis de 233

Garcia, Manuel 235
Gargari, Teofilo 27. *Table 1*
Garrick, David 43
George, Michael 198 n.38
Gilibert, Jean-Pierre-François 87 n.18. *Fig. 13*
Giovannelli, Ruggero 28, 31, 49. *Table 1*
Girodet, Anne-Louis 81 n.11
Giubilato (-i) 8, 123 n.6, 106 n.62, 126, 164
Giustiniani, Vincenzo 39, 210, 233
Gleichauf, Franz Xaver 140, 292
Gluck, Christophe Willibald 84
Goethe, JW von 56
Goncourt, Edmond and Jules 68, 172 n.8. *Fig. 21*
Goodman, Roy 198, 200, 202 n.41, 204 n.53, 206, 213. *Figs. 28, 29*
Gounod, Charles 56, 248, 249 n.29
Grassi, Paride de 8 n.5, 12 n.11, 21–2, 25
Greggiati, Giuseppe 155 n.16
Greuillet, Catherine 211–12
Gros, Antoine-Jean 87
Grossi, Giovanni Francesco ('*Siface*') 17, 247
Gruppetto (-i) 111, 153–4, 181, 233–4, 236, 294, 296–7, 302, 305, 326, 349–50. *Ex. 11*
Guerrero, Francisco 27. *Table 1*
Guest, Douglas 197 n.35
Guest, Sir George 204–6. *Fig 30*

Haas, Robert 137, 196–7, 209, 289
Haberl, Franz Xaver 7 n.2, 27 n.19, 102, 194
Handel, George Frideric 166 n.12
Harvard Glee Club 207 n.59
Hauber, Johann Michael 137
Hauptmann, Moritz 229, 231 n.12, 248, 292
Hawkins, Sir John 33–4, 43 n.15
Haydn, Joseph 92 n.30, 253 n.2
Hensel, Fanny *see* Mendelssohn
Herold, Louis-Joseph-Ferdinand 56, 58 n.10, 124 n.9, 145–6, 158, 162, 227–8, 231
Higginbottom, Edward 212 n.73
Hiller, Ferdinand 131
Holton, Ruth 209

Index   367

Hoffmann, Ernst Theodore Amadeus 244
Hompesch, Nikolaus Joseph 139 n.16, 291
Hugo, Victor 69

Ingres, Jean-Auguste-Dominique 56–8, 87–92, 236, 250
Isaac, Heinrich 17

Jannaconi, Giuseppe 122, 124
Jarves, James 23 n.12, 63–4 n.20, 65 n.24
João V, King of Portugal 76 n.14, 185
Josquin des Pres 10, 17, 28 n.24. *Fig 2*
Junker, Carl Ludwig 55
Juvarra, Filippo 117 n.10. *Fig 1*

Kandler, Franz 126 n.16, 144
Kemble, Fanny 61–2
Keyte, Hugh 208–11
King's College Cambridge (choir) 194, 197–9, 201, 203–4, 206–7, 213. *Figs. 28, 29*
Klein, Bernhard 138–9, 141, 289–91
Kreutzer, Rodolphe 96

La Fage, Adrien de 94 n.33, 99, 121 n1, 124 nn.10 & 13
Laureti, Domenico 127 n.18
Lauriston, Marquis de 94 n.31
Ledger, Philip 203, 206
Leo X, Pope 8 n.5, 11 n.10, 19, 21–2, 25, 32 n.48. *Front cover*
Leo XIII, Pope 170, 173, 175
Leoni, Donato 127 n.20
Leopold I, Holy Roman Emperor 39–41, 76 n.14, 96, 174
Leopold, Prince of Bavaria 174 n.11
Lille 80 n.9, 81, 84 n.13
Lincoln Cathedral 200 n.41
Lindsay, Alexander, Lord 77
Lionnet, Jean 29 nn.26&27, 37 n.1, 100 n.53, 209–10
Liszt, Franz 56, 164
Lorenzani, Paolo 46–7
Luciani, Luciano 12 n.12, 28 n.23, 101 n.56, 243 n.8

Luitpold, Prince Regent of Bavaria 174 n.11

Mainzer, Joseph 66, 67 n.31, 68, 98
La Marque des Anges – Miserere (film) 213
Mancini, Domenico (falsettist) 276
Mancini, Giambattista 233, 248
Manuscripts
  Basel, Universtäts-Bibliothek, *kk XII 22:3* 140, 292, 350
  Basel, Sammlung Rudolf Grumbacher, Mendelssohn letter Nr. 487 157, *Fig. 19*
  Berlin, Staatsbibibliothek,
    Mus. Ms. Teschner 119 138–9, 290
    Mus. Ms. Alfieri 1 152–6, 181, 237, 241 n.3. *App.12*
    Mus. Ms. 550/2 152–4
  Cologne, Hochschule für Musik und Tanz Bibliothek, *R1038* 138 n.10, 139–40, 291
  Dresden, Sächsische Landesbibliothek,
    Mus. Ms. 1474 E3 138, 139 n.13, 290
    Mus. Ms. 1474 E1 139 n.13
  Florence, Conservatorio Luigi Cherubini, *E.I.76* 47 n.23
  Leipzig, Stadtbibliothek - Musikbibliothek *PM 5618* 138 n.10, 104, 292
  London, British Library,
    Egerton MS 2468 43 n.15
    Egerton MS 2470 47 n.23
    Add. MS 31525 51 n.31, 135–8, 142, 144–5, 158, 213, 232, 238, 288, 326. *Apps. 8, 9 & 10*
    Add. MS 31395 149 n.4
    Add. MS 19939 6–7
    R.M.23.f.20 107 n.64
  Manchester, John Rylands Library of the University of Manchester, *MS Italian 45* (**Man**) 3, 77–80, 95, 99–102, 107, 116, 142, 154–5, 181, 200 n.39, 215, 228, 237–9, 251, 253, 261–2, 302, 349–350. *Table 2; App. 6; Fig.11*

Milan, Biblioteca del Conservatorio G. Verdi, *MUSA MS 2-2* (**Mil**) 77 n.1, 106–9, 111, 116, 142, 154, 156, 181, 215, 228, 231, 237–9, 251, 302, 349. *App.7*
Munich, Bayerische Staatsbibliothek,
Mus.Ms.671 137–8, 289
Mus.Ms. 3268(2) 140, 291
Naples, Conservatorio di San Pietro a Majella, *MS 21.6.4* 34 n.37
Paris, Bibliothèque nationale,
D.670 47 n.23
D.14499 (**P**) 3, 77–80, 95–7, 99–102, 106–8, 111–14, 116, 154–5, 181, 200 n.39, 215, 228, 237–9, 251, 253, 261–2, 292, 302, 349–50. *Table 2; App. 6; Fig. 10*
Oxford, Bodleian Libraries,
MS. M.Deneke Mendelssohn d.70 138 n.10, 140, 292
MS. M.Deneke Mendelssohn d.13 161 n.30
Rome, Biblioteca Apostolica Vaticana, *Cappella Sistina (CS)*
CS 38 28 n.24
CS 72 102 n.58. *Table 2*
CS 76 *Table 2*
CS 100 *Table 2*
CS 132 *Table 2*
CS 137 *Table 2*
CS 185 42, 44, 50, 185. *Table 2*, 202
CS 188–189 45 n.18,
CS 192 28 n.24
CS 203–204 46 n.20, 187 n.6
CS 205–206 25, 27–8, 31–2, 34, 35 n.41, 37 n.1, 42 n.11, 43 n.15, 44, 49–50, 72, 96, 114 n.6, 137 n.8, 186 n.4, 187, 194, 208–10, 212, 214, 238, 244, 251, 289, 350. *Tables 1, 2; App.1*
CS 212 *Table 2*
CS 247 *Table 2*
CS 263 41–2, 50, 251. *App.2*
CS 279 100, *Table 2*
CS 280 *Table 2*
CS 286 *Table 2*
CS 302 *Table 2*
CS 331 *Table 2*
CS 340–341 42 n.11, 44, 46 n.20, 50, 78, 114 n.6, 152–3, 185–6, 187 nn.5&6, 208, 212, 239, 251, 350. *Table 2; Apps.3–4*
CS 342 *Table 2*
CS 343 49 n.27, 244
CS 354 42 n.11
CS 371 165 n.7,
CS 375 (**M**) 51, 111, 114, 154, 156 n.17, 162, 169, 171, 173–5, 180–2, 187 n.6, 210–11, 227–8, 230–1, 233–4, 237–9, 245, 249, 251–2, 254, 302, 305, 324–7, 349–50. *App.13/1, Figs. 22–5*
CS 450 124 n.11
CS 483 130 n.25
CS 658 45 n.17, 147–9, 159–60
CS 681 224 n.23
Rome, Conservatorio della Santa Cecilia, *G.Ms.44* 106 n.66
Rome, Archivio della Congregazione dell'Oratorio di S. Filippo Neri, *MS. F.III.4* 107 n.64
Rome, S. Giovanni Laterano, *MS 59* 101 n.56
Venice, Biblioteca Nazionale Marciana, *Cod.It.IV,1339* 34 n.38
Vienna, Österreichische Nationalbibliothek, *Mus. Ms.15604* 148–9, 303–4
Warsaw, Biblioteka Uniwersytecka, *RM 6027* 149 n.277, 304
Massimo, Monsignor Francesco Saverio 149
Marshall, Julian 135–6, 288
Martin, Sir George 193–7, 198 n.36, 200, 350
Martini, Giovanni-Battista (Padre) 71, 73, 76, 101, 107, 122 n.2, 185–7, 350
Martini, Johannes 17
Masini, Antonio 46
Maurice (film) 213
Méhul, Etienne Nicolas 92 n.30
Melba, Nellie 249, 252
Mendelssohn (Hensel), Fanny 57, 114–15, 130, 133, 142, 144, 146, 158–9, 162 n.35, 163 n.1, 224, 230 n.10, 247, 252. *Ex.4*, 7

Mendelssohn, Felix 3, 23 n.12, 24
    n.12, 56, 60, 75, 80 n.8, 111–12,
    114, 128 n.22, 130–3, 139 n.14,
    140, 142, 144–6, 156–7, 159–61,
    187–9, 197, 206 n.58, 209, 211,
    215, 224, 227–8, 230, 232–4, 236,
    238, 241, 245–7, 250 n.31, 252,
    349. *Figs. 19, 26; Ex. 1, 3, 6, 8, 10*
Mercadante, Saverio 164–5
Merlo, Giovanni Antonio 11 n.10
Mesplet, Adelaïde Marie Louise
    Thomas Decressy [wife of
    Louis] 88–9
Mesplet, Hyppolite Louis [son of
    Louis] 89, 97, 99
Mesplet, Louis Hyppolite 77–94,
    96–102, 106–8, 111 n.1, 117, 121
    n.1, 141, 155, 174 n.11, 200 n.39,
    224 *Table 2; Figs. 10–15*
Michelangelo Buonarotti 19, 56, 60,
    61 n.14, 208 n.60
Milner-White, Eric 194 n.26
Mirri, Baldesarre 166
Monge, Gaspard 96
Monteverdi, Claudio 222 n.16
Morales, Cristobal de 14 n.15, 167, 289
Moreschi, Alessandro 3, 112, 112 n.4,
    171–4, 175 n.15, 236 n.22, 238,
    247, 249–50. *Figs. 4, 21*
Morganti, Benedetto 135, 137, 288
Morse, Samuel 236–7
Mozart, Maria-Anna (Nannerl) 73–4
Mozart, Leopold 1, 73–76
Mozart, Wolfgang Amadeus 73–7,
    158, 251, 253
Mustafà, Domenico 3–4, 68, 117, 121,
    136 n.2, 155 n.14, 163, 167–8 n.14,
    207 n.59, 232, 236, 249, 250 n.31.
    Figs. 4, 20, 22–5
  Life 165–70
  MS CS 375 51, 111, 114, 116, 133
    n.34, 136 n.2, 154 n.14, 156 n.17,
    162, 171–5, 180–182, 187 n.6,
    210–11, 215, 228, 231, 233 n.15,
    236–9, 247, 249, 251–4, 324–7.
    App.13/1
  Miserere 162 n.37, 171–5
  Tu es Petrus 183–4
  Peccavimus (after Palestrina) 171,
    231

Naldini, Sante 28, 32, 45, 49. *Table 1*
Nanino, Giovanni Bernardino 29
Nanino, Giovanni Maria 28 n.22,
    28–9, 31, 34, 49, 194–5. *Table 1*
Napoleon (Bonaparte) 4, 12, 61–2, 81,
    82 n.11, 96, 122, 123, 162
Necker, Anne-Louise Germaine,
    baronne of Staël-Holstein 56,
    246
Neroni, Lorenzo di Monte S. Polo 84
New College, Oxford (choir) 194, 212
    n.73
Nicolai, Otto 3, 17 n.27, 56, 113, 115,
    131–2, 140, 142, 144, 158, 164,
    166 n.10, 170–1, 181, 210, 215,
    228, 231, 252–3, 349–50. *Ex.5
    & 9*
Novello, Vincent 28 n.22, 192, 193
    nn.20 & 23, 194–5

Ockeghem, Johannes 17
ORA 212 n.77
Orto, Marbrianus de 17
Ouseley, Sir Frederick Arthur
    Gore 192 n.17
Oxford Camerata 214 n.82

Pacelli, Asprilio 220
Padroni, Don Mariano 3, 109, 142–4,
    146, 156–8, 215–16, 224 n.23, 228,
    247, 349. *Fig. 18*
Palestrina, Giovanni Pierluigi da 1, 7
    n.2, 10, 21, 28 n.24, 29–30, 44,
    61 n.14, 80, 85 n.14, 94, 101, 111
    n.2, 122 n.2, 125, 126 n.16, 128
    n.23, 131, 138 n.10, 161, 164, 166
    n.10, 167, 171, 213 n.78, 225, 229,
    242–3, 248, 289, 292. *Table 1*
  Works:
    Canticum canticorum 220
    Fratres, ego enim accepi 43, 186
      n.4
    Improperia 43, 50 n.30, 100,
      114, 133, 159, 186 n.4, 224, 230.
      Tables 1, 2; Ex. 3, 7
    Lamentations 41, 100–1, 102 n.57,
      141, 229. *Table 2*
    Magnificat II Tono 101
    Missa Assumpta est Maria 100,
      224

Missa dilexi quoniam Table 2
Missa Laudate Dominum 223 n.20
Missa Qual'e il più grande Amor Table 2
Miserere 27, 28 nn.22 & 24, 194. Table 1
Miserere a tre cori 28 n.24
Peccavimus 171, 231
Salvatorem expectamus 100, 102 n.58, 113–14. Table 2
Stabat mater 43, 186 n.4, 208 n.61, 210, 224, 229
Veni sponsa Christi 100–1, 111. Table 2
Paolucci, Giuseppe 221 n.13
Papal Choir (College of Papal Singers, *Cappella Pontificia*) 1–3, 7–8, 10, 14–18, 22, 30, 34 n.38, 36, 43, 60 ,65, 72–4, 82–5, 87, 90–1, 95, 98–9, 108, 135–7, 141–2, 147–51, 166, 214, 242–4, 247–50, 251, 289, 291–2. *Figs 4, 14, 20*
  History and organisation 7–8, 10–13, 21 n.8, 23–4, 28, 32 n.34, 61, 82, 85–6, 90–2, 98, 106–7, 121–8, 155, 163–5, 169–71
  Personnel and repertoire 14–18, 28 n.24, 37, 41, 42 n.11, 46 n.20, 48, 67, 126–7, 131, 139
  Performance practice 10, 14, 15–17, 23–4, 36–41, 49–50, 68, 75, 77, 79, 100–1, 111–17, 127–33, 140, 144–6, 152–4, 156–62, 167, 175, 180–2, 195, 197, 208, 215–6, 217, 223–5, 227–34, 236–9, 241–2, 244–7, 252–4, 324–5, 350. *Ex. 1, 2, 4, 5, 7, 10*
Parca, Biagio di Corchiano 84
Parker, Andrew 200 n.39
Parker, John William 193 n.20
Parrott, Andrew 208
Partecipante (-ti) 8, 106, 123, 163, 165
Pasquali, Innocenzi 165, 170, 173
Patacchiola, Felice da Cantalice 164
Patti, Adelina 238, 249, 252
Paul III, Pope 8, 26
Paul V, Pope 242
Peale, Rembrandt 132
Pesci, Gustavo *Fig. 4*

Perosi, Lorenzo 250 n.31
Philips, Peter 201, 202 n.48, 206, 206 n.58
Pisani, Don Giuseppe di Ferentino di Campagna 84
Pisari, Paschale 46 n.20, 50 n.30, 84, 96, 122 n.2
Pitch
  In the Papal Choir 2, 16–17, 75, 144, 156–9, 181–2, 215, 217–26, 241, 288, 324, 349. *Figs. 18, 19, 22, Ex.2–4, 6–9*
  in Rome 14 n.16, 20 n.22, 158 n.22, 211, 222–3, 225 n.25
Pitoni, Giuseppe Ottavio 67 n.31, 167
Pius VI, Pope 10, 82, 107, 122
Pius VII, Pope 10 n.6, 90, 96–7, 122–4, 126
Pius VIII, Pope 58
Pius IX, Pope 10 n.6, 163–4, 168–70
Pocock, Richard 57 n.7
Poème Harmonique, Le 37, 210
Porpora, Niccolo 41 n.8
Port de voix 235
Porta, Costanzo 80, 101, Table 2
Portamento 38 n.2, 112 n.4, 113–15, 138, 140–1, 181, 210, 232–8, 252–3, 253, 288, 325, 327, 350. *Apps 6–7, 13/1, 13/2, Figs. 22–5, Ex. 2–5, 7, 10*
Potter, John 235 n.19, 252 n.1, 325
Preston, Simon 202, 206
Pro Cantione Antiqua 206–7
Proske, Carl 131
Prosody 2, 49–50, 74, 80 n.8, 97, 116, 153, 193–6, 200, 238–9, 349. *Fig. 30*
Puntatore 12, 90, 106, 107 n.63, 122, 124, 162, 164 n.2, 165, 245 n.14

Raphael (Raffaello Sanzio) 67 n.122. Front cover
Raverio, Alessandro 220
Reali, Francesco 126 n.18
Rellstab, Friedrich 181
Richter, Ernest Friedrich 140, 292
Richter, Jean Paul 244
Risorgimento 169
Ritarossi, Giuseppe *Fig. 4*

Roberts, Deborah 206
Rochlitz, Frédéric 200 n.39
Rockstro, William Smith 187–90, 192–3, 195–7, 205–8, 210, 212–13. *Fig. 26*
Rognoni, Francesco 39, 40 n.6, 111, 210, 233–4, 253
Rombach, William 212
Rota, Andrea 221 n.13
Russell, John 60–1
Rutter, John 206 n.58

Saint John's College Cambridge (choir) 198 n.36, 202 n.46, 204–6
Saint Paul's Cathedral (choir) 192–3, 203
Salvatori, Domenico *Fig. 4*
San Giovanni in Laterano (Cathedral) 7 n.2, 101 n.56, 164, 169, 171, 222 n.17, 223 n.20
San Luigi dei Francesi 29, 34 n.38, 222 n.17
San Lorenzo in Damaso 222 n.17
San Pietro (St Peter's, Basilica) 7 n.2, 16, 28, 34 n.38, 47, 47 n.22 & 23, 69 n.35, 122 n.2, 124, 164, 165 n.5, 166, 169, 171 n.7, 222 n.17, 241 n.3, 242, 243 n.6
Santa Maria Maggiore 222 n.17
Santarelli, Giuseppe 32 n.34, 39–40, 41 n.7, 43–4, 66 n.27, 94, 116, 133, 147–8, 185–6
Santer, Paul 198 n.38
Santini, Fortunato 47 n.23, 99, 122 n.2
Sartori, Baldessare 42 n.11
Santos, Giovanni 16 n.23
Scarlatti, Alessandro 45–6, 50, 161 n.34, 245 n.14
Scarlatti, Domenico 47
Schola Cantorum 7
Secondo servizio 8, 163
Sebastianelli, Vincenzo *Fig. 4*
Severi, Francesco 28 n.23, 37, 208 n.61, 209
Shelley, Mary 56
Sievers, Georg Ludwig Peter 98, 130 n.26, 142–4, 155, 158, 165 n.6, 224–5

Simonelli, Matteo 28 n.24
Sine Nomine, Chorus 212
Sintoni, Carlo 166
Sistine Chapel (*Capella Sistina*) 1–2, 7, 8 n.5, 10, 19–21, 28 n.24, 40, 42 n.11, 45, 56, 58, 60–1, 63–5, 70–1, 73, 77, 79, 82 n.12, 86–7, 90–1 n.26, 96, 108, 113, 121, 137–8, 140, 166 n.10, 167, 169, 171, 173, 175, 185, 188 n.9, 190, 195, 200, 202, 207–8, 214–15, 242–4, 246, 248–9, 289–92, 324. *Figs. 1–3, 9, 11, 20, front and back covers*
Sixteen, The 206 n.58, 207, 212
Sixtus IV, Pope 7, 17
Sixtus V, Pope 11 n.10, 16
Skene, James, of Rubislaw 60 n.12
Soprannumerarî 8, 126, 163,
Soriano, Francesco 94
Soto de Langa, Francisco 15
Source A 109, 135–42, 152, 154 n.14, 155–6, 159 n.26, 181–2, 209, 212–13, 215, 227–8, 233, 236–9, 245, 251, 288–92, 302, 324, 349–50. *Apps. 8, 9, 10 & 13/2*
Sparrow, Bishop Anthony 190 n.12
Spithöver, Josef 153
Spohr, Ludwig 3, 56, 75, 113–14, 140, 145, 158, 181, 227, 229 n.7, 237, 252–3
Spontini, Gaspare 164, 167 n.12
Squire, William Barclay 28 n.22, 194–5, 214
Stainer, Sir John 192–4
Stamp, Alison 206
Stendhal (Henry Beyle) 56, 69, 236
Stowe, Harriet Beecher 69

Tallis Scholars 34, 202 n.48, 206, n.60
Tartini, Giuseppe 46 n.20, 71, 73, 96
Taverner Consort 208, 212
Tenebræ 19–22, 23 n.12, 25, 29, 36 n.44, 42 n.11, 45–6, 49 n.37, 56, 58, 63–4, 94, 101, 145, 162, 173, 214, 244
Teschner, Gustav Wilhelm 138–9, 290
Thibaut, Anton Friedrich Justus 138, 239

372   *Index*

Tifoni, Don Francesco 141 n.21
Titian (Tiziano Vecelli) 61 n.14
Tizio, Sigismondo 19
Tonus peregrinus 35–6, 48–50, 192 n.17, 193. *Fig.7*
Tosi, Pier-Francesco 16 n.22, 223 n.18, 233–4, 248
Traditor autem 21, 23
Tubilli, Giovanni Matteo 165
Turner, Gavin 208, 211 n.72, 243

Urban VIII, Pope 30, 40 n.6

Vaccai, Nicola 234–5
Valentini, Pier Francesco 122 n.4
Vaqueras, Bertrandus 17
Varcoe, Stephen 198 n.37
Viadana, Lodovico 16 n.22, 29, 31 n.31, 37, 40 n.6, 220, 233
Victoria, Tomas Luis da 80, 100–1, 161. *Table 2*
Villa Albani 92
Villa Borghese 87 n.18
Villa Medici 87, 91
Viola, Giovanni Domenico 28 n.23. 36 n.58
Vittori, Loreto 26
Vittorio Emmanuele, King of Italy 169 n.1

Wagner, Richard 165 n.7

Wakefield Cathedral 198 n.36
Walker, Henry Aston 192–4, 200 n.39, 350 n.4
Warren, Joseph 135–6, 145, 158, 288. *Fig 17*
Warren, Thomas 193 n.20
Weerbeke, Gaspar von 17
Westminster Abbey 43 n.15
Westminster Abbey (Choir *and* Consort) 202 nn.44 & 45, 206, 210–1
Westminster Cathedral Choir 206
Wicks, Allan 198 n.37, 203
Willcocks, Sir David 197–8, 200, 203, 206 n.58, 207. *Fig. 29*
William Byrd Choir 208, 210, 211 n.72, 243
Wiseman, Nicholas, Cardinal 64–5, 129–30, 230
Witt, Franz Xaver 131
Worcester Cathedral 194, 195 nn.29 & 30, 197

Zacconi, Lodovico 220
Zarlino, Gioseffe 80, 101, 219 n.8, 220. *Table 2*
Zelter, Carl Friedrich 25 n.12, 139, 144 n.25, 157, 161, 188 n.10, 232 n.14, 290. *Ex.6 & 10*
Zenobi, Luigi 37–8, 40 n.6, 111–12, 210, 234 n.17